THE CAMBRIDGE COMPANION T

HAYEK

F. A. Hayek (1899–1992) was among the most important economists and political philosophers of the twentieth century.
He is widely regarded as the principal intellectual force
behind the triumph of global capitalism, an "anti-Marx"
who did more than any other recent thinker to elucidate
the theoretical foundations of the free market economy.
His account of the role played by market prices in transmit-
ting economic knowledge constituted a devastating critique
of the socialist ideal of central economic planning, and his
famous book *The Road to Serfdom* was a prophetic statement of the dangers which socialism posed to a free and open
society. He also made significant contributions to fields
as diverse as the philosophy of law, the theory of complex
systems, and cognitive science. The essays in this volume,
by an international team of contributors, provide a critical
introduction to all aspects of Hayek's thought.

EDWARD FESER is Philosophy Instructor in the Social Sciences
Division, Pasadena City College. He is author of *On Nozick*
(2003) and *Philosophy of Mind: A Short Introduction* (2005).

The Cambridge Companion to
HAYEK

Edited by Edward Feser
Pasadena City College

 CAMBRIDGE
UNIVERSITY PRESS

CAMBRIDGE UNIVERSITY PRESS
Cambridge, New York, Melbourne, Madrid, Cape Town, Singapore,
São Paulo

Cambridge University Press
The Edinburgh Building, Cambridge CB2 2RU, UK

Published in the United States of America by Cambridge University Press,
New York

www.cambridge.org
Information on this title: www.cambridge.org/9780521615013

First published 2006

Printed in the United Kingdom at the University Press, Cambridge

A catalogue record for this publication is available from the British Library

ISBN-13 978-0-521-84977-7 hardback
ISBN-10 0-521-84977-2 hardback
ISBN-13 978-0-521-61501-3 paperback
ISBN-10 0-521-61501-1 paperback

CONTENTS

ix

NOTES ON CONTRIBUTORS

ROGER E. BACKHOUSE is professor of the history and philosophy of economics at the University of Birmingham in the UK. He is the author of *The Penguin History of Economics* (2002, published in the USA as *The Ordinary Business of Life*) and the editor (with Bradley W. Bateman) of *The Cambridge Companion to Keynes* (2006).

PETER J. BOETTKE is a professor of economics at George Mason University and a senior research fellow at the Mercatus Center. He is also the editor of *The Review of Austrian Economics*.

BRUCE CALDWELL is professor of economics at the University of North Carolina at Greensboro and the General Editor of *The Collected Works of F. A. Hayek*. His 2004 book, *Hayek's Challenge: An Intellectual Biography of F. A. Hayek*, has recently been released in paperback.

MEGHNAD DESAI is emeritus professor at the London School of Economics. He is the author of *The Route of All Evil: The Political Economy of Ezra Pound* (2006).

EDWARD FESER teaches philosophy at Pasadena City College in Pasadena, California. He has been a visiting assistant professor at Loyola Marymount University in Los Angeles and a visiting scholar at the Social Philosophy and Policy Center at Bowling Green State University in Bowling Green, Ohio. He is the author of *On Nozick* (2004), *Philosophy of Mind: A Short Introduction* (2005), and many articles in political philosophy, philosophy of mind, and philosophy of religion.

ANDREW GAMBLE is professor of politics at the University of Sheffield. He is a Fellow of the British Academy and the Academy of Social

Sciences, and a former director of the Political Economy Research Centre. His books include *Hayek: The Iron Cage of Liberty* (1996) and *Politics and Fate* (2000). He was awarded the 2005 Sir Isaiah Berlin Prize for Lifetime Contribution to Political Studies.

GERALD F. GAUS is the James E. Rogers professor of philosophy at the University of Arizona; he was previously professor of philosophy and political economy at Tulane University. During 2005–2006 he was Distinguished Visiting Professor of Philosophy at the University of North Carolina, Chapel Hill. Among his books are *Value and Justification* (Cambridge University Press, 1990), *Justificatory Liberalism* (1996), *Contemporary Theories of Liberalism* (2003), and *On Philosophy and Economics* (forthcoming). He is currently writing a book entitled *Principled Liberalism*.

CHANDRAN KUKATHAS is Neal Maxwell Professor of Political Theory, Public Policy, and Public Service, Department of Political Science, University of Utah. He is the author of *Hayek and Modern Liberalism* (1989), *Rawls: A Theory of Justice and its Critics* (with Philip Pettit, 1990), and *The Liberal Archipelago* (2003). He is also editor of *Rawls: Critical Assessments* (2003), the *Sage Handbook of Political Theory* (with Gerald F. Gaus, 2004), and *Pierre Bayle's Philosophical Commentary* (with John Kilcullen, 2005).

ERIC MACK is a professor of philosophy at Tulane University and a faculty member of Tulane's Murphy Institute of Political Economy. His primary scholarly interests are in moral individualism and the foundation of natural rights, property rights and distributive justice, the scope of justifiable coercion by the state, natural law theories, and the history of classical liberal political theory.

ANTHONY O'HEAR is Weston Professor of Philosophy at the University of Buckingham, director of the Royal Institute of Philosophy, and editor of *Philosophy*. He is the author of many books and articles on philosophy, including *Karl Popper* (1980), *Beyond Evolution* (1997), and *Philosophy in the New Century* (2001).

ROGER SCRUTON has taught philosophy at Birkbeck College, London, Boston University, and more recently at the Institute for the Psychological Sciences in Arlington, Virginia, and is currently teaching a course at Princeton. His works range from academic philosophy, including the aesthetics of music, to fiction and political and cultural commentary. His most recent publications are *Death Devoted Heart: Sex and the Sacred in Wagner's Tristan and Isolde* (2003) and *Gentle Regrets: Thoughts from a Life* (2005).

JEREMY SHEARMUR was educated at the London School of Economics where he also worked as assistant to Karl Popper for eight years. He subsequently held positions at Edinburgh, Manchester, the Centre for Policy Studies, and George Mason University, and is currently Reader in Philosophy in the School of Humanities, Faculty of Arts, Australian National University. He published *The Political Thought of Karl Popper* and *Hayek and After* in 1996.

ROBERT SKIDELSKY is Professor of Political Economy (Department of Economics) at Warwick University. His three-volume biography of John Maynard Keynes was published in 1983, 1992, and 2000. A single-volume abridgment appeared in 2002. He was made a life peer in 1991, and elected a Fellow of the British Academy in 1994. He is chairman of the Centre for Global Studies, and is currently working on a book on globalization and international relations, to be followed by a history of Britain in the twentieth century.

AEON J. SKOBLE is Associate Professor of Philosophy at Bridgewater State College in Massachusetts. He is co-editor of *Political Philosophy: Essential Selections* (1999), *The Simpsons and Philosophy* (2001), and *Woody Allen and Philosophy* (2004), and author of the forthcoming *Freedom, Authority, and Social Order* (2006). He writes on moral and political philosophy for both scholarly and popular journals.

CHRONOLOGY

1899   Hayek is born on May 8 in Vienna to August and Felicitas
von Hayek.

1914   Archduke Ferdinand of Austria assassinated; the First World
War begins.

1917   Hayek begins service in the Austrian army on the Italian
front; Lenin takes power after the Russian Revolution.

1918   Hayek enters the University of Vienna.

1921–23   Hayek earns doctorates in Law and Political Economy, and
begins working with Mises in the Office of Accounts in
Vienna.

1923–24   Hayek does postgraduate research at New York University.

1926   Hayek marries Helene von Fritsch, with whom he will have
two children.

1927   With Mises, Hayek founds the Austrian Institute for
Business Cycle Research in Vienna.

1929   Hayek is appointed *Privatdozent* in Economics and
Statistics at the University of Vienna; *Monetary Theory and
the Trade Cycle* is published.

1931   Hayek lectures at the London School of Economics, where
he will be offered a permanent position a year later; *Prices
and Production* is published.

1935   *Collectivist Economic Planning: Critical Studies on the
Possibilities of Socialism*, a volume edited by Hayek, is
published.

1936   Keynes publishes his *General Theory of Employment,
Interest, and Money*.

1938   Hitler annexes Austria; Hayek becomes a naturalized British subject.

1939   The Second World War begins; the LSE is evacuated to Cambridge.

1941   *The Pure Theory of Capital* is published.

1944   *The Road to Serfdom* is published and Hayek soon becomes an international celebrity; he is admitted to the British Academy.

1945   Labour takes power in Britain; Popper joins the staff of the LSE.

1947   Hayek founds the Mont Pèlerin Society.

1948   *Individualism and Economic Order* is published.

1950   Hayek joins the Committee on Social Thought at the University of Chicago; after divorcing his first wife, he marries Helene Bitterlich.

1952   *The Counter-Revolution of Science* and *The Sensory Order* are published.

1960   *The Constitution of Liberty* is published.

1962   Hayek leaves Chicago to become Professor of Political Economy at the University of Freiburg im Breisgau in West Germany.

1967   *Studies in Philosophy, Politics, and Economics* is published.

1968   Hayek retires from teaching and takes up an honorary professorship at the University of Salzburg in Austria.

1973   *Rules and Order*, the first volume of a trilogy on *Law, Legislation, and Liberty*, is published.

1974   Hayek is awarded the Nobel Prize in Economics.

1976   *The Mirage of Social Justice*, the second volume of *Law, Legislation, and Liberty*, is published.

1978   *New Studies in Philosophy, Politics, Economics, and the History of Ideas* is published.

1979   Margaret Thatcher becomes Prime Minister in Britain; *The Political Order of a Free People*, the third volume of *Law, Legislation, and Liberty*, is published.

1980   Ronald Reagan is elected US President.

1988 *The Fatal Conceit: The Errors of Socialism*, Hayek's final book, is published.
1989 The fall of the Berlin Wall.
1991 The Soviet Union is dissolved.
1992 Hayek dies in Freiburg on March 23.

Introduction

Friedrich August von Hayek (1899–1992) was almost certainly the most consequential thinker of the mainstream political right in the twentieth century. It is just possible that he was the most consequential twentieth-century political thinker, right or left, period. The apparent triumph of global capitalism at the dawn of the twenty-first century owes as much to his influence on policymakers and shapers of public opinion as it does to that of any other intellectual figure. Hayek's semi-popular book *The Road to Serfdom* (1944) was a key text of the emerging New Right, a movement whose influence ultimately made possible the elections of Margaret Thatcher, Ronald Reagan, and George W. Bush. Reagan claimed that his thinking on economics was directly influenced by Hayek's writings. Thatcher famously tried once to end debate on Conservative Party policy by slamming a copy of Hayek's more dryly academic tome *The Constitution of Liberty* (1960) down on the table and exclaiming, "*This* is what we believe!" Even Winston Churchill, long before the New Right's ascendancy, was moved by an (apparently superficial) reading of *The Road to Serfdom* to warn that the election of his opponent Clement Attlee in 1945 might result in the institution of a "Gestapo" to enforce Attlee's socialist economic policy. (Many suggested at the time that this rash charge might have cost Churchill the election; Hayek's influence on politicians did not always entail their political success.) A John Rawls or Isaiah Berlin, however much greater was the esteem with which such thinkers were regarded by most of their academic peers, could only envy such direct impact on practical politics.[1]

No doubt there are many who would regard Hayek's influence, and especially his influence on the political right, as a dubious distinction. But whatever one's opinion of Hayek's political views, no such misgivings can reasonably derive from a dispassionate assessment of the quality of his intellectual output. Hayek's technical work in economics, the field in which he first made his reputation, garnered him the Nobel Prize in 1974 (though he had to share it with his ideological opposite Gunnar Myrdal). Together with his friend and mentor Ludwig von Mises, he developed what is widely regarded (including by many who are otherwise unsympathetic to his views) to be the decisive argument against the very possibility of a socialist economic order. This work eventually led him beyond economics into a wide-ranging examination of the nature of liberal capitalist society, and of the nature of complex systems in general, whether economic, social, or otherwise. The result was an intricate system of thought encompassing worked-out theories not only in economics and social and political philosophy, but also in the philosophy of law, the philosophy of science, and cognitive science. In the last-mentioned of these fields, Hayek is now recognized as having invented, contemporaneously with but independently of D.O. Hebb, the connectionist or parallel distributed processing model of the mind that has become the main rival to the long-dominant symbolic processing paradigm. In the philosophy of social science, he is acknowledged to have made an important contribution to our understanding of the nature of explanations of complex social phenomena. In general social and political theory, he is regarded as the outstanding twentieth-century representative of the classical liberal tradition of John Locke and Adam Smith.[2] Especially in the European context, but increasingly also in the United States, he appears to be regarded by many intellectuals of the left as *the* thinker of the contemporary mainstream right with whose thought they need to come to terms.[3] Despite a long period in the intellectual wilderness following the offense he caused to prevailing sensibilities by publishing *The Road to Serfdom*, there are signs that Hayek is at long last being welcomed, at least tentatively, into the canon.[4]

The breadth and quality of his work are two reasons for this. Its depth and style are two others. Robert Nozick, who derived much of his libertarian philosophy from his reading of Hayek,[5] had a greater direct influence than Hayek himself did on contemporary academic political philosophy, at least within the analytic tradition. But even Nozick's influence has waned, in large part because of his failure to answer his many critics or develop his political philosophy beyond the inchoate state in which he had left it in *Anarchy, State, and Utopia* (1974), and thereby to generate a system as impressively worked out as that of his egalitarian liberal rival John Rawls. Hayek's star has risen in large part because he is not so easily accused of dilettantism; the many years he spent outside the mainstream academic conversation were devoted precisely to developing a thorough and systematic description and defense of a classical liberal economic and political order, first given full-dress presentation in *The Constitution of Liberty* and culminating in what is perhaps his greatest work, the three-volume *Law, Legislation, and Liberty* (1973, 1976, 1979). Hayek also presented his arguments in a fashion calculated to appeal to the secular and scientific (indeed, scientistic) temperament of the majority of his intellectual peers, giving him an advantage over other recent thinkers of the right. Conservative intellectuals of a religious bent could more easily be accused (however unjustly) of merely presenting secular rationalizations for positions whose true motivation was theological; while even a genuinely secular conservative philosopher like Michael Oakeshott, though widely respected, was bound, given his more literary style and eschewal of theory, to be dismissed by his ideological opponents (again, however unjustly) as an obscurantist. Hayek also consistently avoided polemic, and never attributed anything but the best motives to his opponents. Unlike more famous twentieth-century defenders of capitalism like Ayn Rand, Hayek cannot be written off as a shrill ideologue or crude popularizer.

· That Hayek's work deserves the attention of philosophers in particular should be evident when it is remembered how central to it is a distinctive conception of the nature of human knowledge. For Hayek, there is nothing so important to understand about our knowledge as that it is limited, and limited severely wherever it concerns inherently complex phenomena like human minds and human social institutions. Moreover, even the knowledge we do have is fragmented and dispersed, any particular aspect of it directly available only to particular individuals and groups rather than to society as a whole or to its governmental representatives; and much of it is necessarily tacit, embodied in habits and practices, "know-how" rather than data that might be recorded in propositional form. Much of Hayek's work constitutes a sustained reflection on the implications of these facts. In economics, the lesson he drew was that prices generated in a free market encapsulate this otherwise ungatherable information and make it available to individuals in a way that makes it possible for them to act so as to ensure as rational an allocation of resources as is practically possible. In law, he concluded that the piecemeal and organic development of the common law, wherein law is discovered in precedent and settled expectations rather than created in an act of legislation, is the paradigm of a rational and humane legal order. In politics, he held that only abstract and largely negative rules of conduct could reasonably be enforced by government within a free society, given the impossibility, as he saw it, of settling objectively the many disputes over matters of value that characterize modern pluralistic societies. In ethics and social theory, he came to believe that tradition played a role similar to that of the price mechanism, embodying the dispersed and inchoate moral insights of millions of individuals across countless generations and sensitive to far more social information than is available to any individual reformer or revolutionary, so that the radical moral innovator suffers from a hubris analogous to that inherent in socialism. In general philosophy, he took the view that there are inherent and insuperable limits on the mind's capacity to grasp the principles governing its own operations, the bulk of which must remain forever unconscious and inarticulable.

This epistemological emphasis in Hayek's work gives his defense of market society certain advantages. Adam Smith's famous appeal to the invisible hand is often interpreted (however mistakenly) as an apologia for unrestrained greed. The trouble with his argument, or so it is said, is that it assumes that human motives will always be base, so that his claim that market incentives impel us to serve others out of our own self-interest is irrelevant if human beings can be taught to act on more altruistic impulses. Hayek makes it clear that the case for the market has nothing essentially to do with motives. Even with the best wills in the world, we would still need the guidance of prices generated in a competitive market (and the information encapsulated therein), given our incurable ignorance of all the relevant economic circumstances. Furthermore, while Smith's emphasis on the advantages of the division of labor might seem to imply that advances in technology, and in particular the development of ever more ingenious labor-saving devices, might eventually make his case for

the market obsolete, Hayek's emphasis on the division of *knowledge* –
its inherently scattered and ungatherable character – indicates that
the need for market prices and incentives is as unaffected by contingent technological circumstances as it is by motives. This is only
reinforced by the tacit element in economic knowledge; for to the
extent that such knowledge is embodied in practical wisdom and
concrete experience rather than recordable data, it is an illusion to
suppose that advances in computing technology might solve the
calculation problem facing the would-be economic central planner.

It is also worth noting that, to the extent that Hayek's case for
tradition rests on considerations analogous to those underlying his
case for the market, the advantages of the latter accrue to the former
as well. It is tempting to suppose that, while traditional stigmas and
taboos might indeed have had some value in discouraging irrespon-
sible behavior within societies harsher and less compassionate than
we take ours to be, they can be readily dispensed with in a therapeu-
tic culture like our own, where gentle persuasion rather than stern
moral judgment is the order of the day. But as with market prices, the
value of tradition primarily lies in the remedy it supplies, not to our
purported defects of character, but to our defects of knowledge. It is
not because our forebears were hard-hearted that they had to make do
with their austere moral rules; rather, they needed those rules, as we
do, because they embody more information about actual human
needs than is available to any individual, however patient and tender-
hearted. Hayek rescues Edmund Burke, no less than he does Smith,
from the charge of cynicism, and reformulates in hard-headed scientific
terms an argument that unsympathetic critics of Burke have sometimes tended to dismiss as mere romanticism.

These considerations indicate that Hayek was not merely the
most influential of recent mainstream right-of-center thinkers, but
perhaps the most quintessential as well. For it is typical of New Right
thinking to try to combine an emphasis on free markets, limited
government, and individual liberty with the encouragement of personal moral restraint and respect for tradition and religion. Hayek's
body of thought weaves these themes together systematically,
regarding as it does both the deliverances of market competition
and those of tradition as the byproducts of similar selection mechanisms or "filtering processes" (to borrow a term from Nozick),[6]
whose rational superiority to the alternatives (the results of central

planning and moral avant-gardism, respectively) derives from their reflecting a far greater range of information about the concrete details of human life. If Hayek explicitly disavowed the label "conservative" in *The Constitution of Liberty*, he also rejected (and in the same book) the label "libertarian."[7] Moreover, his later writings exhibited a marked tendency toward moral conservatism, and also, despite his personal agnosticism, toward a commendation of traditional religious belief as a bulwark of the moral preconditions of market society.[8] A characteristically New Right combination of classical liberal economics and Burkean conservative social theory seems to have been his settled position, and by the end of his life, the label "Burkean Whig" was the one he indicated best characterized his politics.[9]

At the same time, Hayek was never blind to the potential difficulties inherent in this political synthesis, nor dismissive of the serious criticisms of capitalist society and liberal theory presented by thinkers of the left. He explicitly disavowed the ideal of laissez-faire and distanced himself from the sort of free market utopianism common among more extreme libertarians. He thought it foolish to pretend that capitalism always rewards those who work the hardest or are otherwise deserving, advocated a minimal social safety net for those incapable of supporting themselves in the market, and had no objection to government taking on tasks far beyond those defining the "minimal state" of Nozick's libertarianism, so long as this did not result in monopoly and private firms were allowed to compete with government for provision of the services in question. Like Marx, he believed that liberal capitalist society has a tendency to produce alienation, insofar as the impersonal rules of conduct upon which it rests necessarily eschew any reference to a common social end or purpose, and thus cannot satisfy the deepest human yearnings for solidarity. Unlike Marx, he also thought we nevertheless simply have no alternative to capitalism if we want to maintain the level of individual autonomy and material prosperity that are the most prized characteristics of modernity, and that it is naive and dangerous to pretend otherwise. For Hayek, those who would like to combine the autonomy and prosperity with a deeper sense of community are trying to square the circle. We cannot have our cake and eat it too; tragic as it is, we must either choose to follow out the logic of modernity to its conclusion and forever abandon the hope of satisfying those communal desires hardwired into us while we still lived in bands of hunters and gatherers, or we must return to a premodern form of life and therefore also to a premodern standard of living. There is no third way. Hayek's promotion of a mild Burkean moralism and religiosity would seem to be his way of taking the bite out of this unhappy situation, as far as that is possible; a stolid bourgeois allegiance to what is left in the modern world of the traditional family and the church or synagogue would seem in his view to be all we have left to keep us warm in the chilly atmosphere of liberal individualism and market dynamism.[10]

Clearly, Hayek's thought is rich with nuances; equally clearly, it is open to possible challenges on several fronts. Both the nuances and the challenges are amply explored in the essays comprising this volume.

Bruce Caldwell's "Hayek and the Austrian tradition" lays the groundwork for the rest of the collection by setting out the details of Hayek's personal and intellectual background in the Austria of the early twentieth century. Caldwell recounts Hayek's early family life and education, his encounter with the thought of Ernst Mach and the Vienna Circle of logical positivists, and his relationship to the Austrian School in economics and its controversies with other schools of thought. The central themes that dominated Hayek's thinking throughout the course of his life, Caldwell suggests, bear the imprint of his formation within the Austrian tradition.

In "Hayek on money and the business cycle," Roger E. Backhouse provides an exposition of some of the central themes of Hayek's early technical work in economics, including those bearing on his favored explanation of the great depression. He also addresses certain difficulties with Hayek's work, in particular his theory of capital, and compares it with the Keynesian paradigm to which it ultimately lost out.

Peter J. Boettke's "Hayek and market socialism" considers another facet of Hayek's early work in economics, namely his contribution to the socialist calculation debate. Boettke recounts the arguments of Hayek's mentor Ludwig von Mises against the very possibility of socialism, and the arguments deployed by various "market socialists" in the hope of countering Mises' objections. He then shows how Hayek's own position, developed in order to undermine the arguments of the market socialists, expanded upon and deepened Mises' insights in a way that led eventually to his distinctive epistemologically based conception of liberal political economy.

Marx was, of course, the most consequential of all socialist thinkers, and Hayek is regarded by many as a kind of anti-Marx, a guru and theoretician of capitalism who played a role in its defense analogous to that played by Marx in critiquing it. A systematic comparison of the two thinkers is therefore in order, and in "Hayek and Marx," Meghnad Desai provides just this, focusing on their respective analyses of money, capital, and economic cycles.

John Maynard Keynes was Hayek's great contemporary rival, and their disagreements over economic theory and policy are well known. But as Robert Skidelsky shows in "Hayek versus Keynes: the road to reconciliation," the two men had in common a commitment to liberalism and liberal institutions, and to a great extent their differences concerned means rather than ends. Skidelsky's examination of these agreements and differences focuses on what each man had to say about the great depression, the war economy, and the dangers inherent in state intervention, and indicates respects in which sometimes Hayek, and sometimes Keynes, had the better of the argument.

Andrew Gamble's essay "Hayek on knowledge, economics, and society" provides a natural transition from the more economics-oriented topics of the preceding essays to the broad philosophical and political themes treated in the remaining chapters of the volume. Gamble explores the various aspects and implications of Hayek's theory of knowledge, including his critique of what he took to be the excessive rationalism inherent not only in rival positions in economics, but also in most modern thinking about politics, morality, and the social world generally. He also suggests that Hayek did not entirely succeed in extricating himself from the very tendencies of thought he criticized.

Anthony O'Hear's "Hayek and Popper: the road to serfdom and the open society" compares and contrasts Hayek's arguments in *The Road to Serfdom* with those of one of the other great diagnosticians of totalitarianism in the twentieth century, Hayek's friend Karl Popper. Along the way, O'Hear considers some difficulties with each author's position, but also suggests that, despite the collapse of the systems they criticized, what is of lasting value in their arguments has yet to be fully appreciated.

In "Hayek's politics," Jeremy Shearmur explores the ways in which Hayek's emphasis on the limitations of our knowledge and the moral dangers inherent in central planning influenced his distinctive conceptions of liberty, the rule of law, and the impossibility of realizing an ideal of "social justice" in a market-based society. Shearmur regards the lines of argument Hayek deployed in *The Road to Serfdom* as key to his overall political thought, and traces their development in Hayek's mind in the years leading up to the book's publication. He also considers the tensions in Hayek's thought entailed by his advocacy of a limited degree of "social engineering" in order to bring existing political institutions more into line with his own favored principles.

Aeon J. Skoble's "Hayek the philosopher of law" examines the way in which Hayek's conception of the limitations of knowledge and the dangers of centralized direction led him to a distinctive philosophy of law, one which saw in the English common law a paradigm of a rational legal order and led him to make a crucial distinction between law and legislation. Along the way, Skoble considers several objections that critics have made to Hayek's account and how they might be answered.

Hayek stood in the broad liberal tradition, but on the "classical" rather than the modern and egalitarian side of it. Chandran Kukathas's "Hayek and liberalism" examines Hayek's relationship to this latter, rival brand of liberalism, and suggests that his theoretical differences with it originate from the overriding practical concern he had in countering the dangerous nationalist and totalitarian tendencies that characterized world politics in the twentieth century. This concern led Hayek to be less interested in abstract philosophical foundations than most contemporary liberals are, and more attentive to the concrete features of liberal institutions. It also led him to endorse a thoroughgoing internationalism that would have made him far less exercised by communitarian criticism than some recent egalitarian liberal theorists are.

This internationalism is, in Roger Scruton's view, precisely where Hayek differs most sharply from the conservative tradition in political thought – a tradition to which, as Scruton argues in "Hayek and conservatism," Hayek was otherwise in many respects very close. Scruton also regards it as the greatest potential weakness in Hayek's political philosophy. For citizens' commitment to the liberal institutions Hayek favored arguably cannot be sustained over time without a greater sense of loyalty to the nation in which those institutions are embedded than liberals are usually comfortable with.

In "Hayek on the evolution of society and mind," Gerald F. Gaus presents a systematic exposition of Hayek's account of the interconnected evolutionary processes he saw as molding both social institutions and the individual human mind, laying bare its many subtleties and complex theoretical structure. Gaus argues that the standard objections to Hayek's theory of cultural evolution rest on misinterpretations, and that many of his critics do not appreciate its richness and sophistication because they fail to interpret it in the context of his larger system of ideas.

Eric Mack's "Hayek on justice and the order of actions" provides an equally systematic account of Hayek's conception of just rules of individual conduct and their role in generating and maintaining the sort of unplanned but nevertheless rational large-scale pattern of human actions that Hayek regarded as essential to a free and pluralistic society. In Mack's view, Hayek's defense of his favored conception of justice is teleological without being utilitarian.

Finally, Edward Feser's "Hayek the cognitive scientist and philosopher of mind" examines the philosophical themes contained in Hayek's treatise in cognitive science, *The Sensory Order*. Feser situates Hayek's views firmly within the history of twentieth-century philosophy of mind, relating them to those of Hayek's contemporaries Schlick, Russell, Carnap, and Wittgenstein, and noting the respects in which they foreshadow the views of more recent thinkers. In Feser's estimation, Hayek's philosophy of mind constitutes an impressive synthesis that is superior in many ways to other and better-known naturalistic approaches. But, as he also recounts, Hayek's way of carrying out a naturalistic analysis of the mind opened him up to a possibly fatal set of objections presented by his friend Karl Popper. Yet the upshot of Popper's criticisms if anything only reinforces the critique of scientism that was so central a theme of Hayek's work.

NOTES

1. See Ebenstein 2001 for discussion of Hayek's influence, especially ch. 17 (which deals with his post-*Road to Serfdom* celebrity, including the Churchill episode), ch. 26 (which discusses his general influence on

the New Right), and ch. 37 (which describes his relationship with Thatcher, including the incident mentioned above).

2. As opposed to the modern or egalitarian liberal tradition, which is less enamored of the market economy and limited government than were the classical liberals, and whose greatest twentieth-century representative is John Rawls. See Chandran Kukathas's essay in this volume for discussion of the relative lack of interest in Hayek among modern egalitarian liberal theorists.

3. Gamble 1996 and O'Neill 1998 are two important recent book-length studies of Hayek's work written from a left-of-center point of view. Meghnad Desai (1994, 1997), David Miller (1989a), and Raymond Plant (1994) are three other broadly left-of-center writers who have seriously engaged with Hayek's work. (Gamble and Desai are also represented in this volume.) The currently more-or-less left-wing (or at least anti-right-wing) John Gray has written much on Hayek too, though he started out as a Hayekian. (Gray 1998 is an updated version of his important book-length study of Hayek originally published in 1984, and contains a post-script summarizing Gray's reasons for moving away from a Hayekian position.)

4. Cf. Cassidy (2000), who, writing in the *New Yorker* – no bastion of conservatism – goes as far as to proclaim the twentieth century "the Hayek century" and laments that Hayek's legacy has been "appropriated by the far right."

5. Nozick cited Hayek's *Individualism and Economic Order*, along with Mises's *Socialism*, as the works which converted him away from social-ism while he was in graduate school (Nozick 1986); and of course, Hayek's influence on Nozick's *Anarchy, State, and Utopia* (1974) is obvious, even if there were also other influences. See Feser 2004 for discussion of the relationship between Nozick's views and those of Hayek.

6. See Nozick 1974, pp. 18–22.

7. See the Postscript to Hayek 1960 ("Why I Am Not a Conservative") for the rejection of the "conservative" label, and p. 408 for the rejection of "libertarian." To be sure, the context indicates that his dislike of the latter label was, as of 1960 anyway, mostly due to his finding it artificial sounding. But the conservative direction his thought took in the seven-ties and eighties indicates that his views cannot appropriately be char-acterized as "libertarian" in any case, at least given the connotations that term has come to have. As Gamble has noted, "the arguments by libertarians in the 1980s for scrapping state controls over immigration, drugs, and sexual behaviour find no echo or support in Hayek's writings. He did not favour setting the individual free in the sphere of personal morality" (1996, p. 108).

8. These tendencies are particularly evident in Hayek 1979 (in particular the epilogue on "The Three Sources of Human Values"); 1984d; 1987a; 1987b; and 1988. See Feser 2003 and Roger Scruton's article in this volume for detailed discussion of Hayek's relationship to conservatism.

9. See Hayek 1994, p. 141.

10. That is not to say that Hayek was exactly a traditionalist in his personal life. As is well known, he left his first wife and children in 1949 so that he could marry someone else. Even so, when asked years later whether in his personal life he had always abided by the moral standards he regarded as valid, Hayek acknowledged that "I'm sure that [divorcing his first wife] was wrong" and that "I know I've done wrong in enforcing divorce" (quoted in Ebenstein 2001, p. 169).

1   Hayek and the Austrian tradition

There are two elements of Hayek's background that justify our considering him an Austrian economist: first, that he was raised and went to university in Vienna in the first three decades of the twentieth century, and second, that when he finally decided on economics as his field of study, he was trained within the Austrian tradition in economics.

Hayek spent about a third of his life in Austria, mostly in his early days. When he was thirty-two he moved to England, where he would live for nearly twenty years. (He would later say that it was the place he felt most at home, both intellectually and emotionally.) From 1950 through 1962 he lived in the United States, and then moved to Freiburg, Germany, where (aside from a five-year period in Salzburg, Austria – an altogether depressing time for him, both emotionally and intellectually) he would spend the rest of his life. So the first place to look for Hayek as a distinctly Austrian figure is at the formative early period. Accordingly, I will discuss his family background, his early schooling, and his university days in Vienna. Within economics, of course, the adjective "Austrian" also signifies a specific school of thought. Once he had decided that he would become an economist, Hayek received training that would make him very much a product of that school. So a second part of the story is to examine what being trained as an Austrian economist might mean.

The chapter is divided into four sections. First I will examine Hayek's family life and school experience prior to the war. The second section looks at Hayek's university experiences. In the third we will see what it meant for Hayek to be trained within the Austrian tradition in economics. The Austrian School was a tradition born in opposition, so that being a member of the school was defined as much by what one disavowed as by what one embraced. In the final section I will examine the relationship of the Austrian School to three sets of antagonists: the German Historical School economists, the Austro-Marxists, and the Vienna Circle positivists. Interaction with these groups affected the development of the Austrian tradition, and this affected the way that Hayek saw the world.

EARLY SCHOOLING AND FAMILY LIFE

Hayek was born in Vienna on May 8, 1899 into comfortable circumstances. His family was nominally Catholic, but non-practicing. Hayek suspected that his grandfather "like so many of the scientists of his generation" was "fiercely anti-religious," but his parents were simply non-religious: as a child they never took him to church, and when he expressed interest in a child's Bible he had received from them, "it disappeared mysteriously when I got too interested in it" (Hayek 1994, p. 40). By age fifteen he was a confirmed agnostic, a position he would maintain from then on.

Hayek attended both elementary school and high school (or *Gymnasium*, which consisted of eight grades, or forms) in Vienna. Among the options one faced in choosing a high school were those that emphasized a humanistic curriculum (these required both Greek and Latin) and those that were more scientifically oriented (Latin, but no Greek, was offered). Hayek's father August had received a thoroughly humanistic training, but he was also a natural science enthusiast, so he initially chose a more scientifically oriented Gymnasium for his son. Unfortunately, the school had a required class in drawing, and drawing turned out to be an area in which Hayek had no aptitude. His repeated failures ultimately forced him to find another Gymnasium. His new school, more humanistic in orientation, was in the suburbs and attracted a lower quality of student. Hayek was dubbed "Lex" (short for lexicon) by his classmates for his wide-ranging knowledge on nearly any subject (except, perhaps, the one then being taught). By his own admission he was an exceedingly lazy student, neglecting homework and cramming for special examinations offered to poorly performing students at the end of the year in order to be passed into the next form. One year he failed three subjects and was not permitted to take the end-of-year exam, but was required to repeat the grade. Hayek ultimately attended three different schools before receiving his diploma, but due to the war he was able once again to take a special exam that allowed him to graduate early. This permitted him to volunteer for the army rather than to wait to be drafted. It also gave him confidence that he could "study up" for an area in a short period of time.[1]

If Hayek's poor performance in high school seems difficult to understand, we should recall Malachi Hacohen's description of the typical Austrian Gymnasium of the day as consisting of "strict discipline, tedious memorization, and infinite boredom" (Hacohen 2000, p. 110). It was a system clearly capable of provoking resistance from intelligent students – and indeed, both Stefan Zweig and Karl Popper had similar reactions (Zweig 1943, pp. 24–28; Hacohen 2000, pp. 72–78). When he took an interest in a subject, though, Hayek could pursue it diligently. Biology and its cognate areas were among these, and this seems principally due to his family's influence.

Hayek came from a family of natural scientists, at least on his father's side. His grandfather taught biology and natural history at a Gymnasium. His father was a medical doctor, but devoted all of his spare time to botany, and had hopes of attaining a chair in botany at the university. (This never materialized, though he did obtain an unsalaried *Dozent* position.) August had his own circle, that is, he organized regular meetings of botanists in his own house (Hayek met Erwin Schrödinger as a boy when the latter accompanied his father to one of these meetings), and he also would take his son to lectures at the Zoological and Botanical Society. Hayek would later recall that, "I knew all the biologists in Vienna."[2]

August Hayek was most interested in plant taxonomy; he was what might today be called a plant geographer or ecologist, chronicling which species were indigenous to which habitats and regions. He also owned a large herbarium and ran a business on the side that organized the exchange of pressed plant specimens. From age thirteen to sixteen Hayek helped his father, collecting and photographing specimens, and eventually started his own herbarium. The family's naturalistic expeditions would take place on weekends in the spring and were sufficiently frequent to cause further friction with school authorities, because they meant that Hayek would miss the semi-compulsory attendance at Sunday mass.[3] Hayek's interests were serious; at one point he even began a monograph on a rare variety of orchid, attempting to decipher whether it was a new species. A bit later he developed interests in evolutionary theory and paleontology. In recounting this part of his early history, Hayek concluded that he could easily have imagined becoming a biologist rather than an economist (Hayek 1994, pp. 42–44). Within his family, his ultimate career choice made him an outlier: both of his siblings, and both of his children, went into the natural sciences.

If his father's side of the family influenced him in a scientific direction, his mother's side provided his entrée into the rest of Viennese academic society. His maternal grandfather, Franz von Juraschek, a professor of constitutional law at the university as well as a top-ranking civil servant, was quite wealthy. The family home was "a magnificent, even grandiose, top floor flat of ten rooms" opposite the opera house on the Ringstrasse, and here von Juraschek hosted balls that were attended by the sons and daughters of professors at the university (Hayek 1994, p. 39). Through the Juraschek household Hayek met many people he would encounter again, either at the university or later in his career. He even met Eugen von Böhm-Bawerk there, but he knew him as the climbing companion of his grandfather rather than as a famous economist (Hayek 1994, p. 57).

UNIVERSITY DAYS

Hayek enrolled in the University of Vienna in 1918. He completed his first degree in law in 1921, and another in political economy in 1923. Compared to his earlier educational experience, he thrived at university. The school was flooded with returning veterans, most of whom wanted simply to get their degrees and get out as soon as possible. Hayek was among a small group of students who took his education more seriously. He sought out the best professors, regardless of field, spending his "day at the university from morning to evening ... shifting from subject to subject, readily hearing lectures about art history or ancient Greek plays or something else" (Hayek 1994, p. 51). Perhaps predictably, Hayek was least enthusiastic about his chosen field of study: he ended up hiring a tutor to coach him as he crammed for his exams on Austrian law.[4] His real interests were in psychology and, later, economics.

In the harsh winter of 1919–20 there were fuel shortages that closed the university, and Hayek was sent by his family to Zurich. While there he attended lectures on canon law and on the philosophy of Moritz Schlick (the latter offered not by Schlick but by a Swiss academic). Schlick, the founder of the Vienna Circle of logical positivism, later would become a professor at Vienna, and Hayek would take a class from him. While in Switzerland Hayek also worked briefly in the laboratory of the brain anatomist Constantin von Monakow, dissecting fiber bundles in the brain. It was apparently in Zurich that Hayek wrote most of the essay that would serve as the basis for his 1952 book on the foundations of psychology, *The Sensory Order*.[5]

The Viennese intellectual scene extended far beyond the university, in part because formal professorships (as opposed to the unsalaried *Dozent* positions) were so hard to come by. Study circles formed both within and outside the university, an amalgam of former students, faculty, interested outsiders, and sometimes the best of the undergraduates. While still at university Hayek with his boyhood friend Herbert Fürth formed their own circle, the *Geistkreis*, in which (rather typically) the subjects presented ranged from literature and philosophy to art history and economics. From 1924 until 1931, when he accepted a position at the London School of Economics, Hayek was also a regular member in a circle which formed around Ludwig von Mises. (In late 1921 Hayek took a job in the Office of Accounts, a temporary government office set up to settle various international debt claims, where he met Mises.) In a city in which anti-Semitism was on the increase, it is worth mentioning that Hayek participated in mixed groups, ones that included both gentiles and Jews.

Hayek was at university in the immediate postwar period, an economically desperate and politically tumultuous time. The streets were filled with returning veterans, many of them unemployed, and because embargoes continued even after the war ended, near famine conditions prevailed in Vienna during the first postwar winter. The political situation was extremely volatile, not just in Vienna but across central Europe. In spring 1919 soviet republics were briefly established in both Hungary and Bavaria. Communist agitation in Vienna led to a demonstration on April 17, 1919 in front of the Parliament building that ended in bloodshed, as did an attempted communist coup two months later.[6] Though the various communist revolutions in central Europe all ultimately failed, in the municipal elections of May 1919 the socialists won an absolute majority in Vienna, and undertook the extensive set of social welfare reforms that led to its being called "Red Vienna." Though never as severe as it was in Germany, Austria also experienced hyperinflation in 1921–22, with monthly increases as high as 134 percent.

As a university student Hayek was basically a Fabian socialist.[7] With some friends he briefly toyed with the idea of developing a political party whose platform would lie between the Catholic parties on the one side, and the social democrats and communists on the other. Early on he developed a deep aversion to the communists, however, in part because he witnessed the violence of the first postwar year, but also because the Austrian version of Marxism was so unyielding, at least on paper.[8] Ludwig von Mises' 1922 book on socialism, which appeared soon after Hayek began working with Mises at the Office of Accounts, would begin the gradual process of weaning him from his early socialist sympathies.[9]

We will discuss the influence of various Austrian economists on Hayek's thought in the next section, but here we must also mention the physicist, psychologist, and philosopher Ernst Mach. Mach had died during the war, but his radically empiricist ideas permeated the postwar Viennese intellectual scene. His view that scientific theories are only fictions, useful for organizing complexes of sensations but ultimately to be eliminated as science progresses, directly influenced the views of the logical positivists of the Vienna Circle. Mach's influence was also evident in economist Joseph Schumpeter's 1908 view that sciences do not seek causes but only report on functional relations. Schumpeter used this idea to argue (provocatively, for an economist trained in the Austrian tradition) that the Walrasian general equilibrium approach, which emphasized functional relationships, was the theoretical framework within economics that best exemplified a truly scientific approach. Finally, though Lenin had criticized "empirio-criticism" during the war, the political left in Vienna embraced Machian analysis: the Austro-Marxist variant of "scientific socialism" provided socialist political and economic thought with positivist underpinnings (Caldwell 2004a, pp. 105–6, 136–37).

Mach was important for Hayek, too, in more specific ways. In his student paper on psychology Hayek had argued against the Machian thesis that there is a one-to-one correspondence between an external stimulus and a sensation, positing instead that, when something becomes a part of our consciousness, it assumes a position in relation to our other past impressions. Hayek believed that his own analysis of relations made Mach's recourse to the theoretical construct of "sensations pure and simple" expendable. In making this argument, Hayek was in a sense using Mach's own position within the philosophy of science against his analysis of sensations, an argumentative strategy that Hayek would repeat in certain of his criticisms of both socialism and behaviorism (Caldwell 2004b, pp. 1–5). In addition, in *The Analysis of Sensations* Mach had argued that our commonsense experience of the world (part of what Hayek would call "the sensory order") was a natural product of evolution, a view fully compatible with themes to be found in the mature Hayek's work.

What emerges from these various observations about the economist as a boy and young man? Hayek clearly was an independent and precocious youth, one who could quickly master the basics of a field when he took an interest in it. He was raised in a secular household and had a cosmopolitan outlook, apparently mixing easily with other groups in a society that was growing increasingly anti-Semitic. Perhaps most important, he came from an intellectual household, one that worshiped at the altar of science, and this was reinforced when he went to university – he came of age in a milieu in which the fascination with science was omnipresent. There were reasons for this. The scientific worldview (and with it such economic and political doctrines as liberalism and socialism) challenged both the older tradition-bound Catholic outlook and the doctrines being espoused by various fascist groups (who despised liberalism, socialism, and democracy in equal measure) then emerging across central and southern Europe. The scientific worldview was a bulwark against much that seemed archaic, xenophobic, and irrational, and was a natural draw for the young Hayek.

But it was also contested ground. The mantle of science was being claimed by many contending forces. Who were the real scientists, and how could one demarcate their activities from those of the pseudo-scientists? This question would professionally engage the philosophers of the Vienna Circle and men like Karl Popper, but it was one that touched all who sought to do scientific work.

THE AUSTRIAN TRADITION IN ECONOMICS

When Hayek first enrolled at the University of Vienna, many of the names that we associate with the Austrian School of economics were not on the scene. Though still alive (Hayek saw him once, marching in an academic procession), Carl Menger had been retired since 1903. Eugen von Böhm-Bawerk had died during the war, and Friedrich von Wieser was serving as the Minister of Commerce. The teaching of economics was in the hands of Carl Grünberg, a socialist economic historian, and Othmar Spann. Hayek had little good to say about either; apparently the best thing Spann did for him was to put a copy of Menger's *Principles of Economics* in his hands (Hayek 1994, p. 54).

Hayek briefly was a student of Spann's, but when Wieser returned to the university from his government post Hayek soon settled on him as his major professor. He wrote his dissertation on the theory of imputation, the Austrian approach to marginal productivity theory and a favorite topic for Wieser. Though Hayek greatly admired him as a teacher,[10] Wieser's exact influence on his thought is a bit harder to decipher. Certain affinities are evident. Wieser had argued in his book *Natural Value* that, no matter what the form that social organizations take, the same questions of "management and value" must arise, an argument that is a clear antecedent to Mises' and Hayek's later contributions to the socialist calculation debate. In his theoretical work Wieser followed a methodology of "decreasing levels of abstraction," and Hayek made use of the same method in his own *Pure Theory of Capital* (1941). Perhaps Wieser's treatment of the evolution of social institutions in his 1927 book *Social Economics* also had an impact, for this was an area that Hayek would turn to in later years (Caldwell 2004a, pp. 141–43).

Though Wieser was Hayek's major professor, Ludwig von Mises quickly became his mentor. Mises assisted Hayek in going to America for fifteen months in 1923–24, then helped set him up in a job as the director of an Austrian business cycle institute when the job at the government office was done. As noted earlier, Mises also helped wean him from his youthful dalliance with socialism, a subject to which Hayek would return in the 1930s when he initiated the English language version of the socialist calculation debate.

Mises had made his reputation as a monetary theorist, and this was another area that Hayek chose to investigate. It was perhaps an easy choice: hyperinflation in central Europe, debates over the return to the gold standard and the impact of reparations payments, the emergence of new monetary institutions (the Federal Reserve System in the United States was barely a decade old) and of research and data collection organizations like the newly formed National Bureau for Economic Research and the Harvard Economic Service in the USA, and the London and Cambridge Economic Services in England (similar organizations soon sprang up throughout Europe, as well), all meant that monetary economics was both a hot and an unsettled area, the perfect combination for an ambitious young scholar.

On his trip to the United States Hayek was disappointed to find that theory had not advanced very far beyond what he had already learned as a student. He chose instead to focus on issues of monetary policy as they related to control of inflation and the business cycle. One of the products of his time abroad was a major paper reporting on US monetary policy in the early 1920s, and in it Hayek made reference to the Austrian approach to business cycle theory. In his introduction to a volume of translations of his early papers, Hayek recounted what came next:

[A]nother member of our group with whom I was in daily contact, Gottfried Haberler, persuaded me after reading my first draft that no sufficient exposition of the theory I had used was to be found in Mises' published work, and that if I was to expect to be understood, I must give a fuller account of the theory underlying my report of the events described. Thus arose the long footnote ... containing the first statement of my version of Mises' theory. (Hayek 1984b, pp. 2–3)

Hayek would elaborate his own variant of the Austrian theory of the cycle in his first two books, *Prices and Production* (1931) and *Monetary Theory and the Trade Cycle* (1933). A byproduct of these studies (and also of his trip abroad) was a critique of the theories of two Americans, William Trufant Foster and Waddill Catchings, in a paper published in German that was later translated as "The 'Paradox' of Savings." Lionel Robbins, a young economist at the London School of Economics (LSE), read the paper in German and invited Hayek to give some lectures at the LSE in the spring of 1931. This ultimately led to Hayek's appointment the next year to the Tooke Chair of Economic Science and Statistics there. Hayek's paper providing an Austrian response to the theories of the Americans Foster and Catchings ultimately was responsible for moving him from a *Dozent* position in Austria to a named chair at a major English university. He would remain at the LSE until 1950, when he moved to the Committee on Social Thought at the University of Chicago.

It would be misleading to suggest, however, that Hayek's ideas were exclusively Austrian in origin. For example, his initial statement of the theory of the trade cycle drew on Mises' writings, but also on those of the brilliant Swedish economist, Knut Wicksell. Wicksell published his work in German, and was well known for his 1893 book *Value, Capital, and Rent*, in which he developed the marginal productivity theory of distribution and for his synthetic integration of Walrasian general equilibrium theory with Böhm-Bawerk's capital theory. Five years later he published a book on monetary economics, *Interest and Prices* (Wicksell [1936] 1965), in which he developed the natural rate–market rate of interest dichotomy. Wicksell articulated a more complete version of these theories in lectures that were published in Swedish in 1901 and 1906, and then translated into German in 1922.[11] Hayek had gained considerable institutional knowledge, as well as familiarity with some basic statistical techniques, on his trip to the USA, and was then trying his hand at further integrating monetary theory with an explanation of the business cycle by combining elements of Wicksell's diverse contributions with those of von Mises. His work was integrative and on the cutting edge.

But it also had competitors. Some of these were in Germany, and indeed, I think that one way to read *Monetary Theory and the Trade Cycle* is as an argument directed at German economists, and especially the Kiel School that was forming around Adolf Löwe. Hayek argued that, with the introduction of the "loose joint" of money, a theory of the cycle that was also fully consistent with Walrasian static equilibrium theoretical foundations, was not an oxymoron, as Löwe's work might suggest, but fully viable (Caldwell 2004a, pp. 156–62).

More important in retrospect, however, was the role the book played in leading to Hayek's famous encounter with John Maynard Keynes.[12] In his 1930 book, *A Treatise on Money* (Keynes 1971b), Keynes had also drawn on Wicksell's natural rate–market rate dichotomy, but had left out any reference to Wicksell's earlier work on capital theory. By way of contrast, the effect of divergences between the market and natural rates of interest on the capital stock was a key element of Hayek's story. Hayek offered up his criticisms in a two-part review of Keynes' book, and in his reply Keynes attacked Hayek's own *Prices and Production*, which had just appeared.

The battle with Keynes marked Hayek's entrance into the British academic scene. Of course, Keynes soon swept the field with the publication in 1936 of his *General Theory*. As for Hayek, criticisms from a variety of quarters made him rethink the capital-theoretic foundations of his own model, and in particular his use of Böhm-Bawerk's device of an "average period of production" in explicating how changes in interest rates affect the structure of production. He would work on this project on and off throughout the rest of the 1930s, a project that generated many papers and which ultimately culminated with the publication in 1941 of *The Pure Theory of Capital*. Though he finished the book, the project nearly exhausted him, and he never really achieved what he hoped to do, the construction of a dynamic model of a capital-using monetary economy. Like his earlier work, it drew heavily on the Austrian tradition in economics, but it also integrated the writings of economists working in the traditions of Sweden, Lausanne, America, and Britain. By this point in time, the cosmopolitan nature of Hayek's œuvre was evident.

In the 1930s Hayek also began developing his insights about how a market system with freely adjusting prices coordinates economic activity in a world of dispersed knowledge. These insights led him to question the ability of the static equilibrium analysis of his day, with its assumptions of full information and perfect foresight, to shed light on the workings of a market economy. The origins of these ideas are hard to disentangle, though Hayek's participation in the socialist calculation debate and in discussions with Swedish economists and others about expectations, as well as the challenging claim of Hayek's old classmate Oskar Morgenstern that perfect foresight was logically incompatible with the notion of Walrasian *tâtonnement* (movements towards equilibrium), all deserve mention (Caldwell 2004a, pp. 209–20). In any event, these insights slowly but surely led Hayek to investigate how a host of social institutions in addition to markets assist in the coordination of knowledge, and ultimately to questions about the origins of such institutions. In this later work Hayek was in a sense returning to themes that had initially engaged the founder of the Austrian tradition, Carl Menger. Interestingly, even though Hayek had edited a collection of Menger's writings in the early 1930s and wrote a biographical essay on him, when mentioning predecessors he most often made reference to Scottish Enlightenment philosophers like David Hume, Josiah Tucker, Adam Ferguson, and Adam Smith, rather than Menger (e.g. Hayek [1946] 1948). One suspects that this was because by this time his audience was English-speaking (neither of Menger's books had been translated yet), and because he began these investigations during the Second World War, when reference to German-speaking social scientists, even liberals, might have been viewed as somewhat impolitic.

BATTLES WITH OTHER TRADITIONS

The Austrian tradition was born in opposition; the very use of the term "Austrian" to identify a school of economic thought was begun by its opponents, members of the German Historical School of economics. German Historical School economists rejected a theoretical approach to their subject. Noting that each country has its own distinct and unique history, with different social norms, institutions, and cultural values affecting its course of development, they concluded that the abstract theorizing of classical economists like David Ricardo was simply a mistaken generalization from the narrow experience of one nation at one point in time, Great Britain since the late eighteenth century. They favored instead the detailed study of the development of each nation's economic, social, cultural, and ethical institutions. Some had stage theories of development, others urged the patient collection of facts, but all derided the classicals' desire to articulate a universal theory of economics.

Carl Menger, whose *Principles of Economics* ([1950] 1976) was the founding document of the Austrian School, agreed with the German Historical School economists that the specific theory of value endorsed by Ricardo and the British classicals – most followed some variant of a cost of production theory – was wrong. But he disagreed that this implied that there could be no *theoretical* approach to economic phenomena. In the *Principles* he claimed that a number of economic practices and institutions – these included the origins of money and exchange, the formation of prices, and the development of various market structures – could be explained as the unintended consequences of intentional human action. People in pursuing their own interests do not set out to create such institutions; rather, they emerge as unintended, and in that sense spontaneous, orders. In explaining why exchange occurs, Menger introduced the marginal principle, which would become the foundation for modern microeconomic theory.[13]

Though Menger dedicated his book to Wilhelm Roscher, a leading figure among the older German Historical School economists, it was interpreted by the leader of the younger generation, Gustav Schmoller, as simply a continuation of the errors of Ricardo and other classicals. Disputes between the two schools led eventually to the *Methodenstreit*, or battle over methods – and it was in this battle that the term "Austrian School of economics," originally meant as a term of derision, was coined.

By the time Hayek had come on to the scene, the battle between the Austrian and German Historical Schools was pretty much over. What remained were certain presuppositions that Hayek brought to his studies. Perhaps the most important of these was the Austrian insistence that the proper way to study economics was theoretical.

One can see this view, for example, in the first chapter of *Monetary Theory and the Trade Cycle*, where Hayek both defends a theoretical approach to his subject and offers a scathing attack on "empirical studies" in economics. One of the targets was "the oft-repeated argument that statistical examination of the Trade Cycle should be undertaken without any theoretical prejudice," a view which he claims "is always based on self-deception" (Hayek [1933] 1966, p. 38). For the Austrians, a fundamental conclusion of their debates with the German Historical School economists was that there is no such thing as the presuppositionless observation of reality or collection of data – empirical work always must take place within an existing, even if implicit, theoretical framework.

Though Hayek cited the work of the Harvard Economic Service as an example of the error, his argument was equally directed at the approach advocated by the American economist Wesley Clair Mitchell. Hayek had encountered Mitchell on his trip to America, and even sat in on his history of economic thought class. Though

Mitchell was critical of the German Historical School, he shared their belief that the marginalist approach was simply a continuation of the mistakes of the classicals, especially in their use of the "rational economic man" construct. Mitchell envisioned a future for economics in which the "scientific psychology" of behaviorism would replace subjective value theory, and in which economists would join with natural scientists to use objective statistical data to organize and run society along more rational lines. In his attacks on marginalist theory and emphasis on the use of statistics Mitchell would have reminded Hayek of the German Historical School economists. But in his vision of a future in which science would be used to reconstruct society he would also have reminded Hayek of the positivists, more on whom in a moment.

Another result of the *Methodenstreit* was that the so-called "second generation" of Austrian economists, Böhm-Bawerk and Wieser, increasingly emphasized the marginalist part of the Austrian contribution as opposed to the "social institutions as the unintended consequences of intentional human action" part which had been so important to Menger, and in his later work, to Hayek. They did this to make clear the differences between their own theory and the cost of production theories of value of the classicals. A prominent defender of one variant of the classical theory was Karl Marx, whose utilization of a labor theory of value was central to his explanation of the origin of surplus value, itself a key part of his theory of the exploitation of the proletariat. Marxist value theory then became a natural target for the Austrians. And indeed, after Böhm-Bawerk's devastating 1896 critique of the third and final volume of *Das Kapital*, the Austrian economists were evermore identified as the most prominent critics of Marxism (see Böhm-Bawerk [1896] 1975).

While the criticisms of Marxist value theory by Böhm-Bawerk and others caused some socialists to abandon the labor theory of value (thus provoking the first schism in Marxism), others rose to its defense. Among the most vocal defenders were the Austro-Marxists, and this led to a famous encounter. After years of government service Böhm-Bawerk returned to teaching in 1904, and for the next decade he ran an economics seminar at the university. The first seminar was on the theory of value, and featured an extended debate between Böhm-Bawerk and Otto Bauer, the brilliant young leader of the Austro-Marxists, one who would go on to lead the Austrian

Social Democrats after the war. Other seminar participants included the Marxist theoretician Rudolf Hilferding, who had himself published (see Hilferding 1975) a criticism of Böhm-Bawerk's position on Marx, as well as Joseph Schumpeter and Ludwig von Mises. After these debates on the transformation problem and the Marxian theory of value, the Austrian economists were thoroughly schooled in the nuances of Marxist theory, and indeed defined their own approach at least partly in contradistinction to it.

But the Austrian critique of socialism was ultimately to go far beyond the criticism of its value theory. This was due in part to another seminar participant, Otto Neurath. In the seminar Neurath propounded the doctrine of "war economy," the idea that the massive central planning that typically characterizes an economy in war should be extended into peacetime. Neurath further proposed that money should be abolished, and that the managers charged with directing the economy should rely instead on an extensive body of social statistics that could be used to plan production and distribution, a plan that would particularly irritate a monetary theorist like Ludwig von Mises. By the end of the war many others had joined Neurath in proposing socialization schemes for the reorganization of society, though few were as radical as his. These proposals ultimately provoked von Mises to write an article and later a book on socialism, thereby beginning the German language socialist calculation debate.

Neurath's writings also strengthened the link in the Austrian mind between socialism and positivism, for in the 1920s he was to become the "social science expert" for the Vienna Circle. As recent scholarship emphasizes, the early days of the logical positivist movement had a distinctly political side, and Neurath played a central role in this. In advocating the unity of science, for example, he hoped to enlist all of the sciences to use them to refashion society along socialist lines (Reisch 2005). In any event, for the Austrian School economists, positivist philosophy of science was always aligned in their minds with socialist politics and economics.[14]

How did the conflation of socialism and positivism affect Hayek? Though he had taken a class from Schlick and had participated in political events as a student, Hayek's real exposure to the relevant debates doubtless occurred after he began participating in the Mises Circle. One of his friends from the *Geistkreis*, Felix Kaufmann, was a member of both the Mises Circle and the Vienna Circle, and he kept the former apprised of the latter's activities. In the late 1920s Mises was fashioning his own response to the positivists with his theory of human action, so positivism was a much discussed topic in the seminar. Though Hayek appears never to have been comfortable with the *a priori* foundations that Mises claimed for his program, he imbibed and fully concurred with the view that the positivists were only pretenders to the mantle of science. And because their radically empiricist approach to science had much in common with the naive empiricism of the German Historical School economists, arguments against them came naturally to the lips of anyone trained in the Austrian economic tradition.

One can see the effects of all this in Hayek's work beginning in the 1930s. In the middle of the decade he embarked on his own battle against socialism. His first move was simply to inform his British readers of the German language debates that had already taken place. And his subsequent moves also make sense given his background, for very soon his arguments branched off from the purely economic to a more broad-based attack that focused on the methodological and philosophical underpinnings of socialist thought.

In his Second World War era essay "Scientism and the Study of Society," Hayek grouped together under the common and pejorative label "scientism" a number of doctrines, and did so according to common elements they shared: historicism, objectivism, collectivism, and the planning mentality (Hayek [1942–44] 1952). The advocates of these approaches hoped to use objective, empirically oriented science and the careful collection of historical data and statistics to plan and carry out the efficient production of goods that would then be distributed along more equitable, often socialistic, lines. From Hayek's perspective, positivists, socialists, German Historical School economists, and American institutionalists all shared a similar agenda. For someone raised in the Austrian tradition, he could not see it otherwise.

Hayek and the Austrians were not just critics; they offered an alternative approach to the study of social phenomena, and again, the contrast is well drawn in the "Scientism" essay. In contrast to the objectivism of Neurath's physicalism, say, or Mitchell's behaviorism, there is in the Austrians a stress on subjectivism: people act on the basis of their subjective perceptions of reality, according to their

own subjective tastes, preferences, and knowledge. In place of collectivism, the Austrians offered an analysis that begins with the choices
of purposeful individual agents, of "acting man." Instead of an historical approach, the Austrians proposed the theoretical study of social
phenomena. And in place of the planning mentality, the Austrians
defended the idea that many social phenomena are examples of
spontaneous orders, the unintended consequences of purposeful
human action.

Hayek's commitment to such Austrian themes as subjectivism
and methodological individualism is clear in his work from the
mid-1940s, not just in the "Scientism" essay but also in such pieces
as "The Facts of the Social Sciences" (Hayek [1943] 1948) and
"Individualism: True and False" (Hayek [1946] 1948).[15] His commitment to examining and explicating the formation of complex self-
organizing orders only grew through time, and influenced his work in
psychology, the law, and the philosophy of science. Finally, Hayek's
commitment to theory also never wavered: no matter what the subject matter, his analyses were inevitably framed at the highest, most
abstract level.

Having been raised in the Austrian tradition explains finally why
Hayek fell in so easily with Karl Popper when he read his work. This is
something that needs some explaining because, though both were
Viennese, they did not know each other in Vienna, and Popper's
politics were considerably to the left of Hayek's. If one looks, however,
at the opening chapters of The Logic of Scientific Discovery ([1959] 1968),
Popper's attack there on inductivism (the idea that via the careful
collection of facts one can construct a scientific theory) would have
been completely in line with the Austrian view vis-à-vis the German
Historical School economists and the positivists.

In his LSE inaugural lecture ([1933] 1991) Hayek had attributed
many of the mistaken beliefs of the day to the lingering influence
of the German Historical School economists – in short, their attacks
on economic theory had undermined its authority, opening the door
to the many quack economic policy prescriptions then on offer.
About a year later Hayek was talking to Gottfried Haberler about
the ill effects of positivism, and Haberler told him he should read
the work of Popper. Hayek obliged, and this resulted in Popper being
invited to speak at his seminar at the LSE, where Popper presented
an early version of The Poverty of Historicism. Hayek later was to

recount that when he heard Popper's views about falsification (that is, the idea that for a theory to be scientific there must be some state of the world that can falsify it), he "just embraced his views as a statement of what I was feeling" (Hayek and Weimer 1982, p. 323). I believe that this is equally true for Popper's attacks on inductivism.

A characteristic that Hayek shared with most of his antagonists, at least those identified here, was that he was a full participant in the modernist scientific project. Hayek saw himself as a scientist, and believed in the power of scientific argument. When he attacked socialism, he didn't do so on moral or ethical grounds. Rather, he argued that socialist planning could not accomplish the ends it set out for itself.[16] When he criticized behaviorism in *The Sensory Order* (1952b), his argument was again that it failed to meet its own strictures about science. Behaviorism insists on making recourse only to observable phenomena in order to remain "objective" and to avoid acts of interpretation. But if Hayek's theory is true, all sensory data are themselves products of the mind – they are themselves acts of interpretation. (Incidentally, this argument further reinforces the idea that there is no such thing as brute, uninterpreted facts, a position taken by the Austrians against the German Historical School economists.)

Hayek remained to the end a believer in science; he just thought that many other believers (especially those so ready to label their opponent's beliefs as "metaphysics") were not practicing what they preached. Hayek was a modernist through and through, but one who recognized the importance of interpretation. As a subjective value theorist raised within the Austrian tradition, he was in this sense a fully representative member.

I will close with a final, and very speculative, hypothesis. I have dealt only peripherally with one of the key elements of Hayek's thought, his emphasis on the severe limitations of our knowledge, which implies that there is often very little we can do to shape social phenomena to fit our own designs. One sees this idea running throughout his work. In the Preface to *Monetary Theory and the Trade Cycle*, he says: "[T]he one thing of which we must be painfully aware at the present time – a fact which no writer on these problems should fail to impress upon his readers – is how little we really know of the forces which we are trying to influence by deliberate management; so little indeed that it must remain an open question whether we would try if we knew more" (Hayek [1933] 1966, p. 23). It is there in his essays on knowledge, when he labels the fact of social coordination in a world of dispersed knowledge a "marvel" (e.g. Hayek [1945] 1948, p. 87). One sees it in his claim that often the best we can do in the social sciences, especially when dealing with complex phenomena, is to make pattern predictions or to explain the principle by which the phenomena operate (e.g. [1942–44] 1952, pp. 70–76; [1964] 1967). It is there most evidently in the sorts of statements he was making in interviews toward the end of his life, such as that "what we can know in economics is so much less than people aspire to."[17]

Some may wish to argue that Hayek was simply born with a sort of natural pessimism or cynicism, and that this generated his long-standing belief in the inherent limitations that humans face when they try to intervene in social phenomena. Perhaps. But it is also possible that this view was the product of his having come of age during the final collapse of an already broken-down empire, of having experienced the multiple forms of disaster that surrounded postwar Vienna and enveloped interwar central Europe, and of having witnessed the failures of various high-minded social experiments to achieve anything like what their exponents had promised. In bearing witness to so much tragedy Hayek was again very much a part of the larger Austrian tradition. His famed "epistemic pessimism" may well have been another result of that larger experience.

NOTES

1. These details of Hayek's early school experiences come from an unpublished interview with W. W. Bartley III that took place in Freiburg on February 9, 1983, one of a number that Bartley undertook during the 1980s. I thank Stephen Kresge, who provided me with copies of the interviews, for permission to draw on them here and elsewhere in the chapter.

2. Undated 1983 interview with W. W. Bartley III; cf. also his interview of February 11, 1983. Here and in what follows, any words quoted directly from Hayek appear through the courtesy of the Hayek estate.

3. In an interview with W. W. Bartley III in Freiburg on February 11, 1983 Hayek said that "the Sunday excursions were very much intended by him [August – BC] partly for his own botany and partly to bring up his children [to be] interested in the natural sciences."

4. Interview with W. W. Bartley III, Freiburg, February 11, 1983.

5. Interview with W. W. Bartley III, London, March 28, 1983.

6. In an unpublished 1989 manuscript titled, "Music and politics: Karl Popper meets Arnold Schönberg and the Eislers and gives up communism," W. W. Bartley III noted that Hayek, returning home from university during the April demonstration, was briefly caught in the crossfire.

7. In an interview with W. W. Bartley III in Freiburg on February 10, 1983, Hayek stated that his close friend Herbert Fürth's father was a lawyer in Vienna who was active in various Fabian causes, and that this, together with his reading of the works of Walther Rathenau, were most responsible for his early sympathies for socialism.

8. Austro-Marxists were among the most doctrinaire, with little room for compromise with revisionists, but the actual strategy followed by Otto Bauer, who as leader of the social democrats in Red Vienna did not think that the historical conditions were right for a revolutionary transformation of society, was fairly conciliatory, leading some to blame him for the eventual fascist successes of the 1930s.

9. As Hayek put it in his Foreword to a new English language edition of Mises' book, "It gradually but fundamentally altered the outlook of many of the young idealists returning to their university studies after World War I. I know, for I was one of them" (Hayek 1981, p. xix).

10. See e.g. p. 14 of the 1983 document "Nobel Prize Winning Economist," edited by Armen Alchian, UCLA, Charles E. Young Research Library, Department of Special Collections, Oral History transcript no. 300/224, transcript of an interview with Hayek conducted in 1978 under the auspices of the Oral History Program, University Library, UCLA.

11. Not incidentally, given the importance of Wicksell's work for the controversy between Keynes and Hayek, both *Interest and Prices* and *Lectures on Political Economy* were translated into English in the 1930s. A translation of Wicksell's 1893 book *Value, Capital, and Rent* did not appear until 1954.

12. For more on this episode, see Hayek 1995.

13. For a more detailed discussion of the development of Menger's thought, see Caldwell 2004a, ch. 1.

14. See Caldwell 2004a, ch. 1 for a more detailed discussion of the Austrian economists' debates with Austro-Marxists and positivists.

15. As I argue in 2004a, pp. 279–87, his commitment to "methodological individualism" in later years depends mightily on how one defines the term, and as such is less clear.

16. By utilizing the Weberian means–ends framework, the argument remains value-free. Thus Mises and Hayek argued that the means (socialist planning) would not allow the chosen ends (rational production) to be

accomplished: without freely adjusting market prices, socialist managers would not have the knowledge of relative scarcities needed to
make rational production decisions. Or, as Hayek argued in *The Road to
Serfdom* ([1944] 1962), without common shared values, socialist planners
would not be able to come up with a production plan that would gain
everyone's approval.

17. See p. 258 of the interview cited in n. 10.

2 Hayek on money and the business cycle

Since *The Road to Serfdom* Hayek has been known primarily as a philosopher of freedom. He published ideas about money and macroeconomic policy (for example, his advocacy of the "denationalization" of money) but, though this work may have influenced politicians such as Margaret Thatcher and Ronald Reagan, it was never taken seriously by economists. By the 1970s he was, in the minds of most economists, at best a political philosopher in a world where economics had become highly technical, and at worst an ideologue. Either way, economists did not consider him someone to be taken seriously. Before the Second World War, on the other hand, Hayek was generally accepted, even by those who did not agree with him, as an economist of the first rank, undertaking research in business-cycle theory that demanded their attention. In his controversy with Keynes in 1930–31, Hayek, in a sense, stood on a par with Keynes (in so far as the newly arrived *enfant terrible* could be on a par with an established authority): they offered visions of capitalism and how to remedy its macroeconomic problems that vied for attention at a time when these were more pressing than at almost any other time in history.

This chapter seeks to explain Hayek's ideas on money and the cycle in this period when his work lay at the heart of the field, and which can best be considered independently of his later work. These included his doctoral thesis, published in German in 1929 and translated into English in 1933 as *Monetary Theory and the Trade Cycle*, and the book *Prices and Production* (first edition 1931, second edition 1935) that arose out of the LSE lectures that brought him to the attention of English-speaking economists. Though published later, *Monetary Theory and the Trade Cycle* was the beginning. After a highly charged debate with Keynes, and partly because of his parallel work on socialism, which led to his conception of the market as an information processing mechanism, Hayek's work on the cycle continued though the 1930s, brought together in *Profits, Interest, and Investment* (1939b) and culminated in *The Pure Theory of Capital* (1941), a work constrained by the exigencies of wartime. By this time, not only was the economics profession moving decisively toward Keynesian economics, which differed radically from his, but Hayek was becoming involved in his "abuse of reason" project and *The Road to Serfdom*, which he perceived as his contribution to the war effort.[1]

Hayek's writing on money and the cycle came during one of the most turbulent periods in monetary history. The background was undoubtedly the German experience of hyperinflation in the 1920s, when money lost virtually all its value, ushering in the social and economic disruption out of which totalitarianism emerged. The other defining event of the period was the stock market crash of 1929 and the ensuing depression. Though the immediate causes of this lay in central Europe (the collapse of the Austrian bank, Credit Anstalt), it affected the world; Hayek sought the causes of this catastrophe in the policies pursued, not in Germany, but in the United States. He developed a theory according to which the depression was the inevitable result of the boom that the United States had experienced during the 1920s, when Europe was suffering from persistent depression and economic dislocation. Where Keynes was arguing that interest rate policy and public works expenditure (and at one stage even tariffs to protect industry) could be used to alleviate depression and to promote recovery, Hayek considered these precisely the opposite of what was required. They would merely serve to prolong an expansion that was unsustainable and was bound, eventually, to collapse. To follow such a course would not just postpone something that was inevitable: the longer the maladjustment continued, the worse would be the ensuing crisis.

Hayek had come to this theory by 1930, and sought to develop its foundations during the years leading to his *Pure Theory of Capital*. At this time, economics was much less technical than it became in the second half of the twentieth century. There was a proliferation of theories of the business cycle, each focusing on a different set of factors as its underlying cause. Some economists stressed the "real" shocks resulting from technological innovations, wars, and other causes. Others saw the cycle as rooted in monetary factors, and others explored the role of psychological factors – waves of optimism and pessimism that affected entrepreneurs' expectations of the profitability of investment. With few exceptions, economists did not use any formal framework to explore the relationships between these theories or to test one against the other. Integration was in terms of a narrative, reliance being primarily on verbal not mathematical reasoning. The alternative to upholding a single explanation was thus an eclectic combination of different theories, as represented by Wesley Clair Mitchell.

The same situation held in monetary economics, though here the quantity theory of money (the theory that there is, at least in the long run, a proportionality between the price level and the money supply) provided a framework around which discussion centered. Not all economists were quantity theorists, for in Europe and in the United States there were those who denied such a relationship, and there were many versions of the quantity theory. But it provided a more formal framework for analysis than was available in business cycle theory. Of course, as monetary theories of the cycle demonstrate, the two fields overlapped significantly.

Paradoxically, given the intensity of their disagreement, in the late 1920s, Keynes and Hayek were both turning toward the same version of the quantity theory, developed around 1900 by the Swedish economist, Knut Wicksell ([1936] 1965, [1906] 1978).[2] Though a quantity theory, this focused attention on the role of the interest rate and the role of banking policy in influencing the relationship between savings and investment. Wicksell argued that there was a "natural" rate of interest, at which savings and investment would be equal. If the rate were lower, savers would be unwilling to save as much as entrepreneurs would wish to invest – in buildings, vehicles, machinery, stocks of goods, and so on. If it were higher, in contrast, entrepreneurs' demand for funds to finance their investment activity would be less than savers wished to provide. Only at the natural rate would these be balanced. The problem, however, was that the actual rate of interest (the "market" rate) was determined by the policy of the banking system. If the market rate differed from the natural rate, this would imply that saving and investment were not equal: a monetary disequilibrium.

THE MONETARY THEORY OF THE CYCLE

Hayek's teacher, Ludwig von Mises, was one of those who took up Wicksell's theory, emphasizing the way in which a low rate of interest, set by the banking system below the natural rate of interest, would cause investment to exceed saving (see Laidler 1994, 1999).[3] The difference would be filled by the creation of money by the banking system, for it was the banks' willingness to lend that kept the market rate below the natural rate. Political pressures meant that expansionary monetary policy was more likely than contractionary policy, resulting in a bias toward inflation. However, whereas Wicksell had seen this simply as a theory of inflation in a credit-money economy, Mises transformed it into a theory of the cycle. If saving was too low, consumption must be too high, implying that, at some point, the stock of consumption goods must become exhausted; the price of consumption goods would then rise, bringing the expansion to an end. What was needed for stability was a policy of "neutral" money.

However, the concept of neutral money posed a serious problem of definition. The natural rate could be defined in three ways: (1) as the rate at which savings and investment are equal and therefore no new money is created; (2) as the rate of interest at which prices are constant (no inflation); or (3) as the rate of interest that corresponds to the productivity of real (physical) capital goods. In a stationary economy, the natural rate of interest is simple to define, for the various definitions of neutrality coincide. In a growing economy, on the other hand, they diverge. If the real economy is growing at, say, 4 percent per annum, demand for cash will also be growing at 4 percent per annum. This means that it is possible for the market rate of interest to be lower than the natural rate, for investment to exceed saving, and for the money supply to be expanding, but without inflation. Provided the supply of money does not increase by more than 4 percent per annum, there will be no inflation. There would appear to be monetary neutrality according to one definition (zero inflation) but non-neutrality according to another (saving equal to investment). This was, to quote Laidler (1994, p. 5) "an intellectual muddle of impressive proportions but, as it turned out, a seminal muddle." In the 1920s and 1930s economists responded to it in different ways, producing theories that were very different, despite their common starting point (see Laidler 1999).

Hayek's solution was to argue that neutrality required equality of saving and investment. If investment exceeded saving this meant that, even though there might be no inflation because the economy was growing, monetary policy was distorting the economy. Too many resources were being allocated to investment and not enough to consumption. The reason why this mattered was that the artificially low rate of interest caused the economy not merely to over-invest, but to invest in excessively capital-intensive methods of production. It was this distortion of the structure of production that was the fundamental reason why Hayek argued that neutrality required that investment and saving be equal and that no new money be created, even if this meant, as it would in a growing economy, that prices were falling. To understand why Hayek considered this such a problem, it is necessary to understand in more detail his theory of capital.

THE THEORY OF CAPITAL

As the title of his 1941 book indicates, the theory of capital lay at the heart of his theory of the cycle. The reason is that he attributes the cycle not to changes in aggregate demand, or even to changes in the quantity of capital, but to changes in the *structure* of production and hence the *structure* of the capital stock.[4] In this, his theory was highly unusual: one of the reasons for his failure to engage more effectively with Keynes was the latter's inability to see how the theory of capital could be of any importance for the cycle. Because the theory of capital is so central, and because it is so complex, it needs to be explained carefully. After that, the rest of his theory falls into place comparatively easily.

The most common way to think about the stock of capital is to see it as a list of capital goods: buildings, machinery, vehicles, and other assets that are used in the production process. The stock of capital is the value, calculated using an appropriate set of prices, of the stock of goods existing at any moment in time. If this is higher, so the theory goes, the productivity of labor will be higher. Instead, Hayek, following the Austrian tradition of Böhm-Bawerk and Mises, saw capital as related to time. The essential property of a capital good is that it enables production to take place over a longer period; it is this that causes more capital-intensive methods to raise productivity.

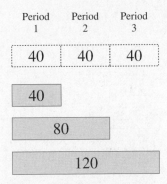

Fig. 1. A three-stage production process

The only simple way to explain this is with an example. Roads can be built, as in China or New Deal era America, by large teams of men with pickaxes and shovels, a labor-intensive process. Or instead, they could be built, as in much of the modern world, with mechanical earth-moving equipment, a much more capital-intensive process. The Austrian theory involves arguing that building roads with mechanical equipment is a longer process of production than doing so with hand tools. The reason is that hand tools can be made very quickly, so that the entire process from first applying labor to making them to seeing the finished road could be very short. In contrast, mechanical equipment takes longer to make, and before it can be made, other equipment (such as machine tools) have to be made. The period from first applying labor (perhaps constructing the factory that made the machine tools that were used to make the mechanical shovels) to finishing the road may be very long indeed.

Hayek represented the capital stock with his "triangles." Consider a process of production that takes three periods (the machine tool is built in period 1; the mechanical shovel in period 2; and the road in period 3). Assume that 40 units of labor are used in each period (for the moment this number is unimportant). The result is the production process shown in figure 1.[5] The machine tools produced in period 1 are the fruit of 40 units of labor; the mechanical shovels produced in period 2 represent 80 units; and the road 120 units. However, time brings in a crucial complication – the rate of interest. By the time that the road is built, the labour employed building the machine tools will have been invested for two periods and the labor used to make the shovels for one period. If the rate of interest is 10 percent, total

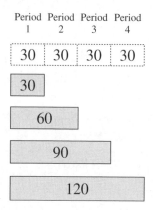

Fig. 2. A four-stage production process

interest payments in building the road will amount to the value of approximately 12 units of labour.[6] If the price of a unit of labor is $1, the cost of the road will be $132.[7]

Now consider the effects of moving toward a four-stage production process. An example is illustrated in figure 2, where the numbers are chosen so that the same total quantity of labor is employed, 30 units being employed in each stage. Assuming the same rate of interest, the interest will be approximately $9 + $6 + $3 = $18 and the total cost $138.

Clearly if the output were the same, entrepreneurs would always choose the labor-intensive process. But suppose that the four-period process is more productive: it produces 1.1 km of road for every unit of labour, whereas the three-stage process produces only 1 km. If roads are priced at $1.20 per km, entrepreneurs using the two processes will earn $158 and $144 respectively. The four-stage process will yield a profit of $20 whereas the three-stage process will yield only $12. Entrepreneurs will choose the former.

The final stage in this abstract argument is to consider the effects of raising the rate of interest to 20 percent. The interest cost on the three-stage process will rise to approximately $24 and that on the four-stage process to $36, yielding total costs of $144 and $156 respectively. At this rate of interest, the three-stage process breaks even, whereas the four-stage process makes a loss. Entrepreneurs will choose the shorter process.

This example is highly abstract and simplified, but it explains several propositions. The first is that the capital intensity of a production process can be measured by the period of production. In more complicated scenarios, different amounts of labor are applied at different stages of production, and the time pattern of labor inputs will be different for each case (compare growing wheat with growing oak trees or vintage port). This means that it is necessary to focus on the average period of production, taking account of when labor is applied, not the overall length of the process. The second is that it suggests a presumption that rises in the rate of interest will cause shorter production processes to be adopted and vice versa.[8] The third is that changing from one process to another does not involve simply having "more" or "less" capital: it involves using different capital goods. The capital goods produced at each stage in the production process will be physically different: it is not merely a matter of having more or less of some homogeneous substance called capital.[9]

THE DEVELOPMENT OF HAYEK'S THEORY

The starting point of Hayek's theory was that economic activity involves time:

All economic activity is carried out through time. Every individual economic process occupies a certain time, and all linkages between economic processes necessarily involve longer or shorter periods of time. (Hayek 1984c, p. 71)

Existing theory, Hayek argued, said nothing about this, dealing only with production and consumption at a specific moment in time. It was necessary to generalize the theory of equilibrium, which explained the set of prices that prevailed at one moment, into a theory of intertemporal equilibrium, explaining how prices evolved over time: the "intertemporal price system."[10] Prices of goods that were physically identical need not be the same at different dates, for there might be changes in production conditions or in consumers' demands. If goods were becoming cheaper to produce, due to technical progress, prices would generally be falling.

Hayek proposed to analyze such price systems using the concept of equilibrium. Equilibrium implies that prices are such that no agent wishes to change his or her production or consumption plans. To extend this to cover production and consumption over time Hayek assumed that agents correctly anticipated any changes that took place, taking such price changes into account when planning their activities. Thus current production and consumption decisions would depend not just on current prices and production costs, but also on anticipated prices and production costs at all future dates. Hayek was particularly concerned with the situation where, due to technical progress, production costs of a particular good were falling. If there were to be equilibrium over time, it was necessary that the price of that good fell pari passu, otherwise it would become progressively more profitable to produce that good. Because this would make entrepreneurs wish to produce more of the good, this would be inconsistent with equilibrium.

In a monetary economy, it was possible that intertemporal equilibrium would require changes in the "general" price level – the price of all goods in terms of money. Prices might need to fluctuate over the year or to change over a longer period in response to changes in conditions of production. Hayek's point was that changes in the general price level played a role in the allocation of resources. Of particular importance, such price changes influenced decisions about whether to produce goods now or in the future. For example, if entrepreneurs expected the price of a good to rise relative to its production cost, they would wish to increase their investment, producing more in the future at the expense of current production. The result was that, if production conditions were changing, a policy of stabilizing the price level would distort the intertemporal price system, with damaging consequences.

In an article the same year, expanded as his thesis, "Geldtheorie und Konjuncturtheorie" (1929), and translated as *Monetary Theory and the Trade Cycle* ([1933] 1966), Hayek extended this argument by turning to the question of how money was introduced into the economy. This, he claimed, was the key to explaining the trade cycle. Here, he turned to what he called the "Wicksell–Mises" theory. The natural rate of interest is the rate of interest that would prevail in equilibrium. At the natural rate of interest, entrepreneurs' demand for funds exactly equals the supply of funds from savers, and the price system is that required for intertemporal equilibrium. However, in a monetary economy, the actual (market) rate of interest will regularly deviate from the natural rate. Periodically there will be rises in the natural rate of interest, caused by real forces, such as innovations that raise productivity. Entrepreneurs will therefore seek greater credit in order to increase their investments to take advantage of the higher profits that they can obtain. Rising incomes will cause additional savings to be deposited with the banks. Competition between banks means that they will not wish to raise their interest rates but will respond to this inflow of cash by increasing their lending. Because banks need hold only a fraction of their deposits as reserves, the total volume of credit can be expanded, keeping the rate of interest from rising. For a while, therefore, the banking system can expand the money supply. Eventually, the banks will run out of reserves and be forced to raise interest rates, cutting back on their lending.

Fractional reserve banking (where banks receive deposits but need retain only a fraction of their deposits as reserves, lending the rest) results in an elastic currency that rises in response to demand. Hayek's point is that an economy with an elastic currency must respond to external shocks "quite differently" from an economy where monetary expansion is not possible and, as a result, the supply of funds is rigidly constrained by what savers are willing to provide. When the natural rate of interest rises, the market rate fails to rise so as to act as a brake on expansion. He drew the conclusion:

The determining cause of the cyclical fluctuation is, therefore, the fact that on account of the elasticity of the volume of currency media the rate of interest demanded by the banks is not always equal to the equilibrium rate, but is, in the short run, determined by considerations of banking liquidity. (Hayek [1933] 1966, pp. 197–80)

The way banking was organized made it inevitable that there would be fluctuations caused by monetary factors. The way to avoid such fluctuations would be to keep the total amount of bank deposits (not the price level) constant. However, Hayek recognized that even if this were possible, it might not be desirable, for it would imply rates of interest that were higher than those actually observed, and a "psychological incentive towards progress" would disappear (Hayek [1933] 1966, p. 191). There were, therefore, both advantages and disadvantages attached to having an elastic currency, and policymakers had to weigh these against each other.

In the 1930–31 academic year, when Hayek gave the lectures that formed the basis for *Prices and Production*, the world was falling into the great depression. Though Hayek's argument was purely theoretical, it makes sense to explain his theory by showing how it could be used to explain the depression. The heart of his argument was that inappropriate monetary policy had distorted the price system, resulting in a misallocation of resources. Depression was an inevitable feature of the process whereby the economy returned to a sustainable allocation of resources.

The 1920s were a period of innovation and prosperity in the United States.[11] Prices had, after the initial postwar cycle, been roughly constant, suggesting that monetary policy had been about right. Drawing on the monetary theory outlined above, Hayek contended that monetary neutrality had required falling prices, and that the constant prices actually observed implied that policy had been too expansionary. The result was an interest rate lower than the natural rate and, according to the theory of capital outlined above, this would result in a lengthening of the period of production. Investment was higher than the level that could be funded by voluntary saving, the remainder being supplied by the banking system. This was unsustainable, for eventually the banking system would be forced to raise interest rates. At this point, Hayek's theory of capital becomes very important to his account.

When the rate of interest rises, long processes of production become unprofitable and entrepreneurs wish to shift resources into shorter processes (such as from that shown in Figure 2 to that shown in Figure 1). The problem with this is that intermediate goods appropriate to the longer processes of production will already have been produced (the motors required to drive mechanical shovels). When entrepreneurs move to building roads with hand tools, these motors will no longer be required: the investment that has already been made has to be written off. However, whilst these longer processes are being terminated, it will take time to build up production using shorter processes: the hand tools needed to build roads using labor-intensive methods may not exist, and it takes time to produce them. Thus old processes are being shut down but new processes are not coming on stream fast enough to absorb the workers who are losing their jobs. Hayek believed that this rise in unemployment would be only temporary, for eventually production methods would adjust to the new set of prices.

Depression arose, therefore, because monetary policy interfered with the price system, causing relative prices to be wrong and distorting the structure of production. In *Prices and Production*, as in his earlier work, his theory was based on the notion of an intertemporal equilibrium. Despite its complexity it was important for Hayek to use the concept of an intertemporal equilibrium in which agents were correctly anticipating future prices and were making plans optimally, for the time structure of production was central to his argument. In a static equilibrium, he argued, there could be no unemployment. During the 1930s, Hayek continued to believe that capital theory was fundamental to any explanation of the business cycle but he modified his views in other respects. The most important change was that Hayek moved away from this extreme faith in equilibrium theory, in the process redefining the notion of equilibrium.[12] In "Economics and Knowledge" ([1937] 1948), he questioned whether the concept of equilibrium had meaning when applied to the actions of a group of individuals, and moved to a broader concept of equilibrium that took account of the subjective character of knowledge. Equilibrium involved consistency of beliefs with outcomes, and hence with the beliefs of other individuals. He therefore focused much more on expectations, arguing that the equilibrium framework of *Prices and Production* was inadequate for analyzing the cycle, and moved instead to a concept of equilibrium based on fulfillment of expectations. Faced with the severity of the depression, he paid greater attention to how downturns in the economy might get amplified, developing theories in which prices and wages and technical coefficients were rigid, and in which perverse expectations might become self-fulfilling; for example, faced with expectations of falling prices, consumption might fall, causing those expectations to be fulfilled (1939b, p. 177). It was even possible that the system might never reach any position that could be described as an equilibrium.

This phase of Hayek's work received its final treatment in *The Pure Theory of Capital* (1941). This offered a more systematic treatment of the subject than had been offered in his previous works, integrating the theory of money with the theory of capital, the link between them being the rate of interest and the price system. This interaction of monetary and real factors was the essence of the theory of the cycle. He did not claim to have solved that problem, merely to have pointed out the importance of real factors. Writing against the background of the success of Keynes' *General Theory* ([1936] 1973) Hayek castigated the way economists focused on the short run and hence on monetary factors. His work, he claimed, had shown that real factors were important and that they severely constrained monetary policy. Economists had gone astray because they assumed that capital was a homogeneous quantity that could easily be switched from one use to another, whereas in fact it comprised a collection of heterogeneous goods, where even the distinction between investment goods and consumption goods was not clear-cut.

The strength with which Hayek held this view, and his difference from what was rapidly becoming the Keynesian orthodoxy, was evident in his conclusions, which are worth quoting at some length:

> I cannot help regarding the increasing concentration on short-run effects – which in this context amounts to the same thing as a concentration on purely monetary factors – not only as a serious and dangerous intellectual error, but as a betrayal of the main duty of the economist and a grave menace to our civilisation ... It is not surprising that Mr. Keynes finds his views anticipated by the mercantilist writers and gifted amateurs: concern with the surface phenomena has always marked the first stage of the scientific approach to our subject. But it is alarming to see that after we have once gone through the process of developing a systematic account of those forces which in the long run determine prices and production, we are now called upon to scrap it, in order to replace it by a short-sighted philosophy of the business man raised to the dignity of a science. Are we not even told [by Keynes] that, "since in the long run we are all dead," policy should be guided entirely by short-run considerations? I fear that these believers in the principle of *après moi le déluge* may get what they have bargained for sooner than they wish. (Hayek 1941, pp. 409–10)

Keynesian theory confined attention to the demand side. Though part of the story, it neglected constraints imposed by the supply side. Hayek's theory of capital was an attempt to analyze the supply side, using the tool of equilibrium analysis, extended to make it appropriate for a dynamic economy. Given this, it is perhaps no coincidence that when Hayekian ideas came back into fashion in the 1970s, it was when economists were once again attaching greater importance to the supply side, even though they were analyzing it using techniques that were very different from Hayek's.[13]

APPRAISAL

Hayek wished to probe beneath the surface of economic phenomena, and in his work on money and the cycle, he relied on the theory of static equilibrium. This was an explicit methodological choice:

It is my conviction that if we want to explain economic phenomena at all, we have no means available but to build on the foundations given by the concept of a tendency towards an equilibrium. For it is this concept alone which permits us to explain fundamental phenomena like the determination of prices or incomes, an understanding of which is essential to any explanation of fluctuation of production. (Hayek 1935a, p. 34)

He went so far as to say that the existence of unemployed resources was "not explained by static analysis, and accordingly we are not entitled to take it for granted" (1935a, p. 34), presumably implying that if it were explained by static analysis, it could be taken for granted, a remarkably strong claim for static equilibrium theory. From 1937, Hayek's attitude changed, but he continued to use a modified concept of equilibrium as a benchmark in analyzing dynamics:

The concept [equilibrium] can also be applied to situations which are not stationary and where the same correspondence between plans prevails, not because people just continue to do what they have been doing in the past [static equilibrium], but because they correctly foresee what changes will occur in the actions of others. (Hayek 1941, p. 18)

Using the concept of equilibrium, Hayek tried to show, using the Austrian theory of capital – perhaps better described as a theory of production – that a capitalist economy would necessarily be subject to periodic spells of unemployment, and that an elastic supply of currency would make this worse, not better.[14]

The main problem with this strategy is that it requires the creation of a rigorous theory of how the capital stock and production will change in a dynamic economy.[15] This problem was beyond anything Hayek could achieve with the methods at his disposal. Intertemporal equilibrium in a dynamic economy with a multiplicity of products and capital goods is extremely complicated, even more so if intermediate goods are specific to different processes and become obsolete when the rate of interest and relative prices change. This problem became even more acute with the shift in his views on markets that took place in 1937. Using advanced mathematical techniques or simulation, it may be possible to say something about such complex models, but such methods were not available to Hayek.[16] As a result, it was impossible to prove the results that he wanted to prove. For example, it can be shown that it is impossible to prove that there is a negative relationship between the rate of interest and the period of production or capital intensity, a relationship that is important in his theory. His theory therefore remained an illustration of what *might* happen (of how a market economy *might* periodically fail), not of what *would* happen. In other words, he pointed to one of the mechanisms that might be operating over the cycle. Possibly, this was as much as any purely deductive theory of the cycle could achieve.[17]

A second problem is an empirical one. Hayek's theory rested, as Garrison (2003) has emphasized, on the assumption that there is some specificity or heterogeneity in capital goods: if there were not, then the idea of a capital structure would be meaningless.[18] Keynes ignored this dimension of capital completely, thereby ruling out problems of the type Hayek was trying to identify. It is clear that some capital goods are heterogeneous, and that they become redundant when production methods change. Highly specialized machinery and many half-finished goods fall into this category. On the other hand, many capital goods can be adapted to new technologies: buildings, much machinery, and many intermediate products. A priori, it is difficult to be sure how much capital falls into each category. Indeed, the answer may be very sensitive to the precise technical changes involved.[19]

Hayek's theory got buried in what has been described as "the Keynesian avalanche" (McCormick 1992). In the years after 1936, whilst Hayek was working on *The Pure Theory of Capital*, most economists were convinced by Keynes, whose theory had an elegance and simplicity that Hayek's did not. Keynes' theory lacked Hayek's theoretical rigor in that it was not based on equilibrium (on individual rationality), and there were places in the argument where Keynes relied on loose, informal arguments, preferring to put his trust in intuition rather than formal theory. Keynesians did not solve the problems with capital theory that Hayek had identified: they just bypassed or ignored them. According to Hayek's methodological criteria, Keynes' theory was decidedly inferior. Against this, Keynes' theory provided opportunities for mathematical and statistical analysis that Hayek's did not. Indeed, though Hayek paid some attention to data, he did so only minimally: he certainly made no attempt to test his theory against statistical data. The choice of Keynesian theory was, at least in part, a methodological one.

If Hayek's capital theory is abandoned, on the grounds that it is impossible to develop a completely rigorous theory of what happens outside a stationary state, let alone outside equilibrium in other senses, it becomes impossible to prove, using a priori methods, that an elastic currency and inflation are harmful, let alone that the great depression was caused by interest rates being too low during the 1920s. It is possible to show that they may be harmful but not that they must have been. The judgment that non-neutral money during the 1920s did cause the subsequent downturn arguably reflected ideology as much as technical economic arguments.[20] If this element of his theory is removed, what is left is his belief, fostered by his experience during the 1920s, that politicians cannot be trusted to keep inflation within safe levels, and that institutions must be developed to constrain it. That, arguably, is a fair characterization of the position he adopted in the 1970s.[21] This later work may not have the theoretical rigor of his work on money and the cycle during the 1930s, but perhaps it retains its most substantial elements: the beliefs that the price system works and that easy money is likely to disrupt it.[22]

NOTES

1. For a detailed account of Hayek's intellectual development, see Caldwell 2004a.
2. They reached this theory very differently: Keynes arrived at it via Cambridge discussions of saving and investment in the 1920s, not via Mises.
3. The literature on Hayek's business cycle theory is much larger than can be cited here. For further references see vol. 3 of Boettke 2000b.
4. All accounts of Hayek recognise this, but Haberler (1986) and Garrison (2003) place particular emphasis on it.
5. This example also assumes that each machine tool produces just one mechanical shovel before being worn out, and that each mechanical shovel produces but one road. The examples given here are simplified versions of those found in Hayek 1935a, where his examples involve longer production periods.
6. Compound interest means the exact figure will be 12.4, but this does not affect the points made here.
7. The shaded rectangles together form one of Hayek's "triangles."
8. These are keenly contested claims that formed the subject of intense debates in capital theory in the 1930s and the 1960s. Though many economists believe that they must in practice be true, it turns out that it is impossible to prove them to be true except under special conditions.

9. All that is necessary for Hayek's theory is that capital goods are not exactly the same. Even if rivets were used in producing both pickaxes and mechanical shovels, the general point would remain.

10. Caldwell (2004a, p. 156) argues that Hayek was strongly influenced by Adolph Löwe (1997, pp. 267–68) who had argued that static theory could not explain the cycle and that a dynamic theory was required. Given Hayek's conviction that theoretical rigor required an equilibrium theory, this led him to a theory of intertemporal equilibrium.

11. In Europe, of course, the situation was very different.

12. For an insightful account of this process, relating it to modern theory, see Desai 1994.

13. The production function that underlies most modern macroeconomics treats capital as homogeneous; it is nowadays critics of the free market, not its supporters, who stress the heterogeneity of capital.

14. Colonna (1994) argues that the use of equilibrium methodology was the distinctive feature of Hayek's theory. His contemporaries argued in terms of disequilibrium states, in which almost anything could happen, contributing to confusion.

15. Trautwein (1994) has identified other problems, but this seems the major one because Hayek made the theory of capital so central to his theory: take it away and his theory had much less to distinguish it from the theories of certain of his contemporaries.

16. For example, Desai and Redfern (1994) use simulations, a method that could be developed using modern information technology.

17. Though they did not make quite this point, this resonates with contemporary criticisms that Hayek's theory of capital was "too cumbersome" and that the conclusions he drew were "too sweeping" (cf. Laidler 1994, p. 14).

18. See also Garrison 1994.

19. Cf. Ebenstein 2001, p. 83.

20. Hayek (1967c, p. 254) himself recognized that ideology could influence economic analysis in ways that led him to argue, in terms reminiscent of Gunnar Myrdal, that political positions should be stated explicitly (cf. Dostaler 1994, p. 147).

21. See the work reprinted in Hayek 1999a and 1999b.

22. This conclusion is close to the one reached by Desai (1994).

3 Hayek and market socialism

F. A. Hayek is perhaps best known for his opposition to socialism. His most famous work is undoubtedly *The Road to Serfdom* ([1944] 1962) and the last work he published, *The Fatal Conceit* (1988), was actually conceived of in the context of attempting to arrange a world-wide debate between advocates of socialism and advocates of capitalism. His founding of the Mont Pèlerin Society in 1947 was an attempt to align the opponents of socialism in the intellectual, political, and business worlds so they could form an effective intellectual bulwark against the rising tide of socialism in the democratic west. He directed his argument against the "hot" socialism of Marxism as well as the "cold" socialism of the social democratic welfare state in the post-Second World War era.[1]

The fact that Hayek was a critic of government command and control over the economy is well known among scholars and intellectuals. Socialism lacked incentives and presented the central planning authority with too complicated a task. As a result socialism was too bureaucratic and cumbersome to operate in an economically efficient manner. Moreover, it is also known that Hayek postulated that the very worst elements within government will tend to take advantage of the situation to rise to power, and thus not only would socialism suffer from a "knowledge problem" but also from an "abuse of power problem."[2] Thus, Hayek's political economy can be summarized by three conjectures:

1. Markets work by mobilizing the dispersed knowledge in society through the price system.
2. Socialism does not work as well as capitalism because without the price system it cannot mobilize the dispersed knowledge in society.

3. Socialism is dangerous to democracy and liberty because economic planning must by necessity concentrate power in the hands of a few, and those with a comparative advantage in exercising that power will rise to the top of the planning bureaucracy.

These "Hayek conjectures" are understood to have emerged in his long battle with socialist economists and intellectuals, and are often invoked as comprising the free market case against government planning of the economy.[3] While they capture, in a superficial way, Hayek's position, the careful student of Hayek is often frustrated with discussions that treat Hayek as an ideological icon as opposed to an economist and political economist. In other words, these conjectures are the byproduct of a network of scientific propositions that Hayek established during his career as an economist and political philosopher and cannot be read as mere statements of ideological opinion. It is this network of scientific propositions, concerning the nature and extent of the economic and political problems that must be addressed for any society to achieve advanced social cooperation under a division of labor, which underlies these "Hayek conjectures" about the policy world.

MISES' CHALLENGE TO MARXIAN SOCIALISM

Hayek inherited his research program from his mentor Ludwig von Mises. While Hayek was not technically Mises' student at the University of Vienna, as a newly minted doctor of jurisprudence with a concentration in economics, he came under Mises' influence at the Vienna Chamber of Commerce. Hayek worked with Mises on questions of business forecasting and what came to be known as the "Austrian theory of the trade cycle." Critical aspects of that theory were: (1) a picture of the capital structure in an economy as consisting of heterogeneous capital good combinations that had to be maintained or reshuffled in more productive and advantageous combinations; (2) a vision of the production process as one engaged in over time, thus generating a need for a mechanism for the intertemporal coordination of production plans to meet consumer demands; and (3) the notion that increases in the money supply work through the economy not in an instantaneous adjustment of prices, but through relative price adjustments.

Each of these elements of the theory of the trade cycle occupied researchers in the first decades of the twentieth century. For example, in analyzing the production process through time the concept of the imputation of the value of producer goods from the consumer goods they produce was developed, and the role of interest rates in coordinating production plans was highlighted. Entrepreneurs rely on price signals to guide them in their production process so that they are allocating scarce capital resources in the most valuable direction and employing the least costly technologies. The capital structure does not automatically replenish itself, but instead requires the careful calculations of economic actors to determine which production projects are the most profitable ones to pursue. If the price signals are confusing, then decisions concerning the maintenance and allocation of capital will be mistaken from the point of view of economic value maximization.

The monetary theory of the trade cycle developed by Mises and Hayek in the 1920s put all the pieces together from the work of Austrian and Swedish neoclassical economists, and contrasted that vision of the capital-using economy with the more mechanistic understanding of a monetary economy associated with economists in the USA and UK and the chaotic vision of economic life associated with the critics of capitalism.

Mises' economic and sociological analysis of socialism ([1920] 1935; [1922] 1951) is based on the subjective theory of value as applied in the context of a capital-using economy. In fact, Mises went as far as to claim: "To understand the problem of economic calculation it was necessary to recognize the true nature of the exchange relations expressed in the prices of the market. The existence of this important problem could be revealed only by the methods of the modern subjective theory of value" ([1922] 1951, p. 186).

Mises provided a comprehensive critique of socialist schemes of all varieties. In his writings one can find a critique based on the perverse incentives of collective ownership, the cumbersomeness of bureaucracy, and the inability to simulate entrepreneurial innovation outside the context of a market economy and the lure of profit and the penalties of loss. But the critical point Mises raised against the most coherent form of socialism was that collective ownership in the means of production would render rational economic calculation impossible.[4] Without private property in the means of production, there would be no market for the means of production. Without a market for the means of production, there would be no market prices for the means of production. Without market prices (reflecting the relative scarcities of capital goods), economic planners would not be able rationally to calculate the most economically efficient investment path. Without the ability to engage in rational economic calculation, "all production by lengthy and roundabout processes would be so many steps in the dark" ([1922] 1951, p. 101). No individual or group of individuals could discriminate between the numerous possibilities of methods of production to determine which ones are the most cost effective without recourse to calculations based on monetary prices. "In societies based on the division of labor, the distribution of property rights effects a kind of mental division of labor, without which neither economy nor systemic production would be possible" ([1922] 1951, p. 101). Monetary prices and profit and loss accounting are indispensable guides in the business of economic administration. "Without such assistance, in the bewildering chaos of alternative materials and processes the human mind would be at a complete loss. Whenever we had to decide between different processes or different centres of production, we would be entirely at sea" ([1922] 1951, p. 102). Socialism in its attempt to overcome the anarchy of production substitutes instead planned chaos. As Mises puts it:

To suppose that a socialist community could substitute calculations in kind for calculations in terms of money is an illusion. In a community that does not practice exchange, calculation in kind can never cover more than consumption goods. They break down completely where goods of higher order are concerned. Once society abandons free pricing of production goods rational production becomes impossible. Every step that leads away from private ownership of the means of production and the use of money is a step away from rational economic activity. ([1922] 1951, p. 102)

Mises' critique was greeted with resistance. In the German language a heated debate ensued in the 1920s and included such figures as Karl Polanyi and Eduard Heimann and Austro-Marxists such as Otto Neurath. In the English language, contributors to the debate in the 1920s and 1930s include Fred Taylor ([1929] 2000), Frank Knight ([1936] 2000), Oskar Lange ([1936–37a] 2000; [1936–37b] 2000) and Abba Lerner ([1934–35] 2000; [1936–37] 2000; [1937] 2000). Amidst the discussion the western capitalist economies were embroiled in the great depression

while the socialist Soviet system transformed a peasant country into
an industrial economy in one generation. Supposedly capitalism was
proved by the events of the 1930s to be not only unjust, but unstable.
Socialist planning, on the other hand, provided the Soviet Union
with the material base effectively to fight the fascist threat that
arose in Germany in the 1930s and 1940s.

It is in this intellectual and analytical context that Hayek started
to develop his own presentation of the issues which Mises had raised.
The reading of Hayek that I want to stress is one that sees him as
groping for answers in an intellectual context that did not make
sense to him. While he was convinced of the power of Mises' argument against socialism, and also that it was government policy
mistakes, and not capitalist instability, that caused the great depression, he understood that many others were not convinced and this
led him to search for reasons why others did not see the power of
Mises' arguments, and for alternative ways to express Mises' insights
so that perhaps they would be more persuasive to those who had
resisted them. In the process, Hayek would, over the coming decades,
refine and extend Mises' foundational work on the methodology of
the human sciences, the analytical method of economics, and the
social philosophy of liberalism.

THE SURPRISING EMERGENCE OF NEOCLASSICAL
MARKET SOCIALISM

In 1931 Hayek visited the London School of Economics at the invita-
tion of Lionel Robbins and he gave a series of lectures that were later
published as *Prices and Production* (1935a). Hayek subsequently
joined the faculty at the LSE assuming the Tooke Professorship in
Economics and Statistics. He and Robbins established the curriculum and considered it part of their mission to introduce the ideas
developed by neoclassical economists in continental Europe to
English-speaking audiences.

In "The Trend of Economic Thinking" ([1933] 1991), Hayek argued
that economics was born in the intellectual exercise of critically
engaging utopian schemes, that the liberal economists are no less
concerned with the disadvantaged in society than are their intellectual opponents on the left, and that economics has vastly improved
as a consequence of the marginal revolution and the development of

neoclassical theory. Ironically, Hayek contended that neoclassical economics had repaired the problems in the classical system identified in the historicist critique, but that the general intellectual world largely ignored these positive developments in the body of economic thought. Instead, the intellectual and policy class proceeded as if the historicist critique held sway over contemporary economic theorizing. As a result, various utopian schemes that would be refuted by careful economic analysis retained a popular support which was far in excess of the merits of the schemes. "Refusing to believe in general laws," Hayek argued, "the Historical School had the special attraction that its method was constitutionally unable to refute even the wildest of Utopias, and was, therefore, not likely to bring disappointment associated with theoretical analysis" ([1933] 1991, p. 125).

The 1930s were a decade of great success for Hayek. He emerged as the major theoretical rival to John Maynard Keynes within the English community of economists. From his intellectual home at the LSE, Hayek, together with Robbins, effectively challenged the "Oxbridge" hegemony in economic research and teaching. Talented students and junior faculty were attracted to the LSE and included such superstars as Ronald Coase, Abba Lerner, John Hicks, Nicholas Kaldor, Ludwig Lachmann, and G. L. S. Shackle. In the early to mid-1930s, students and faculty were attracted to Hayek's monetary theory of the trade cycle and the government-induced credit expansion explanation for the boom–bust associated with the great depression. However, by the end of the decade the Keynesian dominance was beginning to take hold even at the LSE.

Hayek was blindsided by the defection of his students and junior colleagues to the Keynesian argument. But despite his disbelief in the staying power of Keynes' economics of abundance, he could understand that Keynes had written a tract for the times and that serious people could get caught up in the policy concerns of the day. What Hayek could not fathom was the development of schemes for socialism that utilized the very price theory that he had taught. Socialism and neoclassical economics in Hayek's frame of reference were incompatible. He certainly understood that marginal economics was utilized by Fabians at the LSE, but Hayek thought that the English economists had not fully understood the implications of the subjective theory of value and the marginal conditions of equilibrium. The work of Barone, Pareto, and Wieser had established early on that socialism and capitalism faced a formal similarity with respect to the marginal conditions if they wanted to allocate scarce resources efficiently. Formal similarity, though, does not mean that the mechanism and probability of attainment are identical between the different social systems.

In the belief that socialism, if it was to achieve its claimed outcomes of advanced material production, must satisfy the formal conditions of economic efficiency stipulated by marginalist principles, Frederick Taylor, Frank Knight, H. D. Dickinson ([1933] 2000), and Abba Lerner began developing an argument that used modern neoclassical economics to ensure the efficiency of socialist economic planning. Using the same line of neoclassical reasoning, Oskar Lange was able to formulate his critique of Mises.

In deploying the formal similarity argument, Lange provided the following blueprint. First, allow a market for consumer goods and labor allocation. Second, put the productive sector into state hands but provide strict production guidelines to firms. Namely, inform managers that they must price their output equal to marginal costs, and produce that level of output that minimizes average costs. Adjustments can be made on a trial and error basis, using inventory as the signal. The production guidelines will ensure that the full opportunity cost of production will be taken into account and that all least-cost technologies will be employed. In short, these production guidelines will ensure that productive efficiency is achieved even in a setting of state ownership of the means of production.

Lange went even further in his argument for socialism. Not only is socialism, by mimicking the efficiency conditions of capitalism, able theoretically to achieve the same level of efficient production as the market, but it would actually outperform capitalism by purging society of monopoly and business cycles that plague real-world capitalism. Moreover, since the means of production would rest in the hands of authorities, market socialism would also be able to pursue egalitarian distributions in a manner unobtainable with private ownership. In the hands of Lange (and Lerner) neoclassical theory was to become a powerful tool of social control. Modern economic theory, which Mises and Hayek had thought so convincingly established their argument, was now used to show that they were wrong.

MARKET SOCIALISM AND MARKET PROCESSES

Lange's argument presented a formidable challenge for believers in the productive superiority of capitalism, a challenge that Hayek would devote the better part of the 1940s to attempting to meet.[5] Hayek's response to Lange's model for market socialism came in the form of a multi-pronged argument. First, Hayek argued that the models of market socialism proposed by Lange and others reflected a preoccupation with equilibrium. The models possessed no ability to discuss the necessary adaptations to changing conditions required in real economic life. The imputation of value of capital goods from consumer goods represented a classic case in point. Schumpeter (1942, p. 175) had argued that once consumer goods were valued in the market (as they would be in Lange's model), a market for producer goods was unnecessary because we could impute the value of corresponding capital goods ipso facto.

This "solution" was of course accurate in the model of general equilibrium where there is a prereconciliation of plans (i.e. no false trades). Hayek's concern, however (like Mises') was not with the model of general equilibrium, but with how imputation actually takes place within the market process so that production plans come to be coordinated with consumer demands through time. This is not a trivial procedure and requires various market signals to guide entrepreneurs in their decision process on the use of capital good combinations in production projects. In a fundamental sense Hayek was arguing that Mises' calculation argument could not be addressed by assuming it away. Of course, if we focus our analytical attention on the properties of a world in which all plans have already been fully coordinated (general competitive equilibrium), then the process by which that coordination came about in the first place will not be highlighted since the process will have already been worked out by assumption.

This was Hayek's central point. Absent certain institutions and practices, the process that brings about the coordination of plans (including the imputation of value from consumer goods to producer goods) would not take place. Some alternative process would have to be relied upon for decision making concerning resources, and that process would by necessity be one that could not rely on the guides of private property incentives, relative price signals, and profit/loss accounting since the socialist project had explicitly abolished them. In other words, the ipso facto proposition of competitive equilibrium was irrelevant for the world outside of that state of equilibrium. The fact that leading neoclassical economists (like Knight and Schumpeter) had not recognized this elementary point demonstrated the havoc that a preoccupation with the state of equilibrium, as opposed to the process which tends to bring about equilibrium, can have on economic science.

In Hayek's view, the problem with concentrating on a state of affairs as opposed to the process was not limited to its assumption of that which must be argued for, but also included the direction of attention away from how changing circumstances require adaptations on the part of participants. Equilibrium, by definition, is a state of affairs in which no agent within the system has any incentive to change. If all the data were frozen, then indeed the logic of the situation would lead individuals to a state of rest where all plans were coordinated and resources were used in the most efficient manner currently known. The Lange/Lerner conditions would hold – prices would be set to marginal cost (and thus the full opportunity cost of production would be reflected in the price) and production would be at the minimum point on the firm's average cost curve (and thus the least-cost technologies would be employed). But what, Hayek asked, do these conditions tell us about a world where the data are not frozen? What happens when tastes and technologies change?

Marginal conditions, he noted, do not provide any guide to action; they are instead outcomes of a process of learning within a competitive situation. In a tautological sense, competition exists in all social settings, and thus individuals find that in order to do the best that they can given the situation, they will stumble towards equating marginal costs and marginal benefits. This is true at the individual level no matter what system we are talking about. But this says nothing about the first optimality rule proposed in the Lange/Lerner model – that of setting price equal to marginal cost – nor does it address the second optimality rule of the model – that of producing at the level which minimizes average costs. Both rules are definitions of an end point in a certain competitive process, but are not guiding rules for actors caught within that process. Rather than being given to us from above, entrepreneurs must discover anew each day what the best price to offer is, what the least-cost methods of production are, and how best to satisfy consumer tastes.

Effective allocation of resources requires that there is a correspondence between the underlying conditions of tastes, technology, and resource endowments, and the induced variables of prices and profit and loss accounting. In perfect competition the underlying variables and the induced variables are in perfect alignment and thus there are no coordination problems. Traditions in economic scholarship that reject the self-regulation proposition tend to deny that there is any correspondence between the underlying conditions and the induced variables in the market.

Hayek, in contrast to both of these alternatives, sought to explain the lag between the underlying and the induced. Economics for him is a science of tendency and direction, not one of exact determination. Changes in the underlying conditions set in motion accommodating adjustments that are reflected in the induced variables on the market. The induced variables lag behind, but are continually pulled toward the underlying conditions.[6]

The detour on equilibration versus equilibrium in the core of economic theory was important because of the turn the debate took after Lange's paper and the transformation of basic language in economics. Hayek tended to emphasize the dynamic aspects of competition more than Lange did. Market efficiency is adaptive to Hayek, but to Lange and the neoclassicists it is a question of static efficiency. Similarly, to Hayek prices not only represent exchange ratios but also serve a crucial economizing and informational role. For Lange and neoclassical economists they perform merely the former job.

Hayek's fundamental critique of Lange's contribution was that economists ought not to assume what they must in fact demonstrate for their argument to hold. Informational assumptions were particularly problematic in this regard. As Hayek developed his argument, he for the most part steered clear of motivational issues and claimed that individuals (both privately and as planners) would have the best of intentions. However, while assuming moral perfection he refused to assume intellectual perfection. This was quite understandable. If one assumes both moral and intellectual perfection, then what possible objection could anyone raise to any social system of production? In line with our discussion above about equilibration vs.

equilibrium, Hayek argues that perfect knowledge is a defining characteristic of equilibrium but cannot be an assumption within the
process of equilibration. The question instead is: how do individuals
come to learn the information that it is necessary for them to have in
order to coordinate their plans with others?

In "Economics and Knowledge" ([1937] 1948) and "The Use of
Knowledge in Society" ([1945] 1948), Hayek develops the argument
that the way in which economic agents come to learn represents
the crucial empirical element of economics, and that price signals
represent the key institutional guidepost for learning within the
market process. Traditional neoclassical theory taught that prices
were incentive devices, which indeed they are. But Hayek pointed
out that prices also serve an informational role, which is, unfortunately, often overlooked. Prices serve this role by economizing on
the amount of information that market participants must process
and by translating the subjective trade-offs that other participants
make into "objective" information that others can use in formulating
and carrying out their plans.

As the debate progressed, Hayek emphasized different aspects of
the argument developed in these two classic articles and came to
place particular emphasis on the contextual nature of the knowledge that is utilized within the market process. Knowledge, he
pointed out, does not exist disembodied from the context of its
discovery and use. Economic participants base their actions on concrete knowledge of particular times and places. This local knowledge that market participants utilize in orienting their actions is
simply not abstract and objective and thus is incapable of being used
by planners outside that context to plan the large-scale organization
of society.

Hayek's reasons for holding that planning cannot work are not
limited to the problem that the information required for the task of
coordinating the plans of a multitude of individuals is too vast to
organize effectively. The knowledge utilized within the market by
entrepreneurs does not exist outside that local context and thus
cannot even be organized in principle. It is not that planners would
face a complex computational task; it is that they face an impossible
task, because the knowledge required is not accessible to them no
matter what technological developments may come along to ease the
computational burden.

HAYEK AND THE POLITICAL ECONOMY OF LIBERALISM
AND SOCIALISM

The classical economists' argument for liberalism demonstrated its robustness in the face of a world of less-than-benevolent individuals. It is easy to show that liberalism will work well when all individuals are assumed to be perfectly benevolent. But how does it deal with more realistic assumptions? The classical economists sought to show that even in a society populated by completely self-interested individuals, the market would ensure that the desires of men would be satisfied without problem. Smith's famous invisible hand postulate illustrated how, under conditions of respect for property, contract, and consent, each person's pursuing his or her own interests will lead to the promotion of society's interests as a whole. His most famous quote from the *Wealth of Nations* summarizes this point nicely: "It is not from the benevolence of the butcher, the brewer, or the baker, than we expect our dinner, but from their regard to their own interest. We address ourselves, not to their humanity, but to their self-love" (Smith [1776] 1976, p. 18).

Even in the case of knavish men, Smith demonstrated that economic liberalism enabled peaceful social cooperation that leads to increases in productivity. Indeed, he pointed out that liberalism could not only deal with a world of selfish individuals, but actually harnessed man's self-interested motivation for the benefit of everyone. Under liberalism, selfish and rapacious man is "led by an invisible hand to promote an end which was no part of his intention" – the interest of society (Smith [1776] 1976, p. 477). It was within this framework that the classical economists formulated their argument for liberalism. As Hayek stated it:

[T]he main point about which there can be little doubt is that Smith's chief concern was not so much with what man might occasionally achieve when he was at his best but that he should have as little opportunity to do harm when he was at his worst. It would scarcely be too much to claim that the main merit of the individualism which he and his contemporaries advocated is that it is a system under which bad men can do least harm. It is a social system which does not depend for its functioning on our finding good men for running it, or on all men becoming better than they now are, but which makes use of men in all their given variety and complexity, sometimes good and sometimes bad, sometimes intelligent and more often stupid. ([1946] 1948, pp. 11–12)

David Hume's "On the Independency of Parliament" makes it clear that like Smith, he too is interested in developing a case for liberalism that satisfies the hard case rather than the easy one. "In constraining any system of government and fixing the several checks and controls of the constitution," Hume argued, "every man ought to be supposed a knave and to have no other end, in all his actions, than private interest" (1985a, p. 42). In this way, Hume, like Smith, demonstrated how liberalism intended to construct a robust political and economic system.

Hayek restated this argument for the robustness of liberalism in *The Constitution of Liberty* (1960) and later in *Law, Legislation, and Liberty* (1973; 1976b; 1979), where he developed the idea of the importance of particular institutions as the backdrop against which erring and ignorant agents can learn to adapt their behavior so as to coordinate their activities with those of others. According to Hayek, the institutions of private property, contract, and consent, embedded in a system of general rules that protect these institutions, are crucial not only to mobilizing incentives but also in ensuring that economic actors are able to utilize their individual knowledge of time and place in making decisions in such a way that their plans may be realized. These institutions Hayek cites are precisely the institutions of liberalism – private property and freedom of contract protected under a rule of law. And through them, Hayek shows us, liberalism is able effectively to deal with actor ignorance. In fact, Hayek went as far as to state the case for liberalism on the grounds of our ignorance:

If there were omniscient men, if we could know not only all that affects the attainment of our present wishes but also our future wants and desires, there would be little case for liberty. And, in turn, liberty of the individual would, of course, make complete foresight impossible. Liberty is essential in order to leave room for the unforeseeable and unpredictable; we want it because we have learned to expect from it the opportunity of realizing many of our aims. It is because every individual knows so little and, in particular, because we rarely know which of us knows best that we trust the independent and competitive efforts of many to induce the emergence of what we shall want when we see it. (1960, p. 29)

CONCLUSION

Hayek's research program in political economy emerged in his career-long struggle with arguments advocating socialist economic

planning as a corrective to the economic woes of laissez-faire capitalism. Hayek started his career under the guidance of Wieser as a
technical economist, but the issues he worked on were related to
the core questions of the intertemporal coordination of production
plans with consumption demands. In essence, his research path from
the beginning dealt with the essence of the economic arguments
concerning capitalism and socialism.

Once he moved beyond the technical question of the imputation
of value for capital goods, Hayek focused on questions related to the
effects of monetary disturbances on the coordination of plans.
Alongside Mises, Hayek was able to develop the monetary theory
of the trade cycle and offer the most coherent non-Keynesian explanation for the great depression. Hayek rose in scientific stature
quickly, but soon found himself embroiled in debate, with Keynes
on the one side, and market socialists on the other.

In response to these two criticisms of economic liberalism, Hayek
would find himself over the next decades searching for answers, in
the catallactic (or exchange) tradition of economic theorizing as
opposed to the maximizing and equilibrium tradition; in the methodological critique of scientism as opposed to the near-universal
acceptance of methodological monism; and in the institutional analysis of liberalism as opposed to the institutionally antiseptic theory
of post-Second World War neoclassical economics. The debates that
Hayek initiated on methodology and policy continue still.[7] In this
regard Hayek's work remains part of our "extended present," as
Kenneth Boulding (1971) would have put it in discussing the continuing relevance of an economic figure long dead. The plausibility of the
"Hayek conjectures" with which we started this essay is a function of
the plausibility of the network of scientific propositions he weaved
in support of them, in economics, political economy, and social
philosophy. At the end of the day, any evaluation of the former
must wait upon an evaluation of the latter.[8]

NOTES

1. The terms "hot" and "cold" socialism are introduced in Hayek 1960.
2. Lavoie 1985a is perhaps the most comprehensive discussion (beside
   Hayek's) of how "planning does not accidentally deteriorate into the militarization of the economy; it *is* the militarization of economy ... The

theory of planning was, from its inception, modeled after feudal and militaristic organizations. Elements of the Left tried to transform it into a radical program, to fit into a progressive revolutionary vision. But it doesn't fit. Attempts to implement this theory invariably reveal its true nature. The *practice of planning* is nothing but the militarization of the economy" (p. 230, emphasis in original).

3.   The other *economic* arguments invoked in building that case would include the incentive effect of private property rights, the unintended consequences of government intervention in the economy, the rent seeking by interest groups in democratic decision making concerning economic policy, and the failure of discretionary monetary and fiscal policy to stabilize the economic environment. The major contributors in the twentieth century to this literature, in addition to Hayek, would be Ludwig von Mises, Milton Friedman, and James Buchanan.

4.   The emphasis Mises put on economic calculation in his critique of socialist blueprints is a result of two considerations which are sometimes glossed over in the literature on this topic. First, at the time of his original challenge it was considered illegitimate to invoke incentive-based arguments against socialism because advocates of socialism had assumed that man's nature would be transformed by the move to social-ist production. The avarice of a market society would give way to a new spirit of cooperation. Second, for the sake of argument, Mises granted this utopian assumption but pointed out that even if socialist economic planners were motivated to accomplish the task rationally, without the ability to engage in monetary calculation they would not know how to complete the task. There would be no metric with which to measure the result of activity. Here Mises makes an important point about the intimate connection between the calculation argument and the incen-tive argument. "We cannot act economically," he wrote, "if we are not in a position to understand economizing" ([1920] 1935, p. 120).

5.   Hayek's essays are collected in Hayek 1948a. See Caldwell 1997 for a discussion of the development of Hayek's thought that was brought on by his debate over socialism.

6.   Kirzner (1992) provides perhaps the most thorough discussion of this vision of the market process.

7.   On the current status of the debate over markets and socialism, see volume 9 of Boettke 2000c, which is a collection of the main contempo-rary papers on the subject. On the continuing debates over the implica-tions of Hayek's economics and political economy for contemporary scholarship, see Caldwell 2004a.

8.   This chapter draws freely from Boettke, Coyne, and Leeson 2006 and Boettke 2005. The author would like to acknowledge the critical input in

his research on the economics of socialism from Chris Coyne, Peter Leeson, Steve Horwitz, David Prychitko, and the late Don Lavoie. I would also like to thank Edward Feser for the opportunity. Financial assistance from the Mercatus Center at George Mason University and the J. M. Kaplan Fund is gratefully acknowledged. The usual caveat applies.

4   Hayek and Marx

Hayek is recognized as the philosopher/economist who championed liberty and opposed socialism. Marx, especially after the experience of bolshevism, is seen as the high priest, if not the god, of socialism and the enemy of liberty. Hayek is thus anti-Marx as he is also anti-Keynes. Yet there are few direct references to Marx in Hayek's writings; and Marxists, for most of the period when Hayek was writing and beyond, have ignored him. (Gamble 1996 is a notable exception.) Democratic socialists or social democrats engaged in the debates about socialist calculation with Hayek much more in the 1930s (Hayek 1935b; Durbin 1985). By the time Hayek wrote his final book, *The Fatal Conceit: The Errors of Socialism* (1988), the Soviet Union was close to collapse and socialism as a doctrine had become beleaguered. Hayek was celebrated as the philosopher who inspired those who subverted the Soviet empire in Eastern Europe. But it could be argued that by then Marx had little to do with Eastern Europe or the Soviet Union (Desai 2002).

But there is a philosophical lineage to which the two belong, though via different branches. A first antecedent is the Scottish Enlightenment and especially Adam Smith's stadial theory of history. The idea of societies (economies) as self-organizing systems with an autonomous dynamic of movement and change, which is common to both Marx and Hayek, starts here. A second antecedent is the idea taken from a tendency in German philosophy, which begins in the reaction to the Prussian reforms after the defeat at Jena (in the writings of Savigny among others), that argued that laws cannot be imposed but inhere in the slow evolution of the mores of a society (O'Malley 1970). Hegel reformulated this notion as an autonomous movement of the idea through history as it proceeds towards its

progressive self-realization. This requires no outside or human interference. Marx reworked this autonomous dynamic of history, but in
terms of a dialectical development of material forces. But in his
version of the stadial theory of history, the successive modes of
production emerge by an autonomous movement driven by the
forces of history. Any given mode of production produces and reproduces itself as a result of the independent movement of the actors –
classes and individuals belonging to the classes. This is very much as
Adam Smith's invisible hand has it, though with Germanic embel-
lishments. It is later that the Austrians grasp the anti-Hegelian
branch of the same movement starting with Smith and Savigny,
and come up with their version of self-organizing societies and the
dominance of natural law over positive legislation. Either way the
state plays a negligible part in both Marx's and Hayek's story of
how societies evolve and function. The notion of planning by the
state (rather than by a post-capitalist society) is a later addition to
socialist thought and does not have its origin in Marx. Hayek himself
cites Saint-Simon rather than Marx as the progenitor of the idea
(Hayek 1952a).

A more proximate connection between Hayek and Marx is not so
much in the realm of political philosophy as in that of the economics
of money and capital. Each had a vastly ambitious program of understanding the dynamics of capitalism as it experienced accumulation
and cycles. Each also confronted the main economic theoretic orthodoxy of his day – classical political economy for Marx and Walrasian
general equilibrium theory for Hayek – to fashion a better understanding of the capitalist economy as it used money and credit and
went through crises. But each left his ambitious research program
unfinished and, indeed, abandoned it to go on to other seemingly
more urgent tasks – Marx with his delving into Russian history in the
1870s and Hayek into philosophy via his Abuse of Reason program
(Hayek 1952a). Yet what they left behind continues to serve as brilliant insights into the working of capitalism.

In this chapter I concentrate on money, capital, and cycles as a
common theme between Marx and Hayek. Marx's writing on these
topics is strewn across *A Contribution to the Critique of Political
Economy* (CCPE), and *Capital* in all its three volumes (Marx [1859]
1904; [1867] 1887; [1885] 1919; [1894] 1909). Hayek's writings are *Monetary
Theory and the Trade Cycle* (MTTC), *Prices and Production* (PP),

Profits, Interest, and Investment (PII), and *A Pure Theory of Capital* (PTC), as well as some articles of this period collected by Roy McCloughry as *Money, Capital, and Fluctuations* (MCF) (Hayek [1933] 1966; 1935a; 1939b; 1941; 1984c). Marx was actively writing broadly speaking for the ten years between 1857 and 1867, while Hayek wrote these books between 1929 and 1941. In the case of both, the intellectual work occupied a longer time than the writing, but neither ever revisited or resumed the research, instead just abandoning it. Marx lived for another sixteen years, during which time he neither revised nor published his drafts of the second and third volume of *Capital*. Hayek lived another fifty years after he completed PTC, with which he was very unhappy, but he never revised it.

MONEY, CAPITAL, AND CYCLES

Money is the point of departure for both. Marx, in his 1844 *Economic and Philosophical Manuscripts* (see Marx 1975), notices that the presence of money causes many problems but fails to analyze it as yet. By the time of his mature work, he sees money as a crucial form in which separate values produced and embodied in different commodities can be represented in a unified way. So the labor form of value and the commodity form of value can lose their specificities and be dissolved in the money form. Money is the general universal form of value in capitalism. In *Capital*, volume 1, Marx begins by discussing value form and lays out what we now call relative prices of commodities in terms of each other (linen and shoes), but then works out why money is necessary to make these commodities not merely comparable with each other (money as numeraire) but also for exchanging with each other in a mediated fashion (money as means of exchange). This is the C-M-C form of exchange. He then sees money not merely as facilitator of exchange but as the *initiator* of exchange under capitalism, and the new formula is M-C-M' (money as store of value). Thus in simple exchange under petty commodity production, we take a commodity (C), exchange it against money (M), and then exchange it again against another commodity (C). In capitalism, the capitalist (Mr. Moneybags) now starts with a money sum (M) which commands commodities (C) – mainly labor power and means of production – which in turn are transformed in the process of production to a mass of commodities with surplus value (C') which is sold for a sum of money (M') which is larger than what he started with (M). The difference between M' and M is profit, and this is the *money form* of surplus value embodied in commodities but contributed by labor power, which is a singular commodity since it is the only one capable of producing surplus value when employed in production of commodities. The changing form of value from money to commodities (inputs) to commodities with enhanced value (outputs) and then again into money after sale was laid out by Marx in *Capital*, volume 2, in section 1 on "Three Circuits of Capital" (Marx [1885] 1919; see also Desai 1974).

Marx's difficulty with this argument about surplus value was that it gave no active role to capital in the process of generating profits. Thus, capital merely passes on its use value – its wear and tear during the process of production, as it were – to the final value produced. Labor power alone, once expended in production as labor time, passes on more than the use value embodied in its wage. First, this argument led to the question as to why the capitalist would invest in capital, if only labor power produces surplus value. It is also not clear why during a cycle the capitalist replaces labor by capital (increasing the organic composition of capital in the process) if capital does not contribute to surplus value. Secondly, Marx had to go through the so-called Transformation Problem to show that, while the capital–labor ratio differed among different firms ("capitals," as he called them), and hence produced different ratios of surplus value to capital, profit rates in terms of money prices still equalized across firms. This solution was a mess, as Böhm-Bawerk pointed out in a trenchant critique (Böhm-Bawerk [1896] 1975, Sweezy 1949). While the Transformation Problem can be and has been solved several times since, the peculiarly passive role of capital in Marx's theory of profits remains a puzzle (Desai 1991a).

A lesser-known difficulty that Marx faced was the problem of durable capital. This caused Ricardo to revise his labor theory of value in later editions of his *Principles*. Marx took the view in *Capital*, volume 1, that (as one would put it in modern terms) the *flow* of services from the *stock* of capital can be measured (in terms of labor time), and it is this quantity that passes into the final value of output. In his many arithmetical examples in subsequent volumes of *Capital*, he stuck to this view. But in *Capital*, volume 2, section 2, there is a long but inconclusive discussion about the relationship between stocks and flows of durable capital – the turnover of capital and the relation between fixed and circulating capital. Thus the conversion of the stock of capital into the flow of services is not straightforward, but Marx left the problem unsolved.

While the validity of the notions of surplus value and the specificity of labor power as the only commodity producing surplus value have been much debated, the important things which are parallel between Hayek and Marx are the difficulty about durable capital and the attempt to break away from the prevailing orthodoxy about money. In Marx's case, the thing to note is the significant departure from classical economic writing about money which was in the C-M-C mold. Marx was not the first economic theorist to note that the phenomenon of mediated exchange causes a problem of a possible shortfall of demand (John Stuart Mill reflects on this problem in his *Some Unsettled Questions of Political Economy*), but he was the first to carry it through to an analysis of the working of profits as the dynamic driver of capitalism. For Marx, the reproduction of the capitalist mode of production is not easy without the ability to "realize" the surplus value embodied in commodities by converting into its money form as profits.

Hayek too focuses on money as the crucial element missing in Walrasian theory of general equilibrium. His ambition was to integrate money into general equilibrium and provide an explanation of the cycles in capitalism which were ruled out in Walrasian theory. As he wrote in *PP*, "[T]he task of monetary theory is a much wider one than is commonly assumed. Its task is nothing less than to cover a second time the whole field which is treated by pure theory under the assumption of barter, and to investigate what changes in the conclusion of pure theory are made necessary by the introduction of indirect exchange" (1935a, p. 127). In this statement is the essence of Hayek's research program during the 1929–41 period.

Thus MTTC is a survey of the then existing theories of cycles, which are all found to be analytically lacking in rigor, and Hayek promises to provide a theory of cycles which accepts the assumptions of rational economic calculus and eschews arbitrary ad hoc assumptions of rigidities or lags to explain cycles. The key is the presence of money, which introduces uncertainties not present in Walras' equilibrium mechanism. Thus implicitly Hayek attributes a C-M-C logic to Walras and promises to construct a general equilibrium theory with money in it. Hayek is dismissive of the quantity theory of money at this stage, and wants to study the impact of money not so much on the *absolute* level of prices as on *relative* prices. As we shall see, he ultimately failed in his attempt, as did a later generation of theorists (Grandmont 1984).

It has to be noted that money for Marx was mainly gold and only marginally bank credit. By the time Hayek was writing, while the gold standard still existed, commercial banks had become major suppliers of credit to businessmen. Yet governments were not major issuers of money and all money was "inside money." Central banking policy plays no role in the theories of either of them. Of course, after the Second World War, this was to change and money was nationalized, hence Hayek's efforts to argue for the denationalization of money (Hayek 1990).

CAPITAL AND CRISES

Marx was seeking an explanation of profits, that is, of how a capitalist started the production process with a certain quantity of money he invested (or "advanced," as he put it) – the quantity M – and ended up after production and sale with M′, a larger quantity. Of course, after realizing profits, the capitalist reinvested, i.e. "accumulated" capital for the next phase of production and profit making. This process of production and reproduction (in the sense of resumption of the process) resulted in accumulation of capital and enrichment of capitalists, while the workers, crucial to the production of surplus value, did not experience any improvement in their living standards. The key, Marx thought, was the presence of a "reserve army of workers" which kept wages near enough to subsistence. But over the course of accumulation, this reserve army shrank and expanded. Workers experienced cycles of employment and unemployment on a periodic basis. Marx was the first economist, bar none, who noticed cycles in British capitalism and sought an explanation. Before him, there was a curiosity about crises – sudden collapses of confidence and credit. But only Marx gives us the dates for a roughly decennial pattern since 1825. Capitalism had accumulation and cycles as integral to each other. What was the cause?

The explanation in Marx's three volumes of *Capital* proceeds in a sort of zigzag. In volume 1, part 7, we have a one-sector model with no money, and the cycle arises from accumulation draining the reserve army and threatening profitability (upswing and boom), followed by a sudden reversal with retrenchment and refilling of the reserve army and restoration of profitability (crisis and downturn). This is reminiscent of the Phillips curve, and has been deftly modeled by Richard Goodwin in his "A Growth Cycle," which adapts the Volterra Lotka predator–prey model to the struggle between capital and labor (Goodwin 1967; Desai 1973). In *Capital*, volume 2, chapter 23, there is the scheme of expanded reproduction, which is a two-sector model of equilibrium growth with no cycles. This generated a lot of controversy since it seemed that capitalism was shown to be capable of crisis-free growth (Luxemburg [1913] 1951; Desai 1979). Here, too, there is no money in the model. It is in Volume 3, in the course of an explanation of the falling rate of profit, that Marx returns to the cyclical model of volume 1 with money added. But as a posthumous publication, volume 3 lacks the tightness of the volume 1 analysis. It does contain separately a discussion of how there is a struggle between rentiers and capitalists for a division of surplus value as between interest and profits (Panico 1987). This is a higher stage of economy than the one modeled in volume 1, since there is a differentiation within the bourgeoisie.

In this zigzag between a real cycle theory (volume 1), equilibrium growth without cycles (volume 2), and cycles around a falling rate of profit (volume 3), Marx fails to fashion a complete theory of cyclical growth in a money-using capitalist economy. There are insights and half-finished suggestions which are enticing and caused a long controversy. But the research program is abandoned incomplete. Having worked out the rough draft of all three volumes and prepared volume 1 for publication in his polished style in 1867, Marx never returned to the drafts of the next two volumes during the next sixteen years of his life. Despite a superb immanent critique by Rosa Luxemburg, one has to conclude that no subsequent Marxist (or for that matter non-Marxist) author has returned to Marx's incomplete model and finished it (Howard and King 1992).

Hayek's work on cycles is similar to Marx's in its ambition, in the length of time over which it was pursued, and in its abandonment before completion. Just as Marx's use of the labor theory of value (in his own version rather than the standard classical/Ricardian version) has puzzled later readers and led to a reluctance on their part to accept Marx's conclusions, Hayek used an Austrian capital-theoretic approach which equally led to fascination followed by puzzlement and eventually rejection by his contemporaries (Hicks 1967). Hayek tried to integrate money and bank credit (a) into a Walrasian general equilibrium theory; (b) into an Austrian (Böhm-Bawerk) capital theory; and (c) into a proto-rational expectations behavioral theory. He failed in the attempt, but along the way produced some of the most exciting insights into cyclical behavior under capitalism.

The first step in Hayek's quest for a theory of cycles was his visit to the USA, where he followed the new developments at Columbia University about the recent efforts by the Federal Reserve to devise a policy for price stabilization. (See Hayek 1984c for an autobiographical account.) His up-to-date knowledge qualified him upon his return to become the director of a research institute for business cycles in Vienna. His first major piece of writing was a lecture at the Verein fur Sozialpolitik on monetary theory. This became *Geldtheorie und Konjunkturtheorie* (1929, appearing in 1933 as *Monetary Theory and the Trade Cycle*). This is a desk-clearing exercise. Hayek surveys existing theories and finds them unequal to the task of providing an *endogenous behavioral theory* of the cycle. By "endogenous" he meant a theory which did not rely on arbitrary exogenous elements such as fixed lags, and by behavioral, he meant a theory consistent with general equilibrium guaranteed by rational behavior on the part of agents. Thus if lags, for example between order and delivery of durable equipment, were fixed, he wondered (a) why people did not incorporate such information in their calculations and (b) why someone did not take the opportunity to shorten the lags. The following long quotation illustrates the points:

There is a fundamental difficulty inherent in all trade cycle theories which take as their starting point an empirically ascertained disturbance of the equilibrium of the various branches of production. This difficulty arises because, in stating the effects of the disturbance, they have to make use of the logic of equilibrium theory. [Hayek adds in a footnote: "By equilibrium theory we here primarily understand the modern theory of general interdependence of all economic quantities, which has been most perfectly expressed by the Lausanne School of theoretical economics."] Yet this logic, properly followed through, can do no more than demonstrate that such disturbances of equilibrium can come only from outside, i.e., that they represent a change in economic data and that the economic system always reacts to such changes by its well-known methods of adaptation, i.e., the formation of a new equilibrium. No tendency towards the special expansion of certain branches of production, however plausibly adduced, no chance shift in demand, in distribution, or in productivity, could adequately explain, within the framework of the theoretical system, why a general disproportionality between supply and demand should arise. For the essential means of explanation in static theory, which is at the same time, the indispensable assumption for the explanation of particular price variations, is the assumption that prices supply an automatic mechanism for equilibrating supply and demand. (1933 [1966], pp. 42–43)

Hayek's starting point is that, within the Walrasian framework, no disequilibrium behavior can persist for long enough to constitute a cycle. So, any explanation for a cycle must be sought outside the system. Since Walras excludes money from his scheme, here must be sought the explanation of the cycle. Hayek then adapted the theory of Wicksell, which focuses on the divergence between the natural rate of interest and the market rate, to his purposes (Wicksell [1936] 1965). He also borrowed from Ludwig von Mises' theory of money in which the problem is caused by misallocation of credit as between durable and non-durable goods producers (Mises [1912] 1934). Wicksell's is a one-good model and Mises further disaggregates it into a two-sector model. (The parallel with Marx is striking here.) Hayek then makes the crucial break with all previous theories in adopting a multi-sectoral production scheme to generate cycles. He does this in his LSE lectures of 1931 which came out as *PP*.

Hayek adopts an input–output framework (some four years before Leontieff), but it has a triangular structure. The crucial concept is the *period of production*, which in Böhm-Bawerk's theory is an index of productivity. Thus, the longer the period of production as between the initial input and the ultimate output, the more productive the economy. In a progressive economy, as incomes and savings grow, investment is embodied in technologies with a longer period of production. The effect is a higher volume of output at lower prices. Hayek's illustration of this tableau generated much excitement among the younger economists at the LSE at the time, who included John Hicks, Ragnar Nurkse, Nicholas Kaldor, George Shackle, and Abba Lerner (Nurkse 1934; Kaldor 1937; Desai 1982).

Hayek contrasts a steadily growing economy, in which the growth of savings leads to a steady lengthening of the period of production, with one where an artificial stimulation of credit leads to a fall in the market rate of interest and results in a lengthening of the production period based on *forced savings*. The traverse from an economy with a given period of production, say α, to one with a longer period of production β is caused by producers of durable goods with a long gestation period between input and final output having the incentive to pursue their plans because of the artificially low interest rate. As an example, assume that the economy produces a single final good – hamburgers (with apologies to vegetarians). The existing α economy makes hamburgers starting from the cattle being raised on farms and then through all the stages till we get to the hamburger. Someone wants to grow better cattle which yield more, leaner beef, and starts off with bank credit in the β economy which will eventually bring to the market the leaner, meatier hamburger. But while they embark upon their plans, they take inputs (land, labor) away from the α economy. Saleable output comes for the while only from this old economy, and it is being deprived of inputs. Thus, the output of hamburgers falls, while the money supply has gone up due to the credit issue. Inflation results and there is a drop in real wages.

This traverse is frustrated before it is complete, i.e. before the β economy completely replaces the α economy. This is because the banks lose their nerve, perhaps because of outflow of gold abroad, or because of the need to accelerate the credit supply as prices rise. The banks jack up the rate of interest suddenly, and among the producers of the β economy bankruptcy results because their technology is not feasible at the higher rate of interest. There is a crisis. But the capital of the β economy – the work in progress of its unfinished projects – is unusable by the α economy producers. Hence the shortage of consumer goods and inflation continue, while there is unemployed labor and unusable capital. Thus inflation and unemployment coexist.

Yet the cure is not reflation or issuance of credit, since the shortage of the inputs suitable for the α economy can only be eased gradually. The two economies have, in modern terminology, non-shiftable and heterogenous capital. The cure is to wait till the distortions or *malinvestments* caused by false price signals have been cleansed out of the system. Land and labor have to be released by the β economy for use by the α economy. Hayek would not say how long it would take the economy to return to its α equilibrium, but he did not advocate any policy intervention.

The austere theoretical structure of *PP* led to a lot of debate and discussion. Yet it was counter-intuitive in a world faced with a large mass of unemployed and idle capital but falling prices. Credit was, as we now know from the Friedman–Schwartz *Monetary History of the United States*, far from being plentiful (Friedman and Schwartz 1963). In a sharp critique, Sraffa pointed out that Hayek's theory implicitly assumed what we would today call the Homogeneity Postulate. Thus the money supply was super-neutral, and had no effect on the economy except as assumed in arbitrary banking behavior (Sraffa 1932a, 1932b; Hayek 1932a; see also Desai 1982 and 1991b). Sraffa's critique was well taken, but was not generous to the difficulties of what Hayek was attempting in terms of his research program. But Hayek's schema can be shown to be plausible by mapping out the money supply movements along with the specification of the frustrated traverse (Desai and Redfern 1994). This does not prove the inevitability of the crisis occurring but at least the possibility that it could occur.

Hayek proceeded to explain his theory in greater detail through the 1930s, and his articles were collected in *PII*. His difficulties were several. The apparatus of the Austrian capital theory proved too cumbersome for people to follow the argument. Hayek himself did not clarify that the two economies had non-shiftable capital at all stages of production. This was a very severe assumption, since there is no fixed capital in his scheme (the only original inputs being land and labor), and all capital is produced goods or work in progress. Thus, the impossibility of enhancing the output in the α economy by using up the idle resources from the β economy was difficult to understand for his readers. There is also an arbitrary assumption about the behavior of banks; they do not act as rational profit maximizers. That is not to say that we have accomplished the task of constructing a foolproof theory of rational banking behavior yet.

In the middle of his efforts at explaining his argument, Keynes' *General Theory* appeared (Keynes [1936] 1973), and it caught the imagination of the younger members of the economics profession. Keynes exorcised the specter of capital theory by taking capital stock as given. He offered a theory of aggregate output in the short run, with some interesting remarks about the nature of the long run. While he did not offer a theory of cycles, he did suggest a cure for the ills of the economy. Hayek tried in his writings in the late 1930s to counter Keynes' argument, but the result was a muddle in his own argument.

PII takes the interest rate as given but the profit rate fluctuates. (It is at this point that Hayek makes a rare explicit reference to Marx, when he says that the rate of profit was renamed the natural rate of interest by Wicksell because of Marx having made the rate of profit a part of his critique of capitalism.) Wages are sticky but prices are flexible. The economy starts at the point of the crisis of the *PP* story. But now instead of two separate economies, we have two sectors – capital goods and consumer goods. The higher interest rate has made the capital goods sector unprofitable. But with higher prices of consumer goods (due to the previously generated shortage) and fixed money wages, it is profitable to produce consumer goods. Thus the period of production seems to have shortened – a *concertina effect*, as between the two versions of Hayek's model, a long period of production in one and a short in the other. This was a mistake of presentation, not of concepts. In the *PP* story the longer economy starves the shorter one of inputs, and hence the output of consumer goods goes down, causing a temporary fall in the real wage. As real wages try to catch up, the inflation accelerates, increasing the demand for credit, which ultimately leads to the banks stopping the credit flow and putting up the interest rate. Had the β economy been successful, the price level would have gone down as it is the more productive. Its premature demise causes a crisis but no immediate increase in the output of consumer goods because of non-shiftability of capital. In *PII*, the capital goods industries have suffered from a sharp increase in the interest rate, which then remains constant. Only processes which yield profits quickly are feasible. These happen to be in consumer goods of which there is a shortage. There is investment in the shorter processes, e.g. fast-food restaurants serving hamburgers. But Hayek says in *PII* that investment declines due to the shortening of the period of production. What he meant by this and did not clarify is that it is lower than what it would otherwise be had the longer economy continued. It was not investment which fell, but the capital intensity of aggregate output (Desai 1991b).

Hayek's difficulties lie with his capital theory. His Austrian apparatus can now be understood better after Leontieff and von Neumann, but when he was writing, its non-mathematical presentation was tortuous. Nor is it clear that the notion of the *period of production* is soundly based. (See Orosel 1987.) Hayek starts with the assumption that only land and labor are primary inputs and all capital is the intermediate goods produced. It is not clear whether some of this capital is durable machinery, at least in the medium run, although all capital could be produced goods. Hayek then compounds his problem by positing (though not clearly stating that he is doing this) a traverse process between two economies between which capital is non-shiftable and heterogenous. He wanted to show that as interest rates rose and fell there would be a unique (one-to-one) lengthening and shortening of the period of production. But while it is plausible that two economies in steady state may have a higher and a lower capital intensity if they have a persistent difference between their real rates of interest, it is altogether a different proposition to argue that in the short run in which cycles appear you can have a tight correspondence between capital intensity and interest rate.

Hayek spent the next three years trying to write a treatise on capital theory where he might prove his basic proposition. But *PTC* is a failure and Hayek recognizes it as such. Indeed, the rigor with which *PTC* faces up to the difficulties of defining a single capital good outside a stationary equilibrium could have saved a lot of trouble had the Cambridge–Cambridge debate taken account of Hayek. If stationarity is left behind, one enters a complex world, as Hayek recognizes, and if the world is in the dynamic disequilibrium which he wished to model, he finds the task is too formidable to tackle. "The contents of the following pages would perhaps have been more appropriately described as an Introduction to the Dynamics of Capitalist Production provided the emphasis were laid on the word Introduction, and provided that it were clearly understood that it deals only with a part of the wider subject to which it is merely a preliminary" (1941, p. 3). This is a recognition that he has a long way to go before he can substantiate his intuition about crises within a rigorous analytical framework. The Austrian concepts do not help much as they are appropriate to a stationary or at best a steadily growing economy. As Hayek remarks early on in *PTC*, "[I]t is more than doubtful whether the discussion of 'capital' in terms of some single magnitude, however defined, was fortunate even for its immediate purpose, i.e., the explanation of interest. And there can be no doubt that for the understanding of the dynamic processes it was disastrous" (1941, p. 6).

Hayek continues to confront the problems ruthlessly. "With the disappearance of stationary equilibrium, capital splits into two different entities whose movements have to be traced separately and whose interaction becomes the real problem. There is no longer one supply of a single factor, capital, which can be compared with the productivity schedule of capital in the abstract" (1941, p. 10). This being the case, the question as to "what will be the reaction of a given system to an unforeseen change," i.e. the question at the heart of *PP*, cannot be rigorously answered.

The 400-plus pages of *PTC* are a tribute to Hayek's unrelenting but ultimately unsuccessful attempt to square the circle of constructing a usable theory of dynamic disequilibrium with heterogenous capital. These pages bear comparison with the middle part of *Capital*, volume 2. But in this attempt, Hayek neglects the integration of money into capital theory until the very end of the book. Coming back to the old theme of *PP*, he says:

There is little ground for believing that a system with the modern complex credit structure will ever work smoothly without some deliberate control of the monetary mechanism, since money by its very nature constitutes a kind of loose joint in the self-equilibrating apparatus of the price mechanism which is bound to impede its working – the more so the greater is the play in the loose joint. But the existence of this loose joint is no justification for concentrating attention on the loose joint and disregarding the rest of the mechanism, and still less for making the greatest possible use of the short lived freedom from economic necessity which the existence of this loose joint permits. On the contrary, the aim of monetary policy must be to reduce as far as possible this slack in the self-correcting forces of the price mechanism, and to make adaptation more prompt so as to reduce the necessity for a later, more violent reaction. (1941, p. 408)

If we reflect back on the "tasks of monetary theory" quote from *PP* that was given toward the end of the preceding section, we see that all Hayek can now assert is that there is some slack – some loose joint – within the Walrasian equilibrium framework. He has failed to elucidate what this loose joint allows the system to do out of equilibrium, if it allows anything at all. But the policy lesson he draws is the same one which he held before he embarked on these investigations, i.e. money has to be neutral. This may be so, but the previous twelve years of work have not been able to establish this conclusion with the analytical rigor Hayek had wished for. No wonder Hayek gave up any further efforts in this research program, especially as the bombs falling on London made him turn to the more urgent task of developing a philosophy of the abuse of reason.

CONCLUSION

Hayek and Marx are similar in their research programs concerning the dynamics of capitalism, its cycles, and the way in which money is vital to capitalism. They both worked a long time to master the problem, but failed to arrive at a neat solution. Hence they both abandoned the program and went on to other, more urgent, concerns. But along the way, they both left a trail of great insights and unsettled debates.

5 Hayek versus Keynes: the road to reconciliation

[Keynes] was one of the great liberals of our time. He saw clearly that in England and the United States during the nineteen-thirties, the road to serfdom lay, not down the path of too much government control, but down the path of too little, and too late ... He tried to devise the minimum government controls that would allow free enterprise to work. The end of *laissez-faire* was not necessarily the beginning of communism.

– A. F. W. Plumptre, 'Keynes in Cambridge'

INTRODUCTION

The passage of time reduces the Cambridge debates of the 1930s to family quarrels. On the flattened surface stand the twin peaks of Hayek and Keynes. Their intellectual antipody seems the more palpable, because they rarely found a common ground on which to engage. "Both sides launched their broadsides, and that was about it."[1] In economics they were so far apart that, except for one inconclusive and bad-tempered theoretical encounter in 1931–32, they worked out their theories independently of each other. In his brief 1944 comment on Hayek's *Road to Serfdom*, Keynes in effect accused Hayek of lacking a short-period theory of statesmanship; while Hayek accused Keynes (in many writings after Keynes' death) of being blind to the long-term consequences of the "dangerous acts" Keynes sanctioned for a "community which thinks and feels rightly." But again they did not engage directly, because whereas Hayek wrote systematic treatises on political and social theory, Keynes did not live long enough to answer him in his own coin.

Yet the brief encounter of 1944 discloses the common terrain on which they might have fruitfully argued out their differences. This is the grounds on which, and the methods by which, liberalism could most successfully be defended. For both men were liberals in all important senses of the term. They both repudiated central planning, Russian style. They disagreed about whether liberal values could best be protected by more or less state intervention in the economy, but neither gave a very clear indication of where to draw the line.

The common ground was created by the run-up to the war, and by the war itself. The war clarified for both men the values they shared. "Our object in this mad, unavoidable struggle," Keynes declared on December 12, 1939, "is not to conquer Germany, but ... to bring her back within the historic fold of Western civilisation of which the institutional foundations are ... the Christian Ethic, the Scientific Spirit and the Rule of Law. It is only on these foundations that the personal life can be lived."[2] The full employment which the war produced also whittled away their differences in economics. Hayek praised Keynes' anti-inflationary pamphlet *How to Pay for the War*: "It is reassuring to know," Hayek wrote to Keynes after reading it, "that we agree so completely on the economics of scarcity, even if we differ on when it applies."[3] In turn, Keynes cordially welcomed Hayek's *Road to Serfdom*: "It is a grand book ... Morally and philosophically I find myself in agreement with virtually the whole of it; and not only in agreement, but in deeply moved agreement."[4]

This chapter charts the path to their reconciliation.

DIFFERENT TEMPERAMENTS, DIFFERENT BACKGROUNDS

Hayekians argue that Keynes represented the impatient, Hayek the patient, version of liberalism. Hayek liked to think of himself as the hedgehog "who knows one big thing," as opposed to Keynes' fox "who knows many things." The one "big" thing which Hayek "knew" was that all state interference in the market system is evil. The fox, Hayek implied, knew this too, but felt he was clever enough to evade the trap, conjuring up new theories, arguments, policies for each occasion. Hayek, it might be said, was all of a piece; Keynes a man of many pieces. Hayek was infuriated by the rapidity with which Keynes changed his theories. This seemed to show he lacked scientific principles. Statesmanship without principle, Hayek would have said, is the slippery slope to totalitarianism. Statesmanship without prudence, Keynes would have replied, is the royal road to disaster.

The contrast between the fox and hedgehog suggests another: that between the administrator/politician and the scholar/scientist. Keynes came from an activist tradition: the ancient universities saw themselves as part of the British ruling class, pushing their graduates into the higher civil service. Keynes himself had three spells in Whitehall. As an émigré, Hayek had scholarly detachment forced on him. His thinking was never tested by the reality or prospect of action.[5] However, Hayek was not quite so detached as he made out. His fear of inflation, linked to the destruction of his own family fortune and the Viennese middle class by postwar hyperinflation, colored all his supposedly Olympian economics. He went on warning against the dangers of inflation in the 1930s long after deflation had become the problem.

The essential difference between them as theorists was that Hayek's economics was reverential, Keynes' was revolutionary. Hayek added important clarifications to the Austrian School of Böhm-Bawerk, Menger, and Mises; Keynes saw himself as overturning "classical" economics. He was less revolutionary than he thought. Large chunks of Marshallianism – particularly to do with the importance of time (short and long periods), the technique of partial equilibrium analysis, and the cash balances version of the quantity theory of money – were central to his economics and distanced it from the timeless simultaneous-equation general equilibrium theory of Menger and Walras which Hayek regarded as the supreme achievement of the marginalist revolution. The Austrians regarded themselves as the revolutionaries, and Keynes' technique as regressive. Hayek was much more learned than was Keynes in the history of economic thought: he is right to say that Keynes disliked the nineteenth century and lacked knowledge of its economics and economic history. Hayek thought about economic theory within the framework of the Austrian tradition; for Keynes the important thing was to get the argument right on the page (or on the day). Keynes was the more creative thinker. This was partly the result of an innate quality of mind; but it was also partly because his training in economics was so superficial. Keynes had no difficulty in seeing his ideas as original; to Hayek they were simply the latest installment of age-old fallacies.

A final difference was one of intellectual manners. By the early 1930s, Keynes and his followers felt a sense of urgency, almost of desperation, to get their ideas accepted. It became the hallmark of Keynes' coterie to regard every economist outside Cambridge as mad or stupid; argumentative good manners were sacrificed to world salvation. On the other hand, there is near unanimous testimony to Hayek's intellectual hospitality. For example, when Robert Bryce, one of Keynes' students, decided, in 1935, to do some missionary work at the LSE, "Hayek very courteously gave me several sessions of his seminar to expose [the new Keynesian ideas] to his students."[6] Hayek was much impressed by Menger's remark that the final victory of a scientific idea could only be secured by letting every contrary proposition run a free and full course. Hayek's hopes, and expectations, of truth were geared to the long run; the short run was full of error. These errors must be allowed to burn themselves out, because that was how mankind learned wisdom. The Keynesian position – and this partly included Keynes – was much more peremptory: error must be extirpated to prevent catastrophe. The optimism of Cambridge confronted the fatalism of Vienna.

The contrast which sums it up may be expressed by saying that Keynes believed that "in the long run we are all dead," whereas Hayek believed that in the long run we learn wisdom. Hayek never experienced, as a young man, the equivalent of G. E. Moore's liberating touch, which led Keynes to write in "My Early Beliefs": "We entirely repudiated a personal liability on us to obey general rules … We repudiated entirely customary conventions and traditional wisdom."[7] Norman Barry comments: "There could not be a clearer contrast between this extravagant act-utilitarianism, and personalised, anthropomorphic view of the world," leading to the doctrine of the philosopher king and the "social philosophy of impatience," and Hayek's "cautious rule-utilitarianism, with its almost metaphysical belief in the accumulated, but undemonstrable, wisdom, of traditional, impersonal rules of behaviour."[8]

This goes much too far, and the Hayekians never quote Keynes' partial repudiation of his "early beliefs."[9] The sharpness of the contrast they draw between Keynes' "act-utilitarianism" and Hayek's "rule-utilitarianism" is surely untenable in view of what Keynes was saying and writing in the 1930s. It owes too much to Keynes' own interpretation of his "juvenilia."[10] The later Keynes, at least, believed in a system of "Humean" rules, flexibly applied, of which the Bretton Woods system he helped to establish is a good example. Keynes "grew up" and his views shifted with the changing cultural, economic, and political environment. Hayek gives the impression of never having been young.

Their temperamental and philosophical differences can be exaggerated. As has often been pointed out, they maintained cordial relations through all their disagreements. From a distance it is easy to see how many presuppositions they shared. They both came to their economics through philosophy. Neither believed that economics was like a natural science. Both emphasized the importance of subjectivism in economic thinking. Both were critical of econometrics. Both subscribed to procedural theories of justice.[11] Both were inegalitarians, believing in the beneficial spillovers from pockets of wealth.[12] Neither was an ardent democrat. When Keynes wrote of the market system in 1936 that it is "the best safeguard of the variety of life," preserving "the most secure and successful choices of former generations,"[13] it might have been Hayek speaking. Both believed in the overriding power of ideas, and rejected or ignored explanations of events in terms of vested interests and technology. Both men admired Hume and Burke and delighted in the paradoxical wisdom of Mandeville. (Keynes' *General Theory* is full of "unintended consequences," e.g. the "paradox of thrift.") What Hayek would have called Keynes' "constructivist rationalism" was tempered by prudence and regard for tradition. Hayek called himself an "Old Whig," and Keynes had a good deal of whiggery in him. Both came to believe that western civilization was precarious, which they found hard to square with their jointly held conviction that it was an evolutionary success story. In short, both were liberals, and finally understood that, on the great issues of political philosophy and personal freedom, they were in the same camp. It was on the means needed to preserve a free society that they differed. This disagreement centered on their economic theories. They disagreed about the stability properties of market economies, and therefore came to different conclusions about policy. Hayek had a more complete, better-worked-out theory, which is why he held to it so intransigently. But Keynes was more creative,

and in fact a better economist, which is why Hayek eventually
abandoned economics for political philosophy.

STARTING POSITIONS

Hayek believed that the market economy was a smoothly adjusting
machine in the absence of credit creation by the banking system.
Keynes saw monetary management by the central bank, which could
include credit creation, as the only way to keep it stable. This was the
pith of their debate. Keynes won it, because he made the more
relevant statements.

Hayek came to their debate in 1931 equipped with an "Austrian"
intertemporal theory of value which Keynes lacked. This sought to
demonstrate that an unimpeded market system – one in which
relative prices were free to adjust demand and supply simultane-
ously in all markets – secured the full employment of resources
not just at any moment of time but over time. The theory of capital
and interest, which showed how this came about, rounded off
neoclassical value theory, substituting the notion of dynamic for
static equilibrium.[14] The Austrians thus told a much more complete
and confident "market" story than any available in Anglo-American
economics.

In the Hayek story, the rate of interest was the price which
adjusted decisions to save to decisions to invest, in line with individual time preferences. A high rate of saving was key to a progressive economy, insuring that increasing quantities of machinery, and
decreasing quantities of labor, were applied to the production of
consumer goods.

The only problem was that the situation in the 1930s did not fit
Hayek's story. There was massive unemployment of resources. So
Hayek had to introduce money as the "loose joint" in his theory in
order the explain the phenomenon of the trade cycle.[15] Monetary
theory should concern itself with the question of "how and when
money influences the relative values of goods and under what conditions it leaves these relative values undisturbed."[16] The main conclusion he drew from this analysis was that a credit-money economy
will only behave like a barter-exchange economy if banking policy
can keep money "neutral" – that is, provide a constant supply of
money per unit of output, and above all prevent inflation. This was

almost impossible. So the trade cycle was inevitable. The best way of mitigating it – of limiting credit creation – was by rigid adherence to a full gold standard. In Hayek's view, the great depression was the direct result of failing to follow this precept. Credit creation in the 1920s had distorted the system of relative prices, producing depression. There was no alternative to liquidating the inflation even though this might well deepen the depression for a time.

Keynes approached the same phenomena from the standpoint of the quantity theory of money. This states that the price level changes proportionately to the quantity of money. It is purely a theory of the value of money, when the level of output is taken as given. As such it could not explain fluctuations in output. However, there was a tradition, going back to Hume, and latterly reinforced by Irving Fisher, which held that it took time for a change in the money supply to have its full impact on the price level, and that during the interval when prices were rising or falling the economy could either expand or contract.[17] This was the approach Keynes used in his *Tract on Monetary Reform* (1971a). To get his "transitional" results he introduced uncertain expectations. When the price level was changing, uncertainty about future prices prevented the instant adjustment of nominal interest rates and wages necessary to validate the quantity theory of money. Businessmen made windfall profits in the inflationary upswing and windfall losses in the deflationary downswing. "The *fact* of falling prices injures entrepreneurs; consequently the *fear* of falling prices causes them to protect themselves by curtailing their operations."[18] From the *Tract* comes his best-known phrase. Having agreed that the quantity theory of money was "probably true" "in the long run," he went on: "But this *long run* is a misleading guide to current affairs. *In the long run* we are all dead. Economists set themselves too easy, too useless a task if in tempestuous seasons they can only tell us that when the storm is long past the ocean is flat again."[19] This expresses, in typically striking language, his main requirement for a serviceable economic theory: it must be able to account for "tempestuous" as well as "flat" seasons, and prescribe prevention and cure for the former.

The institutional culprit in the *Tract* was the international gold standard, which sacrificed domestic price stability to exchange-rate stability. The policy conclusion was obvious: active monetary policy

was needed to stabilize the domestic price level. This required abandonment, or at least severe modification, of the gold standard.

Both economists suffered from the handicap of using models to
explain phenomena which could not occur if the models were correct. The models could be adjusted to reality only by means of *ad hoc*
additions: Hayek's "loose joint" theory of money, Keynes' "sticki-
ness" of key prices. Keynes' approach was more politically attractive
because it pointed to policies of prevention and cure, whereas
Hayek's enjoined stoicism. Hayek rejected Keynes' policy of stabilizing the price level: a stable price level could disguise inflationary
tendencies when prices ought to be falling. "The banks could *either*
keep the demand for real capital within the limits set by the supply of
saving; *or* keep the price level steady; but they cannot perform both
functions at once."[20] Questions to do with the role of the state in the
economy, of rules versus discretion in monetary policy, of knowledge and ignorance in economics, of prescribing for the long term or
the short term, all of which were to become the battleground
between the Hayekians and the Keynesians, had been posed, though
not yet sharply.

DIFFERENT DOMAINS?

The main issue between Hayek and Keynes comes out in their explanations of the great depression. Both could claim to have predicted it.
Hayek argued in the spring of 1929 that a serious setback to trade was
inevitable, since the "easy money" policy initiated by the US Federal
Reserve Board in July 1927 had prolonged the boom for two years after
it should have ended. The collapse would be due to overinvestment in
securities and real estate, financed by credit creation.[21] For Keynes,
looking at the situation in the autumn of 1928, the danger lay in the
"dear money" policy initiated by the Fed in 1928 in an effort to choke
off the stock market boom. Savings, Keynes argued, were plentiful;
there was no evidence of inflation. The danger was the opposite to the
one diagnosed by Hayek. It was that of underinvestment. "If too
prolonged an attempt is made to check the speculative position by
dear money, it may well be that the dear money, by checking new
investment, will bring about a general business depression."[22] For
Hayek the depression was threatened by investment running ahead
of saving; for Keynes by saving running ahead of investment.

Hayek's attempt to integrate "monetary" and "real" theories of the business cycle, as expounded in his book, *Prices and Production* (1931), has six main elements:

1. Voluntary savings by individuals are decisions to give up a certain amount of consumption now in order to secure a greater quantity of consumption in the future.

2. New acts of saving cause the rate of interest to fall, thus reducing the cost of producer (or investment) goods relative to consumer goods. They thus send a signal to producers to switch from making consumer goods to making producer or investment goods. Capital and labor flow out of the consumer goods into the producer goods sectors, leading to capital deepening. (Hayek variously calls this process lengthening the "period of production," increasing the "roundaboutness of production," or switching to "more capitalistic methods of production.") When completed, the elongated structure of production will make possible a greater amount of consumer goods per unit of capital and labor, i.e. the price of consumer goods will be lower than before and the savers' real income will have gone up.

3. Following the Swedish economist Wicksell, Hayek called the price which secures a balance between saving and investment the "natural" rate of interest. The economy will be in equilibrium when the market, or actual, rate of interest equals the natural rate.

4. This equilibrium condition is continually secured in a barter economy. It may be satisfied in a money economy in which money is neutral. Only a change in the "effective" quantity of money could generate a disequilibrium process. When the banks create credit, a source of funds additional to voluntary savings becomes available to finance new investment. The market rate of interest falls, the money value of investment rises, and resources are attracted to the producer goods industries as before. But now the market rate is below the natural rate. The signals producers get to invest in new productive facilities do not correspond to the willingness of consumers to forgo consumption. Instead, these consumers are "forced to save" by the rise in the prices of consumer goods.

5.   The result is an unsustainable structure of production. As the incomes of wage earners catch up with the rise in prices, they will seek to restore their previous standards of consumption, thus liquidating the saving needed to complete the roundabout processes. The turning point comes when the banks have to restrict credit (or raise interest rates) to protect their cash reserves. The crisis has to run its course, as the structure of production returns to its old proportions. Hayek describes this retrogressive movement as "capital consumption." It necessarily produces an economic crisis, with unemployment appearing quickly in the investment goods sector and only gradually being reabsorbed in the "shorter" processes. Pumping more money into the economy may help temporarily but will make matters worse in the end. "The situation," Hayek writes, "would be similar to that of a people in an isolated island, if, after having partially constructed an enormous machine which was to provide them with all necessities, they found they had exhausted all their savings and available free capital before the new machine could turn out its product. They would then have no choice but to abandon temporarily the work on the new process and to devote all their labour to producing their daily food without any capital."[23]

6.   In an elastic money supply banking system, the business cycle can never be entirely avoided. "Money," wrote Hayek, "will always exercise a determining influence on the course of economic events."[24] There are both technical and political difficulties in keeping money neutral. The natural rate is unknowable; price stability is no proxy, since it can conceal inflationary tendencies. The only practical maxim is that the banks should be overcautious in supplying credit in the upswing. However, the risks of mismanagement can be mitigated by rigid adherence to the gold standard. Hayek rejected fractional reserve banking. All banks should hold 100 percent gold reserves against deposits. This would rapidly reverse credit creation, limit "malinvestment," and ensure that the crisis is shallow and short-lived.

It is a very peculiar story. Hayek was never able to explain properly why the new structure of production made possible by credit creation

was any less permanent than one which reflected voluntary decisions to save. As Keynes' colleague Piero Sraffa pointed out, "One
class has, for a time, robbed another class of part of their incomes;
and has saved the plunder." The "forced" savings of the losers
become the voluntary savings of the gainers; and if wage earners
benefit in due course from the increased flow of consumption
goods made possible by the more roundabout processes, the gainers
do not thereby lose the additional real capital they have created.[25]
Few rejoinders show up more crushingly the limitations of Hayek's
analysis. Even worse, Hayek provides no explanation of why a
change in the quantity of money should have any effect on the
structure of production at all. His story presupposes that changes in
money work themselves slowly and unevenly through the price
system. But this is inconsistent with his assumption of perfect foresight and perfectly flexible prices. On this assumption, he has not
explained the genesis of the cycle; he has simply confirmed the
quantity theory of money![26] A third fallacy was pinpointed by
Keynes in his *General Theory*. This was the confusion of the rate of
interest with the "marginal efficiency" or expected profitability of
capital. An increased desire to save does nothing in itself to improve
profit expectations. *Au contraire*, by lowering the prices of consumer
goods, it depresses the profit expectations of all producers. This leads
to a fall in aggregate income and a fall in actual saving. There is
nothing to cause the rate of interest to change.[27] Yet Hayek never
renounced his early cycle theory and was still using it to explain the
"stagflation" of the 1970s.

Keynes' *Treatise on Money* appeared six months before Hayek's
Prices and Production. The following summary of the *Treatise*
brings out the points of convergence and divergence in the two
theories:

1. Voluntary savings by individuals represent decisions to give
    up a certain amount of consumption now in order to secure a
    greater quantity of consumption in the future.
2. The economy will be in (full employment) equilibrium when
    saving equals investment. This is equivalent to the market
    rate of interest being equal to the natural rate.
3. Saving and investment can diverge for expectational reasons
    unconnected with changes in the quantity of money.

4. When saving runs ahead of investment (the case which particularly concerned Keynes in the *Treatise on Money*) the economy goes into a free fall till something "turns up."

5. Keynes outlines the sequence in his "banana parable." He envisages an economy which only produces and eats bananas. He supposes an increase in saving ("for old age") with no increase in investment in new banana plantations. The price of bananas must fall:

Well, that is splendid, or seems so. The thrift campaign will not only have increased saving, it will have reduced the cost of living ... But unfortunately that is not the end of the story; because, *since wages are still unchanged – and I assume for the moment that the selling price of bananas will have fallen, but not their costs of production –* the entrepreneurs who run the banana plantations will suffer an enormous loss ... equal to the new savings of those people who have saved ... The continuance of this will cause entrepreneurs to try and reduce wages, and if they cannot reduce wages they will [put] their employees out of work. (My italics.)

Keynes then discloses the "full horror of the situation":

However much they [reduce wages] it will not help them at all, because ... the buying power to purchase bananas will be reduced by that amount; and so long as the community goes on saving, the businessmen will always get back from the sale less than their cost of production, and however many men they throw out of work they will still be making a loss. No position of equilibrium is possible until one of four things has happened: either everyone is out of work and the population starves to death, or entrepreneurs combine to keep up prices, or the thrift campaign falls off or peters out, or investment is increased.[28]

6. It was the task of monetary policy to prevent or offset this dire sequence of events by pumping money into the economy; it was, in fact, the only balancer in the system. Keynes explained:

Those who attribute sovereign power to the monetary authority on the governance of prices do not, of course, claim that the terms on which money is supplied is the *only* influence affecting the price level. To maintain that the supplies in a reservoir can be maintained at any required level by pouring enough water into it is not inconsistent with admitting that the level of the reservoir depends on many other factors besides how much water is poured in.[29]

One can see that the two theories diverge with Keynes' third point. Whereas for Hayek savings are smoothly translated into investment, for Keynes there is nothing to align the two except stabilization policy. Hayek was puzzled:

But what does it actually mean if part of current savings is used to make up for losses in the production of consumption goods . . .? It must mean that though the production of consumers' goods has become less profitable, *and that though at the same time the rate of interest has fallen* so that the production of investment goods has become relatively more attractive than the production of consumption goods, yet entrepreneurs continue to produce the two types of goods in the same proportion as before. Mr. Keynes' assertion that there is no automatic mechanism in the economic system to keep the rate of saving and the rate of investing equal might with equal justification be extended to the more general contention that there is no automatic mechanism in the economic system to adapt production to any other shift in demand.[30]

The italicized passage shows that Hayek had misunderstood the key point in Keynes' theory. But his conclusion about the nature of the theory was correct: there was no automatic stabilizing mechanism to be found in it.

Both men confronted the world depression with severely dysfunctional theories. Hayek was right to claim that Keynes had not shown how saving and investment could diverge within the model of the *Treatise*, unless there had been a prior change in the quantity of money.[31] Hayek had not shown why credit creation should start a cumulative process bound to end in depression. But whereas Keynes' policy of pumping purchasing power into a deflating system offered a hope of recovery, Hayek was still warning against Keynes' reflationary remedies.[32] This was to earn him a savage retrospective rebuke from his erstwhile disciple Lionel Robbins:

Assuming the original diagnosis of excessive financial ease and mistaken real investment was correct – which is certainly not a settled matter – to treat what developed subsequently in the way which I then thought valid was as unsuitable as denying blankets and stimulants to a drunk who has fallen into an icy pond, on the ground that his original trouble was overheating. I shall always regard this aspect of my dispute with Keynes as the greatest mistake of my professional career.[33]

One can see how Hayek's intransigent methodological individualism (or what Caldwell calls his "profound epistemological pessimism") hampered his economics. It led him to repudiate Keynes' espousal of macroeconomic remedies for depression, and indeed macroeconomics itself. Hayek claimed that only subjective valuations count as causes: total quantities can exert no influence on individual decisions.[34] This claim pinpoints the weakness in the Austrian economics of the day: the lack of a theory of expectations. Keynes understood that collective expectations entered into individual valuations, and that by controlling aggregates, governments can influence individual expectations. In reviving the neoclassical approach, Milton Friedman never repudiated macroeconomics. Today's "inflation targeting" depends crucially for its success on "managing" expectations, much as Keynes advocated in the *Tract*.

Keynes' (eventual) position was also problematic. He shared much of Hayek's epistemology (wholes have only a fictitious existence, social science is a moral, not natural, science, econometrics is philosophically flawed), yet still believed in macroeconomic policy which depends on national income accounts, econometric modeling, and government manipulation of aggregates. He thought government could manage total spending power only in a rough and ready way which would still be an improvement on laissez-faire. But the next generation carried this project much further. They thought the problem of limited knowledge facing the central manager was a contingent one, and that as statistics improved, so would the possibility of control. This reached its apogee in the "fine-tuning" approach of the 1960s.

Hayek's repudiation of macroeconomics was proclaimed as a methodological principle, but one suspects it stemmed more from his exaggerated pessimism about the results of macroeconomic policy; in contrast, Keynes' embrace of macroeconomics derived from his eagerness to equip governments with the tools of economic management, even before his theory was really up to it. Keynes erred on the right side. He may have exaggerated the wisdom and integrity of governments. But he was surely right to believe that enough collective knowledge existed to improve the working of economies.

In his rejoinder to Hayek's attack on his *Treatise on Money*, Keynes noted that "our theories occupy ... different terrains," Hayek's being a theory of dynamic equilibrium, his own being a disequilibrium theory.[35] Both theories subsequently changed, but brought no meeting of minds. Ironically, Hayek dropped Walrasian equilibrium theory at exactly the moment Keynes embraced it. In his 1936 lecture "Economics and Knowledge" (published as [1937] 1948), Hayek redefined equilibrium as a situation in which there exists a mutual coordination of plans. But given its impossible knowledge requirements, on which Hayek laid increasing stress, it became a purely fictional construction, of no predictive value.[36] His eventual position seems to have been that though an unmanaged market system had no strong tendency to full employment, monetary policy designed to improve the situation would only make matters worse as well as being inflationary. He came to regard his most important contribution to economics as his depiction of the market order as a discovery technique rather than a determinate system.[37]

In Keynes' *General Theory of Employment, Interest, and Money* ([1936] 1973), the economy was always in equilibrium, but this need not be, and mostly was not, a full employment one. Keynes' adoption of the equilibrium method can be seen as the culmination of his attempt to provide a theoretical rationale for activist government. He needed the device of a determinate equilibrium to give government a determinate target. The Keynesian model is taught as a model of output determination. This reconciled Keynes to the mainstream, which craved an economics of certainty, and fitted the growing mathematicization of economic technique. What got sidelined was his most persistent insight, which had to do with the effect of uncertainty on economic behavior.

Hayek had been too badly mauled in his exchanges with Keynes and the Keynesians in 1931–32 to review Keynes' *magnum opus*. But events were finally bringing them back onto the same intellectual and political terrain. Full employment, Keynes thought, occurred only in "moments of excitement." The Second World War was one such moment. The road to reconciliation was opened up by the fact that during the Second World War, the economy *was* fully employed, and the problem which now exercised Keynes was a problem in the theory of value: how to transfer resources to the war effort without inflation.

HOW TO PAY FOR THE WAR

A war economy is faced not by inadequate but by excess demand, by inflationary, not deflationary, pressure. At the same time it needs a high level of saving to effect the transfer of production from consumer to war goods. This transfer can be effected either by inflation-induced "forced saving" or by heavy taxation and other controls on civilian consumption. This is classic Hayekian territory. Keynes sought to avert the twin evils of inflation and confiscation by an imaginative plan for "compulsory saving" or "deferred pay."

His plan was announced in two articles in *The Times* on November 14 and 15, 1939, later expanded into a pamphlet "How to Pay for the War."[38] His analysis of the problem was quite "Austrian." The government had started pumping money into the economy to expand war production. This was equivalent to extra investment in more "roundabout processes" whose aim was to produce a greater quantity of a particular kind of consumption good – guns, tanks, aircraft. However, since this extra investment did not represent any willingness of the public to reduce its consumption of civilian goods, the price level was pushed upward. In Hayekian terms, consumers were "forced to save" by rising prices. But, after a lag, incomes too would start to rise and consumers would want to restore their previous consumption standards. Civilian consumption could then be suppressed only at the cost of further and increasing inflation, or by price controls and rationing, or a mixture of both.[39]

Keynes proposed an ingenious alternative. Consumers would be "forced to save," not by inflation or rationing, but by means of a temporary, graduated surcharge on their post-tax incomes,[40] the proceeds of which would be made available as postwar credits. They would be left free to spend their reduced incomes as they pleased. The great advantage of compulsory saving, as Keynes saw it, over orthodox taxation or inflation, was that workers would not lose the benefit of their higher wages, only be obliged to postpone their spending. This was the plan which Hayek enthusiastically endorsed in *The Spectator* of November 24, 1940, without pointing out that the calculation of how much "money" to take out of the economy was highly dependent on putting numbers to the aggregative analysis of the *General Theory*, one which Hayek repudiated on methodological grounds.[41]

In the expanded pamphlet, *How to Pay for the War*, published on February 27, 1940, Keynes was forced to add sweeteners for the trade unions in the form of family allowances and "iron rations" at subsidized prices; and a concession to the orthodox (including Hayek) in the form of a capital levy to discharge the liability created by the deferred pay. His plan (as opposed to the arithmetic underpinning it) was adopted only in part by Kingsley Wood in his budget of April 1941: in practice, Keynes lost the argument to the central planners, and regulation of aggregate spending took second place to manpower planning, physical allocation of inputs, and rationing of consumer goods. The legacy of his plan, though, was a technique of macroeconomic management, which was not tied to these wartime expedients.

It is the underlying philosophy rather than the details of the scheme that concerns us here, and which won Hayek's approval. Keynes explained to the Fabian Society on February 21, 1941 that he had been searching for an alternative to the "old-fashioned laissez-faire" solution of inflation, the "new fashioned totalitarian" method of comprehensive rationing which would reduce Britain to a "slave state," and the compromise between them of "a totalitarian solution for a narrow range of necessaries and inflation over the remaining field of consumption."[42] "The abolition of consumers' choice in favour of universal rationing is a typical product ... of Bolshevism," he wrote. Similarly the release of deferred pay after the war, "by allowing individuals to choose for themselves what they want, will save us from having to devise large-scale government plans of expenditure which may not correspond so closely to individual need." He wrote: "I am seizing the opportunity to introduce a principle of policy which may be thought of as marking the line of division between the totalitarian and the free economy. For if the community's aggregate rate of spending can be regulated, the way in which personal incomes are spent can be safely left free and individual."

Keynes' most complete statement of his "Middle Way" philosophy came in an article for the American journal *New Republic* on July 29, 1940:

The reformers must believe that it is worth while to concede a great deal to preserve that decentralisation of decisions and of power which is the prime virtue of the old individualism. In a world of destroyers, they must zealously protect the variously woven fabric of society, even when this means that some abuses must be spared. Civilisation is a tradition from the past, a miraculous construction made by our fathers ... hard to come by and easily lost ...

The old guard of the Right, on their side, must surely recognise, if any reason or prudence is theirs, that the existing system is palpably disabled, that the idea of its continuing to function unmodified with half the world in dissolution is just sclerotic. Let them learn from the experience of Great Britain and of Europe that there has been a rottenness at the heart of our society, and do not let them suppose that America is healthy.[43]

These were the very questions which exercised Hayek as he wrote *The Road to Serfdom*.

THE *ROAD TO SERFDOM* DEBATE

Hayek's *Road to Serfdom* arose out of his famous attack on central planning. The early socialist justification of a publicly owned, centrally planned economy was that it would "perfect" the market system by eliminating the "waste" associated with private ownership, monopoly, and booms and slumps. Ludwig von Mises ([1920] 1935) had argued that efficient central planning was impossible, because if all capital were publicly owned there would be no market for capital goods in terms of which competing investment projects could be properly costed. "Instead of the economy of 'anarchical' production the senseless order of an irrational machine would be supreme."[44] To counter this, Oscar Lange ([1936–37a] 2000, [1936–37b] 2000) and A. P. Lerner ([1936–37] 2000, [1937] 2000) said that the planning authority could cause state-run firms to respond appropriately to simulated market signals, provided they were required to minimize their costs and equate marginal costs and market prices. The planning authority would announce starting prices for all capital goods, like an auctioneer. Shortages and surpluses at the initial prices would indicate to the planning authority the need to raise or lower relative prices until, through a process of trial and error, an equilibrium price structure was obtained. Hayek attacked such an idea as utopian: "To imagine that all this adjustment could be brought about by successive orders by the central authority when the necessity is noticed, and that then every price is fixed and changed until some degree of equilibrium is obtained, is certainly an absurd idea."[45] Central planning was doomed to failure because the knowledge necessary to make it work could never be assembled. So it was bound to be inefficient. Further, it ignored the role of market competition in discovering new wants and processes. It thus froze economic development.

In *The Road to Serfdom* Hayek attacked central planning not just because it was inefficient and retrogressive, but on the ground that it was destructive of liberty. This was for two reasons. First, outside wartime or temporary enthusiasm, there is never sufficient voluntary consent for the goals of the central plan. So resistance develops, which has to be suppressed.[46] Secondly, partial planning creates problems which to the planner appear soluble only by more extensive planning. "Once the free working of the market is impeded beyond a certain degree, the planner will be forced to extend his controls until they become all-comprehensive."[47] Thus attempts to direct production into certain channels or achieve a particular distribution of income all involve "progressive suppression of that economic freedom without which personal and political freedom has never existed in the past."[48] Fascism and communism were totalitarian culminations of what had started as democratic socialism. (Hayek had a chapter on the socialist origins of Nazism.) Both involved the "coercive organisation of public life." Western democracies were fighting fascism without realizing that they had started down the same slippery slope. Against the planners, Hayek set out to uphold the "fundamental principle that in the ordering of our affairs we should make as much use as possible of the spontaneous forces of society, and resort as little as possible to coercion."[49]

Hayek was careful not to identify economic liberalism with laissez-faire – a mistake made by nineteenth-century liberals. The state was needed for all sorts of purposes, not least to provide and enforce a legal framework for competition. Hayek distinguished between the rule of law and legality. The rule of law requires that "government, in all its actions, is bound by rules fixed and announced beforehand." But planning requires "discretionary rules to be changed as circumstances change."[50] Thus planning is incompatible with the rule of law. To have a rule of the road is different from a policeman telling people where to go.[51] A liberal order requires a consciously contrived constitution. Hayek thought that a world government would be needed to entrench economic liberalism internationally.[52]

As Hayek saw it, the planning cult arises from the strata of scientists and engineers mistakenly supposing that science can settle matters of politics and morality. But Hayek also acknowledged that capitalist failure to provide security was an important source of collectivist feeling. Minimal indispensable security should be provided "outside the market" for its victims – a rare concession to prudence. But he was deeply suspicious of public works. At this point the argument with Keynes was joined, though not by name.

Admittedly, Keynes was not a central planner in Hayek's sense: he did not want to "direct the use of the means of production to particular ends."[53] But here the slippery slope argument could be used. Keynes was surely the intellectual leader of those "many economists [who] hope ... that the ultimate remedy [for general fluctuations in economic activity and recurrent waves of large-scale unemployment] may be found in the field of monetary policy ... [or] from public works undertaken on a very large scale."[54] But "if we are determined not to allow unemployment at any price, and are not willing to use coercion, we shall be driven to ... a general and considerable inflation [as a way of securing reduction in real wages]."[55] Inflation would suppress information given by the system of relative prices, and so would lead to pressure to fix prices. He warned that on matters of public spending, "we shall have carefully to watch our step if we are to avoid making all economic activity progressively more dependent on the direction and volume of government expenditure."[56]

Keynes read *The Road to Serfdom* while crossing the Atlantic on his way to the Bretton Woods conference of July 1944. It caught him in an anti-collectivist mood. He was annoyed with his more collectivist followers like Thomas Balogh who opposed his plans for reestablishing a liberal world order. (In his last, posthumously published article he even praised the "invisible hand.")[57] The war context is also important to understanding both Hayek's polemic and Keynes' response. For war purposes, economy and society were already highly planned. The question was how much freedom the return to peace would bring. On the necessity of a return to freedom, Keynes was fully with Hayek. On June 28 he wrote him a generous and thoughtful letter, congratulating him on having written a "grand book," and adding that "we all have the greatest reason to be grateful to you for saying so well what needs so much to be said ... Morally and philosophically I find myself in agreement with virtually the whole of it; and not only in agreement, but in a deeply moved agreement."[58]

Keynes would have endorsed all that Hayek wrote of the connection between political and economic liberty, of the importance of allowing the individual to be judge of his own ends, of competition as a better way of adjusting individual efforts to each other than any other, of the advantages of decentralized decision making, and so on. He would have agreed with him that democracy is a means, not an end. He would have applauded his discussion on international freedom, and the conditions needed to secure it. He would certainly have endorsed his strictures against excessive state spending.[59] He might even have agreed with much of Hayek's account of the reasons for the decay of European liberalism.

However, he made several criticisms.

(1) "You admit ... that it is a question of knowing where to draw the line. You agree that the line has to be drawn somewhere, and that the logical extreme is not possible. But you give us no guidance whatever as to where to draw it. It is true that you and I would probably draw it in different places. I should guess that according to my ideas you greatly under-estimate the practicability of the middle course. But as soon as you admit that the extreme is not possible ... you are, on your own argument done for, since you are trying to persuade us that so soon as one moves an inch in the planned direction you are necessarily launched on the slippery path which will lead you in due course over the precipice."

Keynes was suggesting that for Hayek, as for Keynes himself, "where to draw the line" was a matter of judgment, not principle. This is a cogent criticism, which has been echoed by libertarians. Ayn Rand denounced Hayek as a "compromiser." Jasay argues that Hayek leaves the "state's place in society ... *ad hoc*, open-ended, indeterminate."[60] The state, Hayek says, should provide a social safety net. But at what level should it be set? Should it include health care and education? He has only a hazy notion of public goods. As a utilitarian, Hayek rejected restrictions on the scope of the state derived from natural law theory. His justification of liberty is instrumental: the central planner has less knowledge than exists. His is not a negative theory of liberty, but a theory of liberty bounded by the law. Provided the law is properly constituted it is necessarily consistent with liberty. But his distinction between general rules and those designed to benefit particular groups does not do the libertarian work he wants it to: perfectly general rules, like conscription or prices and incomes policies, can be highly coercive.[61] It is hard to extract a theory of liberty or justice from Keynes' scattered remarks on the subject. But there is no suggestion that he ever embraced a positive (or "enabling") theory of liberty, or thought of justice in other than contractual terms.[62] In economics, Keynes' distinctive point of intervention was confined to managing aggregate demand: macroeconomic management was his alternative to microeconomic control. As he wrote in the *General Theory*, "if our central controls succeed in establishing a volume of output corresponding to full employment as nearly as is practicable, the classical theory comes into its own ... [and] there is no more reason to socialise economic life than there was before."[63] This begs the question of how much reason there was before, on which Keynes did not pronounce.

(2) "What we need therefore," Keynes continued, "is not a change in our economic programmes, which would only lead in practice to disillusion with the results of your philosophy, but perhaps even ... an enlargement of them." Keynes had spelled out what he meant in the *General Theory*: "It is certain that the world will not much longer tolerate the unemployment which, apart from brief intervals of excitement, is associated ... with present-day capitalistic individualism. But it may be possible by a right analysis of the problem to cure the disease while preserving efficiency and freedom."[64] Now Keynes accused Hayek of putting ideology ahead of statecraft – a good conservative (and indeed Whig) criticism. Hayek was vulnerable to this charge. He offered no convincing analysis of the forces tending to diminish the attraction of classical liberalism and enlarge the role of the state. He ascribed the retreat from liberalism to intellectual error. His belief that anti-liberal ideas were dysfunctional residues of earlier conditions and would wither away with further evolutionary progress remains to be tested, but does not stand up well in face of Keynes' claim that empires and social systems rise and fall in the short run.

Keynes made the telling point that policies which took no precautions against slumps were likely to produce "disillusion" with liberal values. In fact he might well have pointed out that it was not the habits of mind of the scientist or engineer but the economic consequences of Hayek's liberalism which led to disillusion with liberal philosophy. Whatever the "totalitarian" tendencies in German thought and Weimar practice, it is highly unlikely that Hitler would ever have come to power but for the great depression, which caused six million unemployed and a 40 percent contraction in German industrial output. The socialist creep which Hayek castigates could never have led to totalitarianism without the help of the economic misfortune to which the economic policy of classical liberalism was indifferent. On the other hand, Hayek was right to point out – after Keynes' death – that, by destroying the rules which restrained government economic intervention, Keynes had opened the door to a hubristic form of Keynesianism which took no account of Keynes' own self-imposed limits.

(3) "But the planning should take place in a community in which as many people as possible, both leaders and followers, share your own moral position. Moderate planning will be safe if those carrying it out are rightly orientated in their own minds and hearts to your own moral position ... Dangerous acts can be done safely in a community which thinks and feels rightly which would be the way to hell if they were executed by those who think and feel wrongly." Here Keynes is on much shakier ground. His dictum that "dangerous acts can be safely done in a community which thinks and feels rightly" is obviously right at one level. It *was* safer for freedom to have Churchill running the war than Hitler, even though the wartime organization of Britain and Germany was similar. But this is a static argument. What it ignores is the consideration that that the stock of "right feeling" can be depleted by continuous governmental intervention; it is not independent of the acts being done. A society in which "dangerous acts" by governments become continuous will lose its understanding of why they are dangerous – that is, its sense of what it is to be free. And this has happened to some extent.

(4) "I accuse you of perhaps confusing a little bit the moral and the material issues." The likeliest reference is to the most passionate chapter of *The Road to Serfdom*, chapter 7, in which Hayek attacks socialists for decrying the money motive. Money, Hayek writes, is "one of the greatest instruments of freedom ever invented by man."[65] It is not material abundance that sets us free to choose non-economic ends: we discover our non-economic ends through economic activity, which forces us every moment to choose what is more or less

important for us. Economic planning does not leave us in control of our non-economic ends; by controlling the means for our ends, the central planner will in effect choose our ends for us. Hayek also attacked the doctrine of "potential abundance" – "as palpably untrue as when it was first used over a hundred years ago." "The reader may take it that whoever talks about potential plenty is either dishonest or does not know what he is talking about. Yet it is this false hope as much as anything which drives us along the road to planning."[66]

Much of this was contrary to what Keynes believed. Hayek was a fervent, consistent believer in the virtues of capitalism; Keynes' belief was certainly not fervent, and perhaps only intermittent. He acknowledged that money was useful as a means; but regarded its pursuit as a deforming means, one that skewed life choices away from the valuable to the less valuable, from the concrete to the abstract.[67]

This disparagement of money making goes back to Keynes' student days. It was part of the intellectual atmosphere of his Cambridge and was dominant in the Bloomsbury group.[68] It was characteristic, one might say, of a rentier bourgeoisie, which had already attained a standard of civilization it regarded as good. Keynes' subjectivism did not extend to ethical knowledge. As a follower of G. E. Moore, he believed, unlike Hayek, that certain states of mind were objectively good or bad and that this was intuitively known to those with educated perceptions, prior to experience. One's ethical duty was to maximize good states of mind, for oneself and (more doubtfully) for everyone. In principle, states of mind were independent of material conditions – a poor man could be ethically good, and a rich man ethically bad. In practice, it was easier to be ethically good when free from poverty and irksome toil. Getting to this condition, however, involved bad states of mind. It meant a social system geared to pursuit of the economically efficient at the expense of the morally efficient.

This was how Keynes set up the dilemma in his futuristic essay "Economic Possibilities for our Grandchildren" (1930) and also provided the solution: compound interest was making the world so much richer that our grandchildren, for the first time in history, would be in a position to lead good rather than merely useful lives.

I see us free, therefore, to return to some of the most sure and certain principles of religion and traditional virtue – that avarice is a vice, that the exaction of usury is a misdemeanour, and the the love of money is detestable, that those walk most truly in the paths of virtue and sane wisdom who take least thought for tomorrow. We shall once more value ends above means and prefer the good to the useful. We shall honour those who can teach us how to pluck the hour and the day virtuously and well, the delightful people who are capable of taking direct enjoyment in things, the lilies of the field who toil not, neither do they spin.

But beware! The time for all this is not yet. For at least another hundred years we must pretend to ourselves and to everyone that fair is foul and foul is fair; for foul is useful and fair is not. Avarice and usury and precaution must be our goods for a little longer still. For only then can they lead us out of the tunnel of economic necessity into daylight.[69]

That Keynes accused Hayek of "confusing a little the material and the moral" is understandable in light of the fact that the tension between economics and ethics was central to his philosophy, whereas it simply did not exist for Hayek. For Hayek there was no life beyond capitalism, no knowledge of the good life beyond the discovery process of the market. Subjective preferences applied in an unlimited future. "The end-state cannot be distinguished from the processes which generate it."[70] The market system was a system of discovery, not the most efficient route to utopia. By modern standards, Keynes' formula sounds parochial (he ignored the poverty of the non-western world) and condescending in its claim to privileged knowledge of what is good. But the argument is far from over. Keynes could have pointed out that the constant stimulation of wants through advertising is a recipe for neither happiness nor goodness.[71]

One line of criticism of Hayek fails. This is that he has been proved wrong – that democratic socialism did not collapse into serfdom. Hayek at least safeguarded himself from such retrospective refutation. He was not predicting that totalitarianism would happen, he was warning against the totalitarian implications ("unintended consequences") of trying to direct economic life according to a central plan. He wrote that "the democratic statesman who sets out to plan economic life will soon be confronted with the alternative of either assuming dictatorial powers or abandoning his plans."[72] By the 1970s there was some evidence of the slippery slope . . . and then there was Thatcher. Hayek's warning played a critical part in her determination to "roll back the state." Equally, though, Keynes had earlier given liberalism an economic agenda to fight back against socialism and communism, by demonstrating that societies didn't need public ownership and central planning to secure full employment. Both were lovers and defenders of freedom. Keynes had the grace to acknowledge Hayek's role in its defence, which Hayek, with plenty of time for reflection, never had the generosity of spirit to reciprocate.

CONCLUSION

How should we sum up the debate? In economics Keynes got the better of the argument and this advantage has persisted. Keynes eventually found a way of shaping his intuitions into a logically consistent model, whereas Hayek never improved on the muddle of *Prices and Production*, despite years of effort. Unlike Austrian economics, Keynesianism entered the policy mainstream and has lodged there, albeit in attenuated form. Hayek's rejection of macroeconomics, and macroeconomic policy, marginalized him as an economist. One loss of his eclipse as an economist is the investigation of the effects of inflation on relative prices, which could have been carried out more successfully with modern mathematical techniques. In political economy and political philosophy Hayek is the greater and deeper thinker.

In political philosophy, Hayek was the intransigent, Keynes the flexible face of liberalism. If Keynes' chief flaw was excessive flexibility, which verged on appeasement of antithetical views, Hayek's was excessive rigidity. True to his student criticism of Burke, Keynes was willing, too willing some would say, to sacrifice the "outworks" in order to preserve the "central structure" of a liberal society.[73] He criticized Hayek for never being prepared to sacrifice any outworks. This criticism seems to me to be just. Time and again Hayek carries sensible starting propositions to extreme conclusions. His repudiation of macroeconomics because centralized knowledge is necessarily less than the sum of dispersed knowledge is a case in point. The new phase in the argument between them, hinted at in Keynes' letter on *The Road to Serfdom*, was broken off by Keynes' death. Whether he would have wanted to write a sustained reply to Hayek can never be known for certain. Probably he would have continued to be too distracted by immediate problems. As it is, Hayek, with his wider intellectual range, left a more general message than did Keynes.

Death removed the possibility of what would have been one of the most thrilling, and necessary, intellectual encounters of the twentieth century.[74]

NOTES

1. Ebenstein 2001, p. 72.
2. Quoted in Skidelsky 2000, p. 51.
3. F. A. Hayek to J. M. Keynes, March 3, 1940, Keynes Papers, King's College, Cambridge, HP/4.
4. Keynes 1980, pp. 385–88, JMK to FAH, June 28, 1944.
5. It was also principled. Other members of the Austrian School, like Böhm-Bawerk, Schumpeter, and Mises, had been involved in Austrian public life, but their experiences gave them a permanent distaste for it. These experiences led the Austrians to sharpen the distinction between scholarship and public life.
6. Patinkin and Leith 1977, p. 40.
7. Keynes 1972b, p. 446.
8. Barry 1979, p. 173.
9. Keynes 1972b, pp. 447–50.
10. This, I think, is the chief fault of the interesting paper by Carabelli and Vecchi (1999).
11. For Keynes, "arbitrary" changes in the price level were unjust because they upset contractual expectations.
12. For Hayek, see Barry 1979, p. 149; for Keynes, see Skidelsky 1992, p. 584.
13. Keynes [1936] 1973, p. 380.
14. "The concept of equilibrium is just as indispensable a tool for the analysis of temporal differences in prices as it is for any other investigation in economic theory": Hayek, "Intertemporal Price Equilibrium and Movements in the Value of Money," reprinted in Hayek 1999a and quoted in Caldwell 2004a, p. 156.
15. The best account I have read of Hayek's attempt to "square the epistemological circle" is in Hutchison 1981, pp. 210–13.
16. Hayek 1931, pp. 31–32.
17. In his essay "Of Money," Hume (1904) argued that an increase in the quantity of money (as against a greater absolute quantity as such) need not simply raise prices but can stimulate economic activity in the short run. Irving Fisher (1911, ch. 4) pointed out that, in the transition from lower to higher prices, business profits rise ahead of interest rates and "fixed" incomes, stimulating employment. The check to the upward movement, as banks raise interest rates to protect their reserves, throws the process into reverse.

18. Keynes 1971a, p. 34. For the effect of uncertain expectations see pp. 19–20.
19. Keynes 1971a, p. 65.
20. Hayek 1931, p. 27.
21. Hayek's prediction can be found in Mises 1966, pp. 161–62.
22. Keynes 1973, JMK to C. J. Bullock, October 4, 1928.
23. Hayek 1931, p. 94.
24. Hayek 1931, p. 126.
25. Sraffa 1932a, p. 48.
26. For this demonstration see Hicks 1979, pp. 207–9. Hayek needs sticky prices, lags, and miscalculation to explain the trade cycle, but these are excluded by assumption.
27. Keynes [1936] 1973, pp. 192–93.
28. Keynes' explanation of the parable before the Macmillan Committee, February 21, 1930, in Keynes 1981, pp. 76–79.
29. Keynes 1971c, p. 304.
30. Hayek 1932b, p. 401, my italics.
31. On this see the introduction to Hayek 1995, p. 28.
32. Notably in a letter to the *Times* of October 19, 1932.
33. Robbins 1971, p. 154.
34. Hayek 1931, p. 4.
35. Keynes 1973, pp. 253–54.
36. Caldwell 2004a, p. 214.
37. Brittan 2005, p. 305.
38. Keynes 1978, pp. 41–64; Keynes 1972a, pp. 367–439.
39. In retrospect Keynes conceded that the First World War had been financed by robbing the wage earner of his earnings through inflation and (eventually) rationing.
40. In the case of most workers, who paid no direct taxes, this charge would be levied on gross incomes.
41. Hayek's one criticism was against the proposal to release the deferred pay in cash after the war. Keynes thought that this would guard against the postwar slump. Hayek thought that a much greater danger would be inflation, to which this release would add.
42. Quoted in Skidelsky 2000, p. 63.
43. The quotations in these two paragraphs are from Skidelsky 1992, p. 68.
44. Mises [1920] 1935.
45. Hayek 1935b, pp. 204–5.
46. Hayek [1944] 1962, p. 45.
47. Hayek [1944] 1962, p. 79.
48. Hayek [1944] 1962, p. 10.
49. Hayek [1944] 1962, p. 13.
50. Hayek [1944] 1962, pp. 54–55.

51. Hayek [1944] 1962, pp. 55–56.

52. Hayek [1944] 1962, pp. 172–76.

53. Which is what Hayek means by central planning, [1944] 1962, p. 55.

54. Hayek [1944] 1962, pp. 90–91.

55. Hayek [1944] 1962, p. 154.

56. Hayek [1944] 1962, p. 91.

57. Keynes 1980, pp. 444–45. In this article, Keynes talks of "modernist stuff, gone wrong, and turned sour and silly."

58. Keynes 1980, p. 385.

59. Hayek [1944] 1962, p. 45. Hayek thought 25 percent was the tolerable limit of direct taxation on incomes (Gamble 1996, p. 175). Keynes sympathized with Colin Clark's view that the state could not tax more than 25 percent of the national income, without resistance leading to inflationary pressure (Colin Clark, unpublished lecture of Keynes reminiscences). He arranged for the publication of Clark's "Public Finance and Changes in the Value of Money" (Clark 1945), in which Clark stated this opinion, in the *Economic Journal*.

60. Jasay 1996, p. 113.

61. Barry 1984, pp. 264–67; see also Brittan 1980, p. 39; Epstein 1998.

62. In 1934 he insisted on "preserving as a matter of principle every jot and tittle of the civil and political liberties which former generations painfully secured." Quoted in Skidelsky 1992, p. 518; on his attitude to justice, see Skidelsky 1992, p. 223.

63. Keynes [1936] 1973, pp. 378–79.

64. Keynes [1936] 1973, p. 381.

65. Hayek [1944] 1962, p. 67.

66. Hayek [1944] 1962, p. 73.

67. See unpublished fragment on "love of money," December 23, 1925, cited in Skidelsky 1992, pp. 240–41.

68. See Keynes' paper "Science or Art," read to the Cambridge Apostles, February 20, 1909, cited in Skidelsky 1983, pp. 158–59.

69. Reprinted in Keynes 1972a, pp. 330–31.

70. Barry 1995, p. 566.

71. Layard (2005) is one of a growing number of economists who have used survey data to show that rising real incomes in the west have not produced increased happiness. A distinguished earlier statement, pointing out the tension between "comfort" and "stimulation," is Scitovsky 1976.

72. Hayek [1944] 1962, p. 101.

73. See Skidelsky 1983, p. 156.

74. I would like to thank Sir Samuel Brittan and Lord Lawson for their comments on an earlier draft of this chapter.

6 Hayek on knowledge, economics, and society

Hayek's theory of knowledge is his most distinctive contribution both to economics and to social science. Its foundation is "our irremediable ignorance" (Hayek 1982a, p. 13), both as social actors and as social theorists. "The dispersion and imperfection of all knowledge are two of the basic facts from which the social sciences have to start" (Hayek 1952a, p. 50). The knowledge which members of modern societies possess is *necessarily* imperfect and incomplete, and can never be perfected. This is so for several reasons which are all interlinked; first, because in any modern society knowledge is fragmented and dispersed among millions of individuals; second, because the limits of human reason mean that many things remain unknown and unknowable to individual members of society whether in their roles as social actors or social theorists; and third, because the unintended consequences of human action and the tacit nature of so much of the knowledge that individuals do possess means that modern societies have to be understood as organisms evolving through time, representing extremely complex phenomena which defy the normal methods of science either to explain or to control.

Understanding these characteristics of knowledge in society was for Hayek the principal task of all social and economic theory, and although reason had a key role to play in reforming institutions and guiding policy, it was an extremely limited one and had to be exercised with caution. "To act on the belief that we possess the knowledge and the power which enable us to shape the processes of society entirely to our liking, knowledge which in fact we do *not* possess, is likely to make us do much harm" (Hayek 1978, p. 33). His theory of knowledge provides a thread which runs through almost all his work, the organizing idea which he spent fifty years exploring through a variety of intellectual projects, and to which he returned again in his final work, *The Fatal Conceit* (1988). No other idea is as important for understanding Hayek, his intellectual system, and his mental world. Much of his work is an extended meditation on the problem of knowledge. Hayek's originality has never been properly appreciated beyond a relatively small circle, partly because Hayek continues to be read through ideological spectacles, and partly too perhaps because were his theory taken seriously much of the approach to the study of society in general and economics in particular would be turned upside down. Hayek was a true radical, an uncomfortable thinker for orthodoxies everywhere, including some of those to which he himself subscribed.

Hayek had an ambivalent relationship with economics. Although he spent the first half of his career as a professional economist, he came to adopt positions which were sharply critical of the way the mainstream in economics had developed (Caldwell 2004a; Desai 1994). Hayek wanted to set economics flowing in quite a different direction. Few economists agreed with him, or seem to have understood him. Many like Milton Friedman praised Hayek as a champion of liberal values but were not persuaded by his approach to economics (Ebenstein 2001, p. 273). When he was awarded the Nobel Prize for economics in 1974 many economists greeted the news with incredulity, since he was widely seen as an economist who, sidelined during the Keynesian ascendancy, had turned away from technical economics to immerse himself in social and political philosophy. His 1930s works on economic theory were little studied. Many assumed he had been honored for being one of the leading ideological champions of economic liberalism.

His work has always been controversial, and many different interpretations of it emerged, focused around a number of apparent inconsistencies in his thought, hardly surprising in work that breaks new ground and sees problems in new ways. Just as there is an Adam Smith problem and a Karl Marx problem, so there is a Hayek problem (Caldwell 2004a). One of its first formulations was given by Terence Hutchison, when he detected a significant shift in Hayek's methodological stance, involving the discarding of Mises in favor of Popper (Hutchison 1981). At the heart of every Hayek problem is his theory of knowledge, which became the pivot of his thought.

THE DIVISION OF KNOWLEDGE

Hayek first set out his distinctive theory of knowledge in his seminal 1937 article in *Economica*, "Economics and Knowledge" (Hayek [1937] 1948). The catalyst was his edited volume, *Collectivist Economic Planning* (Hayek 1935b), designed to bring to an English-speaking readership some of the key texts and discussions on the feasibility of centrally planned economies from the socialist calculation debate. With the prestige of Soviet central planning rising in the mid-1930s, Hayek thought it opportune to revive some of the key Austrian School arguments against central planning. It reawakened his interest in some of the broader questions of economic liberalism and the institutional basis of a free economy and free society, and came together with a number of other influences, which included his attempts to theorize how prices changed in the business cycle, the pioneering work of Frank Knight on risk and uncertainty (Knight 1921), and the classical political economists, particularly Carl Menger, Adam Smith, and David Hume.

In "Economics and Knowledge" Hayek addressed his fellow economists about the way in which knowledge was understood and treated in economics. He set out two questions; first, what role did assumptions and propositions about the knowledge possessed by the different members of society play in economic analysis, and second, how much knowledge did formal economic analysis provide about what happens in the real world (Hayek [1937] 1948, p. 33). His answer to both questions was – very little. This was because economists wrongly treated the "data" to be explained as the "objective real facts as the observing economist is supposed to know them." But Hayek argued that the true definition of data had to be subjective: "things known to the persons whose behaviour we are trying to explain" (Hayek [1937] 1948, p. 35). The "data" of economics for Hayek were the facts that are present in the mind of the acting person, not the facts present in the mind of the observing economist.

Economics was a science only to the extent that its theoretical propositions referred to things defined in terms of human attitudes toward them (Hayek [1937] 1948, p. 54). In doing this economists had grasped an essential truth about the ordering of human societies, namely the role played by the knowledge possessed by each member

of the society. Economics had come closer than any other social
science to addressing the central question of all social science:

How can the combination of fragments of knowledge existing in different
minds, bring about results which, if they were to be brought about deliberately, would require a knowledge on the part of the directing mind which no
single person can possess? (Hayek [1937] 1948, p. 54)

This was the issue that had arisen in the course of the socialist
calculation debate, and which Hayek now believed was the key to
understanding the difference between rival economic systems, and
the superiority of market institutions over any other for coordinating
modern societies.

Yet instead of concentrating on how knowledge was acquired and
utilized by the members of a society, economists spent most of their
energies on developing formal models with assumptions about the
knowledge of members of society which were remote from the real
world. Hayek did not dispute that the pure logic of choice was a
powerful analytical tool, but he was concerned about the ways it
was being used, for example in pure equilibrium analysis to construct a set of tautological propositions, remote from any real explanation of social relations (Hayek [1937] 1948, p. 35). The original intent of
equilibrium analysis as developed by Walras and Pareto he felt had
been lost (Hayek 1967c, p. 35; Desai 1994). They had both emphasized
that their models were not a substitute for reality, since there were so
many detailed facts that could not be known. Correct foresight of all
future events was not a precondition of equilibrium, but the defining
characteristic of the concept. This meant that if there was a tendency
toward equilibrium in the economy the knowledge and intentions of
the members of the society were converging. To explain why that
might be so, however, would need careful empirical examination of
the processes by which individuals acquired the necessary knowledge. If this were not done, but simply assumed, the value of the
models would be sharply reduced.

Hayek argued that the modern market economy was founded on a
division of knowledge every bit as important as the division of labor
which had been emphasized by Adam Smith. In subsequent essays,
articles, and books he began to develop and deepen this insight. He
was still refining and restating it when he died. Knowledge was very
different depending on how it arose and where it arose, and it could

not be assumed that because knowledge existed at one level it could be transferred to another. Specifically Hayek argued that the knowledge which was characteristic of a modern market economy was local, dispersed, and fragmented, and much of it was tacit – it could not be articulated. It was acquired and utilized by independent individual agents, but it remained for the most part particular to them. It could not be gathered up and transferred to a central planning board, because it only existed for individuals in particular circumstances, particular places, and particular times. But although this knowledge was dispersed and fragmented, it provided the essential means by which a modern economy consisting of a myriad of individual producers and sellers, who were necessarily strangers to one another, could be coordinated to bring about a tolerable, although always imperfect, order and stability. To make that possible, the right institutions had to emerge, and crucially individuals had to be willing to abandon their instincts and follow abstract rules of conduct, which they had not designed and did not know explicitly (Hayek 1982a, p. 12). Hayek thought that the system of moral rules was, next to language, the most important example of a spontaneous order, an "undesigned growth, a set of rules which govern our lives but of which we can say neither why they are what they are nor what they do to us" (Hayek 1960, p. 64).

This theory of knowledge gave Hayek a new way of stating the case for economic liberalism, as well as a methodology for studying society. By focusing on the way in which knowledge was acquired and communicated in a market economy he was able to mount a critique of central planning as an alternative way of organizing an economy, and direct attention to the very different ways in which the two systems used knowledge. The case for economic liberalism had been distilled into a set of dogmas over the course of the nineteenth century, as befitted the dominant common sense of the age, but by the 1930s it was under increasing attack from various collectivist doctrines, and the older moral arguments for individualism carried less weight. Hayek proclaimed the values of classical liberalism and the case for a free society in a series of polemical works, most famously *The Road to Serfdom* ([1944] 1962). But the reputation he acquired sometimes overshadowed his more fundamental intellectual contribution – restating the classical liberal case by focusing on how individuals acquire and utilize knowledge in a market economy.

Hayek used this focus on knowledge to remind economists that what was important in the workings of an economy was not the knowledge of the economist but the knowledge of the individual agent. Economists should not make assumptions about what that knowledge was, or imagine that they could ever possess it. All they could (and should) do was start from the concepts which guided individuals in their actions rather than from the results of theorizing about their actions (Hayek 1952a, p. 64). Grasping why individuals hold certain views would allow an understanding of "the unintended and often uncomprehended results of the separate and yet interrelated actions of men in society" (Hayek 1952a, p. 59). Such an injunction went against the trend of modern rationalist and scientific thought which believed that the knowledge of the observer and the scientist was potentially much more comprehensive and complete than the knowledge of the actor. The scientist needed to draw on the knowledge of agents but only with a view to propounding a theory which would incorporate and transcend the particular information which the agent possessed. Ideas such as this had long fueled the rationalist belief, the "fatal conceit," as Hayek called it, that human beings could become masters of their fate, acquiring control over both their physical surroundings and their societies. Knowledge could be centralized and put to the service of the whole community to improve every aspect of people's lives. The centralization of knowledge through the practice of science made possible a planned economy and a planned society. Such attitudes had come to permeate most ideologies and most academic disciplines, including economics.

THE KNOWLEDGE OF OTHER MINDS

In rejecting this rationalist conception of knowledge, was Hayek making an empirical claim or a methodological claim? Many philosophers and economists have preferred to treat it as an empirical claim (Watkins 1997), the proposition that modern economies could not centralize knowledge in the way proposed by advocates of central planning without producing results far inferior to those achieved through decentralized institutions of markets and competition. Only an economy organized on the basis of free, competitive markets and private property could sustain the standards of living and population of modern societies. Ludwig von Mises in the 1920s had argued that a socialist economy based on central planning was impossible because without decentralized markets and prices there could be no rational calculation of prices (Mises [1920] 1935). Hayek had accepted the general thrust of Mises' argument but appeared to shift the argument away from Mises' a priori argument that social-ism was impossible by definition, to the empirical claim that it was the different way knowledge was used in the two systems that made a decentralized market economy superior to a centrally planned economy. If knowledge could not be aggregated or centralized then the only way a modern economy could be coordinated was through institutions that took account of the dispersed and fragmented char-acter of knowledge, and which therefore recognized that a modern economy was so complex that most of the knowledge contained within it could never be known to a single mind. What a single mind could grasp was the outcome of the system, the way in which decentralized exchange based on fragmented and dispersed knowl-edge could produce a coordinated, stable, and predictable social order, capable of sustaining and reproducing itself.

But although there are passages where Hayek presents his theory of knowledge as a Popperian hypothesis about the nature of society, there are many others where he continues to make a priori claims about the nature of knowledge. For Hayek, it was never just an empirical question, even assuming an adequate test for it could be devised. There were "constitutional," not just empirical, limits to human knowledge, which formed "a permanent barrier to the possi-bility of a rational construction of the whole of society" (Hayek 1982a, p. 15). The limitations on existing knowledge could be overcome only through the way knowledge was utilized and not through getting more of it. Knowledge was limited because the human mind was limited, and nowhere more so than in analyzing the complex phe-nomenon of society.

Popper thought that the difference between social science and natural science was a question of degree, and that the scope for generating useful knowledge in the social sciences to inform what he called "piecemeal social engineering" was high. Hayek agreed with Popper that the complex nature of the phenomena that social scientists studied meant that what they could learn about society was extremely limited, and that it was theoretically impossible for the social sciences to aspire to the same kind of control over society as the natural scientists claimed over nature. Hayek was firmly opposed to a positivist (or as he termed it, constructivist) conception of social science on two main grounds; first, because it misunderstood the nature of the phenomena social scientists were trying to explain, and second, because it relied on a false conception of reason (Hayek 1952a).

In his epistemology Hayek's general drift throughout his career is toward Popper and Hume, and away from Mises and Kant, but there remains an a priori cast to many of his ideas, particularly his conception of knowledge. Hayek came to his conception that knowledge was limited, not through an empirical inquiry, but because of his a priori stance on the nature of the human mind and of human nature. "Man is not born wise, rational and good, but has to be taught to become so" (Hayek 1982a, p. 21). Human knowledge is limited, and will necessarily remain so, and understanding of societies and economies will always therefore be incomplete. This epistemological pessimism is a fundamental trait of Hayek's thought, though curiously never extended to natural science and the consequences of human domination of the natural world, and contributes to his growing reverence for tradition and his warnings against any kind of interference by governments in the choices that individuals make.

As a methodological postulate it entails that economists and other social scientists should recognize from the outset that they are studying highly complex phenomena which they can never fully know. Knowledge is limited for Hayek in this double sense. The individual agent has limited knowledge of his circumstances (although greater knowledge than anyone else could possess) and limited power to control them (Hayek 1978, p. 13), as well as limited knowledge of the knowledge that other actors have, while the economist has limited knowledge of what individual agents know. Although in other contexts Hayek advocated the use of simplifying models, in this instance he argued that introducing an assumption into economic models that agents have "perfect information" is wrong on two counts. Agents could never have perfect information – the world they face is one of "radical uncertainty"; their knowledge is always fragmentary and incomplete. Second, economists have no way of second-guessing agents. Attributing perfect information to them, even for the purposes of creating a model, assumes that it might in principle be possible for agents to approach having perfect information. Hayek denies that this is possible, and regards it as setting up a series of false trails for economists. Most seriously it leads economists to imagine that there might be a way of remedying the information deficiencies observed within actual markets which cause markets to malfunction, so improving economic efficiency. Hayek attributed this false conception of knowledge in social science to the rationalist bias which inclined economists and social scientists constantly to recommend ways of intervening in market economies to improve outcomes.

Hayek's epistemological pessimism is rooted partly in the Kantian view that human minds cannot know the world as it is but only through the categories which the mind itself furnishes, but mainly in the Humean view that human reason is a frail and limited instrument, and the knowledge it produces is always imperfect and incomplete. From the Kantian perspective, mediated through the work of the Austrian School, Hayek took the argument that all knowledge has presuppositions, that theory always precedes experience, and that therefore all knowledge is informed by theory and predicated upon theory. The social world represents itself to our mind as a series of complex phenomena because these phenomena are not natural phenomena but social phenomena – they are made up of many minds like our own, all of which are limited and imperfect, but all of which have their own capacity to interpret, to value, and to reason. The result is to introduce a potentially unlimited number of variables and details, the totality of which can never be known to a single mind: "No mind can take account of all the particular facts which are known to some men" (Hayek 1982a, p. 16).

One conclusion might be that if social phenomena are really like this, then social science is an impossible project and should be abandoned. Hayek, however, believes that the complexity of the social world makes it a difficult object to study but not an impossible one, so long as its special character is properly understood. The fragmentation of knowledge between many individual minds might seem an insuperable barrier, but Hayek gets across it by suggesting that human minds, although independent and separate, have enough in common that by knowing our own mind we can know the minds of others. This hermeneutic argument in Hayek, which privileges *verstehen* over *erklären*, leads to the uniform minds hypothesis – the claim that the human mind can understand from the inside the way in which another mind reasons. Some philosophers have disputed that minds are uniform in this way (Watkins 1997), but Hayek, although he gave some ground to the criticisms (Hayek 1967c, p. 59), always maintained that there were enough common elements to sustain the idea. As he put it in his essay "Rules, Perception and Intelligibility," the "intelligibility of human action presupposes a certain likeness between [the] actor and the interpreter of his actions" (Hayek [1962] 1967, p. 59). Without this idea Hayek would lose one of the major foundations of his theory of knowledge. Since he is committed to the proposition that the data of social science is the subjective knowledge of individuals, which is always limited and fragmented, and that there are many things that can only ever be known to each individual mind, he is committed to a strong version of methodological individualism (Hodgson 1988). It would be a short step for him to claim that all knowledge is individual knowledge. But since he also thinks that all knowledge is fragmented and dispersed, social science is only feasible if there are enough common and collective elements present in all individuals' minds to make the products of other minds capable of being understood (Hayek 1952a, p. 43).

This aspect of Hayek's theory of knowledge is one of its key elements, and draws heavily upon the tradition of subjectivism in the Austrian School. As he put in "The Facts of the Social Sciences": "We can derive from the knowledge of our own mind in an a priori deductive fashion an exhaustive classification of all the possible forms of intelligible behaviour" (Hayek [1943] 1948, p. 68). Knowledge of the categories of the human mind allowed the principles governing human action to be discerned, and from that came the distinctive Austrian understanding of the nature of value, prices, and costs. Value and costs are to be understood subjectively, the product of the attitudes and preferences which individuals have towards objects. As Hayek explains in "The Facts of the Social Sciences," none of the phenomena which the social sciences study (he cites as examples tools, food, medicine, weapons, words, sentences, communications) can be defined in physical terms. They are all "teleological concepts" in the sense that their meaning depends on the attitude which some person holds towards them. This meaning can only be understood by entering into the minds of others, and since this is impossible, it can only be done by reconstructing the meaning through the knowledge of our own mind. Social scientists use the analogy of their own mind in order to understand social phenomena: "We all constantly act on the assumption that we can interpret other people's actions on the analogy of our own mind" (Hayek [1943] 1948, p. 64).

Hayek maintains that understanding human action is quite unlike understanding natural processes, since for human actions it is impossible to enumerate the physical attributes which would allow the actions to be classified in an objective manner without any resort to the attitudes and intentions of the agent. Hayek was a firm opponent of behaviorism and all forms of positive social science which tried to develop what he regarded as a false objectivism. The core of social science for him has to be subjectivism, and this stems directly from his conception of human knowledge and human action. It follows that the business of social science is not to engage in prediction, or seek to explain individual behavior, or devise ways of measuring human attitudes as though they were physical phenomena. Rather it is to classify types of individual behavior, to uncover patterns and principles:

All that the theory of the social sciences attempts is to provide a technique of reasoning which assists us in connecting individual facts, but which, like logic or mathematics, is not about the facts. (Hayek [1943] 1948, p. 73)

It follows according to Hayek that no social science theory can be verified or refuted by facts. He later modified this position, convinced by Popper's arguments. But in his own practice he found little use for falsifiability:

While it is certainly desirable to make our theories as falsifiable as possible, we must also push forward into fields where, as we advance, the degree of falsifiability necessarily decreases. (Hayek 1967c, p. 29)

He did not seek to collect facts about modern societies or to test theories. As a result his evidence and the conclusions he drew from it, for example on British trade unions, were at times highly questionable (Richardson 1997). He never developed the insight of his economics of knowledge into a research program (Desai 1994). He regarded himself as a theory builder, and for the kinds of theories he was interested in there were no feasible tests. What he sought was social theory which would develop economic reasoning but would not pretend to knowledge it could not possess (Caldwell 2004a). "Economists," he wrote, "often forget the limits of their power and give the unjustified impression that their advanced theoretical insight enables them in concrete instances to predict the consequences of given events or measures" (Hayek 1967c, p. 260).

This emphasis on *verstehen* in Hayek's approach to economics and social science raises the question of why he did not go further and embrace history. But although Hayek is often respectful of history and historians, he is critical of the methods of many historians, in particular their inability to understand the difference between description and theory. Many historians as a result either treat facts quite uncritically, as though they existed in some sense objectively, without any mediation by theory, or impose upon the facts some speculative historicist interpretation, as the German Historical School had done. For Hayek, social theory is indispensable to an understanding of human action, and it does not depend on the accumulation of facts or on the attribution of some objective meaning to history. It depends instead on exploring the logic of human action to understand, if not the detail, at least the general patterns of social interaction.

Social science is therefore the study of complex phenomena that seeks to discover the abstract patterns which govern them. The difference between simple and complex abstract patterns is a matter of degree. Hayek defines it as "the minimum number of elements of which an instance of the pattern must consist in order to exhibit all the characteristic attributes of the class of patterns in question" (Hayek 1967c, p. 25). With simple regularities, statistical techniques may be very effective in establishing connections and testing theories. With complex phenomena, the task is much more difficult. The danger of statistics according to Hayek is that it deals with the problem of large numbers by eliminating complexity, treating all the individual elements uniformly, and misconstruing the complexity of their interrelationship (Hayek 1967c, p. 29). He even declared that no simple regularities were to be expected in social science (Hayek 1967c, p. 33).

These strictures would rule out most of what economists (and some other branches of the social sciences) do. Their mistake, according to Hayek, is to apply the methods of those natural sciences like physics, where a great number of simple relations between a few observables are possible, to society. Instead the social sciences should model themselves on biology or astronomy. What they needed was a cosmology, a theory of the evolution of society, just as astronomy had developed a theory of the evolution of the galaxy:

The problem of how galaxies or social systems are formed and what is their resulting structure is much more like the problems which the social sciences have to face than the problems of mechanics. (Hayek 1967c, p. 76)

Hayek greatly admired Darwin's theory of evolution, not because it could or should be imported directly into social science (he strongly condemned social Darwinism and sociobiology) (Hayek 1982a, p. 23), but because it was one of the best examples of pattern prediction in science. It uncovered not laws but a general pattern (Hayek 1988, p. 26), the detail of which could never be filled in, but which provided an explanatory principle which gained acceptance from fellow scientists. The theory did not predict specific events, but merely described a range of possibilities, its empirical content consisting in what it said could not happen (Hayek 1967c, p. 32; Hayek 1952a). Hayek argued that this was the standard which economics and the other social sciences which sought to be theoretical had to match. They too were studying organisms which evolved, but in this case the organisms were made up of a vast number of individuals, and the interactions between them and the order that resulted could only be explained by understanding the nature of human action, and how coordination of the plans of myriad individuals depended upon them following abstract rules of conduct which had arisen in a process of group selection, because of the fragmented and limited nature of their knowledge.

UNINTENDED CONSEQUENCE: TWO KINDS OF RATIONALISM

Hayek's critique of the assumption of perfect information in models of economic equilibrium and his focus on the "unintended and uncomprehended" character of knowledge drew him inexorably toward a much larger target, the role of reason in modern culture. In attacking rationalism he was aware that he would be misunderstood, particularly as he at first labeled his approach anti-rationalist. He later discarded this in favor of Popper's term "critical rationalism."

This was less confusing, since Hayek always thought of himself as a rationalist, a believer in the value of human reason, the importance of science, and of universal truths. He was never an irrationalist or a nihilist. He believed very deeply in the values of western civilization, and many of the values of the Enlightenment were his values. But he argued that there was not one but two kinds of rationalism in the western tradition, and that the form of rationalism which became dominant after the French Revolution was misguided and dangerous, and had eclipsed true rationalism. If unchallenged it would prevent any proper analysis of the nature of western civilization, its economy and society, and how it might be preserved and strengthened (Hayek 1948a).

Critical rationalism was a tradition that had been lost or submerged, according to Hayek, and for it to be recovered it was necessary to confront what he called variously scientism and constructivism – the belief that in the modern era human beings were able to throw off the chains of tradition, superstition, convention, and precedent and design institutions, choose morals, invent values, and plan societies as though they were starting from a blank sheet (Hayek 1978, p. 5). Rationalism in the form of modern science had come to be associated with the growth of human knowledge and the possibility of subjecting both the physical world and the social world to human purposes and preferences. It was the latter that Hayek thought pernicious. For this kind of constructivist rationalism, nothing from the past should be preserved just because it was from the past. Everything that had been inherited should be interrogated by reason, and if found inadequate or inappropriate should be abolished.

Hayek did not in principle disagree with this. There were many things that liberals achieved in the nineteenth century of which he approved. He did not favour absolutism in any form, or the monopoly of power by church or state, or slavery. He believed strongly in personal freedom, and in reforms which extended it wherever possible. But like many liberals he became concerned about the threat which was posed to liberty by certain aspects of democracy and the spread of collectivist ideas. The powers of reason were not used just against the *anciens régimes* of Europe, but increasingly against the liberal market order as well, and the ideal of a classless planned society run in the interests of all its members took hold. The ferocity of Hayek's assault upon scientism stemmed from his conviction that it mattered hugely which kind of rationalism, and therefore which concept of knowledge, was dominant in western civilization, because he believed only his kind of rationalism was compatible with the further progress of this civilization. If constructivist rationalism was allowed to reign unchecked then western civilization would be launched on a road to serfdom which would end with the extinction of human freedom. For Hayek, rationalism and freedom were very closely connected, but it was a particular kind of rationalism that was required. Intellectual error was for Hayek as much as for Keynes the source of grave social consequences, so in seeking to remedy that intellectual error Hayek saw himself as performing an essential task in the battle for freedom.

Hayek did not invent an alternative rationalism. Instead he drew on an older tradition, the tradition of Mandeville, Smith, Ferguson, and Hume, as well as on Kant and Humboldt. For Mandeville and the Scottish philosophers a major focus of social inquiry was the unintended consequences of social action, the creation of orders which were the result of human action but not human design (Hayek 1948a, p. 7). The great importance of Smith according to Hayek was that he was the first to see that "we had stumbled upon methods of ordering human economic co-operation that exceed the limits of our knowledge and perception" (Hayek 1988, p. 14). The most important problem requiring explanation was how the activities of so many independent agents in modern societies were coordinated so that these societies exhibited high degrees of stability and order. Human agents with their limited knowledge could act in ways that could produce a result which none of them individually had aimed at or could imagine or needed to understand. Rules had over time been selected which led individuals to behave in ways that made social life possible (Hayek 1982a, p. 44). It was a rational process because all agents were acting to obtain the best possible result from their own standpoint, but the order that resulted was not designed or planned or intended by anyone (Bianchi 1994). The modern social order for Hayek was distinctive not just for its complexity, but because the way it had been constituted through the activities of so many minds over so many generations made it in important respects unknowable. The knowledge that was most important for the survival of this civilization was the tacit knowledge encoded in the traditions, conventions, and rules which had been inherited, and were the fruit of human action over millennia, rather than human design in one generation. He was fond of quoting A. N. Whitehead: "Civilization advances by extending the number of important operations which we can perform without thinking about them" (Hayek 1960, p. 22).

Hayek's reformulation of the nature of knowledge in human societies using the insights of economic theory gave him a new way to understand and formulate the insights of classical liberalism. If knowledge was dispersed and fragmented in the Great Society, the society of strangers, it followed that this was a necessary condition for the creation of order in such a society. The market order was imperfect but "the only way so many activities depending on dispersed knowledge can be integrated into a single order" (Hayek 1982a, p. 42). Social scientists and economists should concern themselves with understanding how this order had evolved, what its institutional underpinnings were, and how it might be sustained. Society had to be understood as an organism rather than as a machine. Abstract rules of conduct such as several property, honesty, contract, exchange, trade, competition, and privacy (Hayek 1982a, p. 13) had furnished a new morality which helped human beings to choose among or avoid their instinctual drives. They were the product of a long history of experiments, of trial and error, which embodied a wisdom which could not be arrived at in any other way. Adam Smith's metaphor of the invisible hand, or as Hayek rephrased it less poetically, "the unsurveyable pattern" (Hayek 1988, p. 14), expressed this characteristic of modern societies. The alternative to the invisible hand was the visible hand of human reason, taking control of human societies and remodeling them according to rational blueprints, which, however, lacked the all-important sanction of evolutionary experience, and therefore risked claiming a knowledge which human beings could not possess.

Hayek is sometimes thought to be so pessimistic about the possibilities of human knowledge that he discounts the importance of human reason. But that is a misreading. With Hume he stresses the limited capacity of human reason, but with Kant he acknowledges that recognition of the limits of knowledge also creates the possibility of knowledge. Hayek nowhere suggests that knowledge is impossible, that human reason is unimportant, or that human beings should not seek to act rationally. What he opposes is a conception of human reason which attributes to it powers which it cannot possess. The belief that it can leads to many mistakes, because it means that instead of society, rationality, and action being understood from below, as a spontaneous and unplanned process that can produce order, they are understood from above. The observer and the scientist claim a higher rationality, superior to the rationality of the individual member of society.

ECONOMICS AND POLICY

If this approach were consistently followed it would pose a major challenge to the dominant forms of understanding knowledge and the role of science in the modern world, with far-reaching implications for economics and social science and for policy. It suggests that the problem we face is always too little knowledge rather than too much, and that the limits of our understanding should therefore impose caution on how much we interfere with the delicate organism which is society. Economists and social theorists have to engage in policy discussion and policy advice, but they should be humble about the limits of their knowledge, and cautious about their prescriptions. The failure of economists to have more impact upon policy was because they tried to imitate the procedures of the physical sciences and treated as important only what was accessible to measurement (Hayek 1978, p. 23).

Hayek once wrote how Austrian colleagues used to joke that they were better theorists than their German counterparts because they had so little influence on practical affairs (Hayek 1967c, p. 265). Hayek spent his life as a theorist and only had an indirect influence on public affairs, but he had a clear idea of the role of the theorist in public policy, echoing Keynes' view that the key task for social and economic theory was to distinguish between the agenda and the non-agenda of government (Hayek 1948a, p. 17). Only a social theory which understood the limits of reason in human affairs, the imperfections of human nature, and the character of human knowledge could succeed in doing this. Since the economist would never know all the relevant circumstances, "the economist should refrain from recommending isolated acts of interference even in conditions in which the theory tells him that may sometimes be beneficial" (Hayek 1967c, p. 264). What such an understanding ruled out was any attempt to refashion a whole society according to the dictates of reason, because human beings could never know enough to do this. The only possible course was to try to understand the civilization which had evolved, while always recognizing that there are many aspects of it which would remain unknowable, some of which might appear irrational and incapable of justification. Hayek's advice was to respect the higher wisdom embodied in the rules and institutions which have been bequeathed to us: "If life is to proceed, we must in practice accept much which we cannot justify, and resign ourselves to the fact that reason cannot always be the ultimate judge in human affairs" (Hayek 1967c, p. 130).

Such a stance can seem both fatalist and extremely conservative, and is at odds with Hayek's own practice. *Law, Legislation, and Liberty* contains the outline of a utopian scheme to reform political institutions and remove the defects of democracy. His writings are full of other ideas for redesigning particular institutions and improving the workings of competition, as for example in his proposal for removing the state monopoly on money (Hayek 1976a). This is because Hayek did not oppose planning or rational design or reform as such. Indeed he once declared that the social scientist had the right "critically to examine and even to judge every single value of our society" (Hayek 1978, p. 19). The issue he always maintained was not whether planning should be done or not, but whether it should be done centrally or divided among many individuals (Hayek 1948a, p. 79). There are many passages in his writings where he explicitly defends planning, for example to promote competition (Hayek [1944] 1962, p. 12). He was opposed to laissez-faire which he regarded as a rationalist doctrine taken from the same mold as socialism (Hayek [1944] 1962, p. 27; Hayek 1960, p. 60), and argued instead for a theory which could define the proper functions of the state as well as the limits of state action (Hayek 1960, p. 60). He thought it entirely legitimate that any particular rule inherited from the past could be examined and if necessary abandoned or modified. Without that there could be no progress of any kind. If all rules emanating from the past had to be accepted, then modern societies would still be holding slaves and burning witches. What Hayek rules out is any wholesale junking of rules of conduct and morality and their replacement by a new rational design. Yet attempts at wholesale revolution of the kind Hayek fears are extremely rare. The difficulty for his account of the relationship between theory and practice is that piecemeal, incremental reform is far more common, and here Hayek is a much less certain guide to what we should accept and reject (Kley 1994).

Hayek believed that only those who had studied and fully appreciated the complexity of the organism of modern societies could be trusted with making suggestions for changes to inherited rules. The only way it could be effectively improved was by improving the abstract rules which guide the individuals (Hayek 1967c, p. 92). His own suggestions for institutional reform were put forward in that spirit, as proposals that might find favor and be adopted or which might not. No single person had the authority to prescribe how society should in future evolve. Yet despite Hayek's readiness to turn his hand to institutional design, his lasting message is one of caution. By comparison, German neoliberals like Walter Eucken, whom Hayek admired (Hayek 1967c, p. 252), believed more strongly than he did in the principle of a strong and active state to promote the market order (Streit 1997, p. 60). Hayek, like Hume, recognized the necessity of politics but thought that little good could come from it, and sought ways to minimize the harm it could do (Hayek 1967c, p. 120). His epistemological pessimism about the nature of knowledge was matched by a political pessimism about the possibilities of reform. He was much more struck by the likelihood of human beings unwittingly destroying the basis of the civilization they had created by ill-considered rationalist planning than by their capacity to strengthen the institutions of the market order: "until we have learnt to recognise the proper limits of reason in the arrangement of social affairs, there is great danger that in trying to force on society what we think is a rational pattern we may smother that freedom which is the main condition for gradual improvement" (Hayek 1967c, p. 95). This is why he counseled that we must often accept what appears irrational and unjustifiable and contrary to our sense of justice and desert: "The individual has to be prepared to adjust himself to changes and to submit to conventions which are not the result of intelligent design, whose justification in the particular instance may not be recognisable, and which to him will often appear unintelligible and irrational" (Hayek 1948a, p. 22).

The way in which Hayek approaches the social world is paralleled in the way in which many environmentalists approach the natural world. Both are conceived as extremely delicate, living organisms which have evolved in particular ways and whose operations are imperfectly understood. Human interventions that alter the balance risk destroying the forces that create and sustain the order on which all human life depends. Hayek treats the market order similarly as a social ecosystem which we interfere with at our peril. What he does not address directly is whether the market order is compatible with the natural ecosystem. A liberal market order of the kind Hayek advocates permits constant interference in the natural ecosystem through the ways in which natural resources are acquired and utilized to sustain modern industry and urban lifestyles. Can a liberal market system generate spontaneously in time the innovations, new rules, and changes in behavior necessary to prevent the fatal undermining of the ecosphere on which all human activity ultimately depends?

Hayek saw most environmentalist arguments as new pretexts for intervening in the market order. He was sensitive to environmental problems, but he thought it morally objectionable for rich countries to tell poor ones that they must restrict the growth of either their population or their economy to save the planet (Hayek 1988, pp. 125–26). He argued that most environmental problems are best left to the capacity of the social ecosystem to adapt and experiment. The imposition of controls by the state on the growth of population, or on the use of natural resources, does more harm than good (Hayek 1960, pp. 369–70). Controls will be ineffective and will hinder the emergence of possible solutions. Hayek might have recognized the problem of climate change, but would have rejected recent calls for drastic action by governments to avert potentially irreversible damage to the planet. He fought a long and ultimately broadly successful campaign against the idea that detailed management of the economy by government was necessary to ensure growth, prosperity, and high employment. The contemporary global economy based on neoliberal rules is a success for Hayekian principles. But whether Hayekian principles can preserve the ecosystem poses a new and sterner test, because he never extended to natural science and technology his critique of constructivist rationalism in social science. Although rationalism has retreated in the social sphere, it still has few restraints in its quest to master and control the natural world, posing increasingly serious questions for the civilization that Hayek so valued.

There is a further paradox. Hayek's critique of rationalism is derived from his understanding of the way in which modern societies had evolved and were coordinated, and has major implications for the methodology and practice of economics and social science. Hayek's lasting achievement was to focus attention on the limited and fragmented nature of knowledge in modern societies and the need for social and economic theorists to make that the cornerstone of their thinking. Yet in some ways he remained trapped in the rationalism he was so keen to reject. If our reason is so feeble, and if knowledge is necessarily imperfect and dispersed, how do we know this to be true? To make that claim Hayek has to take up the privileged status of observer that he is so critical of in constructivist rationalism. If he were not prepared to do so he could not justify his project of social and economic theory at all. Despite his denunciation of the ills of scientism and constructivism, Hayek is closer to the rationalism he criticizes than he might like to acknowledge.

7 Hayek and Popper: the road to serfdom and the open society

From the perspective of 2007 it is hard to put oneself in the frame of mind which dominated intellectual life in Britain and much of Europe sixty years ago, particularly over the question of socialism and state planning. Most intellectuals seemed to take socialism for granted. Many were or had been communists; many others were fellow travelers, and many of those who were not were, in Lenin's odious terms, "useful idiots." We in the west were, after all, allies of Soviet communism in the fight against Nazism and fascism, Stalin was familiarly known as "Uncle Joe," and in the British armed forces education officers were vigorously promoting the virtues of leftist approaches to postwar reconstruction. The Spanish Civil War, only a few years earlier, had rallied many European intellectuals to the republican cause, and in Britain at least one would have been hard put to find a voice favoring the nationalists outside the small and supposedly benighted ranks of right-wing Catholicism.

We will leave aside the intriguing question as to what might have been the future of postwar Europe had the communists won in Spain. (With the Nazi–Soviet pact of 1938, had Spain gone communist, would there even have been a postwar Europe remotely analogous to the one which actually arose? And even if there had been, would a communist regime in Spain have confined its influence and activity to the Iberian peninsula?) In 1945, such questions could hardly have been raised at all, and even in 2007, this chapter of counterfactual history might be too hot a potato to handle, and would in any case take us too far from our theme.

Back in the mid-1940s, as all readers of this *Companion* will be aware, there were a few voices, neither Catholic nor reactionary, raised against the political consensus. How influential they were on the audience they were aimed at at that time is perhaps hard to judge, given the almost willful insistence there seemed to be on giving communism an easy ride, and given the uncritical faith there was in central state planning being a key element in reconstruction. But what we can say in retrospect is that Hayek and Popper, along with Arthur Koestler and George Orwell, were telling people all they needed to know about the intellectual weaknesses, the practical difficulties, and the moral defects of collectivism. As time went on, no doubt these ideas entered the intellectual body politic (though to what extent they have been fully absorbed is a question to which we will return). But in the 1940s their enunciation and development was bold intellectually and morally, the more so as they did not depend on any standpoint more contentious than that of a secular liberalism.

The Road to Serfdom (RS) appeared in 1944 (Hayek [1944] 1962) and The Open Society and Its Enemies (OS) in 1945 (Popper [1945] 1966). Although Popper acknowledges the "interest and support" of Hayek, which enabled his book to be published, when he wrote The Open Society (in New Zealand) he had not read The Road to Serfdom, though he had read some of Hayek's earlier writings (cf. OS, vol. 1, p. 285). In the circumstances, as we would expect, there are significant similarities and also significant differences between the two authors and their respective books. As I will attempt to show, both similarities and differences became more pronounced as time went on. But to begin with, I will present an overview of relevant themes from each of the books.

THE ROAD TO SERFDOM

In typically combative spirit early on in RS, Hayek asserts that socialism means slavery and that even in the democratic west we are steadily moving in the direction of socialism (p. 10). The underlying reason for this apparently extreme view is that under socialism, even democratic socialism, the ability and enterprise of individuals will be continually thwarted by the will of others who take it upon themselves to decide who gets what. Hayek goes on to quote de Tocqueville: "Democracy and socialism have nothing in common, but one word: equality. But note the difference: while democracy seeks equality in liberty, socialism seeks equality in restraint and servitude" (p. 18). And he also says that the true nature of our civilization has been seen more clearly by its enemies than by its friends. What he calls "that nineteenth century totalitarian" Auguste Comte spoke of the "revolt of the individual against the species" as being "the perennial Western malady" (p. 12). For Hayek this revolt is no malady, but the very means by which the west has grown, succeeded, and improved socially. It has done so by making as much use as possible of the spontaneous forces of society, creating a system in which competition will work as beneficially as possible, and in which individuals reap the rewards of their successes and pay the cost of their failures. It is just this system that socialists and collectivists are bent on destroying or at least shackling.

Such is the spirit which infuses RS, and for which Hayek is rightly famous, and which permeated his career. As we have already suggested, for many years he was one of a very few voices arguing forcefully and cogently against collectivism and state planning. There is no doubt as to what Hayek's stance would have been on crucial aspects of politics and economics. In view of all this, it is surprising, in reading RS sixty years on, to see how nuanced and "moderate" Hayek's position there actually is in certain crucial respects.

In view of Hayek's reputation as a critic of any sort of planning (to which we will return), at the outset it is worth underlining his comment early on in RS to the effect that everyone who is not a complete fatalist is a planner. "Everybody desires that we should handle our common problems as rationally as possible, and that in doing so we should use as much foresight as we can command" (p. 26). The question, of course, is the extent to which we can rationally use foresight, the distinction in other words between good and bad planning. Thus far what Hayek says would be consistent with complete laissez-faire, a state in which the only planning admitted is that undertaken by individuals, with the state opting out of economic and social arrangements entirely.

No doubt arguments could be mounted for laissez-faire and, more generally, for anarchism. But such is not, and never was, Hayek's position. In fact, Hayek's specific repudiation of these extreme positions leaves him vulnerable to the criticism that his own position is, contrary to appearance, consistent with quite a high degree of state control and interference (and, as we will also see, Popper's espousal of negative utilitarianism and piecemeal social engineering is open to similar uncertainties). What Hayek says is that while we should not plan for particular goals for society as a whole (such as controlling prices, setting centralized production targets, or getting incomes or wealth to conform to some standard), what we should do is to plan for those social conditions which would permit the highest exercise of individual freedom, so that individuals can then best make their own plans. (A similar distinction between what we might call planning for freedom by means of what Popper calls protective institutions, as opposed to planning which interferes with freedom by imposing the designs of the rulers on others, is also a cornerstone of Popper's social philosophy – cf. OS, vol. 2, p. 131, and the later reference to Hayek in Popper's appendix 29 to ch. 17, p. 331.)

Initially this Hayek-approved type of planning is glossed in terms of rules to ensure universal entry to markets (so no cartels), but he immediately goes on to say that there could legitimately be rules to prohibit abuses (of liberty?) such as overlong working hours or the use of certain poisonous substances. It is true that Hayek does say that we will have to look to see whether in specific cases regulation and prohibition impose too high a social cost for the advantages they bring about. But the trouble is, as we see in the recent wrangles over the European working time directive, there is unlikely to be agreement on this calculation. What for one man is a matter of ensuring fair competition by means of a level playing field is for another a restriction of competition and its advantages.

But this is not the only uncertainty in Hayek's prescriptions for planning. He immediately goes on to add that the preservation of competition is not incompatible with "an extensive system of social services," to which an immediate riposte might be, "What about competition within the social services themselves?" In fact, as we see later in RS (p. 76), Hayek thinks that there is a strong case for the state to act so as to reduce inequality of opportunity "as far as congenital differences permit" and so far as doing so does not impede the impersonal system of rules under which all are to operate. He also thinks that the state should ensure certain minimum standards in physical necessities and also organize "a comprehensive system of social insurance" (p. 90).

One might not object to these proposals on a priori grounds (whatever doubts one might have fifty years later about the state's ability actually to provide extensive systems of social services and the rest).

The difficulty with all this from Hayek's point of view is that those who set up the post-1945 welfare state in Britain might well have described their ambitions in terms very similar to those of Hayek. Even worse, equality of opportunity – to which we are all these days supposed to adhere as the unobjectionable side of equality – proves to be increasingly difficult to distinguish from equality of outcome, for working toward such equality will inevitably mean attempting to reduce the differences which result from previous unequal outcomes (such as the wealth of one's parents and the education one has received). I suspect that there is not going to be a third way here. Those who believe in freedom and, like Hayek, dislike the prospect (or reality) of groups of politicians and bureaucrats determining who should have what and at what time are simply going to have to drop talk of equality of opportunity (as opposed to talk of opportunity), however inconvenient this may be politically and electorally. And, with fifty years of experience in Britain of monolithic state provision of health and education, at ever-increasing cost and ever-decreasing satisfaction, we should surely heed Hayek's warning of the treacherousness of the apparently reasonable proposition that there is a "middle way" between "atomistic" competition and central direction – and this half a century before Professor Giddens and Mr. Blair.

In RS, as in his later writings, Hayek marshals a number of arguments against central planning of the economy. Of these perhaps the most fundamental, but also the least developed, is an epistemological argument to show that rational planning by a central agency is impossible. It is impossible because the type of knowledge it would need to be rational simply cannot be had. The only way a large society can be effectively coordinated is to allow the workings of competition. Precisely because a large society is so complex and composed of so many different individuals all making their individual choices, it would be impossible to centralize the information needed for rational planning. Competition works by diffusing the information about the myriad uncoordinated choices and actions of millions of consumers and entrepreneurs throughout the whole of society. In this way labor and capital will be pulled to their most productive uses, entrepreneurs will succeed only if they produce goods and services consumers want, and as a result consumers will be offered the biggest range of goods at the best prices. Hayek does not pretend that markets are perfect, even if they are circumscribed by good rules; there will inevitably be waste and failure in the system, as things are tried and found wanting. Though many will gain, and the system overall will be beneficial, some will lose, even catastrophically for those individuals. But the alternative of a system run by a government or a committee of bureaucrats will be far worse. By its interference it will impede the flow of information, and in its pretension to have knowledge which simply cannot be had, its activity will in fact be tantamount to the arbitrary exercise of power by a few over the many. And Hayek thinks that arbitrary power constraining individual freedom is far worse than all of us submitting to the impersonal forces of the market, forces which are not rational, to be sure, but forces which do not in themselves and by their very nature constrain freedom.

Some may, of course, dispute this last point, particularly if central state planning affords them some security against failure in the market. There is, as both Hayek and Popper say, a yearning deep within many of us for a more organic form of society than that of economic liberalism. To this Hayek would no doubt reply that in the modern world the only form an organic society could take would be a form of despotism, more or less mild, more or less arbitrary. But is Hayek actually right in his epistemological argument? It surely cannot just be because of the unsurveyability point, for that is purely contingent. The unsurveyability Hayek refers to is not that of the mathematical unsurveyability of infinite sets. Though very large, the numbers we are talking about in the market are not infinite. Maybe with the tremendous power of modern data processing it would be possible to survey all the choices and purchases consumers make almost instantly and to direct production accordingly.

What Hayek clearly needs at this point is some argument as to the intrinsic unpredictability of the human world, irrespective of its size. There are well-known arguments – which Popper toyed with at various times – about the inability of a predictor within a system to predict the future states of the system, because of the way its own predictions will interfere with the system, and will do so regressively. The disturbance factor of the predictor will obviously increase to the extent that the predictor is itself an agent within the system, as would certainly be the case were the predictor also the agent who planned the system. Intriguing as these arguments are, though, they may not get to the heart of the matter. They certainly carry some weight in the sort of case which Hayek envisages, for the predictor is undoubtedly, directly or indirectly, going to affect the system. But in themselves the arguments do not produce the link between unpredictability and freedom which we seem to need, because the "Tristram Shandy effect," as Popper calls it, would not show that a system was not in fact determined or even that a predictor insulated from the system and observing it from outside could not accurately predict its development. Furthermore, the basic reason Hayek is arguing against planning is because of the way it interferes with human freedom. It would be nicely symmetrical if the reason why planning is bound to fail is because human freedom itself makes prediction impossible.

There are indeed good reasons to think that human behavior is both free and unpredictable, indeed that over and above the interference effect of prediction, human behavior is unpredictable because free. We can point to the basic fact that before a consumer actually makes a choice, no one will know whether or not he or she will. Until he or she is in the position of choosing, maybe not even the subject himself or herself knows what will be done. Given that this basic fact is replicated many times each day by millions of individuals in a given market and by millions of others throughout the world, it is going to be very hard to come up with more than very broad-brush probabilistic predictions of the behavior of markets. And to what might seem the caprice of individuals acting in markets, we can add the phenomenon noted by Popper in the Preface to *The Poverty of Historicism* (Popper 1957), that, namely, of the unpredictability of scientific and technological development. As Popper points out, one reason we cannot know these things in advance is because if we did, we would know them already, and so they would not be future developments. Intriguing as this point is, however, the underlying cause of all this uncertainty is that in the human world developments in any sphere depend on all sorts of uncertain factors, including luck, chance meetings of events and people, and above all human creativity. If anyone doubts this, we have only to consider the amazing developments in computing and the internet, developments which even now we can hardly comprehend or survey, but which stemmed originally from the application of some apparently very rarefied and abstract mathematics to the needs of code-breakers in military intelligence in the Second World War and then from the discovery that mechanical valves in the first computers could be replaced by electronic chips. It was – and is – a story full of all the factors just mentioned, and one which has changed the world in ways which would have defied any attempts to predict in advance.

If the epistemological argument is the cornerstone of Hayek's argument against planning, it is supplemented by a strong protest of a moral nature. Hayek is a pluralist about values. There is no single and complete ethical code. People are individuals and should have the freedom to make their own choices and to follow their own values and preferences without being dictated to by others. In this context, a planner, however "expert," will be just one more player in the game, with no more right to impose his vision as to the correct distribution of goods, say, than any one else. And democracy is no safeguard here, for it is all too easy in a democracy for a majority to trample on the rights of minorities, an all too common result of economic planning. Fundamentally, economic planning is objectionable because it treats individuals and their work as means to some end they have not chosen, and in so doing it deprives them of their freedom, for economic freedom is neither more nor less than the freedom to act.

Freedom depends on the individual being able to plan, and to know probable outcomes of his actions. It is precisely this knowledge which is impeded by the actions of planners who constrain and regulate him according to plans of their own, arbitrarily from the point of view of the individual. On the other hand, planning requires a framework of rules and laws to provide a firm context for individuals to plan. So, to reemphasize the point already made, Hayek is not saying that the state should not act and rule, but that it should do so in order to create a stable and fair context for individuals to act and pursue their own ends.

Strangely enough, in RS Hayek says little about the inefficiency of planning, as opposed to its assaults on the freedom of individuals. But he does take up another theme which has also become prominent in recent years, that of demoralization. For if the state provides all sorts of services and functions for individuals, which individuals could better provide for themselves, this deprives individuals of responsibility, creating a culture of irresponsibility. Part of the reason the state might do this is because of a yearning for security on the part of citizens, a nostalgia for a more organic form of society. But this is an idle dream. Far from producing real security, the state will undermine individual freedom and responsibility in its provision of "services," without producing any satisfaction with what it provides. This is because of its inbuilt inefficiency and hostility to the sort of competition which would improve those services or even keep them at a reasonable standard. And unsuspected by the politicians who set up the National Health Service in the 1940s, arguably intending to provide a minimum basic service for genuine emergencies, there is also the insatiable demand on the part of the public for an ever-increasing provision for which it is not directly paying. The result inevitably is a provision which simply becomes thinner and more stretched, and less able to provide even the minimum levels regarded acceptable when it was originally set up.

THE OPEN SOCIETY AND ITS ENEMIES

Hayek's observations about the desire of people to be freed from the burden of economic cares (and hence in practice freed from their own freedom) are a good place from which to start our analysis of OS. For an important and prominent theme of OS is what Popper refers to as tribalism and the desire to avoid what he calls the strain of civilization (OS, vol. 1, p. 176). While tribal societies are based on organic structures and face-to-face contact, and are typically small enough to operate in these ways, what Popper calls abstract societies are far too large for any of this. Accordingly, personal links are far weaker. Many of the people I deal with and whose actions affect me I do not know at all, and our dealings are through the impersonal mechanisms of trade. For an abstract society to operate effectively, what is needed are sets of rules governing these impersonal transactions which will afford agents expectations of outcomes and allow them to plan in the absence of personal dealings and agreements.

It is surely significant that for Popper as for Hayek the condition of possibility of an abstract or Great Society is trade, for trade breaks down tribalism and heralds an era in which old boundaries and customs melt away. The abstract society, with its inherent drive to cosmopolitanism and universalism, is for Popper the basis on which an open society can emerge. Old certainties and old taboos will not survive the sense that we are now operating in a much wider arena in which people from all sorts of different backgrounds are intermingling and dealing with each other. Popper, of course, had experience of just this sort of effect in New Zealand when he was writing OS, and also of what he regarded as the benighted efforts of some to preserve Maori ways inviolate, benighted apart from any-thing else because Maori ways had never been inviolate, but had always been changing in response to changing circumstance; as one of these benighted individuals was his own head of department, with whom he had appalling relations, it is perhaps surprising that in his discussion of tribalism he never mentions the tribalism on his own doorstep. Fifth-century BC Sparta, not twentieth-century Maori, is the focus of his discussion, perhaps unfortunately for the Maoris, as the dilemmas Popper explores in OS are if anything further from being resolved in New Zealand in 2007 than they were in 1945. Nevertheless it can be said that in his writing Popper shows an acuity of awareness of the human dimension of the topics he is discussing which Hayek never approaches.

The strain of civilization is a strain, and people yearn for an atmosphere of security. But once a society has moved away from tribalism, tribal values can be restored only by reasserting the differ-ences between the tribe and the rest, by restoring or reinstating hierarchies and taboos within, by the attempt to be independent of trade, and in general by what Popper calls "anti-humanitarianism," shutting out all "equalitarian, democratic and individualistic ideologies" (OS, vol. 1, p. 182). Looked at from this angle, the strain of civilization is simply the strain of being human, of recognizing a world of Kantian universality in which all are, first and foremost, rational agents, in that respect equal, and in which all must bear the responsibility and burden of their own freedom. What is interesting in OS, and where Popper perhaps comes closest to Hayek, is the way Popper sees the abstract universalism of Kant, in which humanity is defined in terms of shared rationality pertaining to individuals as individuals, as emerging historically from the development of the abstract and boundary-blind relations of trade and commerce.

However, the very point at which Popper seems closest to Hayek is actually the one from which a significant difference emerges. It is Popper's Kantian interpretation of trade and its effects and his Kantian analysis of human individuality which actually distance him from Hayek. Popper is a believer in the logical separation of facts and values; so values cannot simply be derived from any sort of teleology and even less from anything like divine commands. Like Kant, Popper believes that we, as rational agents, would still have to make our own judgments as to the validity of the commands or the desirability of the ends proposed by nature. In that sense, humans do, for Popper, create values (which anyone with Platonistic leanings, such as Iris Murdoch, would find objectionable). But – and this is where Popper is quite different from Hayek – although we choose our values in the sense of having to determine them for ourselves, values are not simply a matter of individual choice or preference. They are not arbitrary or relative.

I do not think that Popper could agree with Hayek's claim in RS (p. 42) that as values exist only in individual minds, nothing but partial and, hence, different and inconsistent sets of values exist. Hayek later criticized what he took to be Popper's excessive rationalism, according to which rationalist thinkers will not submit blindly to any tradition (Hayek 1988, p. 61). It was just that which Hayek came to advocate, that we submit to values we do understand and cannot justify, in the hope that doing so might lead to successful results. Even a conservative traditionalist might have difficulties with this notion, if only because of the uncertainty in any concrete case that it was the value we did not fully understand which was actually responsible for the result we liked. For Popper, by contrast, values can always be argued about, in themselves and independently, one assumes, of dubious inferences concerning their effects. And without ever being sure we are absolutely right at any given time, these discussions are (or should be) rational, and progress can be made, and in Popper's view has been made. (Cf. OS, vol. 1, pp. 64–65, and the 1961 appendix to vol. 2, especially pp. 384–86.) In other words, Popper is not a subjectivist about value. In this respect, as in his cosmopolitanism, he is a Kantian, sharing none of the sense of the Austrian Economic School of the ultimate undecidability of values which we find in Hayek. He is a rationalist, albeit a critical rationalist here, and this is inconsistent with any form of subjectivism or relativism, even the rather attenuated and roundabout form we find in Hayek.

Popper's open society is premised on the assumption that its citizens are Kantian rational individuals, free to conduct their own lives and to work out their own systems of value, and also, it emerges, liberated from the typically conservative bonds of nation or roots, and prepared to take the strain of civilization without lapsing into the warmth and comfort of tribalism. They are also fallibilists. That is, they are prepared to admit that they might be wrong and ready, as Popper put it, to listen to "the other fellow's point of view." For this reason, too, they will typically be democracies, societies best adapted to discussion of this sort. But discussion as Popper envisages it is something which can make progress. Without having a blueprint for a good society, any more than scientists have criteria for the truth of their theories, in both science and politics progress can be made. We can, through attending closely to the consequences of theories and to the effects of policies, especially to the effects on those they impinge on, get nearer the truth, nearer to what is good. Or so Popper, like Mill, believed (cf. OS, vol. 2, p. 386).

Popper is as hostile to central planning as Hayek, but his hostility derives from no a priori dislike of state activity or of policies designed to do more than simply set up the rules within which individuals and groups will compete. Indeed, it has often been pointed out that, while Popper himself may have become more opposed to state activity in his later years, there is little or nothing in *The Open Society and Its Enemies* which is inconsistent with the sort of social democracy of the socialist parties of Western Europe – so long as their activity was conceived in terms of piecemeal social engineering, their policies open to criticism and development, and the government itself dismissible at regular intervals by electorates. Indeed, one could argue that the open society itself might require a degree of state activity quite repellent to Hayek in order to bring disadvantaged and marginalized groups up to the level at which they could effectively participate in its deliberations and discussions. In more general terms, as we have already seen, Popper is quite happy in OS to advocate what he calls "equalitarianism," and he also speaks of the moral demands for equality and for helping the weak as being moral demands (OS, vol. 1, p. 65). There is nothing in any of this to rule out state activity in these areas, any more than in the case of what we earlier called Hayek's more nuanced description of the state. And with Popper, there is a further difficulty over "piecemeal" social engineering. When is a policy a piecemeal one (and hence, for Popper, permissible)? As with so much else in this area, what for some would be an absolutely essential step to removing a manifest evil or to securing participation in the open society or the economy might for others be a piece of objectionable large-scale planning and interference with essential freedoms. While we might know (or think we know) where Popper or indeed Hayek might have stood on such issues, it is not so clear that their arguments alone secure their conclusions.

Popper's hostility to large-scale central planning derives jointly from his fallibilism and his individualism, but it is fallibilism which seems to be more fundamental. Although he is a rationalist, he is a critical rationalist. That is, he does not believe that we can ever justify our beliefs. Rationality consists in criticism, and central planners, irrationally convinced of the rightness of their vision, tend to suppress criticism of it. They tend, in other words, not to take a fallibilist attitude to their plans. At the extreme they may be totalitarians, so convinced of the rightness of their ideals that criticism can come only from those who out of moral or intellectual blindness cannot see the truth (and so must be suppressed). Furthermore, as we cannot foresee the consequences of any policy, policies limited in scope are preferable to grandiose blueprints for the whole of society. Both are likely to have unforeseen and unintended consequences, but correction of limited actions is easier, and the harm they might do is less as well.

Although, in practice, Popperian openness and Hayekian limited government might look very similar, there is I think a significant difference between the two. Both are indeed convinced that the knowledge required by central planning cannot be had, but for Hayek there is, in addition, ineradicable value pluralism. In fact, Hayek seems more realistic here, for Popper's faith in the efficacy of openness and discussion to solve problems and overcome disagreements with "the other fellow" can seem shallowly optimistic. Of course, there may be people unprepared to discuss at all, and who would rather simply shoot their opponents, but this is not where the problem lies. In this case, Popper can appeal to his Kantian humanitarianism, and simply assert that the terrorist or dictator is acting irrationally and inhumanely. The problem for Popper arises where both parties to a discussion are as well mannered and as Kantian in spirit as possible. However long and painstaking the discussion, this may not be enough to produce agreement or progress on issues on which there are radical differences of perspective. Consider, for example, the differences which exist on matters such as abortion and stem cell research. Some people, for perfectly good (and not necessarily religious) reasons, believe that these things are wholly wrong and that their legalization is a step toward the dehumanizing of society. Others, also for defensible reasons, believe just the opposite. One could, of course, in a democracy simply accept that there is an impasse here, and legislate permissively; and maybe the objectors will eventually die out. But neither of these things would in any clear sense constitute progress from the rational point of view. Kantian discussion may not be as powerful a tool as Popper hoped.

In his own later reflections on morality (particularly in *The Fatal Conceit* [Hayek 1988]), Hayek does not offer justifications, even of a negative sort, of moral principles. What he gives us is the outline of an account of their genesis, along with a functionalist analysis of their operation. The underlying idea is that societies are held together by their moral codes, which are in turn formed by an invisible hand to respond to circumstances in ways the protagonists may well not understand. Nevertheless, particularly in the case of successful societies, the morality on which they are founded is disturbed at our peril. In reconstructing our morality we may well remove the very things which made our society strong and successful, examples being the traditional family and the ethic of work and personal honesty associated with some forms of Christianity. Indeed, though an agnostic himself, Hayek writes in favor of the role religion had and might still have in supporting property and the family. Hayek's whole approach here, in some contrast to RS, is to suggest that value pluralism, if taken too far, can lead to the erosion of a society; but this is not because he is able to argue that some values are more rational (or less criticizable) than others. In that sense he retains the stance of RS. But in contrast to RS and to the optimistic liberalism and Kantianism of Popper in OS, he came eventually to appreciate the pitfalls inherent in trying to hold a society together on no more than a shared commitment to reason. Humanly and socially speaking that would be too slender a support, powerless against the fissiparous effects of competing and conflicting sets of values.

In short, in the spheres of morality and values, Hayek, the pluralist convinced of the intellectual unassailability of pluralism, despite his well-known disclaimer, becomes a conservative, unconvinced of the possibility of justifying our values or of knowing their truth, but convinced of their necessity. In this context, it is interesting to record that in the 1950s Popper was privately defending Hayek against some of his left-inclined students: a liberal society, Popper himself urged then, needed a framework of conservative values. Indeed, as I have myself argued (O'Hear 2004), Popper had himself moved some way from the rationalism of *The Open Society and Its Enemies* even as early as 1949, with his essay "Towards a Rational Theory of Tradition" (Popper [1949] 1968). There, in rather Burkean terms, Popper castigates rationalists – even, I surmise, of a critical sort – for disparaging tradition and thinking that they can do so on the basis of pure reason, through their own brains, so to speak. It seems to me that there is tension here with the thoroughly untraditional and rootless Kantian cosmopolitan citizen of OS, who is supposed to keep everything under constant review, but unfortunately I cannot see where Popper was able to resolve or even explore this apparent tension. No more than the Hayek of *The Fatal Conceit*, in whose direction Popper may have moved over the years, is Popper able to explain just which traditions and values we need as the framework for our liberal society. Perhaps in neoconservative fashion they just assumed they would be the ones of Anglo-American society since, say, the eighteenth century; but that might not cut much ice with those unconvinced of the worth of such a society.

In this essay, I have tried to bring out some significant differences between the political and social views of Hayek and Popper, differences which may be the more remarkable given their similarities on many points, and particularly in their conclusions. Both are politically and methodologically individualists. Both are passionate in arguing against collectivism and totalitarianism, and also in warning against tendencies within liberal democracies which tend in that direction. Both show as clearly as need be shown that socialism in its communistic form is not a good idea which went wrong, but that it was a rotten idea from the start, rotten because in its pretensions to knowledge of a universal blueprint, it could produce nothing but tyranny and tears.

Certainly part of their joint message has got through. At least we will find few now arguing in favor of Marxism or Leninism, and the names of Hayek and Popper will often be cited as prophets in this respect, along with Orwell and Koestler and, among those who know at least, with Aurel Kolnai and Michael Oakeshott. But it remains questionable how far the Popper–Hayek message has really got through, in Western Europe at least and at least as regards freedom and individualism. The dream of an unattainable organic security combined with freedom remains; where the state has given up direct ownership of resources, it doubles its hold through regulation; welfarism remains an intractable problem holding its clients in penury and demoralizing them at the same time; and the state commandeers and mostly wastes 40 percent of GDP. All this is dressed up in talk of third ways, compassionate conservatism, "New" Labour, and the rest. All this goes to suggest that *The Open Society and Its Enemies* and (above all) *The Road to Serfdom*, for all their obvious faults and lacunae, some of which we have examined here, are as worth pondering now as they were in the 1940s. Faced with the angst of globalization and the problems of those who cannot cope in modern societies, we may feel that freedom and individualism are not what we want. But we should at least know what it is we are rejecting, and the likely cost.

8 Hayek's politics

In this chapter I offer a brief account of some central issues in Hayek's political thought, by way of discussing four important building blocks which play a role in their construction. I discuss several strands that go to make up his work, and some of the problems to which they give rise. I conclude with a suggestion about the relative priority that different themes might usefully be given, and with some remarks about the more narrowly political implications of Hayek's work. What are these different strands?

First, there are ideas stemming from the debate about economic calculation under socialism, and Hayek's related views concerning the use of knowledge in (commercial) society. Hayek thought that there was no alternative – for commercial societies – but to make use of price mechanisms, to aspects of whose significance he drew attention. At the same time, Hayek argued – for example, in his "Trend of Economic Thinking" ([1933] 1991) – that these also imposed certain constraints over what we might be able to accomplish, politically. This strand of argument – and its later extension into the claim that within such commercial societies the ideal of "social justice" is unrealizable – plays a significant role in his political thought.

A second strand of argument stems from a different concern. It was developed by Hayek in the course of his reflections upon Nazi Germany, and on the lessons that he thought developments there offered for Britain during and after the Second World War. It grew into his *Road to Serfdom* ([1944] 1962), although his account was developed in large measure in a series of earlier papers. This may usefully be contrasted with the first strand of argument. The first strand related to the key role of the price system in the sustaining of any society like our own, to the idea that there was no alternative for societies

like ours but to make use of such a system, and to the constraints
that we should understand this as imposing upon us. The second
strand of argument dealt with what occurred if one attempted to
introduce social planning into a market-based society. Hayek's concern here was not to argue that a fully planned society would not
work, but, rather, with what the consequences would be if the
attempt were made to introduce such planning systematically.
Hayek believed that if one persisted with such a course of action,
it would have the unintended consequence of limiting human
freedom, introducing a political system that is incompatible with
democracy, and requiring the use of coercion. Hayek offered a theory
of what he took to be significant features of Nazi Germany as
the product of the pursuit of policies which were popular – not
least among critics of Nazi Germany – in the England in which he
was living.

Hayek referred to *The Road to Serfdom* as a political book.[1] In so
doing, he did it a disservice. Not only was the argument of the book
impeccably scholarly, but it played a key role in the development of
his work; in fact, two such roles. For in *The Road to Serfdom* Hayek
was critical of laissez-faire, and had a positive agenda for governmental action.[2] This included a program for the rational improvement of
existing institutions,[3] and also various measures of a broadly welfar-
ist character.[4] This, however, posed a problem which was pressed
home upon him by John Maynard Keynes. Keynes, in a well-known
letter to Hayek,[5] after indicating a good measure of agreement, posed
a problem. It might be put thus: given that, you, Hayek, also have
an agenda for governmental action, how is it that you are not also
yourself on the "road to serfdom"? I will argue that this question
plays a key role in the subsequent development of Hayek's political
thought. Indeed, one can see Hayek's response as constituting a third
building block in his political views; for it led to his addressing the
problem of just what kinds of governmental action are and are not
problematic. Hayek was preoccupied with it in work undertaken
between *The Road to Serfdom* and *The Constitution of Liberty*
(1960). His answer becomes something like: the way to distinguish
between governmental action that poses a threat to liberty and governmental action that does not is in terms of its compliance with
Hayek's understanding of the rule of law. I write, here, "Hayek's
understanding of the rule of law," just because this was distinctive.

As commentators on Hayek have made clear, what he invoked was not this idea as it was understood in contemporary Anglo-American jurisprudence.[6] Rather, Hayek's concern was with this notion as understood in the (Kantian) *Rechtsstaat* tradition.[7] In this, one had a rich and moralized theory of the rule of law: it isn't enough that such law not be retrospective, and so on, be universal in its character, and apply to governmental action. But in espousing these ideas, Hayek was offering something akin to what has recently been championed as a "Republican" theory of liberty, for example by Philip Pettit and Quentin Skinner.[8]

Compliance with the rule of law, so understood, was for Hayek a necessary but not a sufficient condition for good government.[9] Hayek recognized – especially in the face of criticism – the limitations of a formalistic approach to liberty. He also stressed that compliance with the rule of law was not a guarantee of good policy. That, rather, also depended on other substantive matters. What these are is not altogether easy to sum up briefly. In part, it is a matter of their not having an adverse effect upon the inherited institutions of what, for want of a better term, I will call commercial society.[10] These institutions, however, are on Hayek's account themselves also open to piecemeal improvement. Exactly how this is to be done is, though, a somewhat complex matter. The overall goal seems to be something like a preference utilitarianism. However, Hayek's exposition of this is muddied by his concern about the limitations of our ability to design institutions and the dangers of overrating our rational capacities, which he at times expresses by way of attacks on both utilitarianism and rationalism.

This introduces a further element into our discussion. For Hayek's views are complicated by the anti-rationalistic strand to his work. This enters his work with the way in which he understood some of the lessons of the economic calculation debate in "The Trend of Economic Thinking,"[11] and from his work on Carl Menger in connection with his preparation of an introduction to an edition of Menger's writings that was published by the LSE.[12] One has, in these writings of Hayek's, an appreciation of certain important human institutions as the products of human action but not of human design. The non-rationalistic tendency of this work is, in turn, reinforced in his subsequent denunciations of the hubris of rationalistic planners, and by tendencies in his work on both the development of rule-governed conduct and human cognition which could be seen as anti-rationalistic.

All this would be striking enough on its own. But it becomes particularly challenging given that, on Hayek's account, we stand in need of a rational appreciation of the character of these inherited institutions, and the limitations that they impose upon us. We may need, however, to improve them and even to undertake more radical forms of social engineering, inspired by some of their characteristics. The result might seem to call for the skeptical liberal to become a philosopher king! But Hayek is a democrat – which introduces the further problem of what all this means for a democratic politics. I conclude with a suggestion as to how these problems might be resolved, and with some reflections on the more directly political thrust of Hayek's work.

THERE IS NO ALTERNATIVE

When Mrs. Thatcher was the leader of the British Conservative party, some people, when addressing issues of public policy, came out with the mantra "TINA." This stood for "There is No Alternative": for the (contestable) idea that there was no alternative but to adopt the kinds of market-orientated policies that they favored. In the context of Hayek's work, the theme of "TINA" has a more interesting and sub-stantive content. For it was Hayek's view – set out, particularly per-ceptively, in his inaugural address at the LSE, "The Trend of Economic Thinking" – that for a society such as that in which he was living, there was no alternative but to deploy the price system that lay at the heart of commercial society. I will not, here, review the details of Hayek's views about economic calculation, as this topic is treated elsewhere within the present volume. Suffice it to say that Hayek – in his early days attracted to a form of mild Fabian socialism – had initially been shaken by Mises' *Socialism*, and by his article on the problems of economic calculation under socialism.[13] Hayek tells us that he was not fully convinced by Mises' argument. He also went on to develop his own ideas about this topic. These were striking in themselves, and also led him to his interest in problems about eco-nomics and knowledge. What is most significant about these develop-ments in the present context is his view of their political implications as is explored in "The Trend of Economic Thinking."

I will paint a picture here with a fairly broad brush, and will extend my account to later work of Hayek's which also explores this theme.

First, Hayek thought that one consequence of his and Mises' arguments was that there was, for a society *of the kind within which he was living*, no alternative but to make use of market mechanisms. What is involved relates in part to the idea, set out in works from John Locke's *Second Treatise of Government* to Leonard Read's "I, Pencil," that market relations make possible a form of cooperation among innumerable people without their entering into face-to-face relations.[14] Hayek added the idea of the price mechanism as serving to harness knowledge – including various forms of tacit knowledge – that was distributed across the whole "Great Society" that is created by such means. All of this information, including people's effective demand for different goods and services, is, albeit in a somewhat rough and ready way, not only aggregated, but also then disaggregated. It makes available to social actors, in their various different social situations, an overall picture of how other people's plans and decisions, as expressed in the marketplace, currently relate to what they may do, and in a manner that constantly changes to reflect changes in those people's actions and decisions.

Second, Hayek took the message from his own work, and the work of Mises, to be that there really was no alternative to this system. One approach popular at the time (not least because of the influence of Marxism) was that the benefits of commercial society could be taken for granted – such that, say, they would be available to central planners to redeploy as they might wish. Hayek, by contrast, argued that we – as distinct, say, from those in much smaller, more face-to-face societies – could only organize ourselves on the basis of the price system. The thrust of the argument about socialist calculation was that the view that there is an alternative was simply erroneous.

This leads to a distinctive feature of Hayek's political ideas, in which there is something in common with those of Marx.[15] In each case, what plays a central role in their approach to politics is an understanding of the character of the society in which we are living, the constraints that this imposes on us, and the possibilities that are (or in Hayek's case, are not) then open to us. This may be contrasted with the more common view that puts our values at the center of things, and then considers how these values should be realized. Clearly, in Hayek and in Marx, values are there; but in each case, once the issues of social organization are explicated, it is almost a "no brainer" what should or should not be done. There was, however, more in common between them. Each took the view that we need to see the actions of individual agents as giving rise to social structures that constrain them, and that the current economic organization of our society also constrains what can be accomplished within it politically without fouling it up.[16]

Third, then, such arrangements indeed impose constraints. In a striking line of argument in his inaugural address, Hayek suggested that the development of economics – and its discovery of the role and character of such arrangements – was starting to make clear that we are subject to constraints of a character that we had not previously suspected. From Hayek's perspective, these arrangements are themselves a product of human action but not of human design, but they then serve both to enable us and to limit what we may do. It is this which furnishes the parallel to Marx's view of there being constraints on what may be accomplished by (ordinary) politics. But as distinct from the view of Marx, while we may – in Hayek's view – come to appreciate that these things are not natural in the sense of innate, and also that they are not the products of deliberate human planning, there is no possibility of a transformation of our situation to one in which we somehow have the advantages of such an economic order without its constraints. Rather, not only is there no alternative, but there is, on Hayek's account, a cost to doing things as we do. For example, Hayek argued that – pace the wishful thinking of some conservatives – there simply is no *moral* merit to the distribution of wealth within such a society, and that one cost of such a society may thus be that it generates forms of economic inequality that we find morally unattractive.[17] In a manner that parallels certain themes in Karl Popper's work, the price of life in an open commercial society is a certain moral unease.[18] For, on both their accounts, there are certain very attractive moral ideals – e.g. for certain kinds of security, and for the characteristics of life in a more organic community – which simply cannot be satisfied within societies like ours.

There is another aspect to this, as well. There has been much discussion of the claim made by Hayek that the ideal of social justice is meaningless. I have elsewhere argued that Hayek expressed himself poorly when making such statements,[19] and that what he should be understood as claiming is that the ideal of social justice – understood as people being rewarded on the basis of what they merit – cannot be realized within a commercial society. Hayek's argument is clearly *not* that there cannot be non-market welfare provision; for of this he was an advocate.[20] Rather, it is his view that many significant occurrences in societies like ours are the products of disaggregated action, and that this may have profound implications for what can – and what cannot – be achieved in such societies.[21] If we make use of certain kinds of social institutions – from the price system to all kinds of "spontaneous orders" – the significance of which Hayek has stressed, then we may find that there are other prima facie desirable things which we simply cannot bring about. We may find that they are not achievable because within such a society there is no mechanism that can be created to bring about the kind of distribution that we favor, or that no one possesses the kind of knowledge that would be required to make such a thing work. Alternatively, if we set up institutions to try to accomplish such purposes, we may find that our intentions are systematically frustrated by the disaggregated actions of individual citizens.

All this may have been particularly poignant for Hayek himself, for he had initially been impelled into economics by a wish to improve people's social conditions, and he had been a moderate Fabian when he was young. Even after he had published his *Road to Serfdom*, Hayek, in a talk to students at the LSE, made it clear that he still had emotional sympathy with certain socialist ideals.[22]

Fourth, Hayek regarded the market – functioning along the lines that Mises had indicated – as working like an "organism."[23] This is significant, in two respects. First, it is something that has not been designed; indeed, in Hayek's view, it is only with the gradual development of economic understanding that we came to understand that there was something that we had inherited that both empowered and constrained us. Second, on Hayek's (developing) understanding, markets also exemplified a distinctive kind of order, one which served as an alternative to detailed planning, and of which there are also various other examples. Thanks to the work of Bruce Caldwell, we can now track the way in which Hayek's interest in and understanding of such ideas developed, not least during his period on the Committee on Social Thought, where he had the opportunity to interact with people from a wide variety of disciplines who had interests in these issues.[24] A key – and persisting – concern of

Hayek's became that we should recognize the existence and the importance of such phenomena, and that we should not operate with a simple dichotomy between what is natural and what is designed. Such thoughts led Hayek in several directions. He became interested in the character of such orders, and in the kind of theoretical understanding that we could have of them. He became interested in the link between their development and various rules of conduct – an investigation that in turn connected to his interests in cognition and in *The Sensory Order* (Hayek 1952b). He became critical of what might be called the planning mentality, and also of overinflated ideas about the capacity of human reason associated with it. He also became interested in various quasi-evolutionary ideas about the development, over time, of "spontaneous orders."

All this, however, at times spilled over into an attack on "rationalism" as such; for example, in his "Individualism: True and False" ([1946] 1948) and later in parts of *Law, Legislation, and Liberty* (1973; 1976b; 1979). This strand in his thought alarmed his friend Karl Popper, who in an unpublished lecture was led to defend his own "critical rationalism" against Hayek's strictures against rationalism in the former work.[25] This was also significant because Hayek was also, in some respects, a proponent of a kind of rationalism himself.

Hayek was in part a critical rationalist. By this I do not mean someone who subscribed wholesale to Popper's ideas. Rather, I mean someone who favored a program of piecemeal critical improvement of social institutions, rather than their comprehensive redesign. Hayek, for example, stressed quite clearly that inherited legal arrangements might, in some respects, not be fully functional for a commercial society.[26] Even in some of the writings of his old age, Hayek was keen to suggest the need for their critical improvement. There was, however, a difference here from Popper, in that Hayek typically looked to the improvement of our laws and institutions as such – i.e. to the creation of better frameworks within which individuals might act – as contrasted with Popper's more direct concern for the improvement of society by way of "piecemeal social engineering."

Hayek also favored a distinctive program of social reform, in which he thought that we should learn from the working of "evolved" spontaneous orders, and make use of the principles upon which they operated in the design of new social institutions. His ideas about the "denationalization of money" are an interesting example of such an approach, as – to a degree – are his ideas about a distinctive kind of second parliamentary chamber.[27]

There is, however, a tension between the "critical rationalist" and "anti-rationalist" strands in Hayek's work. Not only did some of the things that he said against rationalism in his work just after *The Road to Serfdom* (in "Individualism: True and False," and in *The Counter-Revolution of Science* [1952a]) pose some problems for his own, more critical, use of reason. But there is also a tendency, in the work of his old age, to take a somewhat uncritical view of the operation of non-rational selective mechanisms, and to downplay the role that can be played by rational activity.[28] However, such ideas were to be found alongside other themes that seemed to call for the exercise of the very kind of rationality that he was calling into question, and thus cannot be seen as superseding it.[29] I will return to this issue in the final section of this paper.

THE ROAD TO SERFDOM

There is also a separate line of argument feeding into Hayek's political thought, relating to the argument of his *Road to Serfdom*. Hayek has told us this book stemmed from a memorandum that he wrote for Lord Beveridge, when he was the Director of the LSE.[30] Bruce Caldwell has identified this memo.[31] It turns out to be something that Hayek had initially written in 1933, under the title "Nazi Socialism." The memo, however, is rather disappointing. It does little more than point out the role, in the Nazi party, of a statement of "twenty-five points" which included some socialist ideas, and document that some of those involved with the party came from a socialist background. There is nothing there which significantly anticipates *The Road to Serfdom*. The argument of that work, rather, is first set out clearly in Hayek's article "Freedom and the Economic System," published in *Contemporary Review* in 1938, and further elaborated in a pamphlet published under the same title in 1939.[32] This work – and *The Road to Serfdom* – contain a striking analysis of what, in Hayek's view, are the problems implicit in certain demands for economic planning. These ideas, as I will explain, also play a further distinctive role in the development of Hayek's political thought.

However, it seems to me understandable enough that Hayek may have overrated the degree to which these ideas were anticipated in his short note of 1933. For Hayek came to see the argument that he set out in "Freedom and the Economic System" as a diagnosis of what had happened in Nazi Germany. Let us look at how his ideas about this develop. In that memo, Hayek was, understandably, somewhat ambivalent about the character of the social ideals to which the Nazi regime would be led, when in power. He suggested that while it appealed for support to the lower middle classes and championed the idea of private property, it would be likely that shopkeepers and others would find themselves placed in some kind of guild structure, while the larger owners of property might find themselves subject to state control and the restriction of their income. He comments, however, that the National Socialist party had increased dramatically in size and had embraced people with very different ideas, such that "at ... present ... it is ... difficult to say which view will predominate." However, Hayek mentions the possibility that "the scare of Russian communism has driven the German people unawares into something which differs from communism in little but name."[33] Indeed, Hayek also commented on the contrast between his view of National Socialism and that of some of his colleagues at the LSE in the following terms. "They ... tended to interpret the National Socialist regime of Hitler as a sort of capitalist reaction to the socialist tendencies of the immediate post-war period, while I saw it rather as the victory of a sort of lower-middle-class socialism."[34]

Later, Hayek had occasion to review two books about Nazi Germany: Paul Einzig's *Hitler's "New Order" in Europe*, and Claude Guillebaud's *The Social Policies of Nazi Germany*. In his joint review, "Nazi Order," Hayek discusses how Guillebaud, in particular, emphasizes features of German social policy that go "far to explain the hold which National Socialism undoubtedly still has on the great mass of German workers." Hayek describes the book as offering an "objective account" which may upset the way in which official British propaganda "has represented Hitler as the very antithesis of socialism."[35] Hayek comments further that: "Guillebaud's reader will sometimes feel, that something good at least must come from measures which in themselves are so similar to what has long been advocated by social reformers elsewhere." Hayek himself comments, however:

Is it not possible that all that planning and direction, which in Germany longer than elsewhere has been universally demanded, necessarily require a "totalitarian" regime, arbitrary preferences, the use of force, and the institution of a new hierarchical order of society, and that only the most ruthless and unscrupulous are capable of satisfying the clamour of the masses for "action," while the decent falter and fail when faced with the concrete task?

This line of thought, which draws on Germany as a model of the consequences of the political implementation of then popular ideas about "planning," achieved its fullest development in an unpublished paper of Hayek's, entitled: "A Note on the Significance of the German 'New Order.' "[36] In this, we indeed find the argument of "Freedom and the Economic System" offered as an account of how broad developments in Germany can be seen as a consequence of the pursuit of ideas about top-down planning. Hayek concludes his discussion of this theme in that paper by claiming: "The ideas now so widely advocated in this country of an international 'organization' of the different industries, of the central control and distribution of the supplies of raw materials etc. etc., would ultimately lead to essentially similar results, that is to a totalitarian organization of life in the interest of whoever exercises these controls."[37]

This account parallels the core ideas of The Road to Serfdom, which were set out, initially, in Hayek's "Freedom and the Economic System." They are not an unconditional prediction of what will take place, but rather an analysis of what would be the consequences if the kind of conscious direction of the economy for which people were calling were systematically put into place. Hayek's broad line of argument is as follows. Central planning, on his account, "presupposes a much more complete agreement on the relative importance of ... different ends than actually exists, and ... in consequence, in order to be able to plan, the planning authority must impose upon the people that detailed code of values which is lacking."[38] From this Hayek sketches – by plausible moves – an account of how the responsibility for such planning will shift away from democratic political control. Further, Hayek argues that the power to impose a program where there is, in fact, no possibility of rational agreement about it leads the planners into propaganda and if necessary force, with the result that only the kind of people whom one would not wish to be in power will undertake it.

The argument of the two versions of "Freedom and the Economic System," and of The Road to Serfdom itself, also addresses an issue that becomes characteristic of Hayek's work, and which in some ways

parallels his *economic* analysis in his "Trend of Economic Thinking."
It is that Hayek becomes concerned with the problem that in liberal
societies we have achieved something significant which we have taken
for granted. However, we typically don't understand its character – i.e.
in this case the theoretical character of a liberal *social* order. Hayek is
thus also led to try to explicate a theory of liberal society, at least in
part so that we do not inadvertently harm it by undertaking political
measures which will damage it without knowing that this is what
we will be doing. The argument, here, parallels his concern, in "The
Trend," for the inherited but vulnerable price system and its associated economic order. In *The Road to Serfdom* Hayek, in addition to
his critical analysis of measures that he thinks will damage such a
society, thus also furnishes an account of how a liberal society
functions and also of constraints that this imposes upon us.

It is in this connection that Hayek sketches ideas about the functions of government that led Keynes to offer his criticism. How
Hayek responds to them seems to me also of significance for
Hayek's political thought from that point on. Keynes noted that,
in *The Road to Serfdom*, Hayek is critical of laissez-faire (indeed,
Hayek's *Road to Serfdom* endorses a welfare state, and a fairly extensive agenda of governmental activity).[39] But Keynes commented to
Hayek, à propos of government action:[40] "You admit here and there
that it is a question of knowing where to draw the line. You agree that
the line has to be drawn somewhere, and that the logical extreme [i.e.
laissez-faire] is not possible. But you give us no guidance as to where
to draw it." Keynes then goes on to argue that "as soon as you [Hayek]
admit that the extreme is not possible, and that a line has to be
drawn, you are, on your own argument, done for, since you are trying
to persuade us that as soon as one moves an inch in the planned
direction you are necessarily launched on the slippery slope which
will lead you in due course over the precipice."

HAYEK AND KEYNES' PROBLEM

Hayek did not, as far as we know, respond directly to Keynes.[41] But he
was concerned with this problem – or something very like it – in the
years between *The Road to Serfdom* and *The Constitution of Liberty*.

In a talk that Hayek gave about *The Road to Serfdom* in the
United States in 1945, he referred to the need for a clear set of

principles to distinguish between the legitimate and illegitimate fields of governmental activity. In fact, he describes himself as having addressed that task in his book.[42] At the same time, there is a note of ambivalence in Hayek's account, in that he *also* indicates that this is a task that is still to be undertaken. Hayek tries to resolve this problem by arguing that compatibility with the rule of law is a necessary (but not sufficient) condition for policy to be in order: from time to time he refers to policies that would be permissible on this basis, but which he thinks would be unwise. At the same time, the ideal of the rule of law has, in his view, the dual characteristic of safeguarding people's freedom of action and of being incompatible with a centrally planned economy. The task of explaining how it also resolves Keynes' problem, I conjecture, thus becomes the agenda that Hayek addresses in his writings on political issues during the late 1940s and 1950s.

Consider first Hayek's unpublished "Postscript to *The Road to Serfdom* (1948)." Here, after briefly discussing his ideas about monetary policy, Hayek states that he attaches great importance to the idea that monetary policy should be guided by known rules, and he is sharply critical of a discretionary approach.[43] That is to say, he is bringing out that his own favored response to problems of trade cycles is compatible with the rule of law.

Second, there is a paper of Hayek's, dated 1950, entitled "The Meaning of Government Interference."[44] In this, Hayek raises the question of what kind of governmental action is legitimate, and answers it in terms of the idea of equality before the law. He stresses again – as was done in *The Road to Serfdom* (and also in the unpublished "Postscript") – that in saying this, he does not mean that all action that is permissible on this basis will be wise. Hayek also points out that if such a restriction is imposed, it may mean that we prevent government from doing things that we would judge to be good. However, he thinks that such a restriction would also be incompatible with economic planning of the kind of which he is critical. For example, it would be incompatible with the discretionary granting of licenses, permits, and allocations, with price fixing, and with most forms of quotas and subsidies (unless the latter were offered to everyone who wished to undertake the activities in question). He again recognizes that some arrangements which would pass his test nevertheless might well be problematic even if formally in order (e.g. if a legislature were to keep changing the character of such restrictions on a frequent basis), and he argues that rules should be kept stable for extensive periods of time.[45]

Third, there is a paper, "Planning and Competitive Order," which is not dated, but which would appear to stem from much the same period.[46] In it, Hayek poses directly the question of how to distinguish between those kinds of governmental action which are compatible with a free economic system and those which will lead to a planned economy, and he answers the question in terms of the rule of law. He also mentions that this may well only be an ideal that we can approach, rather than something that can be fully realized. When discussing its characteristics, he writes of government as laying down rules of behavior, enforcing them, and itself being limited by them. The rules would apply equally to all people, and they are also intended to remain the same over long periods of time.

It is obvious enough how all this relates to Hayek's subsequent concern with the development of the ideal of the rule of law in his *Political Ideal of the Rule of Law*, and, further, with his *Constitution of Liberty*.[47] What is worth spelling out is that the ideal of the rule of law turns out to play a remarkable role in Hayek's work after *The Road to Serfdom*. For it serves three functions. On the one side, it offers a clear-cut answer to Keynes, in that, as Hayek's account develops, it is by reference to the ideal of the rule of law (interpreted in the light of *Rechtsstaat* ideas) that he offers a demarcation between those kinds of governmental activity that are permissible (although not necessarily wise) and those that are not. Second, he thinks that it would rule out the kinds of planning that would be damaging to people's liberty. Third, it turns out also to be just what is required by Hayek's positive account of individual liberty, too. For as he develops his ideas about this in *The Constitution of Liberty*, it turns out that freedom, for Hayek, is preserved if people are faced with laws that are universal in their form and which, more generally, fit his ideas about the rule of law. This grapples with an issue that is of continuing importance, even today when enthusiasm for a centrally planned economy – the immediate target of his earlier work – has faded.

Hayek has also written – for example, in his discussion of David Hume[48] – about the significance of law operating as a system that will generate particular tough cases. Hayek's view, here, is that we need to resist the impulse to try to change the law to avoid them. His views are very much in line with Hume's point:

All general laws are attended with inconveniences, when applied to particular cases; and it requires great penetration and experience, both to perceive that these inconveniences are fewer than what result from full discretionary powers in every magistrate, and also to discern what general laws are, upon the whole, attended with fewest inconveniences.[49]

Such ideas might seem most obviously understandable in terms of the functional requirements of a commercial society. In a smaller, more face-to-face society, there is room for the more discretionary administration of the law. While the provision of guidelines for future conduct is important, if people know a lot about one another's circumstances they are likely to be able to anticipate the kind of discretion that might be exercised by a judge in relation to particular difficult cases. By contrast, once we are in a full-fledged commercial society, typified by the kinds of relationships between strangers that we have met in Locke and in Leonard Read, and when Hayekian themes of the price-system mediated use of knowledge in society are in full play, an abstract and rigidly enforced system of law would seem to be essential if we are to be able to coordinate our actions with those of others. This, however, looks close in its character – if not its usual rationale – to the *Rechtsstaat* ideal that Hayek favors and which we have just discussed.

SOME PROBLEMS

I will conclude by discussing three broad themes concerning Hayek's politics, which emerge from this material.

First, there are problems of reason, reform, and the kind of institutional design that Hayek favors. As we have noted earlier, there is a reformist side to Hayek's view of the law and of our inherited institutions. While he stresses the significance of arrangements that we have inherited and which may, in some sense, be the historical products of human action but not of human design,[50] he believes that they may also need revision and improvement. The brief quotation from Hume also brings out the need for discernment in the selection of laws, and in our attitudes to their application. One might see Hayek's approach – in *The Road to Serfdom* and in *The*

Constitution of Liberty – as offering an account that might serve to guide those concerned with such issues. It suggests what is needed for a liberal society, as he understood it, to flourish. Above all, it indicates the kinds of things that we should do, and the way in which we should do things, in order to avoid damage to its economic operation and to its freedoms.

The *Rechtsstaat* interpretation of the rule of law which came to play such a role in his work was, historically, identified with a codified legal system (especially if it is contrasted with its "historical" opponents).[51] In *Law, Legislation, and Liberty*, Hayek, influenced it would seem by Bruno Leoni's criticism of the ability of legislatures to secure the stability of the law,[52] shifted his own views in the direction of the more "historical" common law tradition. He also offered a distinctive account of the reasoning that should handle the development of the law – an odd but engaging mix of common law reasoning and Karl Popper's epistemology. In this, a legal system with the characteristics that we had become used to from Hayek's work on Hume and on the *Rechtsstaat* tradition was pictured as the product of such reasoning.

At the same time, some other interesting – but strange – things start to take place in *Law, Legislation, and Liberty*. The book opens with an argument that traditional constitutional inhibitions concerning limited government have broken down. This leads to a concern for constitutional reform, to which Hayek contributes his striking proposals for a second parliamentary chamber structured round age-based cohorts. Such a body would have also to respond to Hume's problem of how to choose the right legal ideas. Seen in such terms, however, it does not seem adequate, just because what is needed is the best *theoretical* knowledge that we have to hand. That is to say, what should ideally play the role of determining the content and character of our laws and public policy measures would, from Hayek's perspective, be the best version of the *kind* of enterprise that Hayek himself was undertaking in *The Constitution of Liberty*. (Suppose his ideas were found compelling, and that successive versions of those arguments were to undergo an ongoing process of critical scrutiny and improvement from the community of scholars.)

What is also needed, on Hayek's account, is an appreciation of the various heritages of evolved rules of conduct and traditions, and also the ability to reflect upon them, to understand them theoretically, and to modify them where necessary. This, however, looks like a recipe for rule by philosopher kings, or by a Hayekian version of Saint-Simonian scientists. One feature that we noted in Hume's comments on law is particularly significant in this context. It is that a system of laws of the kind that Hayek favors will, indeed, generate particular consequences which may be morally problematic, such that it may take an experienced person, or perhaps better a social theorist, to understand why our impulse to remedy them should be resisted. There would seem no reason to suppose that such knowledge will be possessed in a tacit form by Hayek's age-based cohorts, not least because Hayek's own account in *Law, Legislation, and Liberty* starts from the idea that our instinctive ideas about the need for constitutional limitations have broken down.

Second, there is the problem of reason. Hayek, in the course of his appreciation of institutions that have *developed* "spontaneously" and also of the *current* working of such "spontaneous orders" – such as the price system – was led to stress their advantages when compared to what could be achieved through rational planning. In addition, he delivered an extended critical commentary on the limitations of reason. This involved his criticism of the follies of would-be rational planners, his own work on features of our processes of cognition, and his stress on the role of selective, evolutionary-like operations in history. However, Hayek himself also seems to require the existence on our part of rational capacities that may both play a critical, improving role, and also undertake at times heroic efforts at Hayekian social engineering (such as the introduction of Hayek's own constitutional proposals).

What is to be done about this contrast in Hayek's work? Let me offer a brief suggestion. My starting point is with a theme that Hayek described in "The Trend of Economic Thinking" and which I have argued is to be found in *The Road to Serfdom* and *The Constitution of Liberty*. It is that we are in some ways the products of various forms of tradition, various forms of social selection, and so on. We, however, become aware of this through the growth of our theoretical knowledge, and may thus come to understand what we have been doing, what intrinsic limitations it imposes upon us, but also that there are problems that require theoretical work and practical experimentation. This may include a need to appreciate, understand, and possibly improve the workings of various systems of "spontaneous order," and may also lead us to wish to set up various kinds of new institutions which work upon these same principles.

Clearly, such a picture draws on much that is familiar from Hayek, not least from what I have described above. But it gives it a distinctive twist. For it identifies clearly with Hayek's wish to spell out – and to convince us of – a theory of commercial society and of the operation of a liberal society more generally. It is within the compass of such an account that non-rationalistic forms of learning would then have their important role to play, that is, they would be seen as subject to the critical control of this kind of reflective public reason. The line of argument that I am suggesting contrasts with what sometimes emerges from Hayek's later work, because there the appreciation of "spontaneous order" mechanisms sometimes seems to overflow and leave no space for the kind of reflective rationalism to which I am here suggesting we accord a key position in the interpretation of Hayek's approach.

Such a view will involve our recognizing ourselves as having genuine – albeit limited and fallible – rational capacities. These may enable us to understand, again fallibly, our society, our current problems, and also what has been achieved by various unplanned social institutions. We may, then, set about trying to remedy problems – in some cases directly, within our limitations as we currently understand them to be, albeit typically by way of the formation or reform of institutions. If we do this, we will be engaging in an institutional form of what Karl Popper called "piecemeal social engineering," and will, as he stressed, need to be on the lookout for problematic unintended consequences of our actions, and to be ready to learn what we have got wrong, and to remedy it. However – as Hayek has stressed, following Hume – our theoretical knowledge may inform us that some of what we rightly see as problems are things that would prove more problematic if we were to try to remedy them.

More positively, we may be involved in one of two things. First, we need to develop an appreciation of the characteristics of spontaneous orders, and – as Hayek has suggested – the use of principles suggested by them, to design institutions to address new problems. Second, we may take a lead from Hayek's more conservative themes concerning the significance of various forms of learning by trial and error. The lead that I would suggest that we take from this, however, is that we should set out to *create* space – and institutions – within which such learning can take place. On the one side, this is likely to involve a securing of property rights, and freedom for individuals and groups to pursue ideas, projects, and forms of life – traditional or innovative – that appeal to them. On the other, it will involve an absence of political interference from the rest of us who may disapprove, unless they are creating negative externalities in a pretty direct way. We may, however, need to take steps to secure the freedom of people to escape from such "experiments in living" if they find them oppressive, and to provide a judicial system for the enforcement of contractual arrangements that they have made with those running such experiments. In this sense, Hayek's more conservative themes lead us in the direction of some quite radical arrangements, and indeed here suggest a point of similarity with the unjustly neglected "utopia" section of Nozick's *Anarchy, State, and Utopia* (1974).[53]

One further feature of all this, however, needs spelling out. Such a reading of Hayek's political ideas calls for a clear recognition of something that is implicit within his work. As his approach is democratic, those interested in it face an interesting challenge. It is that of how – and where – such ideas are to be legitimated in the public sphere. In the light of the content of Hayek's views, this presents us with a remarkably difficult challenge, though one which I cannot attempt to address here.

Finally, there is a further and somewhat vexed issue: that of the more specific character of Hayek's politics, in the sense of the political views to which Hayek's thought should lead us. Hayek dedicated *The Road to Serfdom* to "Socialists of All Parties." His reason for so doing was, surely, that he thought that the ideals about planning of which he was critical were to be found right across the party-political spectrum. Hayek set out an account of what people needed to do in the pursuit of their political ideals, if they were not going to compromise the basis on which a commercial society functioned, nor compromise people's freedom. Hayek was concerned to be heard by those on the left of politics, and seems to have been a bit disconcerted that he initially made an impact largely on the political right.[54] He would presumably have been heartened by the way in which – thanks in large part to the espousal of his ideas by Mrs. Thatcher – several writers on the left of politics subsequently came to take his views seriously.[55]

Hayek himself gradually identified with classical liberalism in a more specific sense. But it seems to me an open question just where his arguments should lead us. Hayek himself started with socialist concerns and sentiments. He also clearly favored extra-market welfare provision, at least within rich countries, and his *Road to Serfdom* allows for government to play quite a considerable role. I would have thought that his arguments point us in the direction of ideas that everyone should pay attention to, rather than just offering a positive program for one specific view of politics.[56] At the same time we may find that the kind of structural characteristics that he discerns in our society, and the kind of freedom we need in order to learn, may make *certain* kinds of otherwise attractive ideals difficult to pursue. They may also, however, make it difficult for us to solve certain other kinds of problem – such as some issues concerned with the environment.[57] But this leads us into issues that I cannot take further here.[58]

NOTES

1. See Hayek [1944] 1962, preface, p. v. Andrew Gamble has, however, rightly stressed to me just how significant it was as an intervention in politics.
2. See, for some detailed documentation, Shearmur 1997.
3. See for example Hayek [1944] 1962, pp. 13 and 27.
4. See notably his broad endorsement of the idea that a society that is as wealthy as his own should guarantee economic security to all "outside of and supplementary to the market system." Cf. Hayek [1944] 1962, pp. 89–90.
5. Cf. Keynes 1980, pp. 385–87.
6. Compare Joseph Raz's criticism of Hayek in Raz 1979.
7. As Hayek makes clear in *The Road to Serfdom*; see [1944] 1962, n. 1 to ch. 6, "Planning and the Rule of Law."
8. Cf. Pettit 1997 and Skinner 1998.
9. It is of course a matter of debate how successful such a formalistic approach could be, and Hayek himself expresses some reservations about formalism – without, however, indicating what is to be done.
10. Particularly illuminating upon which are Hont and Ignatieff 1983 and Ignatieff 1984, pp. 107–31.

11. On which see Caldwell 1988 and my discussion in Shearmur 1996a.

12. On which compare Shearmur 1986.

13. For detailed discussion of these issues, see ch. 2 of Shearmur 1996a.

14. John Locke discusses this issue in the context of the number of people indirectly involved in the making of bread, in his *Second Treatise of Government*, sect. 43; Leonard Read's "I, Pencil," published in *The Freeman* in December 1958, is available online at: http://www.econlib.org/library/Essays/rdPncl1.html.

15. Karl Popper, who in other respects was in agreement with Hayek, remarked critically on this point, in correspondence.

16. Compare here also Hayek's argument, from his later work, that the lives of millions of people depend upon commercial societies being retained.

17. It is instructive in this context to contrast the views of Kristol (1972), who seems affronted by Hayek's argument, but seems also to have nothing whatever of substance to say in response.

18. Compare on this the theme of "the strains of civilization" in Popper's *Open Society and Its Enemies* ([1945] 1966). For a brief comparative discussion of Popper's and Hayek's ideas on this point, see Gellner 1991.

19. See, for discussion, Shearmur 1996a, pp. 133–51. And see the exchange between Feser (1997, 1998), Johnston (1997a, 1997b), and Lukes (1997) for a debate over the merits of Hayek's argument concerning social justice.

20. See, for example, *The Road to Serfdom*, chs. 3, 8, and 9.

21. There is an obvious parallel with Robert Nozick's discussion of Wilt Chamberlain in his *Anarchy, State, and Utopia* (1974), in terms of issues not about rights, but about the kinds of constant state action that would be required if certain things are not to occur.

22. Compare on this his "On Being an Economist," which dates from 1944 and is now available in Hayek 1991; see also, for discussion, Shearmur 1996a, pp. 40–41.

23. See Hayek [1933] 1991, pp. 27–28 and the reference there to Mises' *Socialism* (Mises [1922] 1951).

24. See, notably, Caldwell's discussion "The Crucial Decade of the 1950s" in Caldwell 2004a, pp. 297–306.

25. Popper discussed this in a lecture on the topic of "Rationalism: True and False," as part of a series of lectures delivered at Emory University in 1956. This lecture was delivered on Tuesday, July 3rd. Some information about the lectures is available in Hoover Institution, Popper Archive, box 45, folders 16–24.

26. See, for example, his discussion in *The Road to Serfdom* ([1944] 1962), ch. 3.

27. See, for example, Hayek 1979, ch. 17.

28. See, notably, his "Epilogue: Three Sources of Human Values," in Hayek 1979.

29. For more detailed discussion on these themes, and documentation, see Shearmur 1996a.
30. Cf. Hayek 1994, p. 102.
31. See for discussion the edition of *The Road to Serfdom* in *The Collected Works of F. A. Hayek* (Hayek [1944] 2007). Caldwell reproduces the memo – a copy of which is held in the Hayek Archive at the Hoover Institution – as appendix A in this volume.
32. Both are now included, as chs. 8 and 9, in Hayek 1997.
33. The quotations are from "Nazi Socialism," in Hayek [1944] 2007.
34. See "The Economics of the 1930s as seen from London," in Hayek 1995, p. 62.
35. See Hayek, "Nazi Order," in "Documents Relating to the War," sect. 7, in Hayek 1997, pp. 173–75.
36. Hayek, "A Note on the Significance of the German 'New Order,'" Hoover Institution, Hayek Archive, box 128. The material in this part of the Hayek collection is not subdivided into folders, but the six-page double-spaced typescript bears an old number B4 on its right-hand corner.
37. Hayek, "A Note on the Significance of the German 'New Order,'" p. 5.
38. "Freedom and the Economic System," in Hayek 1997, p. 182.
39. See, for example, *The Road to Serfdom*, chs. 3 and 9. It is interesting that Hayek, when writing an introduction to the 1976 reprint of *The Road to Serfdom*, comments on the original text: "I had not wholly freed myself from all the current interventionist superstitions, and in consequence still made various concessions which I now think unwarranted." Compare Hayek, *The Road to Serfdom: Fiftieth Anniversary Edition* (Hayek [1944] 1994), which reprints the 1976 introduction; see p. xxiv.
40. Keynes 1980, pp. 386–87.
41. For a fuller discussion of these issues, see Shearmur 1997. The material here about the period between *The Road to Serfdom* and *The Constitution of Liberty* draws in part upon that account.
42. See "The Road to Serfdom," address before the Economic Club of Detroit, April 23, 1945. Hoover Institution, Hayek Archive, box 94, folder 38; see pp. 6–7. The paper is a transcript of Hayek's talk taken by a shorthand reporter. I have in Shearmur 1997 offered a reconstruction of what his view was in *The Road to Serfdom*.
43. See "Postscript to *The Road to Serfdom* (1948)," Hoover Institution, Hayek Archive, box 93, accession no. 86002–8M.40; the material is included in the brown folder inscribed "Road to Serfdom." The material referred to in the text is on pp. 12–13 of the Hoover Archive material.
44. Hoover Institution, Hayek Archive, box 94, folder 46.
45. This suggests that Hayek was already open to the argument that Leoni was later to press against his preference for legislation (i.e. that the

problem with legislatures was that they as a matter of fact could not be depended upon to leave such things alone and thus to provide stability); see below, and for discussion, Shearmur 1996a, pp. 88–92.

46. "Planning and Competitive Order," Hoover Institution, Hayek Archive, box 108; the folder in which this is held is labeled "Planning and Competitive Order."

47. Hayek 1955 and 1960.

48. See Hayek [1963] 1967.

49. Hume 1985b, p. 116.

50. Hayek, in some of his later writings, offers an account of legal and of other institutions as if they had simply evolved. But his own earlier accounts, such as in Hayek 1955, give an account – which is surely much more realistic – of critical intellectual reflection, and various human ideals, as having played a significant role in all this.

51. Compare, here, the discussion in Shearmur 1996a, pp. 88ff.

52. See, again, Shearmur 1996a, pp. 88ff.

53. For more on this argument, see Shearmur 1996a and 1996b.

54. See, on this, Shearmur (forthcoming).

55. Compare, for example, David Miller (1989a and 1989b), Raymond Plant (1994), and Andrew Gamble (1996).

56. Although clearly, one may – as I have done in Shearmur 1996a – explore what would be needed to develop his views into a telling argument for classical liberalism.

57. It is obviously an interesting question how far "free-market environmentalism" and the use of spontaneous order models can take us.

58. I would like to thank Bruce Caldwell for his encouragement and for some particularly useful suggestions in connection with my discussion of the material relating to *The Road to Serfdom* (although he is in no way responsible for what I have produced). I would also like to thank him for permission to make brief quotations from Hayek's unpublished work in this paper, copyright in which is held by Hayek's literary executors. I also wish to thank members of the Australian Society for the History of Economic Thought for their comments when a fuller discussion of the material about Hayek on the German New Order was presented at their conference in July 2005, and Andrew Gamble and Jeff Friedman for some most useful comments on an earlier version of this chapter.

9   Hayek the philosopher of law

Although Friedrich Hayek received the greatest recognition for his work in economics, he wrote several books on political theory and jurisprudence (as well as other philosophical areas). His writings on law and the philosophy of law have been widely discussed in the last decade or so, and represent a crucial contribution to this area of philosophy. Although Hayek's degree was not in philosophy, his writings are clearly philosophical. Inasmuch as he writes about the law in a philosophical way, asking justificatory, methodological, and normative questions about the nature and practice of law and legal systems, he is writing as a philosopher of law.

THESIS VERSUS NOMOS

In his three-volume study *Law, Legislation, and Liberty* (1973, 1976b, 1979), Hayek makes a key distinction between what he calls *thesis*, the law of legislation, and *nomos*, the law of liberty. The former is imposed by the sovereign, in what Hayek describes as a top-down, coercive process; the latter is evolved, a spontaneously-emerging (or bottom-up) process. While *thesis* reflects primarily the interests of the sovereign (or ruling class generally), *nomos* arises out of human interaction – the many iterations of people seeking more effectively to coordinate their actions and to resolve disputes peaceably. (Some legal historians have argued that Hayek conflates common law and customary law, but this doesn't undermine the *thesis/nomos* distinction.) As we shall see, Hayek argues that it is *nomos* that is critical for liberal political and economic theory.

Hayek had argued in earlier works that, like markets, society in general can be seen as an example of "spontaneous order" – that is, the product of human interaction but not of human design. Chapters 10 and 11 of *The Constitution of Liberty* (Hayek 1960, cited herein as CL) are concerned with the same themes, and provide Hayek's analysis of the origins of the rule of law. These matters receive more thorough and systematic treatment in *Law, Legislation, and Liberty*. Volume 1 deals with "Rules and Order" (cited herein as RO) and is the primary source of the *nomos/thesis* distinction. Hayek derives this via another distinction, to which I have alluded, between spontaneous order (*kosmos*) and designed order (*taxis*). Volume 2 deals with distributive justice and the market order. Volume 3 deals with democracy, separation of powers, and several policy issues. The three-volume set as a whole is truly a comprehensive work on the political economy of a free society, though it is really volume 1 which is the chief source for Hayek as philosopher of law. In particular, the *nomos/thesis* distinction represents an important contribution to how we ought to think about law.

We ordinarily tend to think of law as the commands issued by the sovereign, whether the "sovereign" in question is a monarch, or the whole of the people, or some representative assembly. It is Hayek's historical analysis of the English common law which in large measure informs his distinction between *nomos* and *thesis*. First, let's clarify what Hayek means by order. Then we can turn to his understanding of law as a spontaneous order, and see what the ramifications of that might be.

KOSMOS VERSUS TAXIS

Let us begin with the distinction between spontaneous order (*kosmos*) and planned order (*taxis*). Hayek defines "order" generally as "a state of affairs in which a multiplicity of elements of various kinds are so related to each other that we may learn from our acquaintance with some spatial or temporal part of the whole to form correct expectations concerning the rest, or at least expectations which have a good chance of proving correct" (RO, p. 36). Hayek makes the twin observations that every society needs to have order, and that such order will often exist without having been deliberately created. The first observation of that pair seems uncontroversial: social living depends on our having stable expectations regarding how to act and how to anticipate the actions of others. Hayek notes that part of the very function of social living is to enable us to meet each others' needs. We need other people partly because we cannot do everything by ourselves. We cannot live above a subsistence level without a division of labor. Plato makes this observation in the *Republic*, and of course economists since Smith and Ricardo had discussed the advantages of division of labor. But for society to realize a division of labor, we must be capable of cooperation, and this requires order as Hayek has defined it.

But more interesting is his follow-up observation that there are two possible sources of order: planned order and spontaneous order. Hayek notes that both biologists and economists have been concerned with the development of orders which are not the result of deliberate planning. Spontaneous orders may also be understood as "self-generating orders" or "grown orders" or "endogenous orders," but he thinks that the most felicitous ways of expressing the concept are via the English expression "spontaneous orders" or by invoking the classical Greek word *kosmos*. Similarly, a planned order may be understood as a "construction," or "artificial order" or "exogenous order," but is best described, according to Hayek, as a "planned order" or "made order," or by the Greek word *taxis*.

A paradigm case of planned order might be the order of a battle, as designed by a general. Any organization that is the result of deliberate design is *taxis*. But what Hayek finds exciting is the "discovery that there exist orderly structures which are the product of the action of many men but are not the result of human design" (RO, p. 37). He cites as a relatively uncontroversial example language. There was no historical moment in which some past genius invented language, yet languages do have an order. Of course, Hayek also sees markets as examples of spontaneous order, yet notes (with some dismay) that this is poorly understood:

[M]any people still treat with suspicion the claim that the patterns of interaction of many men can show an order that is of nobody's deliberate making; in the economic sphere, in particular, critics still pour uncomprehending ridicule on Adam Smith's expression of the "invisible hand" by which ... he described how man is led to promote an end which was no part of his intentions. (RO, p. 37)

Similarly, biologists characterize organisms as spontaneous orders (even if this idea is controversial in some segments of the larger culture). Hayek's larger point in noticing that some spontaneous orders are not well understood is that if we think that the social order, which really is necessary, can only arise as the result of the deliberate planning of some person or persons, then we invite authoritarianism. He sees our tendency to ascribe deliberate planning to *all* orders as a lapse of critical reasoning, one with pernicious consequences.

Clearly, one aspect of society that is necessary to facilitate cooperation, and social living generally, is the law. Laws help create stable expectations for the conduct of others, and can serve as guides to one's own conduct. What kind of order is law? Hayek argues that the *kosmos/taxis* distinction applies to the law as well. Some laws, to be sure, are the deliberate makings of a person or group of people, the product of human design. Hayek calls this "legislation," and distinguishes it from law. Legislation, Hayek says, is the deliberate making of law, but he argues that law is older than legislation, and that there is also a "grown" law which we need to consider.

What is law? One sense of "law" is "enforced rules of conduct," which, Hayek notes, "is undoubtedly coeval with society; only the observance of common rules makes the peaceful existence of individuals in society possible" (RO, p. 72). But whereas legislation is made law, "grown law" is law that is itself a spontaneous order. Law can be understood as a spontaneous order when it is the result of the evolved mechanisms for resolving disputes and enabling the peaceful coexistence of the members of a given community. Hayek argues not only that it is a pernicious threat to the freedom of a people to assume that law must be a *taxis*, but also that this assumption is factually mistaken. Many aspects of today's legal order are the result of deliberate planning, but many others are the result of no one's design. Custom and precedent may yield stable practices and rules, and would thus be *kosmos* – an order that is the result of human action, but not of human planning. Different societies develop differently, even within a single continent like Europe, but Hayek argues that all societies show some *kosmos*, even in their law.

THE COMMON LAW

The clearest example, according to Hayek, is the English common law. The common law is overtly an enshrining of evolved practices which enable peaceable dispute resolution, and not the product of legislation or deliberate planning. In what ways is the common law a *kosmos*? Rules of law arise through repeated human interaction. Patterns, and expectations of adherence to patterns, emerge. Juries are asked to apply the commonly accepted rules for settling disputes which, in principle anyway, embody the general consensus about what is fair as revealed in actual practice. Judges are expected to follow precedent when applying principles in their rulings. Hayek speaks of "judge-made law" as something different from legislation: his point is that judicial rulings only have the force of law because it is part of the common law tradition to respect them. Judges themselves, unlike executives, cannot enforce their rulings. While the explicit enforcing is performed by some delegated agent of the people (such as the police), in more general terms it is the tradition itself which is facilitating the enforcement. As Arthur Hogue points out, "The doctrine of *stare decisis*, or the practice of looking to precedents while formulating a legal procedure ... assumes that court decisions have been reasonable" (Hogue [1966] 1985, p. 9). (Where made law, legislation, is at odds with either common law traditions or community sensibility, executive enforcement can of course take the place of tradition.) The common law is both stable and vital; that is, it contains elements that carry on across time, enabling people to have reasonable expectations about the future, and also elements that enable the procedures and policies to adapt to changing times. Without being the product of any intentional design, it nevertheless comes into being ("spontaneously") and produces order.

John Hasnas has recently argued that Hayek confuses the concepts "common law" and "customary law," and that his failure to note the distinction between them weakens his normative case (Hasnas 2004). In particular, Hasnas says that Hayek confuses the judge-made "law" which results from the presumption of respect for judicial decisions (common law), with the true bottom-up evolved praxis by which communities arrive at dispute-resolving or rights-respecting mechanisms (customary law). This confusion is harmful, in Hasnas' view, because it makes it difficult for Hayek to make a coherent positive argument for the "law of liberty"; specifically, Hasnas says it's a mistake to think that "neutral, objective rules of just conduct" will spontaneously evolve through the common law process, since the judges may very well act in such a way as to enshrine their biases or class interests or the like, just as legislators do. Indeed, *stare decisis* is not historically a part of the customary law – Hasnas notes that *stare decisis* as a formal rule is less than 200 years old – but the general point Hayek is making about the emergence of patterns in legal decision making is nevertheless a sound one. Hasnas is, as far as I can tell, correct in making the distinction Hayek fails to make, and he may be correct also in concluding that this oversight on Hayek's part weakens the overall argument Hayek wants to develop in *Law, Legislation, and Liberty*. He is, in a sense, arguing for a more Hayekian position than Hayek himself did – a truer understanding of the evolutionary nature of bottom-up law. But the English common law is intended merely as an *example* of what Hayek means by grown law, so we can acknowledge Hasnas' scholarly criticism while still finding value in the particular distinction Hayek himself wanted to make.

LAW AND LIBERTY

The sort of law that evolves, a "grown" law which is a spontaneous order, is what Hayek calls *nomos*, or the law of liberty: that is, the sort of law which is most conducive to the values of a liberal society. *Nomos* allows for stability of expectations, yet is fluid, adaptable, and, almost tautologically, acceptable to the members of a society. But Hayek argues that it is a mistake to conflate *nomos* with what he calls *thesis*, the law of legislation. The latter is made by design. Note that Hayek is not merely critical of legislation with an ill-intentioned design. His point is that the very mechanism of top-down imposed law will have a tendency to be antithetical to liberty. The obvious dimension of this is overtly coercive tyranny. But even democratic *thesis* can be antithetical to liberty, just because it *is* top-down. According to Hayek, the law of legislation is necessarily less fluid and less vital, and since by definition it is not grown, it will be less compatible with liberal principles. Legislators necessarily lack all the information necessary to accomplish their ostensible goal. While the judge's function in a grown law setting is constrained by the evolved rules, the legislator not only *can* overreach, but is virtually sure to do so. Invoking an observation he had previously made in the economic context,[1] Hayek notes in this context that even well-intentioned legislators will fail to make good laws, as they lack the requisite knowledge of all relevant concrete circumstances. In other words, the knowledge-problem argument against central planning of a nation's economy is also Hayek's argument against the idea that law must come from legislation. *Thesis* may be right or wrong, but in either case it will surely be incomplete, due to the lack of knowledge – an inevitable hazard of what Hayek refers to as "naive" constructivism. *Nomos*, on the other hand, is more likely to be a discovery – "either in the sense that they [grown laws] merely articulate already observed practices or in the sense that they are found to be required complements of the already established rules if the order which rests on them is to operate smoothly and efficiently" (RO, p. 123). They will thus be, in some sense, part of the natural world, the *kosmos*, as opposed to the inventions of the mind of the legislator.

More significantly, though, the evolved law of *nomos*, the bottom-up law, is the law which actually allows people to coordinate their actions, to successfully engage in cooperative enterprises and form stable expectations of the behavior of others. This is what is truly needed by any society. Hayek regards this *nomos* as the law of liberty precisely because it is the kind of law that is most consistent with respect for liberty. It does not coerce, since it is an embodiment of established norms, and, perhaps more importantly, because it is not the product of human design. Hayek argues in *The Constitution of Liberty* that coercion occurs "when one man's actions are made to serve another man's will, not for his own but for the other's purpose ... Coercion implies both the threat of inflicting harm and the intention thereby to bring about certain conduct" (CL, p. 133). Why is this bad? The coerced person, Hayek says,

is not altogether deprived of the use of his capacities; but he is deprived of the possibility of using his knowledge for his own aims ... Most human aims can be achieved only by a chain of connected actions, decided upon as a coherent whole ... It is because, and insofar as, we can predict events, or at least know probabilities, that we can achieve anything ... [I]f the facts which determine our plans are under the sole control of another, our actions will be similarly controlled ... Though the coerced will still do the best he can for himself at any given moment, the only comprehensive design that his actions fit into is that of another mind. (CL, p. 134)

Thus Hayek is objecting not only to the morally problematic features of the control, but to its negative practical consequences as well.

Thesis, the top-down imposed law, is coercive in just this sense, even when well intentioned, but *nomos*, even when incomplete, is not coercive, as there is no coercer.

It is fair to note that Hayek's understanding of coercion is not without its critics, even among those generally sympathetic to his general project and values. Ronald Hamowy, for example, has argued that by defining "coercion" without reference to a theory of rights, Hayek is (inadvertently) saddled with a subjective theory on which virtually anything might be said to qualify – or not (Hamowy 1978). But even with a more rigorous definition of coercion, it would nevertheless be true that *thesis* is coercive in a more thoroughgoing way than *nomos*.

LAW AND LEGISLATION

The general superiority of grown law does not mean, however, that legislation can be done away with entirely. The grown law may occasionally require "correction" by legislation. Hayek says that one reason for this is that "the process of judicial development of law ... may prove too slow to bring about the desirable rapid adaptation of the law to wholly new circumstances" (RO, p. 88). A more important reason, he says, is that it is both "difficult" and "undesirable" for "judicial decisions to reverse a development, which has already taken place and then is seen to have undesirable consequences or to be downright wrong" (RO, p. 88). It is difficult, of course, because there would be no rule or precedent in place which would allow a judge to do this without its being transparently contrary to the common law tradition, and undesirable in the sense that it would violate the function of judges in a common law system for them to act in such a manner. But Hayek seems to have in mind here, as a sort of example in which there nevertheless would be a clear case for "correction," something perhaps like the recent *Kelo v. New London* decision,[2] in which precedent following by the judicial branch led to a clear erosion of property rights. In such a case, legislation could be an appropriate corrective measure. This presupposes, of course, that the legislative body shares Hayek's concern for the utility of property rights and would be interested in the codification of such values in the first place. But he thinks that a government with limited powers, in a society which does take liberty seriously, would be a reasonably reliable mechanism for these "corrections."

One critical question that arises is whether Hayek can make the distinction between good *thesis* and bad *thesis* in a principled way. The natural tension between his advocacy of both grown law and (some) made law requires some principle of resolution. The ostensibly corrective legislation comes from a ruling body which may well be more interested in enhancing its own power than in the liberty of the citizens. One way Hayek's theory might address this tension would be to emphasize the idea of constitutional limits on the scope of legislation. This seems to be the point underlying his analysis of the American constitution in *The Constitution of Liberty*: "The constitution [of the United States] was thus conceived as a protection of the people against all arbitrary action, on the part of the legislative as well as the other branches of government" (CL, p. 178). Hayek further notes that the constitution thus restricts both the methods and the aims of the legislature. On a strong reading of this theory of constitutionalism, the "corrective" legislation could, in principle, be limited to that conducive to individual liberty.

That there is a limited but valuable role for *thesis* is relevant to Hayek's distinction between what he calls "private law" and "public law." Immediately upon introducing these categories, he acknowledges that the labels are potentially misleading: he stipulates that the distinction does *not* entail that "private law serves only the welfare of particular individuals and only the public law the general welfare" (RO, p. 132). Rather, he intends "private law" to be understood as that part of the law concerned with rules of just conduct and "public law" as that part of law concerned with rules of organization. The spontaneous order that generates most social institutions will provide the bulk of these rules, but for preservation of the peace there may be a need for legislated institutions, and these will require legislated organization. Hence, "the public law as the law of the organization of government requires those to whom it applies to serve deliberately the public interest, while the private law allows individuals to pursue their respective individual ends and merely aims at so confining individual action that they will in the result serve the general interest" (RO, p. 133). Note the similarity between the latter idea and Smith's description of the invisible hand: by restricting individual conduct to non-coercive activities, mutual respect and cooperation are facilitated, even though no one intentionally directs the cooperation. Hayek notes that "it is an error to believe that only actions which deliberately aim at common purposes serve common needs" (RO, p. 132). What Hayek is here calling public law is well suited to *thesis*, whereas what he is calling private law will best be served by *nomos*, subject to the correction mechanism of occasional legislation. The public law, he says, might be better described as the regulations or bylaws of the government, so that it does not function in the same way as the laws which are intended to restrain individual conduct. However, it is easy to confuse the two, letting *thesis* substitute for *nomos* in a coercive way. Hayek argues that one consequence of this confusion has been the rise of legal positivism in jurisprudence, according to which all laws properly enacted by *thesis* are presumptively legitimate, regardless of their impact on liberty. Another consequence is the strengthening of "the socialist and totalitarian ideologies implicit in" positivism (RO, p. 134), because, again, *thesis* reflects primarily the interests of the sovereign or ruling class.

To forestall this confusion and the attendant pernicious consequences, Hayek recommends a constitutional regime in which "social legislation" is strictly limited. What he is especially concerned about is not legislation which serves some social purpose, such as providing for the police function, but rather legislation the aim of which is "to direct private activity towards particular ends and to the benefit of particular groups" (RO, p. 142), which would first of all substitute *thesis* for *nomos*, and would second of all be necessarily coercive. In such cases, he says, what we see is a "gradual transformation of the purpose-independent rules of just conduct (or the rules of private law) into purpose-dependent rules of organization (or rules of public law) ... [making it] necessary for governments to treat the citizen and his property as an object of administration" (RO, p. 142). This erosion results not only in an actual decline in liberty, but also in a decline in the society's understanding of liberty. If we are attentive to these distinctions, though, then in Hayek's view we can establish constitutionally limited *thesis* while letting *nomos* provide the means for peaceably coordinating our conduct. It is this understanding of the nature and structure of law which he thinks will best serve human freedom, and thus human needs, and prevent us from traveling down the "road to serfdom" he spent his career warning us against.[3]

NOTES

1. For example, in Hayek [1944] 1962 or Hayek [1945] 1948.
2. A controversial U.S. Supreme Court decision in which it was ruled that the Takings Clause of the Fifth Amendment to the U.S. Constitution permits the transfer of land from one private owner to another in the interests of fostering economic redevelopment.
3. I am grateful to Ed Feser for his helpful suggestions on this essay.

10 Hayek and liberalism

> In particular you should not assume that in times of crisis
> exceptions should be made to principles
> – F. A. Hayek, "The Rediscovery of Freedom"

F. A. Hayek occupies a peculiar place in the history of twentieth-century liberalism. His influence has, in many respects, been enormous. *The Road to Serfdom*, his first political work, not only attracted popular attention in the west but also circulated widely (in samizdat form) in the intellectual underground of Eastern Europe during the years between the end of the war and the revolutions of 1989. His critique of central planning has been thoroughly vindicated, if not by the demise of communist economic systems, then at least by the recognition by socialists of many stripes of the importance of market processes.[1] Books and articles on his thought continue to appear and there is plenty of evidence that his ideas are widely discussed in Europe, South America, and even in the United States. Hayek's political influence has been no less remarkable. He persuaded Antony Fisher to abandon his plans for a political career and to devote himself instead to establishing an organization for the dissemination of classical liberal ideas. The Institute of Economic Affairs founded by Fisher not only played an important role in changing the policymaking climate in Britain but also became the model for many classical liberal "think-tanks" around the world. But Hayek also influenced political leaders and activists more directly through his writings and public speeches,[2] and also through personal correspondence. By any reasonable standard, Hayek has been a significant public intellectual whose influence has roamed across the disciplines of social science into the realms of public policy.

Yet in spite of all this, Hayek is also a figure who has gone unrecognized by most contemporary political theorists as a contributor to liberal thought – or indeed to political thought – in the twentieth century. His work has not attracted commentary of the quality or quantity of that elicited by the work of John Rawls. One is unlikely to see university courses on Hayek's political thought and, as likely as not, his name will fail to appear in books and papers discussing issues in liberal political theory. In the academic mainstream of contemporary political theory, Hayek is a marginal figure. In Rawls' work, including *Political Liberalism* (Rawls 1993), Hayek does not rate a mention; nor are Hayek's ideas and concerns addressed in any of the major critiques of liberalism which have appeared over the last three decades.[3]

All this raises a number of questions about Hayek and modern liberalism. Why has Hayek not been taken more seriously by modern liberals or by their critics? Is Hayek in fact an important figure in twentieth-century liberalism and, if he is, what has been his contribution? What, in the end, is Hayek's liberal legacy? My purpose here is to show that Hayek has something important to contribute to liberal thought in the twentieth century. To do this I begin, in the first section, with a brief account of the fundamental tenets of Hayek's liberalism. I then turn, in the second section, to explain how Hayek came to this liberalism and how the genesis of Hayek's commitment to liberal ideals shaped the development of his political thinking. The third section examines modern liberal theory more broadly conceived and tries to explain what have been its primary concerns (and presuppositions), particularly since the work of John Rawls. This should afford us a firm base from which to look at why Hayek and contemporary liberal theory have failed to engage one another. From here I shall turn, in the fifth section, to broach more directly the question of what Hayek has to offer.

HAYEK'S LIBERALISM

Hayek's liberalism is best understood as a response to socialism. The distinctive feature of socialism, in his understanding, is its aspiration to organize society in accordance with some common purpose. What he finds implausible about the socialist ideal is the thought that attempts at such organization will achieve their purported goals.

What he finds objectionable about socialism is that it is incompatible with individual freedom as he understands it.

Implicit in all this are two assumptions, which Hayek has tried to bring out explicitly in his social and political philosophy. First, order is possible without design or central command. Hayek, more than any other thinker in this century (with the possible exception of Ludwig von Mises), attempted to show the feasibility of a social order understood as a means-connected system without a common hierarchy of ultimate ends.[4] Indeed, Hayek has gone further, arguing that demands for conscious control or direction of social processes can never be met and that attempts to gain control or to direct social development can only result in the loss of liberty and, ultimately, in the destruction of civilizations. In some respects, Hayek's theory here is not especially novel: he offers an account of invisible-hand processes which Mandeville, Hume, and Adam Smith had identified as crucial to the understanding of social order as the undesigned product of human interaction. Hayek's distinctive contribution is his account of social institutions and rules of conduct as bearers of *knowledge*. Society may profitably be viewed as a network of practices and traditions of behavior that convey information guiding individual conduct. These institutions not only facilitate the matching of means with established ends, but also stimulate the discovery of human ends. Hayek's argument is that it is vital that society not be brought under the governance of a single conception of the ends of life which is held to subsume all the various purposes human beings pursue, for this can only stifle the transmission and growth of knowledge.

The second assumption underlying Hayek's political philosophy is that individual freedom is not to be understood in terms of man's capacity to control his circumstances, nor in terms of collective self-government. Rather, freedom obtains when the individual enjoys a protected sphere or domain within which others may not interfere, and he may engage in his separate pursuits in accordance with his own purposes.

This liberalism stands in clear contrast to the socialism of Karl Marx. For Marx, human freedom would only be achieved when man gained control of those social forces which, as products of his own creation, had worked to dominate and control him. Alienation would be overcome, and freedom achieved, only when the autonomous life of social objects and forces was destroyed. This would be accomplished under socialism, when we would see the conscious, purposive ordering of production by the producers. As Marx put it in *Capital*, "the life process of society, which is based on the process of material production, does not strip off its mystical veil until it is treated as production by freely associated men, and is consciously regulated by them in accordance with a settled plan."[5] Hayek's liberalism suggests that this hope is delusory. Man will never acquire the capacity to control or redesign society because of the limited powers of human reason. The fact that no single mind can know more than a fraction of what is known to all individual minds sets limits to the extent to which conscious direction can improve upon the results of unconscious social processes. Liberalism as a social philosophy, in Hayek's conception, rests on this understanding of the "spontaneous" character of social processes. Any answer to the question of what are the best social and political arrangements for human beings must be based on this understanding. The answer that Hayek gives is that human relations should be governed by arrangements which preserve liberty, with liberty understood as "independence of the arbitrary will of another."[6] More precisely, Hayek argues that a liberal society is one governed by the rule of law, and that justice is served only if the law operates to delimit the scope of individual freedom. In short, liberalism upholds the idea of a free society in which individual conduct is regulated by rules of justice so that each may pursue his own ends or purposes in peace.

The ideal of equality has a place in this scheme of things only insofar as Hayek concedes that "The great aim of the struggle for liberty has been equality before the law."[7] Individual differences provide no reason for the government to treat them differently: "people should be treated alike in spite of the fact that they are different."[8] What has to be recognized, however, is that this cannot but lead to inequality in the actual positions people occupy. The equality before the law which freedom requires leads to material inequality. Hayek's argument is that "though where the state must use coercion for other reasons, it should treat all people alike, the desire of making people more alike in their condition cannot be accepted in a free society as a justification for further and discriminatory coercion."[9] His objection is not to equality as such, but to all attempts to impose upon society a chosen pattern of distribution.

The objection to institutions for the distribution of goods according to merit is of a similar nature. If the principle of reward according to merit were to be accepted as the just foundation for the distribution of incomes, for example, we would end up with attempts to control remuneration that would, in their turn, create the necessity for even more controls on human activity.[10] "This would produce a kind of society which in all essential respects would be the opposite of a free society – a society in which authority decided what the individual was to do and how he was to do it."[11]

The fear of this outcome is also the basis for rejecting demands for equal distribution based on the contention that membership in a particular community or nation entitles the individual to a particular material standard that is determined by the general wealth of the group to which he belongs. Membership of some national community does not, in Hayek's liberalism, confer rights or entitlements to any sort of share of national wealth. "The recognition of such claims on a national scale would in fact only create a kind of collective (but not less exclusive) property right in the resources of the nation that could not be justified on the same grounds as individual property."[12] Moreover, the result of such recognition would be that, "Rather than admit people to the advantages that living in their country offers, a nation will prefer to keep them out altogether."[13]

The liberal ideal, in Hayek's conception, has no room for such nationalist sentiments. On the contrary, it must resist them. Indeed, it is a characteristic of the liberalism Hayek upholds, and which he describes as "liberalism in the English sense," that it is "generally opposed to centralization, to nationalism and to socialism."[14]

There is, of course, more to Hayek's liberalism than this brief outline reveals. To understand the character of this liberal philosophy more fully, however, requires a deeper investigation not only of its tenets but also of its origins.

THE GENESIS OF HAYEK'S LIBERAL COMMITMENTS

A little has now been written about the intellectual origins of Hayek's ideas. Hayek himself has discussed his indebtedness to earlier economists of the Austrian School – including, most famously, Ludwig von Mises, Friedrich von Wieser, and Carl Menger.[15] And Jeremy Shearmur has investigated aspects of Hayek's intellectual background in a number of papers, as well as in his study of Hayek's thought.[16] We also have two popular biographies of Hayek by Alan Ebenstein, as well as Bruce Caldwell's magisterial study of the origins and development of Hayek's economic thinking.[17] Yet to understand Hayek's liberalism, it is important to understand not only its origins in the world of European ideas, but also its genesis in Hayek's life and, more particularly, in his practical concerns.

Hayek's first major political work, *The Road to Serfdom*, was not published until 1944. By this time Hayek, having turned forty-five, was an established scholar, a Fellow of the British Academy, and an economist whose reputation had rivaled that of Keynes. We need to ask what it was that prompted an economist whose original interests lay in trade-cycle research to turn his attention to political theory – and, indeed, to devote himself to political theory for the next forty-five years.

An important part of the answer to this question is that it was not his theoretical preoccupations that led him to his political writings but his practical ones. In the 1930s, observing the Nazis' seizure of power, Hayek clearly became increasingly concerned about political developments in Europe. In his own terms, he saw "civilization" coming under threat from two significant forces: nationalism and totalitarianism. The danger lay not merely in the victory of a particular political party but in the victory of ideas which had the capacity to undermine European civilization. By the time war erupted in September 1939, Hayek had some clearly formulated views about the nature of the problem, and about how it had to be confronted. Addressing the problem was something that dominated Hayek's intellectual and political energies for the next twenty years – up until the publication in 1960 of *The Constitution of Liberty*.

The problem, as Hayek perceived it, was how to combat the ideas that provided the basis for totalitarian institutions. The answer, he thought, would have to involve at once subjecting those ideas to sustained criticism, and developing and promoting the liberal alternative. It is very important to note here two things: first, Hayek did not see this as essentially or primarily a philosophical task, but rather as an intellectual task which required the contribution not only of philosophers but also of economists and other social scientists, as well as (perhaps most importantly) historians. Second, Hayek believed quite firmly that for this task to meet with success it was necessary that the battle of ideas be engaged not merely in academia but in the broader public realm.

These points come out very clearly in some correspondence between Hayek and the British Broadcasting Service less than a week after the declaration of war following the German invasion of Poland. On September 9, 1939 Hayek wrote to Mr. F. W. Ogilvie of the BBC offering to help with its propaganda broadcasts into Germany.[18] Enclosed was an additional memorandum (dated September 1939) entitled "Some Notes on Propaganda in Germany."[19] Hayek also wrote to the Director General of the Ministry of Information,[20] again enclosing his memorandum on propaganda in Germany, and to the Minister of Information, Lord Macmillan,[21] offering his services as a propagandist.

The advice Hayek offered in his "Notes on Propaganda" is instructive. The purpose of the propaganda, he thought, should be to defend and explain the principles of liberal democracy. To be effective it would have to show how the principles that Great Britain and France stood for were also those held dear by the great German poets and thinkers. He also stressed that accuracy was vital: the German people were largely ignorant of the more discreditable acts of the Nazi regime and needed to be made aware of the facts in a sober, dispassionate, and matter-of-fact way. That this process of "propaganda" seemed too academic, he thought, did not matter. The important thing to do was to tell the truth, to admit mistakes when they were made, and to be sober and accurate in a way that Nazi propaganda was not.[22]

Hayek's advocacy has two interesting features. First, it is persistent: indeed, he felt strongly enough about the problem to continue the correspondence into 1940 (at one point warning that he would continue to make a nuisance of himself until the BBC got it right!). Second, it betrays a very strong conviction that for propaganda to be effective it must be truthful and accurate. Thus in a letter to Ogilvie on September 22, 1939 he expressed distress at hearing the current anti-Nazi broadcasts, stressed again the need for propaganda telling Germans what had been happening in Germany since 1933, and recommended establishing a committee of British, German, and neutral scholars to do this.[23] When a Major Gifford wrote to Hayek saying that the value of the creation of a commission would not be in proportion to the size of the "machinery" needed to set it up, he responded that the only way to convince Germans was by presenting not just examples of Nazi crimes but details, names, and overwhelming evidence – enough to persuade them of the terrible nature of the regime.[24]

What is also revealing about this correspondence, however, is Hayek's practical interest in Germany and its fate. His concern was not simply how propaganda might best be employed to sap German morale and to weaken its capacity to sustain a war effort – though that may well have been important. The problem for him was how to strengthen the internal forces of German resistance to Nazism. As the war wore on, and it became clear (at least to Hayek) that Germany was going to be crushed, it became even more important in his mind that something be done to recover and restore German moral and intellectual life. However, Hayek's concern was not simply for Germany's own well-being. The fate of Germany was entangled with the fortunes of Europe, and Germany could not be lost if Europe was to survive the war. This concern was presented very clearly in a paper Hayek read to the Political Society at King's College, Cambridge University, on February 28, 1944. There he wrote:

Whether we shall be able to rebuild something like a common European civilization after this war will be decided mainly by what happens in the years immediately following it. It is possible that the events that will accompany the collapse of Germany will cause such destruction as to remove the whole of Central Europe for generations or perhaps permanently from the orbit of European civilization. It seems unlikely that, if this happens, the developments can be confined to Central Europe; and if the fate of Europe should be to relapse into barbarism, though ultimately a new civilization may emerge from it, it is not likely that this country would escape the consequences. The future of England is tied up with the future of Europe, and, whether we like it or not, the future of Europe will largely be decided by what will happen in Germany. Our efforts at least must be directed towards regaining Germany for those values on which European civilization was built and which alone can form the basis from which we can move towards the realization of the ideals which guide us.[25]

Hayek's concern at this point was that certain moral ideals were in danger of being lost, particularly in Germany, and that the effects of this loss would be to push people into nationalist camps that would provide harbor for totalitarian ideas. What was needed, he thought, was the reassertion and reestablishment of those moral ideas that were antithetical to totalitarianism.

But it would not be enough to pursue this task in a single country. In the case of Germany the problem was that Nazism had left behind a "moral and intellectual desert" in which the "many oases, some very fine, [were] almost completely isolated from each other."[26] The absence of any common tradition – beyond opposition to the Nazis and to communism – made it difficult for people of good will to accomplish very much: "nothing will probably be more conspicuous than the powerlessness of good intentions without the uniting element of those common moral and political traditions which we take for granted, but which in Germany a complete break of a dozen years has destroyed, with a thoroughness which few people in this country can imagine."[27] For this reason it was important that Germany be brought back into the fold of European civilization, so that it might draw upon the resources of that wider tradition. Isolation could have disastrous consequences. (After the First World War, Hayek suggests, "the expulsion of all Germans from several learned societies and their exclusion from certain international scientific congresses was among the strongest of the forces which drove many German scholars into the nationalist camp.")[28]

Having made these points in an academic paper, however, Hayek then took up the task of finding practical means of reintegrating Germany into European cultural life. His Cambridge paper was sent out to a number of academics and public figures,[29] seeking comments on his proposals for the reintegration of Germany. Moreover, he raised the idea of establishing an international society to the furtherance of this end.

The difficulty of persuading others to join in such an endeavor at the time should not be underestimated. Michael Polanyi, for example, wrote back expressing his unwillingness to meet other Germans – saying that he could forgive but not forget.[30] And Hayek was well aware of the suspicion with which Germany and Germans had come to be regarded – as he makes clear in a review published in March 1945, "Is There a German nation?" The review begins: "Difficult as it is for the ordinary man to believe that all he has heard of the Germans can be true, it becomes almost impossible for those who have direct acquaintance with a particular side of German life."[31] And once again Hayek argued that most Germans approved of little in Hitler's program but were taken in by appeals to nationalist sentiment, and that the problem this has created can be remedied only by a concerted effort on the part of Europeans to put "the common house in order."[32]

Whatever the difficulties, Hayek set about trying to organize an international society of liberal-minded intellectuals. He was able eventually to raise the money to fund a meeting of sympathetic scholars in April 1947 – a meeting that saw the founding of the Mont Pèlerin Society. But a great deal of Hayek's energies between the publication of *The Road to Serfdom* in 1944 and the formation of the Mont Pèlerin Society were spent working toward or arguing for the reintegration of German scholarship – and particularly historical scholarship – into the intellectual life of Europe.

Hayek's writings and activities in this period covering the rise and fall of Nazi Germany are important because they reveal how much his efforts as a political theorist emerge out of the worries and fears of an active public intellectual. Especially revealing is his "Memorandum on the Proposed Foundation of an International Academy for Political Philosophy tentatively called 'The Acton–Tocqueville Society.' " Dated 1945, it sets out Hayek's basic proposals to bring German scholars and German cultural life back into the fold, to fight "totalitarianism," and to preserve the liberal tradition. The tone of the memorandum is one of anxious urgency, as is made clear in the opening paragraph:

In large parts of the European Continent the former common civilization is in danger of immediate disintegration. In the rest of the Western World, where it still seems secure, many of the basic values on which it is founded are already threatened. Even among those who are aware of these dangers there exists an uncertainty of aim and a lack of assured basic convictions which makes their isolated endeavours to stem the tide largely ineffective. The most sinister sign is a widespread fatalism, a readiness to treat as inevitable tendencies that are merely the results of human decisions, and a belief that our wishes can have no power to avert the fate which an inexorable law of historical development has decreed for us. If we are not to drift into a state which nobody wants, there is clearly urgent need for a common effort at reconsideration of our moral and political values, a sorting out of those which must in all circumstances be preserved and never sacrificed or endangered for some other "advances," and a deliberate effort to make people aware of the values which they take for granted as the air they breathe and which may yet be endangered if no deliberate effort is made to preserve them.[33]

Throughout the memorandum Hayek expresses his concern that, even after victory in war, the situation is precarious because totalitarian ideas have gained a foothold and a mighty effort is still needed to combat their influence. This comes out even more clearly in a second memorandum, probably written in 1946, entitled "The Prospects of Freedom."[34] Here he quotes the words of "a great man whom we have recently lost," Lord Keynes, who had written of the power of ideas, observing that "the world is ruled by little else," and that "it is ideas and not vested interests, which are dangerous for good and evil."[35] Hayek was entirely in agreement with Keynes on this point, and this also helps account for his eagerness to get on with the task of developing alternatives to totalitarian ideas – particularly since there was always a lengthy "interval between the time when ideas are given currency and the time when they govern action."[36]

So it is out of his anxiety and fears about the future of Europe and modern civilization, and a conviction that that future depended upon the salvaging of a tradition of humane values whose vitality had been sapped by war and the influence of totalitarianism, that Hayek's liberal social and political philosophy emerges. And this, I think, accounts for a number of important and persistent features of his thought. First, it accounts for Hayek's repeated attempts to *restate* the principles of liberalism rather than to offer a new liberal theory. *The Constitution of Liberty* opens with the words: "If old truths are to retain their hold on men's minds, they must be restated in the language and concepts of successive generations." And *Law, Legislation, and Liberty* is, in a similar vein, subtitled *A New Statement of the Liberal Principles of Justice and Political Economy.* In these, and other, works Hayek sees himself not as setting out to devise a new theory of justice or social order *de novo*, but as seeking to keep alive and refine a tradition of ideas of whose importance as a bulwark against totalitarianism he was profoundly convinced. It is his concern with the moral and spiritual[37] threat of totalitarianism over and above any concern with abstract philosophical problems of liberal theory that also shapes his attempt to draw, through his restatements, as many sympathizers as possible into the liberal camp. Thus, in his first "Memorandum on the Proposed Foundation of an International Academy," he asserts that although "Without some ... common basis no fruitful discussion of the problems with which we are concerned is possible, ... within these limits there ought to be room for many shades of opinion from, to mention only two instances, some 'liberal socialists' at one end to some 'liberal catholics' on the other. The group should, in other words, combine all people who are united in the opposition to totalitarianism of any kind."[38] Hayek's ambition has not been to redefine the liberal tradition but to halt the drift of people away from it.[39]

Secondly, Hayek's anxieties about totalitarianism help to account for his interpretation of liberalism as an outlook at whose heart is a refusal to seek to control or shape human development. The idea of providing society with a "conscious" direction toward a particular aim is what, in Hayek's thinking, unites collectivist doctrines such as fascism and communism which, in seeking to organize society, refuse "to recognize autonomous spheres in which the ends of the individuals are supreme"; and these doctrines are "totalitarian."[40] Liberalism is, therefore, presented as a tradition that recognizes the significance of human ignorance, and appreciates that civilization is something which emerges without the help of a designing mind. Indeed, Hayek tries to argue, particularly in *The Constitution of Liberty*, that civilization's creative powers depend upon social processes not being brought within the control of human reason.[41]

Thirdly, Hayek's concerns about the influence of totalitarianism and the dangers facing European civilization account for the persistent internationalist – and anti-nationalist – character of his liberal thought. This is where Hayek's thought is, perhaps, most distinctive within – and out of step with – modern liberalism. Early on in his assessment of the problem of totalitarianism Hayek decided that the threat it posed could only be met by an international movement, and that a relapse into national isolationism would be fatal for free societies and give succor to collectivist forces. This is why he asked, as early as 1939:

But now when nationalism and socialism have combined – not only in name – into a powerful organization which threatens the liberal democracies, and when, even within these democracies, the socialists are becoming steadily more nationalist and the nationalists steadily more socialist, is it too much to hope for a rebirth of real liberalism, true to its ideal of freedom and internationalism...?[42]

But if these concerns are what have shaped Hayek's thinking, they are also what have kept him in important ways out of step with much of contemporary liberal thought. To understand why this has been so, however, requires a closer look at recent developments in liberal theory.

CONTEMPORARY LIBERAL THEORY

Liberal theory, over the past quarter-century, has been dominated by the work of John Rawls. For the most part, political theorists have approached liberalism by considering the problems, methods, and conclusions developed by Rawls in *A Theory of Justice*. The literature reveals two major concerns among political philosophers. The first is with the substantive question of the nature of the just regime, which leads these writers to ask what is the proper role of government, what rights individuals have, and how the benefits and burdens of social life should be distributed. The second concern has been with the procedural or methodological problem of *justifying* such arrangements. The two concerns are not always easily distinguished, however, since methodological strictures are often adopted because they lead to certain substantive conclusions – or, at least, rule out others.

The debates over these questions have focused for much of the time on the issue of "neutrality." Many have argued that neutrality is fundamental to liberalism. Two kinds of claims have been asserted. The first is that the liberal state must exemplify neutrality inasmuch as its laws must not prefer any particular conception of the good life as superior to others: the various conceptions of the good to be found in a pluralist society must be accorded equal respect. "Liberalism dictates official neutrality among the projects to which individuals might come to commit themselves."[43] The second claim is that the principles governing a liberal polity must be principles chosen under "neutral" conditions: they must be principles whose selection is not determined by any particular conception of the good life, even though the principles themselves will rule out some ways of life (indeed, they would be pointless if they did not). Rawls' original theory is most readily interpreted in this way.

Yet many liberals have rejected neutrality as unattractive or philosophically unpersuasive. William Galston, for example, has argued that a coherent defense of liberalism requires a stonger commitment to a particular, liberal, conception of the good life; and Stephen

Macedo has tried to show that a liberal regime presupposes the existence (and encourages the development) of distinctively liberal virtues.[44] For the most part, however, criticisms of neutrality have come from critics of liberalism, who see the idea of state neutrality as neither attainable nor desirable, and procedural neutrality as philosophically incoherent. These critics have challenged liberalism's fundamental assumptions, arguing that any plausible conception of a political order cannot aspire merely to neutrality among competing conceptions of the good life. A society, they insist, is more than an association of individuals bound together by contractual ties; it is a community that coheres because people share common practices and beliefs. At some deep level, they suggest, people must share an understanding of the character of the good life if they are to be able to associate in human communities. Politics is not simply about protecting or enforcing individual rights but about securing the common good. And they emphasize that we cannot justify political arrangements without referring to common purposes or ends.

This challenge from the so-called communitarian critics[45] of liberalism has had a substantial impact on contemporary liberal theory. It has persuaded some that, if liberalism is defensible, it can only be so for existing liberal societies, which should endorse the practices and values of their own traditions.[46] To a significant extent it has also persuaded Rawls to re-present his own theory of justice as a response to certain important features of the modern world – notably, its pluralism and its religious diversity. In *Political Liberalism* (Rawls 1993), the principles of justice as fairness are offered as the basis for securing an "overlapping consensus" which would make for the stability and social unity of a democratic regime.

In the discussions and debates over the basis and the content of liberal theory, it would be fair to say, the dominant issues have concerned the moral foundations of liberalism. Or, to put the matter less grandly, liberal theorists have focused on the moral justification for particular social entitlements and obligations of governments and individuals within a democratic state. In all of this, a number of presuppositions about the important concerns of theory ought to be recognized. First, it is assumed that pluralism is a significant – perhaps the most important – issue, since there are within a society different conceptions of the good associated with different ways of life or preferences. Second, it is assumed that the question of how to deal with pluralism is raised – and must be handled – within the context of existing states, which are treated, for the purpose of argument, as closed societies. Indeed, the question posed is often: what should the government do? Third, questions concerning the institutional arrangements appropriate for a liberal society are not generally approached. Rawls, for example explicitly set aside the question of what kind of economic system was appropriate if society were to be governed by his principles of justice. Issues of institutional design are typically left out of consideration: questions about the structure of authority and the mechanisms necessary for its operation and its delimitation (for example, federalism, the division of legislative and executive powers, independent associations within civil society) are not discussed by Rawls, nor, for that matter, by most prominent liberal writers.[47]

What all this amounts to is a liberal theory whose style and preoccupations are a good way from Hayek's method and indeed from his very concerns. First, for Hayek the main problem confronting the modern world was not diversity or pluralism but totalitarianism. Diversity, far from being a problem, was potentially a solution – provided the right institutions were in place. Secondly, Hayek refused to theorize on the basis of a working assumption that society was a closed system whose internal principles of justice might usefully be specified before theory was extended into the international realm. For Hayek, liberalism was not merely a universalist creed but an internationalist one which did not recognize the moral significance of national boundaries. Thus Hayek tries to develop an account of liberalism as the tradition of the Open Society. This is not to say that Hayek ignores the existence of national boundaries; it is rather that his theory recognizes national states not as presupposed by liberalism but as problems which liberal theory must deal with. Thirdly, then, Hayek places great importance on problems of social theory which liberalism must address if its general concerns are to be met.

Seen in this light, it is not surprising that Hayek and contemporary liberal theory have failed to engage or connect. This is a pity because Hayek has more to offer than modern liberals have generally recognized. We should turn then to look in more detail at what Hayek has to say to appreciate better his contribution to modern liberalism.

The motivation for Hayek's efforts to defend liberal principles, as we saw earlier, was a concern about the state of the postwar world. Hayek's fear was that the forces of nationalism and separatism could still triumph, and destroy modern civilization. The only way to combat these forces was with the ideas which were their antithesis: the universalist, egalitarian, and libertarian ideas of liberalism.

To espouse these ideas was to espouse the idea of an "abstract order." This point is especially important for Hayek, for he noted very early that if moral values were to be shared across a wide range of people, the scope for agreement on substantive questions would be reduced. This, he argued in *Law, Legislation, and Liberty*, was one of the reasons why liberal ideas were difficult to defend.

"The resistance against the new morals of the Open Society was strengthened also by the realization that it not only indefinitely enlarged the circle of other people in relation to whom one had to obey moral rules, but that this extension of the scope of the moral code necessarily brought with itself a reduction of its content."[48] The human craving would always be for a more personal, a more particularistic, morals. In Hayek's terms, there is a fundamental conflict between tribal morals and universal justice which has manifested itself throughout history "in a recurrent clash between the sense of loyalty and that of justice."[49]

Nonetheless, the nature of the extended society as an abstract order, Hayek thinks, has to be recognized. An abstract order is one governed by abstract rules of just conduct. Abstract rules of just conduct are so called because when they come into dispute the issue is settled by appealing to other rules that share some abstract features with the present issue. Disputes are thus settled without any appeal to, or agreement about, the importance of the particular aims pursued by the disputing parties.[50] The persistent application of abstract rules over time produces an abstract order which, as a whole, serves no particular end, but which nevertheless facilitates the peaceful pursuit of diverse ends. The nature of the extended society as an abstract order has to be explicitly recognized, however, because it must be understood that this order is *not* a community. The abstract order is Hayek's term to characterize what he otherwise calls the Open Society or the Great Society. And his writings in general counsel against attempting to turn this kind of society into a community in which substantive or concrete goals or purposes are held in common. This would be a danger to liberty; worse, "all attempts to model the Great Society on the image of the familiar small group, or to turn it into a community by directing the individuals towards common visible purposes, must produce a totalitarian society."[51]

There are two other related reasons why Hayek is so insistent in his work on the importance of not closing the borders of the Open Society to turn it into a community, and of not going down the path of nationalism. The first has to do with Hayek's views about the growth of knowledge. The expansion and development of human knowledge he thinks is generally stifled by attempts to control it or direct it. The growth of knowledge is greatest when spontaneous interaction among individuals and institutions to solve problems of adaptation leads to solutions which were unforeseen and unexpected.[52] The threat to this process comes from attempts to organize the social process; and the greatest attempt – and threat – comes from the state. "In the past, the spontaneous forces of growth, however much restricted, could usually still assert themselves against the organized coercion of the state."[53] But the fear Hayek expresses is that, with the development of the technological means of control available to government, the balance of power may change. "We are not far from the point where the deliberately organized forces of society may destroy those spontaneous forces which have made advance possible."[54] The restriction of human interaction within the confines of state borders in the name of community is thus something Hayek views with suspicion, if not alarm.

The second reason for Hayek's insistence on the importance of keeping open the Open Society and avoiding the nationalist road has to do with his sympathy with Lord Acton's views on nationalism and the state, and his hostility to John Stuart Mill's. In his *Considerations of Representative Government* Mill had argued that "It is in general a necessary condition of free institutions that the boundaries of government should coincide in the main with those of nationalities."[55] For Hayek, one of the problems with Mill was that he had accepted more of nationalist doctrines than was compatible with his liberal program. Acton, however, had seen more clearly that liberty required diversity rather than uniformity – or even consensus.

He had argued, rightly, that "the combination of different nations in one State is as necessary a condition of civilized life as the combination of men in society," and that "this diversity in the same State is a firm barrier against the intention of the Government beyond the political sphere which is common to all into the social department which escapes legislation and is ruled by spontaneous laws."[56] Diversity was the bulwark of resistance to social organization.

But the question is: how does one deal with the fact that the state exists, and exists in the context of other states? Boundaries have been, and will continue to be, drawn. What does liberalism have to say about this? In Hayek's view it has a good deal to say; and what it has to say is largely in defense of the idea of interstate federation.

"The idea of interstate federation as the consistent development of the liberal point of view should be able to provide a new *point d'appui* for all those liberals who have despaired of and deserted their creed during the periods of wandering."[57] So wrote Hayek in 1939, when he was convinced that the rebirth of "real liberalism, true to the ideal of freedom and internationalism" required the development of some form of federal union of states. Hayek had a number of theoretical arguments to advance in defense of this view; but his concerns were also very much practical, particularly during the years surrounding the war, and this is reflected in a number of writings of this period. It is worth looking at both dimensions to understand why Hayek saw liberal ideas as the great hope for European civilization, and why he saw federalism as an integral part of them.

The clearest application of federalist ideas to the solution of practical problems is to be seen in Hayek's assessment of what to do about the problem of Germany, whose return to the fold of European civilization, as we have already noted, he thought vitally important for everyone. In an essay entitled "A Plan for the Future of Germany" he suggested that there were three aspects to the long-term policy problem of guiding the Germans back: political, economic, and educational or psychological.[58] The political problem was largely one of directing German ambitions away from the ideal of a highly centralized German Reich unified for common action. But here there was a dilemma:

The direct method of breaking Germany into parts and prohibiting their reunion would almost certainly fail in the long run. It would be the surest way to reawaken the most violent nationalism and to make the creation of a reunified and centralized Germany the main ambition of all Germans. We should be able to prevent this for some time. But in the long run no measure will succeed which does not rest on the acquiescence of the Germans; and it surely must be our fundamental maxim that any successful settlement must have a chance of continuing when we are no longer ready to maintain it by the continuous exercise of force.[59]

In Hayek's view, there was only one solution to this dilemma. This would involve, in the first instance, placing Germany's common central government under Allied control, but making clear to the Germans that they could progressively escape this control by developing representative and democratic institutions on a smaller scale in the individual states of which the Reich was composed. Over time, however, all these states would, at varying rates, earn their emancipation from direct Allied control and the Allied control would become more and more like that of a "government of a federation or even of a confederation."[60] Moreover, Hayek thought, it would be preferable if, upon emancipation, the German states had the option of joining some other federation of European states that was ready to receive them. In the course of time, he suggested, they might become a part of a much more comprehensive European federation which included France and Italy.[61] The aim would be to so "entangle" the states with their non-German neighbors that they would become "far from anxious once again to merge their individuality in a highly centralized Reich."[62] A policy of crucial importance here is free trade. This is not for the economic benefits it would bring but because giving the power of foreign trade to the states would give them too much power over the economic system. And to retain a common tariff system for the whole of Germany's economic system would build up a highly centralized and self-sufficient system – which was precisely what had to be prevented.[63]

Whatever the merits or difficulties of Hayek's practical proposals, they do reveal some important general concerns, and a view about the desirable course of liberalism. His most general concern was undoubtedly the danger of the rebirth of a powerful totalitarian state. The solution was to decentralize power through the development of federal institutions. And he clearly thought that "an essentially liberal economic regime [was] a necessary condition for the success of any interstate federation."[64] But more importantly, he also thought, and argued explicitly, that the converse was no less true: "the abrogation of national sovereignties and the creation of an effective international order of law is a necessary complement and the logical consummation of the liberal program."[65]

These matters are addressed most directly by Hayek in his essay on "The Economic Conditions of Interstate Federalism." Here he makes plain that the "main purpose of interstate federation is to secure peace: to prevent war between the parts of the federation by eliminating causes of friction between them and by providing effective machinery for the settlement of any disputes which may arise between them and to prevent war between the federation and any independent states by making the former so strong as to eliminate any danger of attack from without."[66] To achieve this, federation had to involve not only political but also economic union. The most important reason for this was that economic seclusion or isolation of any state within a union would produce a solidarity of interests among the inhabitants of that state, and conflicts with the interests of other states.

Economic frontiers create communities of interest on a regional basis and of a most intimate character: they bring it about that all conflicts of interests tend to become conflicts between the same groups of people, instead of conflicts between groups of constantly varying composition, and that there will in consequence be perpetual conflicts between the inhabitants of a state as such instead of between the various individuals themselves arrayed, sometimes with one group of people against another, and at other times on another issue with the second group against the first.[67]

The removal of economic barriers would do a great deal to reduce the potential for conflict.

Political union and the abrogation of national sovereignty, on the other hand, would work to reduce the scope of intervention in economic activity. Planning or central direction of economic activity presupposes the existence of common values, "and the degree to which planning can be carried is limited to the extent to which agreement on such a common scale of values can be obtained or enforced."[68] Diversity within a federation, however, would militate against the sharing of common substantive values to any extent that would make extensive planning possible. And this would offer certain safeguards for individual freedom.

All this is possible, however, only if there is widespread agreement on some values. These are the values which lie at the core of liberal political philosophy, and which include the respect for the idea of individual freedom and an opposition to totalitarianism. Federation would not be possible without some minimal level of acceptance of these values. Indeed, it is questionable whether a voluntary federation of non-liberal states would be at all possible. For this reason it was important not only to work to secure the conditions which made consensus on substantive goals or ends on the national level less likely, but also to secure widespread acceptance of the fundamental principles of liberalism across all boundaries. This, of necessity, meant presenting liberalism as an ideal that was in no way confined in its outlook to the interests of nations or national groups. It would be best to present it as what it was: a doctrine of individual liberty.

While the plausibility and consistency of Hayek's arguments ought not to be taken for granted – and important criticisms have been made of a number of aspects of Hayek's liberalism – it is, nonetheless, worth noting why they should be taken seriously and why his work is deserving of closer study.[69]

Hayek's liberalism repays examination, first, because it mounts a comprehensive attempt to address a large range of complex and interrelated problems in moral, social, and political theory. More seriously than any other liberal thinker since Weber, he has grappled with the difficulties confronting liberalism as a philosophical doctrine in a world in which ethical demands have often come into conflict with economic and political reality. Hayek has certainly addressed the ethical problems of liberty and justice; but he has attempted to deal with them not as isolated philosophical problems but in relation to issues of social and economic organization, and problems of national and international political conflict. In this respect his work presents an important challenge to contemporary liberal theory, which has, for much of the past thirty years, been locked in abstract discussions of liberalism's moral foundations and has neglected to relate these questions to institutional issues.

Secondly, Hayek's views should be considered because, in addressing institutional questions, he has not made the mistake of confining the problems of liberalism within national boundaries. The question is not: what should a liberal democratic regime do? Nor is it: what should be the institutions of a liberal democratic society?

The question is: what are the appropriate institutions if the most important liberal values are to survive? Fundamental discussion of the nature, role, and authority of the state should be addressed from this standpoint. Hayek has accurately perceived that, in the modern world, moral, economic, and political systems do not – indeed, cannot – exist in isolation. His social philosophy thus attempts to address questions of moral, economic, and political theory in a way which takes this fact as an important given. In some ways it might be said that Hayek's work as a political thinker and activist has been intended to recover and strengthen the liberal tradition by building a coalition – or an overlapping consensus – of ideas which might nourish it. That consensus, however, was always, in his mind, an international consensus since the traditions of liberalism were themselves fundamentally not nationalist.

Finally, then, Hayek should be taken seriously because he has correctly identified as the most serious problems confronting civilization in the twentieth century the problems of nationalism and totalitarianism. Even with the dereliction of European communism at the end of the twentieth century, the problems which remain or are reemerging in the shape of ethnic conflict, separatist national movements, and regional trading blocs stem from practices and ideas which the liberal tradition has consistently criticized: ideas hostile to individualist, universalist, and egalitarian moral principles. While thinkers like Hannah Arendt have also recognized the threat and moral danger posed by totalitarianism, it is in Hayek's work that we have the most thorough attempt to understand the logic of its institutional alternative.

NOTES

1. See for example the work of David Miller (1989b) arguing for a form of "market socialism."
2. See for example Stockman 1986.
3. None of the so-called communitarian critics of liberalism have taken Hayek to be an important target. An interesting exception is Crowley (1987), although this work focuses on Hayek and Sidney and Beatrice Webb, and argues (mistakenly, in my view) that they share premises which compromise their different *liberal* theories.
4. I borrow this phrasing from Larmore 1987, p. 107.

5. Marx 1967, p. 80.

6. Hayek 1960, p. 12.

7. Hayek 1960, p. 85.

8. Hayek 1960, p. 86.

9. Hayek 1960, p. 87.

10. This is a point David Hume recognized in his *Enquiries Concerning the Principles of Morals*, where he writes: "The most rigorous inquisition too is requisite to watch every inequality on its first appearance; and the most severe jurisdiction, to punish and redress it ... so much authority must soon degenerate into tyranny, and be exerted with great partialities" (1976, p. 194).

11. Hayek 1960, p. 100.

12. Hayek 1960, p. 101.

13. Hayek 1960, p. 101.

14. Hayek [1946] 1948, p. 28.

15. See Hayek 1992, part I, especially Hayek's essays on "The Economics of the 1920s as Seen from Vienna" and "The Austrian School of Economics," and also the essays on Carl Menger, Friedrich von Wieser, Ludwig von Mises, and Ernst Mach.

16. See for example Shearmur 1986.

17. See Ebenstein 2001 and 2003; Caldwell 2004a.

18. Letter to Ogilvie is unpublished. It may be found in the Hoover Institution, Stanford University, Hayek Archive, box 61, folder 5.

19. Hoover Institution, Hayek Archive, box 61, folder 4.

20. Letter to Director General, Ministry of Information, September 9, 1939, Hoover Institution, Hayek Archive, box 61, folder 5. Interestingly, Hayek notes in this letter that the Austrian intelligentsia generally had, unfortunately, been deluded by "Hitlerism" and could be of little help.

21. Letter to Macmillan, September 12, 1939, Hoover Institution, Hayek Archive, box 61, folder 5.

22. "Some Notes on Propaganda in Germany," Hoover Institution, Hayek Archive, box 61, folder 4.

23. Letter to Ogilvie, September 22, 1939, Hoover Institution, Hayek Archive, box 61, folder 5. In another letter to Ogilvie sent on the same day Hayek complained that BBC broadcasts were too mild – but argued against violent and abusive broadcasts. Three weeks later, in a letter to Ogilvie dated October 15, he noted the improvement in BBC propaganda broadcasts, but argued that they could still be better. (For example, he argued against using one of the voices which Germans might think sounded Jewish.)

24. Letter to Major Gifford (Ministry of Information?), January 3, 1940, Hoover Institution, Hayek Archive, box 61, folder 5.

25. Hayek 1992, p. 201.
26. Hayek 1992, p. 202.
27. Hayek 1992, p. 202.
28. Hayek 1992, p. 207.
29. These included David Mathias, G. N. Clark, E. K. Bramstedt, Denis Brogan, F. M. Stenton, Ernest Barker, Charles Welsley, G. P. Gooch, E. L. Woodward, Michael Polanyi, G. M. Trevelyan, and Herbert Butterfield, all of whom replied with comments on Hayek's paper. Their letters may be found in the Hoover Institution, Hayek Archive, box 61, folder 7.
30. Letter from Polanyi to Hayek, July 11, 1944, Hoover Institution, Hayek Archive, box 61, folder 7.
31. In Hayek 1992, pp. 219–22, at p. 219. The review, first published in *Time and Tide*, March 24, 1945, was of Edmond Vermeil's *Germany's Three Reichs*.
32. Hayek 1992, pp. 221–22.
33. Unpublished memorandum dated August 1945, London School of Economics, pp. 1–13, at p. 1. The MSS is held at the Hoover Institution, Hayek Archive, box 61, folder 8. Marked "confidential," the memorandum was never published, although it was distributed among a number of people sympathetic to Hayek's efforts to form an international society.
34. In a letter to A. Hunold dated October 9, 1946, in which he was seeking help with funding for his proposed international society, Hayek enclosed copies of this and also his earlier memorandum for consideration. It may be found in the Hoover Institution, Hayek Archive, box 61, folder 9.
35. Quoted in Hayek's memorandum, "Prospects of Freedom," at p. 2.
36. "Prospects of Freedom," p. 3. Hayek continues: "It is usually a generation, or even more, and that is one reason why on the one hand our present thinking seems so powerless to influence events, and why on the other so much well meant effort at political education and propaganda is misspent, because it is almost invariably aimed at a short run effect."
37. It may seem like an exaggeration to suggest that Hayek saw totalitarianism as a spiritual threat. Yet this is precisely what he suggests in a two-page "Explanatory Memorandum" he wrote for an International Liberal Conference at Wadham College, Oxford, April 9–14, 1947. Noting the decline of liberalism, the progress of collectivist ideas, and the tendency "towards national isolationism and away from the broader conception of international cooperation," Hayek remarked that the causes of this were deep. They lie less in the actions of rulers than in "a mass retreat from the spirit and tradition of liberalism which has been the ruling force in European civilization since the Middle Ages. The conception of the free individual living in a free society, and of free

societies working together for their mutual good is being replaced by the doctrine of the compulsory subordination of the individual to the group, and the consequent disintegration of the world into antagonistic societies. Men and women are losing faith in the old doctrine of personal freedom coupled with personal responsibility, and are giving up their hard-won right of personal choice in favour of communal control ... The crisis in human relationships is, therefore, largely a spiritual one, and is less concerned with the activities of particular parties than with the basic outlook on life of the average citizen."

38. "Memorandum on the Proposed Foundation of an International Academy," pp. 7–8.
39. This was essentially Hayek's response to Pierre Goodrich's criticisms of a draft of *The Constitution of Liberty*. In a letter to Goodrich dated April 4, 1959 Hayek wrote: "I don't think it is considerations of political expediency or possibility or any temporizing which make me draw the line at a point which admittedly still leaves much that I dislike inside the range of the permissible. The fact is that in my present state of thinking I cannot yet state with any clarity a general criterion which would exclude all that I dislike. I believe much would be gained and further drift prevented if agreement among sensible people could be achieved on the criteria which I suggest, even if in the long run they should not be proven altogether sufficient."
40. Hayek [1944] 1962, p. 42.
41. See especially ch. 2, "The Creative Powers of a Free Civilization." Even in 1946, in "Prospects of Freedom," pp. 6–7, Hayek had lamented that "The current interpretation of recent history as much as the very language in which we now discuss public affairs are so much permeated with the conception that nothing can be satisfactory unless it is 'consciously controlled' by some super-mind, that even if we to-day defeated all the schemes for government control of economic life existing or proposed, we would to-morrow be faced by another crop, not less dangerous or harmful."
42. From Hayek [1939] 1948, pp. 270–1.
43. Lomasky 1987, p. 167.
44. See Galston 1992 and Macedo 1990.
45. The literature of communitarianism is voluminous. For a useful survey see Mulhall and Swift 1992.
46. See for example, John Gray, who has argued this in Gray 1989.
47. In Rawls 2001, Rawls does indicate that his theory is incompatible with certain kinds of institutional arrangements, including both free market capitalism and the welfare state; and that he is most sympathetic to the idea of a property-owning democracy.

48. Hayek 1976b, p. 146.
49. Hayek 1976b, p. 147. This idea is also a guiding theme of Hayek 1988.
50. Hayek 1976b, p. 15.
51. Hayek 1976b, p. 147.
52. This is the general line of argument of ch. 2 of *The Constitution of Liberty*, "The Creative Powers of a Free Civilization." It is arguably a general theme of the entire work; at one point Hayek contemplated using the title of ch. 2 as the title (and later as the subtitle) of the book.
53. Hayek 1960, p. 38.
54. Hayek 1960, p. 38.
55. Quoted in Hayek [1939] 1948, p. 270n.
56. Acton, in *The History of Freedom and Other Essays*, quoted in Hayek [1939] 1948, p. 270n.
57. Hayek [1939] 1948, p. 271.
58. First published, with the subtitle "Decentralization Offers Some Basis for Independence," in the *Saturday Review of Literature*, June 23, 1945, pp. 7–9, 39–40; this reference to the reprinted essay in Hayek 1992, pp. 223–36, at p. 223.
59. Hayek 1992, p. 225.
60. Hayek 1992, pp. 225–26.
61. Hayek 1992, p. 226.
62. Hayek 1992, p. 226.
63. Hayek 1992, p. 227. Compare Oakeshott's observation: "But of all the acquisitions of governmental power inherent in collectivism, that which comes from its monopoly of foreign trade is, perhaps, the most dangerous to liberty; for freedom of external trade is one of the most effective safeguards a community may have against excessive power. And just as the abolition of competition at home draws the government into (and thus magnifies) every conflict, so collectivist trading abroad involves the government in competitive commercial transactions and increases the occasions and the severity of international disharmony." See Oakeshott 1991, p. 400.
64. Hayek [1939] 1948, p. 269.
65. Hayek [1939] 1948, p. 269.
66. Hayek [1939] 1948, p. 255.
67. Hayek [1939] 1948, p. 257.
68. Hayek [1939] 1948, p. 264.
69. I have offered a detailed critique of Hayek's political theory in Kukathas 1989; for a different, though no less critical, analysis, see Kley 1994.

11 Hayek and conservatism

In the well-known postscript to *The Constitution of Liberty*, entitled "Why I Am Not a Conservative," Hayek states what he calls "the decisive objection to any conservatism which deserves to be called such," which is "that by its very nature it cannot offer an alternative to the direction in which we are moving ... The tug of war between conservatives and progressives can only affect the speed, not the direction, of contemporary developments." He adds that while the conservative "generally holds merely a mild and moderate version of the prejudices of his time, the liberal today must more positively oppose some of the basic conceptions which most conservatives share with the socialists."[1]

At the time when those words were published – 1960 – they expressed an understandable distrust of European conservative parties, which seemed unable to offer an alternative vision to the collectivism that had prevailed in Europe since the Second World War. Hayek dedicated his book to "the unknown civilisation that is growing in America," and he showed his impatience with the old elites of Europe, whose principal concern, in Hayek's eyes, was to rescue from the jaws of the socialist machine as many of their privileges as they could, but who had no adequate rival notion as to how we should be governed. It is true that *The Road to Serfdom*, published toward the end of the war as a warning against the collectivism that had caused it, had been excitedly endorsed by conservatives and proposed as their bible by Winston Churchill. But Hayek did not believe that it had really changed the conservative agenda, and was acutely aware, in any case, of the damage that it had done to his own career in England, where the left establishment united to oppose this continental outsider who knew nothing of the road to Wigan pier.

Since that time, however, it has become increasingly apparent that it is people called conservative who have endorsed the arguments of the *Constitution of Liberty*, while those who campaign under the "liberal" banner are usually the first to espouse the egalitarian values and statist politics that Hayek was attacking. Although it is true that labels are less significant than the things they stand for, it is nevertheless important to recognize that Hayek's core arguments and ideas belong to the conservative tradition, and that his defence of freedom begins from premises, and arrives at conclusions, which align him with Burke against Paine, de Maistre against Saint-Simon, and Hegel against Marx. In this chapter, therefore, I will defend the view of Hayek as a major theorist of conservatism, while suggesting ways in which his philosophy is also open to criticism from the conservative standpoint.

SPONTANEOUS ORDER AND EVOLUTIONARY RATIONALITY

For Hayek, liberty is not the antithesis of order but a specific form of it. He contrasts two kinds of order: the planned order – *taxis* – which is dictated from above, usually by a government, and the "spontaneous order" – *kosmos* – which arises from below, by the free interactions of sovereign individuals. The inspiration for this contrast is Adam Smith's conception of the "invisible hand" – the process that generates, from our myriad intentional actions, a distribution of wealth, power, and accountability that is no part of anyone's intention. It is Hayek's firm belief that – while there are malign spontaneous orders, such as the networks of corruption that arise under state bureaucracies – spontaneous orders survive if and because they are beneficial. They may require correction at the margins; but they are also self-correcting, since they adapt to changing circumstances in ways in which no planned order is capable of doing. He even compares his account of spontaneous order to the Darwinian theory of evolution, making the interesting suggestion that the inevitable collapse of the planned economy will come about, like the extinction of a species, from the failure to adapt. Spontaneous orders, he argues, do not derive from a rational plan; but they are rational in spite of this, and also because of it. They exhibit "evolutionary rationality" – which consists not in a plan but a process, whereby individual plans adapt to the plans of others.

Hayek's principal opponents try to undermine this defense of spontaneity by developing theories of "market failure," many of which have their origins in the Marxist critique of "the crisis of capitalism." It is therefore often alleged that Hayek is proposing the market as the root of social order, and so exposing himself to the obvious criticism that long-standing institutions and moral ties are vulnerable to "market erosion" as cheaper, less demanding, or more exciting alternatives appear to replace them. However, the market exists side by side and in competition with other spontaneous orders in which value is not reducible to price. Thus, in volume 1 of *Law, Legislation and Liberty*, Hayek defends the common law against legislation, the first being a form of spontaneous order, the second an attempt to organize society according to an overarching plan. He defends ordinary morality against the "social justice" of the socialists, and recognizes the constraints that ordinary morality places upon the market. His attack on egalitarianism is not based on any defense of the market economy but on the belief that inequality is the spontaneous outgrowth of peaceful exchange in every area of human intercourse, and that the attempt to suppress inequality is both bound to fail and also bound to threaten the collective accumulation of socially useful knowledge. And although he sometimes identifies himself as a "progressive," Hayek recognizes tradition as another form of spontaneous order, and a repository of knowledge that cannot be contained in a single head.[2]

THE FREE MARKET

The Austrian defense of the market reached its culmination in the "calculation debate," initiated by Mises and Hayek in response to socialist proposals for a centrally planned economy. The Austrian response to these proposals turns on three crucial ideas. First, economic activity depends upon knowledge of other people's wants, needs, and resources. Secondly, this knowledge is dispersed throughout society and is not the property of any individual. Thirdly, in the free exchange of goods and services, the price mechanism provides access to this knowledge – not as a theoretical statement, but as a signal to action. Prices in a free economy offer the solution to countless simultaneous equations mapping individual demand against available supply. When prices are fixed by a central authority, however, they no longer provide an index either of the scarcity of a resource or of the extent of others' demand for it. The crucial piece of economic knowledge, which exists in the free economy as a social fact, has been destroyed. Hence when prices are fixed the economy either breaks down, with queues, gluts, and shortages replacing the spontaneous order of distribution, or is replaced by a black economy in which things exchange at their real price – the price that people are prepared to pay for them.[3] This result has been abundantly confirmed by the experience of socialist economies; however, the argument given in support of it is not empirical but a priori. It is based on broad philosophical conceptions concerning socially generated and socially dispersed information.

The important point in the argument is that the price of a commodity conveys reliable economic information only if the economy is free. It is only in conditions of free exchange that the budgets of individual consumers feed into the epistemic process, as one might call it, which distils in the form of price the collective solution to their shared economic problem – the problem of knowing what to produce, and what to exchange for it. All attempts to interfere with this process, by controlling either the supply or the price of a product, will lead to a loss of economic knowledge. For that knowledge is not contained in a plan, but only in the economic activity of free agents, as they produce, market, and exchange their goods according to the laws of supply and demand. The planned economy, which offers a rational distribution in place of the "random" distribution of the market, destroys the information on which the proper functioning of an economy depends. It therefore undermines its own knowledge base. It is a supreme example of a project that is supposedly rational while being not rational at all, since it depends on knowledge that is available only in conditions that it destroys.

One corollary of this argument is that economic knowledge, of the kind contained in prices, lives in the system, is generated by the free activity of countless rational choosers, and cannot be translated into a set of propositions or fed as premises into some problem-solving device. As the Austrians were possibly the first to realize, economic activity displays the peculiar logic of collective action, when the response of one person changes the information base of another. Out of this recognition grew the science of game theory, developed by von Neumann and Morgenstern as a first step toward an

explanation of markets, but pursued today as a branch of mathematics with applications (and misapplications) in every area of social
and political life.[4]

Hayek's epistemic theory of the market does not claim that the
market is the only form of spontaneous order, nor that a free market
is *sufficient* to produce either economic coordination or social stability. The theory asserts only that the price mechanism generates and
contains knowledge that is *necessary* to economic coordination.
Coordination can be defeated by business cycles, market failures,
and externalities, and is in any case dependent on other forms of
spontaneous order for its long-term survival. John O'Neill, defending
a mitigated socialism against Hayek's advocacy of the free economy,
argues that the price mechanism does not communicate all the
information necessary to economic coordination, and that in any
case information is not enough.[5] There are good conservative
reasons for agreeing with O'Neill's claims; but they are reasons
that Hayek accepts. The market is held in place by other forms of
spontaneous order, not all of which are to be understood simply as
epistemic devices, but some of which – moral and legal traditions, for
example – create the kind of solidarity that markets, left to themselves, will erode.

COMMON LAW JUSTICE

This conservative aspect of Hayek's argument is best understood
through the argument for common law justice that dominates volume 1 of *Law, Legislation, and Liberty*. "To modern man," Hayek
argues, "the belief that all law governing human action is the product
of legislation appears so obvious that the contention that law is older
than law-making has almost the character of a paradox. Yet there can
be no doubt that law existed for ages before it occurred to man that he
could make or alter it."[6] People cannot form a society and then give
themselves laws, as Rousseau had imagined. For the existence of law
is presupposed in the very project of living in society – or at least, in a
society of strangers. Law is real, though tacit, long before it is written
down, and it is for the judge to discover the law by examining social
conflicts and laying bare the shared assumptions that permit their
resolution. Law in its natural condition is therefore to be construed
on the model of the common law of England, which preceded the

legislative powers of Parliament, and which for many centuries looked upon Parliament not as a legislative body but as another court of law, whose function was to resolve the questions that could not be answered from a study of existing precedents.

Hayek says many true and interesting things about common law justice, pointing out that written law and sovereign legislation are latecomers to human society, and that both open the way to abuses which, in the common law, are usually self-correcting.[7] The distinction between law and legislation has been tacitly recognized in many European languages – *diritto* versus *legge*, *droit* versus *loi*, *Recht* versus *Gesetz*, *právo* versus *zákon*, and so on. Interestingly enough, however, it has no such clear marker in English, even though English law is nearly unique in preserving common law procedure. The legislator sees law as a human artifact, created for a purpose, and may endeavor to use law not merely to rectify injustices but also to bring about a new social order, in conformity with some ideal or plan. There is nothing to prevent such a legislator from passing laws that fly in the face of justice, by granting privileges, confiscating assets, and extinguishing deserts in the interests of some personal or political agenda. One sign of this is the adoption of "social justice" in the place of plain justice, as the goal of law. For Hayek, justice is an attribute of human conduct, and the attempt – inherent in the concept of "social" justice – to apply the concept to a state of affairs, without any reference to the human actions that produced it, does violence to our understanding of responsibility and choice. The goal of the common law is not social engineering but justice in the proper sense of the term, namely the punishment or rectification of unjust actions. The judge, examining the specific case, attempts to find the rule that will settle it. According to Hayek, such a rule is part of a network of abstract rules, all of which are implicitly counted upon by those who engage in free transactions. The judge rightly thinks of himself as discovering the law, for the reason that there would be no case to judge had the existence of the relevant law not been implicitly assumed by the parties.

Hayek's theory of law, which is laid out with considerable erudition, has several distinct parts. For example, there is the notion of law as implicit in human intercourse, and discovered in the act of judgment. There is the idea of law as abstract rule. There is the theory that the abstract rules discovered by the methods of common law judgment are the true rules of justice. And there is the criticism of modern styles of legislation, which see law as a policy-enforcing rather than justice-endorsing device. Clearly these ideas are independent of one another, though they all connect to an underlying conception of law as an essentially negative institution, concerned to prevent and rectify wrongdoing rather than to build some new form of social order.[8]

In the English system it is certainly true that the law is discovered, rather than invented, by the judge.[9] It is true too that the law is formulated as a rule – the rule in *Rylands v. Fletcher*, for example, which tells us that "the person who for his own purposes brings on his lands and collects and keeps there anything likely to do mischief if it escapes, must keep it in at his peril, and, if he does not do so, is prima facie answerable for all the damage which is the natural consequence of its escape." But it is also true that a judge may find for one of the parties, without formulating explicitly the rule that justifies his judgment: it may be a matter of controversy what the *ratio decidendi* is, of a case that all agree to have been rightly decided. To point to this interesting fact is not to criticize Hayek's theory, but on the contrary to provide further support for the idea that the law exists prior to its judicial determination, and that the belief that this is so both guides the judge and limits his ambitions. You cannot use the common law procedures to change the nature of society, to redistribute property that is justly held, to violate ordinary understandings, or to upset longstanding expectations and natural relations of trust. For the common law is the working out of the rules already implicit in those things. It is a network woven by an invisible hand.

ABSTRACT AND INSTRUMENTAL RULES

Abstract rules, as Hayek calls them, govern conduct without specifying some independent end to be achieved by it. In a way it is unfortunate that Hayek chooses the term "abstract" in this context, since it creates the erroneous impression that the common law is a system of deductively related norms, which can be expressed in terms that make no reference to the history and affections of a given human community. Against that a conservative (at least a conservative of my persuasion) would urge that the common law is, in contrast to the civilian system, essentially *concrete*. Its ultimate authorities are embedded in the history and experience of a human community, and although it aims to universalize its judgments, and so to achieve the abstract *form* of law, it is inseparable from a given *content*, which derives from conflicts within a shared historical experience. The distinction here is, to be sure, a distinction of emphasis, but it connects with a broader and deeper objection to Hayek's method to which I return below.

The important contrast for Hayek is not that between the abstract and the concrete, but that between the abstract and the instrumental. And his target here is both legal positivism, in the forms defended by Bentham, Austin, and Kelsen, and the legislative systems that have derived from it.[10] For the positivists, law is not discovered but made, and made for a purpose: hence they dismiss the common law as "judge-made" law, implying that its force and validity are not implicit in its origins but dependent on the legislative decision to enforce it. However, when the English Parliament first began to turn itself into a legislative institution it regarded law as an independent and preexisting system, to which it was adding new rules by the same process of discovery and adjustment that was exemplified by the courts. The aim was to provide remedies to the victims of injustice, and to emphasize the will of the sovereign to enforce and uphold the law. Law was an independent domain, which appointed the sovereign and stood over him in judgment. Legislation was regarded as law only if it derived from and harmonized with the thing rightly so called, which was the body of precedents discovered in the courts. Such was explicitly said by Lord Chief Justice Coke, and reaffirmed by Blackstone in his commentaries. And such was assumed by the English Court of Chancery, through which appeals were made to the sovereign when the existing legal record seemed to provide no remedy. Indeed, the existence of equity, and its ability even today to qualify and marginalize the decisions of Parliament, testifies to the deep commitment of English jurisdiction to the Hayekian view of law as a system of negative side constraints.

The legal positivists reversed the old order of things. For them a rule becomes law only if it is announced or confirmed as such by the legislature. For Hayek, this theory is both mistaken and pernicious. It confuses the abstract rules of a legal system with the instrumental rules of a social engineer. It divorces law from the underlying conception – that of justice and the rectification of injustice – on which it depends for its authority and its sense. And it places in the hands of the legislature an indefinite authorization to issue commands in every sphere of social life, and to compel general obedience to them. Hitherto the judge had been guardian of the law, and the law had been the shield that protected the subject from the arbitrary misuse of power by compelling the sovereign to provide remedies for injustice. The appropriation of law by the legislature was at the same time an expropriation of the judicial power. And that is what the positivists set out to justify. Hence "the evil of positivism is that it made the guardians of the law unable to resist the advance of arbitrary government."[11] Hayek saw the rise of positivism as the triumph of an anti-liberal view of sovereignty – the view that he associated with Hobbes, according to which sovereignty is exercised by a body that stands above the law, instead of being an attribute vested in the law itself, arising by an "invisible hand" from the free transactions of individuals.

Hayek's attack on positivism and the legislative order should not be understood merely as a further argument against the socialist state. Although Hayek was deeply opposed to the idea of using the law to enforce socialist redistribution, this was in part because he was opposed to using the law to enforce *any* kind of social order, other than the one already implicit in the law's discoverable rules. The law could be so used, of course, but only by ceasing to be an exercise of justice and so ceasing to be law *proprement dite*. Moreover, the instrumental use of law occurs in an epistemological vacuum – a vacuum created by itself. By destroying the base of the law in abstract rules of justice, instrumentalism renders the use of the law profoundly unpredictable. Whatever the goal, be it social equality, economic progress, the destruction of religion, or the elimination of some "enemy within," this goal will be fulfilled only by accident, and as an unforeseeable consequence of actions that destroy the ability either to predict or rationally to intend it. Sometimes, it is true, Hayek writes as though law has a purpose, and he quotes with approval Hume's view that, while individual laws and judgments cannot be evaluated in terms of their consequences, the law as a whole serves a beneficial function.[12] But this thought should be understood as an anthropologist might understand it. Law has a social function; but it is not by appeal to this function that laws or the judgments that flow from them are justified. For the function can be fulfilled only by those who treat laws as *intrinsically* valid, and open to neither correction nor justification from the consequentialist standpoint.

LAW AND PRACTICAL KNOWLEDGE

Hayek's argument picks up thoughts that form the core vision of a certain kind of very English conservatism. As Hayek frequently observes in the footnotes to *Law, Legislation, and Liberty*, German jurisprudence in the nineteenth and twentieth centuries had not always made room for that English vision. One result of this could be seen in Carl Schmitt's frightening theory of sovereignty (he is sovereign who "decides on the exception," i.e. who takes power in emergencies, in particular those emergencies created by himself).[13] It can also be found in the view of German jurists in the thirties, such as G. Radbruch, that the sovereign power can make any law it pleases, so long as it is consistent in enforcing it. This positivist view was endorsed by British socialists, in terms borrowed from well-meaning and not-so-well-meaning German jurists. Thus Harold Laski, subsequently to become Hayek's arch-enemy at the London School of Economics, could write in 1934 that "the Hitlerite State, equally with that of Britain and France, is a *Rechtsstaat* in the sense that dictatorial power has been transferred to the Führer by legal order."[14] Of course, not all Germans at every epoch have endorsed the positivist theory – Hayek explicitly exempts Kant from the charge, and to that illustrious example we should add Hegel, Schopenhauer, and Gierke, the third of whom goes unmentioned by Hayek, perhaps because his *Deutsches Genossenschaftsrecht* takes too firm a step in the conservative direction that I too shall take at the end of this chapter.[15]

The extended argument about law and rules is by no means secure from criticism. Nor, as the work of Ronald Dworkin shows, does the theory of judicial discovery necessarily lead in a conservative direction, or necessarily create a divide between the pursuit of common law justice and the pursuit of public policy.[16] But Hayek's argument is a tour de force of erudition and imagination, and entirely rescues him from the charge that he was merely an economic liberal, concerned to replace all forms of order with that of the free market. It adds concretion and depth to Oakeshott's celebrated distinction between civil and enterprise association,[17] and shows the intrinsic connection between civil association and the rule of law. Furthermore, it has an interesting and highly conservative corollary, which is only occasionally given by Hayek with the clarity that it deserves. Abstract rules, as Hayek calls them, are not part of a plan of action, but arise from the enterprise of social cooperation over time. They are the parameters within which the cooperation of strangers to their mutual advantage becomes possible. As with the market, the benefit that they confer is in part epistemic: they provide knowledge that has stood the test of time, by permitting the resolution of conflicts and the reestablishment of social equilibrium in the face of local disturbances. By following these rules we equip ourselves with practical knowledge that will be especially useful when venturing forth into the unforeseeable – namely, knowledge how to conduct ourselves toward others, so as to secure their cooperation in advancing our aims.

To put the point in another way, the law condenses into itself the fruits of a long history of human experience: it provides knowledge that can be neither contained in a formula nor confined to a single human head, but which is dispersed across time, in the historical experience of an evolving community. Just as prices in a market condense into themselves information that is otherwise dispersed throughout contemporary society, so do laws condense information that is dispersed over a society's past.[18] From this thought it is a small step to reconstructing Burke's celebrated defence of custom, tradition, and "prejudice" against the "rationalism" of the French revolutionaries. To put Burke's point in a modern idiom somewhat removed from his own majestic periods: the knowledge that we need in the unforeseeable circumstances of human life is neither derived from nor contained in the experience of a single person, nor can it be deduced a priori from universal laws. This knowledge is bequeathed to us by customs, institutions, and habits of thought that have shaped themselves over generations, through the trials and errors of people many of whom have perished in the course of acquiring it.

TRADITION, MORALITY, AND THE MARKET

For a contemporary conservative, the most profound aspect of Hayek's extended epistemological argument is the alignment between the defense of the market and the defense of tradition. Indeed, as Edward Feser has argued, the defence of tradition, custom, and commonsense morality could well constitute the most important aspect of Hayek's social and political thought.[19] Hayek's theory of evolutionary rationality shows how traditions and customs (those surrounding sexual relations, for example) might be reasonable solutions to complex social problems, even when, and especially when, no clear rational grounds can be provided to the individual for obeying them. These customs have been selected by the "invisible hand" of social reproduction, and societies that reject them will soon enter the condition of "maladaptation," which is the normal prelude to extinction.

Implicit in Hayek is the thought that free exchange and enduring customs are to be justified in exactly the same terms. Both are indispensable distillations of socially necessary knowledge, the one operating synchronously, the other diachronically, in order to bring the experiences of indefinitely many others to bear on the decision taken by me, here, now. Hayek emphasizes the free market as part of a wider spontaneous order founded in the free exchange of goods, ideas, and interests – the "game of catallaxy" as he calls it.[20] But this game is played over time, and – to adapt a thought of Burke's – the dead and the unborn are also players, who make their presence known through traditions, institutions, and laws. Those who believe that social order demands constraints on the market are right. But in a true spontaneous order the constraints are already there, in the form of customs, laws, and morals. If those good things decay, then there is no way, according to Hayek, that legislation can replace them. For they arise spontaneously or not at all, and the imposition of legislative edicts for the "good society" destroys what remains of the accumulated wisdom that makes such a society possible. It is not surprising, therefore, if British conservative thinkers – notably Hume, Smith, Burke, and Oakeshott – have tended to see no tension between a defense of the free market and a traditionalist vision of social order. For they have put their faith in the spontaneous limits placed on the market by the moral consensus of the community. Maybe that consensus is now breaking down. But the breakdown is in part the result of state interference, and certainly unlikely to be cured by it.

It is at this point, however, that conservatives may wish to enter a note of caution. Although Hayek may be right in believing that the free market and traditional morality are both forms of spontaneous order and both to be justified epistemically, it does not follow that the two will not conflict. Socialists are not alone in pointing to the corrosive effects of markets on the forms of human settlement, or in emphasizing the contrast between things with a value and things with a price. Indeed, many of the traditions to which conservatives are most attached can be understood (from the point of view of Hayek's evolutionary rationality) as devices for rescuing human life from the market. Traditional sexual morality, for example, which insists on the sanctity of the human person, the sacramental charac- ter of marriage, and the sinfulness of sex outside the vow of love, is – seen from the Hayekian perspective – a way of taking sex off the market, of refusing it the status of a commodity and ring-fencing it against the corrosive world of contract and exchange. This practice has an evident social function; but it is a function that can be ful- filled only if people see sex as a realm of intrinsic values and sexual prohibitions as absolute commands. In all societies religion, which emerges spontaneously, is connected to such ideas of intrinsic value and absolute command. To put the matter succinctly, that is sacred which does not have a price.

It follows that the "game of catallaxy" does not provide a complete account of politics, nor does it resolve the question of how and to what extent the state might choose to interfere in the market in order to give the advantage to some other and potentially conflicting form of spontaneous order. This question defines the point where conser- vatism and socialism meet and also the nature of the conflict between them.

SOCIALISM AND SOCIAL JUSTICE

Hayek's routine dismissal of "social justice" has both an economic and a philosophical foundation and, although in later writings he sometimes refers (even approvingly) to the work of Rawls, it is clear that his account of justice is entirely incompatible with that expounded in *A Theory of Justice*. There is, for Hayek, no such thing as a just distribution, conceived independently of the deliberate choices that bring it about. It is human actions that are just or unjust, and just actions, reiterated over time, will produce, by an invisible hand, an unequal social order.[21] Attempts to rectify this by legislation will invariably involve injustice, whether by expropriating people without their consent, or by forcing people to do what they otherwise would not do with their time, abilities, or energy. And such attempts are doomed to failure, since (to return to the root conception) they inevitably destroy the information that they will need for their own success.

Moreover, Hayek adds in later writings, there is something wrong with the very word "social," attached like a mantra to otherwise desirable things: social justice, social market, social morality, social conscience, social liberalism. Hayek describes it as a "weasel word," one that sucks the meaning from whatever term it is attached to, "as a weasel sucks eggs."[22] Words to which this parasite attaches itself are turned from their referential purpose, and made to perform a task that is the opposite of the one for which they were designed. In the name of social justice any amount of injustice can be inflicted; in the name of the social market the market itself can be destroyed; and so on. And the word "social," used in this way, does not merely destroy its successor – it destroys itself. It no longer refers to society, that benign and spontaneous byproduct of human sympathy, but to the state, which acts in the name of society but to society's detriment. Social justice means state control, the social market means state distortion, and social morality means the chilling puritanical edicts with which socialists bar the way to success.

In this and related ways Hayek extended his attack on socialism from the narrow territory of the original "calculation debate" to the realm of philosophy and culture. Hayek came close to Orwell in seeing that state socialism goes hand in hand with the corruption of language. Much of the difficulty the Austrian economists had encountered in making themselves heard in modern Europe arose from the fact that they were using words with their normal meanings, and without the ideological commitments that had been instilled by their systematic misuse. But this brings me to a problem that Hayek frequently addressed, but to which he never found a satisfactory answer: namely, what explains the triumph of socialism in his day, and of its more liberal derivatives in ours? Hayek was aware of the obvious fact that the validity of an argument does not guarantee its widespread acceptance, and was fond of quoting Hume's remark that "though men be much governed by interest, yet even interest itself, and all human affairs, are entirely governed by *opinion*."[23] Difficult truths, such as those presented by the Austrian defense of the market or the Burkean defense of custom, are unlikely to influence events when more emotionally satisfying or exhilarating falsehoods compete with them.

In an article first published in the *University of Chicago Law Review* in 1949,[24] Hayek addressed the problem of "The Intellectuals and Socialism," and made the following suggestion. First there is a distinction, of recent provenance, between the scholar and the intellectual. The scholar is interested in knowledge for its own sake, and is often master of some narrow, outwardly unexciting, and in any case publicly inconspicuous field. The intellectual is a "second-hand dealer in ideas" interested in exerting his mind in the public sphere, who will be naturally drawn to those theories and ideas that make thinking the avenue to action. He will be prey to visionary and utopian conceptions, and drawn to those theories that give to the intellectuals a special role in the redemption of mankind. Hayek points out that no socialist ever loses credibility with his fellows by the impracticality or extravagance of his ideas, while liberals (in Hayek's sense of the term), who are dependent on the good will of existing institutions and have no utopian formula for their improvement, will instantly damn themselves by an impractical suggestion. He also notes the prevalence of people "who have undeservedly achieved a popular reputation as great scientists solely because they hold what the intellectuals regard as 'progressive' views," adding, "I have yet to come across a single instance where such a scientific pseudo-reputation has been bestowed for political reasons on a scholar of more conservative leanings." In the competition for influence, therefore, liberals (in Hayek's sense) and conservatives are constantly eliminated while socialists advance from strength to strength. And because intellectuals effectively set the terms of political debate, both inside and outside the universities, they are able to make it seem as if all disputes are internal to the socialist program.

Much of what Hayek says in this bold and interesting essay is undeniably true. However, he fails to give an adequate explanation of the crucial item of socialist doctrine, which is the commitment to social equality. This commitment has shown an ability to survive quite out of proportion to its intrinsic plausibility, and outlasts all the theories that have risen and fallen in the attempt to enclose it in an argument. Indeed, the theories of socialism stand to the belief in

social equality rather as theology stands to the belief in God. They
are *ex post facto* attempts to give a rational foundation to a dogma
that will survive every rational attempt to refute it. Equality is, for
the socialist intellectual, a matter of faith, and Hayek has no real
explanation as to why this faith should have arisen or why it should
have attracted to itself such an ardent priesthood. He himself is a
believer in equality before the law, and recognizes that this is a
consequence of the individualism that is the major premise of his
thinking. But he rejects most other forms of equality as either unobtainable or undesirable – interferences, at best, in the natural working of the spontaneous order. Moreover, he adds, "equality of the
general rules of law and conduct ... is the only kind of equality
conducive to liberty and the only equality which we can secure
without destroying liberty."[25]

THE CONSERVATIVE CRITIQUE

In *The Constitution of Liberty* Hayek shows himself to be a mas-
terly, if uncommonly long-winded, exponent of the principles of
classical liberalism. He rightly sees that liberty does not require,
but on the contrary is threatened by, majority choice, and that the
primary task for the classical liberal thinker is to devise a constitution that will both permit the effective exercise of political power,
and also limit the areas in which it can be asserted, so that society
can flourish according to its innate and "spontaneous" principles. On
the Hayekian view, it is only within the spontaneous order of civil
society that the information needed by the state can be generated.
Moreover, he believes, even democrats must accept this truth, and
therefore cooperate in searching for a constitution that will resist the
pressures to conformity that arise when too much respect is paid to
majority opinion. "The ideal of democracy rests on the belief that the
view which will direct government emerges from an independent
and spontaneous process. It requires, therefore, the existence of a
large sphere independent of majority control in which the opinions of
the individuals are formed."[26]

The problem for all liberal thinkers is contained in those remarks.
What holds the "large sphere" of "spontaneous" processes together,
and how does it defend itself against fragmentation? Classical liberals have tended to follow Locke in arguing for a society founded in a

social contract. However, contract does not create the bond of society, but depends upon it. Without membership there is no motive to obey the contract, rather than to pretend to obey it in order to reap the advantages of other people's obedience. It is this bond of membership that conservatives have traditionally sought to define and defend, believing liberal individualism to be a potential threat to it. Relations seen in contractual terms are subject to the constant erosion of self-interest; those based in membership are fortified by trials and by the love of neighbor and home.

Hayek does not exactly ignore this problem, which had been brought to the fore by Hume, both in his criticism of the social contract and in his theory of justice as an "artificial" virtue. Indeed, Hayek's approach helps to make the Humean objection to the social contract theory more precise. The social contract is supposed to explain what it is for a society to be founded on the consent of its members. It does so by envisaging a social order that is the object of a single act of collective consent, rather than the byproduct of myriad consensual transactions. It is an attempt, as one might put it, to construe the invisible hand as a visible handshake. But Hayek's approach conceals what is really at stake in the Humean (and one might add Hegelian) objections to social contract theory. Hayek begins from the assumption of "methodological individualism," as Joseph Schumpeter called it: the assumption that facts about collectives are to be explained in terms of individual plans. I don't say that this assumption is erroneous, or that it does not have an important role in the search for genuine explanations, as opposed to enchanting descriptions, in the social sciences. But it causes those who adopt it to overlook the many ways in which individual plans depend upon collective states of mind. Hayek is suspicious of the Hegelian fashion in German social thinking, which attributes to the *Volk*, the *Gemeinschaft*, and the state a kind of identity above and beyond their constituent members. As a result he does not give sufficient weight to the truth that, however willing people may be to live with their neighbors on terms of free association under a rule of law, they will always make, and will always need to make, a distinction between the true neighbor and the interloper.

Hayek writes that "a group of men become a society not by giving themselves laws but by obeying the same rules of conduct."[27] But that states neither a necessary nor a sufficient condition of social membership. The rules of conduct that prevail in Britain are for the most part followed in France. And there are societies such as the Italian in which the rules change from town to town and season to season. What makes Britain, France, and Italy into three separate societies is the emergence in each of them of a politically pregnant first person plural. The British, the French, and the Italians all recognize a distinction between those to whom they are bound by history, territory, language, and allegiance and those against whom they might one day have to defend themselves. Only when this sense of membership is in place are people disposed to submit to a common rule of law and willing to place contractual obligations to strangers above tribal and family ties.

It is true that membership is a form of spontaneous order. But it is radically different from, and often in conflict with, the spontaneous orders studied by Hayek. It comes to us with imperative force. For some it has a religious meaning; for others it speaks of home, neighborhood, language, and landscape. Where the experience of membership is absent society fragments into families, gangs, and clans, as in Africa today. And there is no instance of a catallactic order in the modern world that does not depend upon national loyalty – a loyalty that may very well be threatened by too great an emphasis on the free and sovereign individual.

Now conservatives will, I hope, agree with Hayek's defense of the catallactic order. They will support the free economy, the rule of law, and the precedence of tradition and custom over state control. However, they may be more concerned than Hayek was to emphasize the tensions that arise between these several spontaneous orders, and the frequent need for a standpoint above and beyond them from which their rival claims can be brokered. Moreover, it is characteristic of conservatism to suggest that free exchange and the rule of law require a sense of togetherness that they themselves do not generate. While tradition, the market, and "abstract" rules are all rational solutions to problems of social coordination, and maybe even unique avenues to socially necessary knowledge, the same is not true of the bond of membership. This is not a solution to a coordination problem, but the condition from which both problem and solution arise. The alternative to membership is the Hobbesian social contract, which creates a sovereign above and beyond the social order, a solution that Hayek expressly and rightly rejects, not least because it tries to replace evolutionary rationality – the rationality of a society that solves its problems by spontaneous adaptation – with a constructivist rationality that wishes to embody the solution to all future problems in a master plan. And when the conditions of membership are abused or ignored – as when a ruling elite allows uncontrolled immigration from disloyal minorities and antagonistic religious groups – then all the benefits of a liberal social order are at risk.[28]

The motives of membership are love, gratitude, and fear – love of country, language, neighbors, family, religion, customs, and home, gratitude toward these things as the source of life and happiness, and fear of their dissolution and of the anarchy, enmity, and predation that would then ensue. All of those feelings flow into a common reservoir of loyalty, which maintains the community in being and overcomes the problem of the "free rider." For some this loyalty takes a religious form – the loyalty of the "creed community," as Spengler called it. For others, who have passed through the Enlightenment experience, loyalty is directed to the nation and the homeland. Others still lack the feeling altogether, and identify themselves as in some way outside the society by which they are nevertheless surrounded and on which they depend for their groceries. Loyalty brings the capacity for sacrifice. And sacrifice means the preparedness to lose control of your budget, to cease to maximize your own utility, to lay down your life, *in extremis*, for your unknown friends. It is part of the business of politics to sustain the conditions under which this loyalty arises, and liberals (in Hayek's sense of the term) have argued, on the whole, as though loyalty did not matter, or as though it could be costlessly replaced by relations of a purely contractual kind.

MEMBERSHIP

There is a tendency in Hayek, encouraged by his methodological individualism, to see spontaneous order as the default position of human society – the position to which we naturally revert when the distorting pressures of political control and egalitarian planning are lifted. In this Hayek resembles those American neoconservatives who believe that democracy is the default position of government, to which even a Middle Eastern society will revert when the gangsters have gone. In fact, however, spontaneous order, like democracy, is a rare achievement, extracted at great cost from the true default position of mankind, which is priest-haunted tyranny. One of the goals of conservative political thinking in our time, therefore, has been to give a coherent and humane account of the kind of pre-political membership that will sustain free institutions and a rule of law. Many conservatives have been attracted by the arguments of Wilhelm Röpke, in support of a "social market economy": an economy in which the free market is combined with welfare provisions designed to retain the loyalty of those who might otherwise lose out.[29] Others have seen the welfare state, even in the mild form proposed by Röpke and Beveridge, as a threat to the shared loyalty on which social survival ultimately depends. The question who is right in this confrontation is, by its very nature, not one that can be resolved by Hayek's mode of argument. Classical liberalism of Hayek's kind begins from the assumption that society exists, and that the distinction between the member and the non-member is securely established in the thoughts and emotions of those who are facing the future together – so securely established that it need not be mentioned.

Membership brings a vital piece of knowledge to those joined by it, namely knowledge that they are so joined, and therefore can trust each other. From that knowledge the catallactic process can begin. But membership involves altogether more visceral and less calculating feelings than those that drive the market, feelings that cause us to espouse policies and causes that could never stand up to examination under the withering eye of methodological individualism. Hence those thinkers who have taken membership seriously have tended to emphasize other aspects of law, custom, and tradition than those singled out by Hayek. While Hayek points to the role of the common law in providing remedies to injustices suffered by the individual, Maitland, for example, is more interested in the role of equity in protecting the rights, property, and identity of institutions.[30] Gierke, the most articulate defender of the German common law, saw this law in similar terms, as arising from the need to protect the community, the *Genossenschaft*, against predation by the sovereign power. This is not the place to expound Gierke's interesting analysis.[31] But I mention it in order to draw attention to the fundamental weakness in Hayek's argument, which is his failure to take proper note of the emotions and motives that are presupposed by the enterprise of free association, and which will inevitably surface in, and draw limits to, the institutions and laws of a free society.

THE PERSISTENCE OF EGALITARIANISM

This same weakness infects Hayek's response to socialism. As I remarked above, Hayek fails to account either for the passion among intellectuals for equality, or for the resulting success of socialists and their egalitarian successors in driving the liberal idea from the stage of politics. This passion for equality is not a new thing, and indeed pre-dates socialism by many centuries, finding its most influential expression in the writings of Rousseau. There is no consensus as to how equality might be achieved, what it would consist in if achieved, or why it is so desirable in the first place. But no argument against the cogency or viability of the idea has the faintest chance of being listened to or discussed by those who have fallen under its spell. Why is this? I shall conclude with a suggestion.

Hayek is right to distinguish the intellectual from the scholar, and to see the intellectual as striving for an influence that the true scholar may abhor. And in his introduction to *Capitalism and the Historians* he argues plausibly for the view that recent historians, like other intellectuals, have been animated by an anti-capitalist bias.[32] This bias has caused them to misrepresent capitalism as a form of exploitation, and private profit as achieved always at the expense of the workforce that helped to produce it. Indeed, it seems to be characteristic of a certain kind of intellectual to perceive all economic activity as a zero-sum game. If someone gains, another loses. This zero-sum vision underpins Marx's theory of surplus value, and crops up again and again in the socialist attacks on private enterprise, selective schools, inheritance, and just about anything else that creates a benefit that not everyone can enjoy. The idea that inequality (of reward, status, advantage, or whatever) might be in the interest of both parties, the better off and the worse off, is either not accepted, or seen as irrelevant to the charge against the capitalist order. It is to the credit of Rawls that he believes that inequality can be justified. Yet, according to the Difference Principle, the justification must show that inequality benefits the worse off. But why does inequality have to be justified? And why must the justification be framed in terms of the benefits brought to the underdog, and not in terms of those enjoyed by the dog on top of him? These questions suggest that the belief in equality is being *built in* to the arguments offered in support of it. Like a religious belief, it is being protected rather than questioned by the arguments adduced in its favor.

Hayek sees that the zero-sum vision is fired by an implacable negative energy. It is not the concrete vision of some real alternative that animates the socialist critic of the capitalist order. It is hostility toward the actual, and in particular toward those who enjoy advantages within it. Hence the belief in equality remains vague and undefined, except negatively. For it is essentially a weapon against the existing order – a way of undermining its claims to legitimacy, by discovering a victim for every form of success. The striving for equality is, in other words, based in *ressentiment* in Nietzsche's sense, the state of mind that Max Scheler identified as the principal motive behind the socialist orthodoxy of his day.[33] It is one of the major problems of modern politics, which no classical liberal could possibly solve, how to govern a society in which resentment has acquired the kind of privileged social, intellectual, and political position that we witness today.

If you accept the Nietzschean explanation of egalitarianism, then you will perhaps accept the burden of my conservative critique of Hayek, which is that he pays too much attention to the search for rational solutions to socially generated problems, and not enough to the motives that prompt people to believe or disbelieve in them. For all his brilliance in uncovering a thread of argument that (in my view) decisively establishes the intellectual superiority of liberal-conservative over socialist politics, Hayek does not engage with the real, deep-down conflict between conservatism and socialism, which is a conflict over the nature and conditions of social membership. In this conflict liberalism must learn to fight on the conservative side. For liberalism is possible only under a conservative government.[34]

NOTES

1. Hayek 1960, p. 398.
2. See Hayek 1976b, p. 12, and also the arguments marshalled in Feser 2003.
3. The argument that I have here condensed is spelled out in detail in Mises [1922] 1951, and in the essays in Hayek 1948a, especially the three essays on "Socialist Calculation" there reprinted.

4. Neumann and Morgenstern 1944.
5. O'Neill 1998, pp. 134ff.
6. Hayek 1982a, p. 73.
7. Ancient writers on the whole concurred with Hayek's view of law. According to Demosthenes, "every law (*nomos*) is a discovery and a gift of the gods" (*Antiphon* I, iii, 27), a view maintained by Plato in *The Laws*, by the Greek tragedians, and many other ancient sources. See the discussion in Brague 2005.
8. See Hayek 1976b.
9. I have argued for this position in Scruton 2000, ch. 6.
10. Bentham 1907; Austin 1954; Kelsen 1945.
11. Hayek 1976b, p. 55.
12. Hayek 1973, pp. 112–13.
13. Schmitt [1922] 1985.
14. Laski 1934, p. 177.
15. Among German opponents of positivism special mention should be made of A. Reinach, whose book *The A Priori Foundations of the Civil Law* appeared in 1913, and also Max Scheler.
16. See especially the argument of Dworkin in "Hard Cases," reprinted in Dworkin 1978. For an overview of Dworkin's theory of law in a study that deals also with Hayek and Oakeshott, see Covell 1992.
17. Oakeshott 1962 and 1975.
18. Of course the processes involved are different in either case. Prices are informative partly because those who overprice or underprice their goods are quickly driven from the market; the common law is informative because judgments that create conflicts are gradually overruled, and judgments that reinforce the implied social order gradually assume the status of precedents.
19. Feser 2003. Others have written of a tension between liberal rationalism and conservative traditionalism in Hayek – notably Kukathas (1989) and O'Neill (1998) – though it seems to me that the concept of evolutionary rationality is designed precisely to defuse this tension.
20. Hayek 1976b, pp. 108–9.
21. Those looking for points of vulnerability in Hayek's argument might question the idea of the "just action," rather than the "just person," as the fundamental application of the concept. To explore this topic would, however, take us too far from the present argument. Suffice it to say that the Aristotelian approach to morality, in terms of the virtues and vices of the human character, made little impact on thinkers brought up in the atmosphere of "methodological individualism."
22. Hayek 1983b. The quotation is from Jacques in *As You Like It*.
23. Hume 1985c, p. 51.

24. Republished as a pamphlet (Hayek 1971).
25. Hayek 1960, p. 85.
26. Hayek 1960, p. 109.
27. Hayek 1960, pp. 106–7.
28. See Scruton 2002.
29. See Röpke 1960, and the papers in Peacock and Willgerodt 1989. For a contemporary defense of this position, see Gray 1992.
30. Maitland 1911.
31. I have made the attempt in "Gierke and the Corporate Person" (Scruton [1990] 1998). *Das deutsche Genossenschaftsrecht* was published over many years, the last volume appearing in 1913 when the author was seventy-three years old. It has never been fully translated, though important parts are available in Gierke 1900 and 1934.
32. Hayek 1954.
33. Nietzsche, *The Genealogy of Morals* (Nietzsche 1994), pt. 1, sec. 8; Scheler 1998.
34. I have benefited greatly from comments from Kevin Mulligan, Barry Smith, and David Wiggins.

12 Hayek on the evolution of society and mind

INTRODUCTION

As a rule, Hayek has not been treated kindly by scholars. One would expect that a political theorist and economist of his stature would be charitably, if not sympathetically, read by commentators; instead, Hayek often elicits harsh dismissals. This is especially true of his fundamental ideas about the evolution of society and reason. A reader will find influential discussions in which his analysis is described as "dogmatic," "unsophisticated," and "crude." In this chapter I propose to take a fresh start, sketching a sympathetic interpretation of Hayek's accounts of social evolution and mind as fundamental to his thinking. My basic claim is that Hayek's views on social evolution and reason are not only intimately bound together, but they also depend on his analyses of complex orders, scientific explanations of such orders, and the place of rules in complex orders. Because so few commentators recognize that his claims about evolution are embedded in a system of ideas,[1] most misunderstand him.

THE COMPLEX ORDER OF ACTIONS

Complex phenomena

Hayek repeatedly refers to "the twin ideas of evolution and spontaneous order."[2] Although some commentators question whether these ideas are related, Hayek's insistence on the link between evolutionary analysis and spontaneous orders in writings spanning a number of years indicates that we need to make sense of the "twin ideas thesis" if we are to grasp what he has in mind.[3]

Hayek tells us that attempts to understand human interaction through the ideas of evolution and spontaneous order are the main tools for dealing with complex phenomena.[4] It is, I think, the notion of complex phenomena that is the key. Hayek's analysis of complexity, especially of social complexity, is built on seven key claims, most of which are part of current analyses of social complexity.[5]

I. Complex phenomena, according to Hayek, display abstract patterns composed of a large number of variables.[6] Hayek goes so far as to define complexity in terms of a large number of variables. This is perhaps the least adequate feature of his analysis. Although complex systems typically involve a large number of elements, it is the character of the elements' interactions and the resulting patterns that are fundamental.

2. Organized complexity occurs "when the character of the structures showing it depends not only on the properties of the individual elements of which they are composed, and the relative frequency with which they occur, but also on the manner in which the individual elements are connected with each other."[7] Hayek, then, certainly sees that complex systems arise because of the nature of the interactions of the elements. Importantly, he points to the idea of an emergent property:

The "emergence" of "new" patterns as a result of the increase in the number of elements between which simple relations exist, means that this larger structure as a whole will possess certain general or abstract features which will recur independently of the particular values of the individual data, so long as the general structure (as described, e.g., by an algebraic equation) is preserved. Such "wholes," defined in terms of certain general properties of their structure, will constitute distinctive objects of explanation for a theory, even though such a theory may be merely a particular way of fitting together statements about the relation between individual elements.[8]

This is crucial: in analyzing something as a complex phenomenon our concern is the pattern of relations that pertains among the elements. It is the abstract, emergent, pattern that is the crux of complexity. The abstract pattern cannot be predicted from a small sample of the individual elements. Contemporary complexity theorists, for example, see liquidity as an emergent property of a huge number of related water molecules; although liquidity is a property that causally arises out of the interaction of a very large number of individual molecules, the precise properties of waves and ripples could not be predicted from what we know about molecular chemistry, nor does the property appear in a small sample of the molecules.[9] The same emergent property may obtain at times t_1 and t_2 even though none of the individual elements at t_1 persist at t_2. The complex order – the pattern of relations – is this emergent property, not the individual elements.

3.   Complex systems can be tightly coupled. As Hayek notes, in a complex order the state of the system at any one time depends on a number of factors, and if even one is varied, there may be profound changes throughout the system.[10] The behavior of tightly coupled systems is difficult to predict as they are characterized by error inflation: a small error in predicting one variable can lead to drastic errors in predicting the overall system's state or, as Hayek would say, its pattern.[11]

4.   Complex systems are apt to be self-maintaining.[12] By this Hayek meant that such systems have a tendency to persist and to respond to a range of exogenous and endogenous changes.[13] This is fundamental to the idea of a *spontaneous* order (though not all spontaneous orders are complex).

5.   In many complex systems we cannot measure how close the system is to equilibrium, though we have good grounds to suppose it is never in equilibrium.[14] The most our theories can do is tell us that the system moves towards equilibrium. Thus our theories of equilibrium (say, price theory) will not allow us to reliably predict actual prices.[15] It is important to realize that Hayek accepted the legitimacy of mathematical modeling of the economy; what he dismissed was any claim that we could reliably estimate actual values and so employ our model to generate fine-grained predictions.

6.   Complex systems such as the economy are characterized by constant novelty.[16] We need to remember that Hayek, like the Austrian School of economics in general, insisted on the importance of dynamic and unknown factors in economic life. "The solution of the economic problem of society . . . is always a voyage of exploration into the unknown, an attempt to discover new ways of doing things better than they have been done before."[17]

7. Because of the complexity of the system, there is "no global controller that can exploit all opportunities or interactions."[18] This brings us to the very heart of Hayek's economics: global planners could not secure and employ sufficient information to direct individuals to employ capital and labor in an efficient way. Thus Hayek's position in the socialist calculation debate: "the 'data' from which the economic calculus starts are never for the whole society 'given' to a single mind which could work out the implications and can never be so given."[19]

Explanation of the principle

Given the features of complex phenomena, the scientific study of complex orders cannot aim at the prediction of the "specific" future states or values of the individual elements. Hayek realized that the idea of a "specific" prediction is context dependent; his claim, though, was that in many natural sciences (such as parts of physics), "it will generally be possible to specify all those aspects of the phenomenon in which we are interested with any degree of precision we may need for our purposes."[20] In contrast, when dealing with complex phenomena we are simply unable to specify the values (in contemporary terms, the system is modeled in non-linear equations which have no unique solution);[21] we can only predict the "range of phenomena to expect."[22] We can understand the general principles on which the system operates, and with this knowledge we can predict the parameters within which the system will settle. This is, as Hayek says, an idea of "great importance for the understanding of the theoretical methods of the social sciences."[23] It is the failure to understand the limits of social prediction that leads to an ill-fated attempt to employ science to engineer society.

The emergent order of actions

Hayek subtitles his "Notes on the Evolution of Systems of Rules of Conduct," "The Interplay between Rules of Individual Conduct and the Social Order of Actions."[24] Given what we already know, we can grasp Hayek's distinction between specific rules of conduct that individuals follow, and the "social order of actions" – the emergent property – that arises from a system of rules. Hayek says that (1) it is conceivable that the same social order of actions might be produced by entirely different sets of individual rules; and (2) the same set of individual rules may lead to very different social orders, depending on the environment in which it operates.[25] Both points, of course, are fundamental to the idea of a complex phenomenon: it can be produced by different sets of individual elements and the same set of individual elements may produce very different emergent features.

Throughout his long career – and certainly since the 1950s – Hayek's overriding concern was the analysis of the emergent property he called "the order of actions":

> It is the resulting overall order of actions but not the regularity of the actions of the separate individuals as such which is important for the preservation of the group; and a certain kind of overall order may in the same manner contribute to the survival of the members of the group whatever the particular rules of individual conduct that bring it about.[26]

Hayek's fundamental insight is that the survival of a society depends on the emergent property of orderly cooperation of different individuals which has a complex relation to the rules of conduct individuals follow. Thus it is a serious misunderstanding of Hayek to claim, as does one commentator, that

> Hayek's distinction between the group (in the sense of an order ...) and its institutions (such as rules and paradigms) is pointless. The distinction is redundant because the group neither acts as an individual nor operates as a cohesive form. It is merely, given external circumstance, a mirror image of the rules adopted by the individuals.[27]

Although the order of actions arises out of the set of rules and institutions, it is not just the mirror image of them (as we have seen, the same order might arise from an entirely different set). So far from being pointless, the fundamental interest of Hayek's account is that his analysis of complexity allows him to distinguish the pattern (emergent) property from the set of rules which gives rise to it, and so his analysis focuses on the pattern property.[28] This order does not depend on the predictability of individual actions, which is one reason why Hayek can advocate a dynamic social order in which individuals are constantly doing new things in new ways (and this is one reason why he is not a conservative).

SOCIAL EVOLUTION

Evolutionary accounts as "in principle explanations"
of dynamic and open complex orders

Recall Hayek's insistence that the twin ideas of a spontaneous order
and evolution are the main tools for understanding complexity.
Theories of spontaneous order (e.g. economics) – which explain
how the complex order of social actions can be self-organizing and
self-maintaining – are essentially what Hayek calls "models" of the
complex phenomenon of the social order of actions, providing general accounts of how the elements relate.[29] As Hayek remarks, all of
economics can be understood as modeling the complex order.[30] But
to understand the workings of the social order of actions as a spontaneously organized and self-regulating complex phenomenon is, still,
essentially a static explanation. Moreover, Hayek insists that any
such model of a spontaneous order is incomplete because the behavior of the order does not simply depend on the internal relations of
the system but on exogenous (outside) forces; indeed, it may have
been shaped by the specific series of environments it passed through.
"Though it is reasonable to believe that structures of the kind will
in a definable environment always behave as they do, the existence
of such structures may in fact depend not only on that environment,
but also on a definite sequence of such environments."[31]

Hayek is so attracted to evolutionary accounts of the order of
actions because they hold out the promise of providing "in principle
explanations" of the alteration and development of complex orders
without supposing anyone fully understands the working of the
order.[32] As Hayek sees it, evolutionary accounts provide the real
alternative to design theories,[33] and they articulate precisely the
"explanations of principle" that are appropriate to complexity.[34]
In biology, Darwinian theory allows us to understand the principles
that regulate the development of species, shows us that some
developments are outside the possible range of values (e.g. that
horses will suddenly give birth to winged offspring), but it is unable
to generate specific predictions about the future of individuals or
species. Hayek's analysis was path-breaking here, showing how evolution is a case of complexity theory. Compare a recent writer on
evolution:

Algorithms must always produce the same result if they start from the same point. This seems to suggest that, if evolution follows an algorithm, its results must be predetermined and predictable. This is not the case and chaos theory explains why not. There are many simple processes, like dripping taps or moving gases, or the path drawn by a swinging pendulum, which are chaotic. They follow simple and mindless algorithms but their end results are complex, chaotic and unpredictable. Beautiful shapes and patterns can emerge, but although the *kind* of pattern may be repeatable, the detail cannot be predicted without running the procedure right through. And since chaotic systems can be highly sensitive to initial starting conditions, a tiny difference at the beginning may lead to an entirely different outcome. Evolution is like this.[35]

The core idea

Before we get into details, complexities, and problems, it will be helpful to get clear about the outline of Hayek's account of social evolution. We have seen that the *explanandum* (that which is to be explained) is the rise and development of an emergent property, namely, the social order of actions. As Hayek says, "the selection process will operate on the order as a whole."[36] This is the "Great Society": an overall spontaneous order of adaptations that allows for coordinated action.[37] The *explanans* (that which does the explaining) is an evolutionary account whereby the rules and institutions that give rise to this order (i.e. this emergent property) are selected via a competition ("in the widest sense")[38] among social orders. The emergent property, we have seen, arises out of a system of rules; therefore the competition among these social orders is determined by their constituent rules and institutions as they operate in specific environments. Social orders of actions are typically differentiated by their constituent rules and institutions; variation in the rules and institutions can provide a competitive advantage in the competition between social orders, leading to selection of a social order of actions with certain sets of rules.

There is a rough and ready analogy here with one understanding of Darwinian evolution. On the face of it (remember, complications will come later), in Hayek's account rules play a role analogous to genes in biological evolution; whereas individual organisms are constituted by following the instructions of genes, a Great Society is constituted by following the instructions of rules.[39] And just as genetic variation can give an advantage to an individual organism in its competition with others, rule variation can perform the same role in competition between social orders of actions.

Like evolutionary explanations in biology, it is easy to confuse Hayek's evolutionary theory with a functionalist account.[40] In a functionalist biological explanation, the presence of, say, the heart is explained by its function in the overall system – the role of the heart in keeping animals alive. A functionalist may claim that the heart exists because it is needed to pump blood. Thus it may seem that when Hayek says that practices have been maintained "because they enabled the group in which they have arisen to prevail over others,"[41] he is saying that the practices are there because they are needed for the group to prevail. Consequently, many suppose that Hayek's *explanandum* is why we have the specific rules we have, and his *explanans* is that they are needed for the complex order. This, I think, gets things precisely backwards. Evolutionary theories are not functionalist: they are causal explanations of the development of an organism. However, once the evolutionary account has been given, over a wide range of traits, we will be able to see that the trait performs a function. Hearts do indeed perform a function. But in the evolutionary theory the existence of the heart is not explained in terms of its function, but in terms of the history of the organism and the competitive pressures that selected those with certain genes that developed into hearts. Similarly for Hayek. Once he has provided an evolutionary account of the rise of the social order of actions, he then has grounds for saying that the rules and institutions we find in this order generally have served a function that has given the order an advantage in the environment in which evolutionary selection occurred.

Units and mechanisms of selection

If this core idea is to be filled out in a convincing way, Hayek must specify and explain two crucial mechanisms: the selection and replicator mechanisms. Let us first consider the selection mechanism. It would seem that any evolutionary explanation of the rise of X_α (entity X with feature α) must be able to identify at least one mechanism according to which in some past environment E, mechanism M selected X_α over some X_β. Hayek is often criticized for not identifying "the" selection mechanism, but an adequate evolutionary theory need not rely on a single mechanism. Darwin himself proposed both natural and sexual selection as mechanisms, and these apparently can work in opposite directions. Biologists are still debating whether sexual selection can produce traits such as male bird feathers that do not render the male fitter to survive in its environment and may actually result in traits that make the male less fit to survive. As Hayek often reminds us, though, we ought not to take Darwinianism as the template for all evolutionary accounts.[42] For Darwin, one selection mechanism involves differential survival rates: those Xs with α have a higher probability of survival than those with β. But a non-Darwinian evolutionary account also could be based on, say, differential growth rates. Suppose we begin in E with a limited amount of space, and five entities (X_1-X_5) that cannot reproduce or die, but can grow to some maximum or shrink down to some minimum. We could still have an evolutionary explanation of why X_1 takes over the space, even though there is no difference in reproduction or survival rates; evolutionary accounts thus need not be based on natural selection.

I stress this because even careful commentators are apt to suppose that either Hayek's evolutionary account must closely parallel Darwin's, or else it is simply metaphorical or confused. We must be careful to consider Hayek's selection mechanisms on their own terms. Three possible selection mechanisms can be identified.

(1) *Group survival.* Although Hayek generally insisted on the distance between his theory of "cultural" evolution and Darwin's account of biological evolution, he also stressed that both rely on competition for survival.[43] Of course the difference – and why Hayek is not a social Darwinist[44] – is that the competition is not between individuals, in which "fitter" individuals survive, but between social orders of actions. Unfortunately, Hayek often employs the more accessible notion of competition between "groups," in which one group prevails over another.[45] He writes:

> The rules of conduct have ... evolved because the groups who practiced them were more successful and displaced others. They were rules which, given the environment in which men lived, secured that a greater number of the groups or individuals who practiced them would survive.[46]

This passage presents problems. By simply talking of "groups," and then adding at the close that "a greater number of the groups or individuals" survive, Hayek appears to be directly falling prey to problems of group selection and collective action.[47] It looks as if Hayek is claiming that an individual's chance of survival is maximized if she belongs to a group that maximizes its own chance of survival.[48] But this raises familiar problems of collective action and the rationality of free riding. If individuals are confronting prisoner's dilemmas, it may be rational for each person not to do that which is good for the group, even though this leads to a situation which is disadvantageous for all. One of the lessons of game theory is that what is good for the group may not be rational for anyone.

Space does not allow us to go deeply into these issues; even simply in terms of rational choice narrowly understood, they are much more complex than the above suggests.[49] In relation to Hayek, however, we must keep two points in mind. First, Hayek's concern is not simply groups, but "the order of actions of a group."[50] This means that our units are systems of cooperation – arising out of a system of rules – and for Hayek this means that the rules actually regulate people's actions.[51] Secondly, as we shall see in the sixth section, Hayek repeatedly insists that our reason is itself evolved, and is itself shaped by the order of actions. This does not mean simply that the degree to which people are moved by reason is shaped by the order of actions. When Hayek tells us that "individual reason is a product of inter-individual relationships,"[52] he is arguing that our conception of rationality is produced by social life. Mind is a product of the social order in which it has evolved.[53] Successful orders of action evolve conceptions of reason that induce general rule following.[54]

It is not clear in what sense Hayek advocated group selection. The idea of group selection is not pellucid, but we probably should not understand an evolutionary theory to raise the problems of group selection just because the theory selects among groups. Group selection is controversial in biology because it refers to selection among group traits that leads to the selection among individual traits. A typical group selection story would be that because *groups* of altruists do better than groups of selfish people, *individuals* in those groups do better than individuals in selfish groups, *and this explains why these surviving individuals have an altruistic trait.* The idea is that individual characteristics are explained by group membership. Sometimes Hayek seems to uphold group selection in this sense:

Although the existence and preservation of the order of actions of a group can be accounted for only from the rules of conduct which individuals obey, these rules of conduct have developed because the individuals have been living in groups whose structures have gradually changed. In other words, the properties of the individuals which are significant for the existence and preservation of the group, and through this also for the existence and preservation of the individuals themselves, have been shaped by the selection of those individuals from the individuals living in groups which at each stage of evolution of the group tended to act according to such rules as made the group more efficient.[55]

So it looks as if Hayek's claim is that group selection leads to the selection of individual traits – a full-fledged group selection account. I think, though, that this is misleading. Group selection accounts in biology claim that, *because* it is better for an individual to be a member of an altruistic group, an individual who has the altruistic trait will do better, and that is why the individual has the trait. And this is what raises the prisoner's dilemma problem: it is *even better* to be a non-altruistic member of an altruistic group. Hayek's claim, though, is different. As I have mentioned – and more on this anon – Hayek has a general theory that reason is significantly shaped by culture. Because of this, if it is advantageous for the group to be characterized by a way of reasoning, this will be instilled into the individual by the culture: the option of reasoning in an individually advantageous but uncooperative way is undermined, at least to some extent, by the account of the social roots of reason.[56]

(2) *Group growth.* Hayek tells us that comparative increase of wealth and population are means of evolutionary selection.[57] An evolutionary account of customs, he holds, must show the "distinct advantages by those groups that kept to such customs, thereby enabling them to expand more rapidly than others and ultimately to supersede (or absorb) those not possessing similar customs."[58] However, this is not really a different mechanism from survival – these are specific traits that tend toward survival. There is certainly a good case for wealth and population growth being understood as traits that are conducive to the survival of social orders (just as good nutrition is a trait that is conducive to the survival of an organism). Those that are

wealthier will be able to expand, fend off external threats, and their culture may come to dominate others. We also would expect them to attract immigration: Hayek suggests that this *attractor* trait is probably more important than internal population growth.[59]

These claims have not been well received (many take them to be an unfortunate feature of *The Fatal Conceit*, a book completed during Hayek's final illness, and some of which seems to reflect the views of his editor, Bartley, who finished the manuscript).[60] The analysis, though, is not really implausible, whereas many of the critiques are. For example, it is sometimes offered as a criticism of Hayek that the liberal western world has much lower birth rates than many less developed countries, and China, an authoritarian state, is the most populous country. But these criticisms miss the mark. Selection mechanisms select by giving an advantage to some trait over a time span. Evolutionary selection is not subject to particular counter-examples. No doubt there were cases in which Neanderthals beat out *Homo sapiens* for survival: this would not show that we were not more fit in the evolutionary environment in which we competed. So too we may find that because of drastically reduced death rates combined with traditional birth rates, some countries may experience a population explosion. The question is whether, over the long term – and remember, Hayek thought that the most important achievements of cultural evolution occurred before recorded history[61] – certain sorts of cooperative orders are better able to sustain larger populations, and whether this gives them an advantage that leads to their greater survival. Given the collapse in recent times of Soviet-style command economies, which were manifestly unable to produce sufficient wealth to support their populations, Hayek's idea should not be lightly dismissed.

(3) *An endogenous mechanism.* Reflect again on the rough analogy according to which rules are to orders of actions as genes are to organisms. Keeping that in mind, we need to be clear whether our aim is to explain how (a) a specific gene evolved or (b) how a trait of the organism evolved. It might seem that these are just different sides of the same explanation: if we explain how X_α (an organism with a specific trait) was selected by an evolutionary mechanism, we must explain how the α-gene was selected.[62] The evolutionary account of how X_α arose must ipso facto be the evolutionary story of how the α-gene arose. Interestingly, things are not so simple. We

might have some story about the selection of α-genes that did not entirely depend on a story about, say, the competitive advantage of X_α. Suppose that there was a competition between genes that was not determined by the competition of X_α with its rival X_β. Imagine that we are biological organisms of a somewhat different type. We still have genes that determine our traits, and natural selection still works in the familiar way. But we also have homunculi floating around in us. These homunculi have their own aims and, importantly, to survive a gene must receive a general endorsement from the homunculi population. Unless the homunculi endorse the gene, the gene dies out, and so the organism (us) loses a trait. Now we have genes that are pressured in two directions. They are pressured in natural selection: they will be maintained in the gene pool only so long as no competitor pops up that confers a survival advantage on the organism. On the other hand, they will only be maintained if they garner endorsement from the homunculi. Of course what the homunculi want, and what causes them to endorse a gene, will be crucial in filling out the story (we would expect that they are not too prone to reject genes that give rise to traits that have an advantage in the competition between organisms).

Such an evolutionary account would be complicated, but it is by no means confused, and it is certainly not crude. True, sometimes the "unit of selection" will be the *organism's traits* and sometimes the *genes*. Now there is reason to think that Hayek's account of social evolution is similar to this more complex picture. Hayek writes that a person's "thinking and acting are governed by rules which have by a *process of selection been evolved in the society in which he lives*."[63] Understood thus, it looks now as if his project is to explain how each rule (not the order of actions itself) evolved within the society. That this project may rely not only on the rule's ability to produce a competitive order of actions, but the rule's attractiveness to individuals, is suggested by Hayek's remark that "[t]he competition on which the process of selection rests must be understood in the widest sense. It involves competition between organized and unorganized groups *no less than competition between individuals*."[64] This stress on individual competition and the evolution of *rules* suggests that, instead of a competition between social orders, Hayek has in mind a competition between individuals within a social order that leads to the *selection and evolution of rules*. So we seem to have two evolutionary competitions, pressuring rules from two different directions. First, a competition exists between social orders which are, as it were, carriers of rules (as individual organisms are carriers of genes). The rules give a social order a certain competitive advantage, but the rules are only selected insofar as they are part of the evolved social order of actions. Second, there is also a competition between individuals and groups, and *this* competition selects certain rules as conducive to individual/group success.

If we allow ourselves to forget biology for a moment, the basic idea seems sound. Orders of actions are emergent properties constituted by a system of rules. What rules exist in an order of action is determined both by how well that order of action fares in competition with other orders and by the ability of the rules to garner support from the individuals who follow them and are competing with other individuals within the society. So rules will have selection pressures from two very different directions. I think this is probably Hayek's settled view. Admittedly, he typically insists on the competition between social orders account, though in *The Fatal Conceit* he does say that "cultural evolution operates *largely* through group selection,"[65] suggesting a non-group mechanism. In *The Constitution of Liberty* he writes:

[I]t is, in fact, desirable that the rules should be observed only in most instances and that the individual should be able to transgress them when it seems to him worthwhile to incur the odium this will cause ... It is this flexibility of voluntary rules which in the field of morals makes gradual evolution and spontaneous growth possible, which allows further modifications and improvements.[66]

And in the epilogue to *Law, Legislation and Liberty*, he argues that the steps in cultural evolution toward large-scale coordination "were made possible by some individuals breaking some traditional rules and practising new forms of conduct – not because they understood them to be better, but because the groups which acted on them prospered more and grew."[67] There are three ways this individual-initiated change might be understood:

1.   It might be that the development of new practices by individuals is aimed at a better order of actions. This is the interpretation Hayek explicitly rejects, and given his analysis of complexity, he is right to do so.

2. New rules might be conceived, à la Darwinian evolution, as random mutations – simply a source of variation and not involving another selection mechanism at all. Hayek's insistence toward the end of his career on group selection suggests this. But this looks somewhat implausible. We would expect, for example, that there will be some mechanisms that make some rules more likely to catch on in a group than others (ones that are easier to learn, ones that allow the individual more room to satisfy his own interests, ones that serve individual interests in their competition with others). It is not simply that groups with rules such as "Don't satisfy your self-interest" lose out to groups that have competing rules, but that such rules have a hard time getting the support of enough homunculi.

3. So the account might claim that though individuals do not innovate, or imitate the innovations of others, *because they have a grasp about how to improve the overall order of actions*, the conditions under which rules lose or gain the support of the constituent individuals are non-random and relate to local perceived individual benefits. Rules that allow individuals to locally satisfy their interests are apt to catch on, and those that are parts of badly performing orders are apt to be violated. This would add a useful non-Darwinian element to Hayek's account: the occurrence of "mutations" (i.e. new rules) would be non-random: they occur more often when they are needed. (When things are going badly for people, they break the old rules more often and try new arrangements.) This makes the wealth criterion more plausible: Hayek does not have to say that the less wealthy societies are simply overwhelmed by the wealthier, but that as societies lose their ability to produce wealth, defections from existing rules increase, leading either to swift changes into other orders or to collapse.

Rules as replicating instructions

Let us return again to Darwinism to orient ourselves. We have seen that an adequate evolutionary account must identify units of selection and selection mechanisms. In addition, a Darwinian account must include a high-fidelity replicator – in contemporary biology, the gene.[68] To say the gene is a replicator is to say that it copies itself; it has high fidelity because its copying is highly accurate. However, it is not perfect: its imperfection is a source of variation in genes – the faulty copies are what we call "mutations." Darwinian evolution is based on differential reproduction, and so copying is crucial. This is a part of Hayek's account of social evolution: he details how norms of trade spread in the ancient world, and this included colonization: a sort of copying of rules from one society to another.[69] This, though, is not at all central. What is really important is that the rules have high-fidelity replication insofar as they must be accurately "copied" by each individual subject to them. Cultural evolution, says Hayek, "simulates" Lamarckian evolution because acquired characteristics – rules and institutions – are transmitted from earlier to later generations.[70] This is done, he indicates, through the ability to imitate.[71]

The worry is that the imitation of rule-following behavior does not possess high fidelity. Imitating the results of another's actions – his output, as it were – is a low-fidelity way of copying.[72] If each generation simply observes the previous generation's behavior, and infers from this what the rule is, we would expect large drifts in the interpretation of the rule over many generations. Imagine a game of "Do what I do" in which there is a long line of people. The first person performs some relatively complex action, and the second person copies her, the third person copies the second, and so on. By the end of a long line we would expect a very different performance, because of the low fidelity of the replicating method.

It is hard to overestimate the importance of this to an evolutionary account. If from generation to generation there is a great deal of random drift in how the rule is interpreted, then even if we grant everything Hayek tells us about the selection mechanism it will be to no avail, for the advantages of adopting the rule will be lost by random changes. It is no good to adopt a good rule that quickly mutates into a bad rule. Now language greatly improves fidelity: instead of simply copying the results, we copy a set of instructions about how to do so. (Susan Blackmore compares trying to copy the soup of a good cook with copying down his recipe: we expect much higher fidelity from the latter.)[73] The apparent problem for Hayek is that he insists that the rules which guide the members of a society are largely unconscious. A rule, Hayek says, is a "propensity to act."[74] Customs and habits, which Hayek repeatedly sees as central to an order of actions, are "unconscious rules."[75]

That rules in this sense exist and operate without being explicitly known to those who obey them applies ... to many of the rules which govern the actions of men and thereby determine a spontaneous social order. Man certainly does not know all the rules which guide his actions in the sense that he is able to state them in words.[76]

Hayek, then, cannot avail himself of the fidelity of language, since so many rules are not conscious. How, then, can he ensure high fidelity?

MIND AND EVOLUTION

Neural network models

To understand Hayek's sophisticated solution to this problem, we need to reflect on his theory of the mind. Hayek is recognized today as an early neural network modeler.[77] Neural network theory, or connectionism, can be seen as a development of the associationist psychologies of Locke, Hume, and James Mill, according to which thoughts are connected by the laws of association (such as similarity, continuity, and so on).[78] The crux of associationism has been summed up thus:

Events that occur in space or time become connected in the mind. Events that share meaning or physical similarity become associated in the mind. Activation of one unit activates others to which it is linked, the degree of activation depending on the strength of association. This approach held great intuitive appeal for investigators of the mind because it seems to capture the flavor of cognitive behaviors: When thinking, reasoning, or musing, one thought reminds us of others.[79]

Unlike traditional associationism, connectionism abjures any appeal to primitive qualitative differences between sensations or thoughts. Connectionist systems are composed purely of neurons that simply have on/off states:[80] qualitative differences (e.g. between thoughts) are the results of a complex pattern of neural activation. As one contemporary cognitive psychologist describes them:

Each unit ["neuron"] receives "activity," both excitatory and inhibitory, as input, and then transmits activity to other units according to some function (usually nonlinear) of the inputs. The behavior of the network as a whole is determined by the initial state of activation and the connections between the units. The inputs of the network also gradually change the "weights" of the connections between the units according to some *learning rule* ... The units have no memory in themselves, but earlier inputs are represented indirectly via the changes in the weights they have caused.[81]

The relevance of Hayek's neural network model

Our concern here is not the adequacy of neural network models in relation to their competitors,[82] but the way that Hayek's early (and, I think, path-breaking) neural network account meshes with his overall social theory.[83] Four features of his connectionist theory of mind are relevant here.

(1) *Mind, classification, and rules.* The fundamental aim of Hayek's neural network theory is to explain "the kind of process by which a given physical situation is transformed into a certain phenomenal picture."[84] A certain state of the external world W exists at time t: how is W_t transformed into a sensory experience S of W_t, and how does $S[W_t]$ relate to sensory experiences of other states of the world, and when will these be perceived as the same, and when will the sensation be different? The key to Hayek's analysis is "classification" via neuronal connections, "a process of channeling, or switching, or 'gating,' of the nervous impulses so as to produce a particular disposition or set."[85]

By "classification" we shall mean a process in which on each occasion on which a certain recurring event happens it produces the same specific effect, and where the effects produced by any one kind of such events may be either the same or different from those which any other kind of event produces in a similar manner. All the different events which whenever they occur produce the same effect will be said to be events in the same class, and the fact that every one of them produces the same effect will be the *sole* criterion which makes them members of the same class.[86]

Thus two events are the same just in case they trigger the same neuronal configuration. The central nervous system, then, takes what we might think of as an undifferentiated world and, via the connections in the neuronal network, creates a formal structure of classes of sensations.[87] But this is to say that the mind is rule governed: the neuronal connections constitute perceptions of patterns. In a fundamental sense the mind *is* a set of rules that takes sensory inputs and yields perceptions. It is important to understand here that Hayek refuses to identify mind and consciousness. In fact – and this gives a contemporary flavor to his theory – Hayek advances a somewhat deflationary theory of consciousness.[88] Consciousness – "higher mental processes" – operates on the same connectionist principles as unconscious or pre-conscious mentality; both are defined by the relevant neural networks.

Some might wonder how this analysis of the formation of sensory *experience* (inputs) could be relevant to *action* (outputs). (Our concern, it will be remembered, is learning action-guiding rules.) Hayek has no real problems here, as his theory denies any fundamental distinction between the neural basis of sensation and output or "motor behavior." Action also follows from neural connections and so human action is inherently rule based: it is regulated by a network that is based on classification of types of sensation and how they relate to types of responses. Practical rules identify "patterns of actions" that are classified as having the same meaning; the activation of such rules disposes the agent to act.[89] And, again, because so much mental life is unconscious, we can see how Hayek is led to his famous claim of the fundamental importance of unconscious rule following (third section, above): rule following involves dispositions to act. It is mistaken, however, to see this as evidence of behaviorism.[90] As Hayek points out, although his theory concurs with the behaviorist claim that psychology must not focus (solely) on the conscious, unlike behaviorism, he makes no effort to avoid the mental: quite the contrary – his entire theory of rule following is based on an analysis of the mental, albeit a conception of the mental that has a large role for the unconscious.[91] To learn a social rule, then, is to form a neural network uniting a pattern of inputs with a pattern of output behaviors.

(2) *Learning.* Neural network theories, including Hayek's, place great stress on learning: the connections and attendant weights that form the network are shaped and reinforced by the environment – the stimuli that the agent encounters.[92] The mind can be understood as a map of the world. The particular environment in which the mind

has been formed shapes the neural connections that form the map.[93] Thus we can say that "the apparatus by which we learn about the external world is itself the product of a kind of experience."[94] This sheds light on Hayek's often-quoted remark that reason not only shapes culture, but is shaped by it.[95] To be a reasoning creature is to have neural networks of a certain complexity; our environment is crucial in shaping the networks, forging pathways through repeated experiences that give rise to a pattern of connections. Given this, we can see how social rules have high, but not perfect, fidelity. They have high fidelity because we are not simply imitating the behavior of others, trying to copy their products (recall the discussion from the third section). Rather, our similar environment impresses on us similar maps of the world, which include similar perceptions of instances as "the same" and similar types of actions as "the same" response. In a fundamental sense, we have similar sets of instructions – neural networks. However, these are by no means identical:

The different maps which will thus be formed in different brains will be determined by factors which are sufficiently similar to make those maps also similar to each other. But they will not be identical. Complete identity of maps would presuppose not only an identical history of the different individuals but also complete identity in their anatomical structure. The mere fact that for each individual the map will be subject to constant changes practically precludes the possibility that at any moment the maps of two individuals should be completely identical.[96]

We can see how, on such an account, the evolution of the order of actions, which can yield new rules, can lead to corresponding changes in mind. Thus "cultural selection ... creates reason."[97] The evolution of society is the driving force behind the *evolution* of mind. This is not to say that the mind is passive: we have seen how individuals are sources of variation and changes in rules. We might say that the development of the mind "feeds back" into the further evolution of culture. It is hard to see in Hayek's writings, however, a case for the mind as evolving independently from culture (i.e. via an independent selection mechanism). Thus *"the brain is an organ enabling us to absorb ... culture."*[98]

(3) *Decentralization*. It should be obvious that neural network theories are decentralized accounts of the mind: the mind *is* the entirety of neural networks – the complex of relations.[99] It is important that

Hayek conceives of intelligence itself as decentralized in a complex network. Consequently, his famous analysis of the rules of society as possessing "much more 'intelligence'" than do people's thoughts about their world[100] is entirely at one with his analysis of reason. Reasoned mental life itself is not subject to a central controller but is dispersed throughout a system of rules.

(4) *Complexity again.* The mind itself is another example of a complex phenomenon, about which we can only give explanations in principle.[101] Again, we see the importance of the theory of complex phenomena, which informs his account not only of society, but of the mind itself. Hayek advances an additional argument that the mind can never fully understand itself. Any modeling of an X, Hayek argues, must employ neural networks that are not a part of X: the model operates on X by employing additional mental processes that model X. But this means that our mind can never form a complete model of itself, since any model must employ mental processes outside the thing modeled, which we cannot do in respect to our own mind. Moreover, because Hayek advocates a mental holism, in which mental states depend on the total activated neural networks, we cannot even form an adequate model of part of the mind.[102] Thus he concludes that "the whole idea of the mind explaining itself is a logical contradiction – nonsense in the literal meaning of the word."[103] However, this limit on self-understanding would not preclude us from building artificial intelligence systems as complex, or even more complex, than our own mind, since there would be no self-subsuming modeling involved.[104]

CONCLUSION: MISUNDERSTANDING AND UNDERSTANDING HAYEK

I have tried to show how Hayek's work is a sophisticated (and was often path-breaking) system of ideas involving complexity, prediction, evolution, and the nature of the mind. In light of these, I think we can see how the standard criticisms of Hayek's theory of social evolution are misconceived.

It is sometimes claimed that Hayek's thought is, at bottom, contradictory: he insists on our ignorance of social processes but, out of his analysis of ignorance, he generates prescriptions about what we should do.[105] If we know enough to say why socialism won't work, then we must have good enough insights into the economic order to intervene to promote social goals. This, though, is wrong. As we have seen, Hayek believes that we can know quite a lot about the principles on which complex orders operate, and this theoretical knowledge allows us to say that some system states cannot be achieved and that some ways of organizing social cooperation are more efficient than others; we also know that we are unable to predict the course of, or control, the complex order itself. Thus the analysis of complexity provides sound reasons against planning – seeking to control the emergent order. There is nothing contradictory about a mix of knowledge of principle and ignorance of what is a good plan or optimal policy.

Others believe that Hayek must be a rigid traditionalist, since given his evolutionary account no one has grounds for objecting to the rules of one's own society.[106] We have seen that Hayek certainly provides grounds for taking the existing norms of society seriously. This is not only because they have been selected in the competition between orders of actions, but because they form a network of actions producing an order that we cannot fully understand. Hayek's main claims, though, are (a) that we cannot devise a reasonable plan to reform our rules *in order to develop a better order of actions*, and (b) because we cannot fully understand our system of rules, we will be largely in the dark about the overall effects of any change, so we often act in ignorance of the most important consequences.[107] Complexity theory teaches us that we do not have good grounds for fine-grained predictions. The analysis of the economy as a complex phenomenon generates a strong presumption against claims of the expediency of change. None of this, however, shows that individuals must display rigid adherence to existing rules.[108] Hayek's endogenous selection mechanism requires that individuals sometimes abandon rules and do things in new ways. Although he is much more suspicious of centralized coercive changes of rules (e.g. legislation), there is no theoretical reason why changes in response to proximate (i.e. non-systemic) concerns should be barred.

More subtly, others question whether there is any good reason to take the outcome of social evolution as having any normative importance for us.[109] Even if it is a fact that our society evolved such rules in competition with other social orders, it does not follow that they are morally good rules. In evaluating this important criticism we must remember that on Hayek's view, cultural evolution shapes our understanding of reason, morality, and our values. It is not as if we have access to an Archimedean perspective from which we can evaluate *in toto* our evolved morality.[110] Mind cannot stand outside the order of actions. It is in this sense that we cannot justify our entire morality.[111] We can employ part of our morality to criticize other elements, but this is not to stand back and criticize the outcome of evolution – it is to employ the outcome. Moreover, given Hayek's holist account of the mind and the order of actions, any proposal to give one element of our traditional morality absolute supremacy and so remake the rest of society on the basis of it alone must involve misunderstanding the rule, whose importance and meaning depend on being embedded in an overall pattern of rules and actions.[112]

My aim has not been to correct all the misunderstandings of Hayek's account of social evolution – that could become one's life work. Rather, I have tried to show in this chapter how Hayek offers a system of sophisticated and complex analyses. Because the theories of complexity, spontaneous order, evolution, mind, and rule following form their own complex pattern, commentators are apt to focus on just one or two elements which, not too surprisingly, they find inadequate. It is only when we appreciate the genius of Hayek's linking of complexity theory, spontaneous ordering, social evolution, and neural networks into an overall account of mind and human society that we will be, finally, in a position to see the true difficulties of his system of ideas, and move beyond, by building on, his great work.

NOTES

1. John Gray (1998) recognizes the systematic character of Hayek's thought.
2. Hayek 1967a, p. 77; in [1967] 1978, p. 250, Hayek writes of "the twin ideas of evolution and of the spontaneous formation of an order." See also Hayek 1973, pp. 23, 158. In Hayek 1988, p. 146, he writes of "the twin concepts of the formation of spontaneous orders and selective evolution."
3. For doubts about their connection see Paul 1988; Hodgson 1993, pp. 177ff. Vanberg (1994, p. 78) agrees that the two ideas are intimately related. See also Kukathas 1989, pp. 88ff.
4. Hayek 1988, p. 146.
5. Caldwell (2004a, p. 363) correctly argues that Hayek never developed a full-fledged theory of complexity. Hayek's writings did, however, display many of the ideas that were later crystallized into complexity theory. J. Barkley Rosser, Jr.'s observation seems more accurate:

"Hayek . . . was an early and independent developer of complexity theory in something resembling its current form, albeit without computers" (1999, p. 185n.).

6. Hayek [1964] 1967, pp. 23–24; Hayek [1975] 1978, pp. 26–27; Hayek 1988, p. 148.
7. Hayek [1975] 1978, pp. 26–27.
8. Hayek [1964] 1967, p. 26. Note deleted.
9. Waldrop 1992, pp. 81–83.
10. Hayek [1964] 1967, pp. 24ff.
11. This is the so-called "butterfly" effect. See Smith 1998, p. 16.
12. Hayek [1964] 1967, p. 27.
13. Hayek 1973, p. 63.
14. Hayek [1945] 1948, p. 87.
15. Hayek [1975] 1978, p. 27. This is identified as an element of contemporary economic analyses of complexity by Rosser (1999, p. 176).
16. Rosser 1999, p. 176.
17. Hayek 1948b, p. 101.
18. Rosser 1999, p. 176.
19. Hayek [1945] 1948, p. 77. As Kukathas (1989, p. 57) points out, in comparison to von Mises, Hayek's critique of socialism is not so much that in the absence of a market prices could not be calculated, but that in the absence of a market the necessary information to determine prices could not be collected.
20. Hayek [1955] 1967, p. 8.
21. Vaughn 1999, p. 245.
22. Hayek [1955] 1967, p. 11; Hayek [1964] 1967.
23. Hayek 1952a, p. 43.
24. Hayek 1967a.
25. Hayek 1967a, p. 68.
26. Hayek 1967a, p. 68.
27. Khalil 1996, p. 194.
28. I put aside here the debate among Hayek scholars whether this is consistent with Hayek's methodological individualism. See Vanberg 1994, ch. 5; Hodgson 1993, pp. 156ff.; Witt 1994, p. 185; Gray 1998, pp. 52–53; Khalil 1996, pp. 191ff. I think Caldwell (2004a, pp. 281ff) is right that Hayek's version of methodological individualism is complicated: given his theory of complexity, the properties of wholes cannot be reduced to the properties of individuals, though those properties result from individuals in relations.
29. Hayek [1955] 1967, pp. 14ff.
30. Hayek 1967a, p. 72. I think it is a mistake to distinguish the market order from the social order of actions; as Hayek suggests, all cooperation is economic. Hayek 1960, p. 35. Cf. Hodgson 1993, p. 176.

31. Hayek 1967a, pp. 74–75.
32. See Witt 1994, pp. 181–83.
33. Hayek 1960, p. 59.
34. Hayek [1964] 1967, pp. 31ff.
35. Blackmore 1999, p. 12.
36. Hayek 1967a, p. 71.
37. Hayek 1973, pp. 2ff.
38. Hayek 1960, p. 37.
39. For doubts, see Hodgson 1993, pp. 164ff. I believe that Hodgson's doubts are based on his misunderstanding of Hayek's account of rationality, which I take up in the fourth section, below.
40. On Hayek's supposed functionalism, see Vanberg 1994, p. 84; Hodgson 1993, pp. 168, 171; see also Gray 1998, pp. 44ff., 137ff. Hayek's analysis of complex phenomena, which employs systems theory, may strike some as functionalist. See Hayek [1955] 1967, p. 20; Hayek 1988, p. 28.
41. Hayek 1973, p. 9.
42. Hayek 1988, pp. 23ff.; Hayek 1973, p. 22.
43. Hayek 1988, p. 26.
44. Hayek 1988, pp. 23ff. For interpretations of Hayek as a social Darwinist, see Paul 1988; Miller 1989a. Those who reject this view include Whitman 1988; Hodgson 1993, pp. 161–62.
45. Hayek 1973, p. 9.
46. Hayek 1973, p. 18. See also Hayek 1988, p. 25.
47. See Vanberg 1994, ch. 5; Hodgson 1993, pp. 170ff; Witt 1994, p. 184; Whitman 1988.
48. Hayek 1967a, p. 72.
49. A crucial question is whether the prisoner's dilemma is really the proper model for understanding cooperation. There is also a question about whether we should model individuals in terms of their best (self-interested) move in response to others or, as Hayek himself suggests, whether we should suppose that individuals imitate the successful. The analysis of the evolution of cooperation is dependent on these issues. See Skyrms 1996; Skyrms 2004.
50. Hayek 1967a, p. 72.
51. See Hayek [1964] 1967. See the fourth section, below.
52. Hayek 1952a, p. 91.
53. Hayek 1973, p. 17.
54. Hayek 1967a, p. 72. Thus Hayek (1960, p. 63) argues that morality is a presupposition of reason.
55. Hayek 1967a, p. 72.
56. Kurt Baier (1995) has recently provided a philosophical account of the social roots of reasoning that leads to some similar conclusions.

57. Hayek 1988, p. 6. See also Hayek 1973, pp. 3, 17.
58. Hayek 1988, p. 43.
59. Hayek 1979, p. 159.
60. Caldwell 2004a, pp. 361ff.
61. Hayek 1979, p. 156.
62. For simplicity's sake I assume, counterfactually, that each trait of the organism is produced by a distinct gene.
63. Hayek 1973, p. 11. Emphasis added.
64. Hayek 1960, p. 37. Emphasis added.
65. Hayek 1988, p. 23. Emphasis added.
66. Hayek 1960, p. 63. This seems to conflict with his insistence on inviolable rules in *Rules and Order* (1973, p. 57). But in the passage quoted in the text, Hayek is concerned with individual violation; collective and coercive violation by the state, he goes on to say, is not permissible.
67. Hayek 1979, p. 161.
68. For a useful account, see Blackmore 1999, ch. 2.
69. Hayek 1988, ch. 3.
70. Hayek 1988, p. 25.
71. Hayek 1979, p. 157.
72. See Blackmore 1999, pp. 61–62.
73. Blackmore 1999, p. 61.
74. Hayek 1973, p. 74.
75. Hayek [1964] 1967, p. 56.
76. Hayek 1973, p. 43.
77. Pinker 2002, p. 292.
78. See Pinker 1999, p. 113; Gärdenfors 2004, p. 40; Hayek 1952b, p. 151.
79. D. Dellarosa quoted in Gärdenfors 2004, p. 41.
80. Hayek 1952b, p. 57.
81. Gärdenfors 2004, p. 41. Emphasis in original.
82. On this see Pinker 1997, pp. 112ff; Gärdenfors 2004, pp. 40ff.
83. Hayek insisted on the link to his social theory. See Hayek 1952b, p. v.
84. Hayek 1952b, p. 7.
85. Hayek [1964] 1967, p. 51.
86. Hayek 1952b, p. 48.
87. Hayek 1952b, p. 51.
88. Hayek 1952b, ch. 6. Compare Pinker 1999, pp. 131ff.
89. Hayek [1964] 1967, p. 57.
90. As does Hodgson 1993, p. 165.
91. Hayek 1952b, pp. 23ff.
92. Hayek 1952b, p. 64.
93. Hayek 1952b, p. 108.
94. Hayek 1952b, p. 165.

95. Hayek 1979, p. 155.
96. Hayek 1952b, p. 110.
97. Hayek 1979, p. 166.
98. Hayek 1979, p. 157. Emphasis in original.
99. Hayek 1952b, p. 35.
100. Hayek 1979, p. 157.
101. Hayek 1952b, pp. 19, 43ff., 185ff.
102. Hayek 1952b, p. 190.
103. Hayek 1952b, p. 192.
104. Hayek 1952b, p. 189.
105. See Hodgson 1993, p. 183.
106. See Paul 1988, p. 258.
107. Hayek 1973, p. 57.
108. Although one should rigidly adhere to the system as a whole. Hayek [1965] 1967, p. 91.
109. See O'Hear 1997, pp. 146ff.
110. Hayek 1988, p. 8.
111. Hayek 1988, pp. 60ff.
112. Hayek 1967a, p. 71; Hayek 1960, p. 63.

13 Hayek on justice and the order of actions

INTRODUCTION

In this chapter I provide a constructive account of F. A. Hayek's views on justice.[1] Hayek does not have a thoroughly developed and persuasive theory of justice. (Who does?) Nevertheless, I hope to show that Hayek has interesting and illuminating things to say about justice – especially about the justification of the rules of just conduct – and that his views about justice play a more central role in his evolved teaching than has generally been recognized. The rules of just conduct are essentially the fundamental norms compliance with which generates peaceful coexistence and mutually beneficial coordination in large-scale pluralistic societies in which (almost) every individual comes into contact with and interacts with many individuals who are unlike himself in circumstances, knowledge, skills, preferences, and personal codes of value.[2] Although the particular articulation of these norms will vary with time and place, they are essentially general prohibitions against trespass on persons and their liberty and property and against violations of persons' contractual rights. I shall maintain that Hayek rejects anything that can appropriately be called a utilitarian vindication of these norms and proposes an alternative teleological (but non-utilitarian) justification for rules of just conduct. I do not claim that everything that Hayek says about justice and the rules of just conduct fits into the specific account that I shall offer.

I shall take Hayek's three-volume work, *Law, Legislation, and Liberty* (1973; 1976b; 1979) as my primary text. This work is Hayek's culminating pronouncement in social and legal theory,[3] and the first two volumes of this work, *Rules and Order* (RO) and *The Mirage of*

Social Justice (MSJ), together provide Hayek's most sustained examination of the rules of just conduct and their possible rationales. We should note at the outset that the general subtitle of *Law, Legislation, and Liberty* is, *A New Statement of the Liberal Principles of Justice and Political Economy*. Since these volumes do not even attempt to provide a new statement of principles of political economy, the point of the subtitle must be that *Law, Legislation, and Liberty* offers a new statement of liberal principles of justice. Hayek says as much in his general introduction. He there characterizes his project as a new effort to ground liberal constitutionalism. This effort must overcome the problems to which past liberal constitutionalism has succumbed; and the most fundamental reason for the unraveling of past liberal constitutionalism has been "the loss of belief in a justice independent of personal interest" (RO, p. 2). So any new effort must center on a new vindicating statement of liberal principles of justice. This new statement, I maintain, turns upon the identification of a special justifying telos for the rules of just conduct, namely, the abstract order of actions that will be manifested in some particular but unpredictable way whenever there is general compliance with those rules. This abstract order of actions is the pattern or structure of peaceful coexistence and cooperative interaction that respect for these rules facilitates. This "guiding conception of the overall order to be aimed at is ... not only the indispensable precondition of any rational policy, but also the chief contribution that science can make to the solution of the problems of practical policy" (RO, p. 65).

I will proceed as follows: in the second section, I recount some of Hayek's basic insights about social order and law. According to Hayek, the "great tragedy of our time" has been the "destruction of values by scientific error" – especially social-scientific error about the nature of social order and law. This "scientific error tends to dethrone" the values which are "the indispensable foundation of all our civilization" (RO, pp. 6–7); but the correction of this error will re-enthrone these vital values. In the third section, I distinguish among various forms of utilitarian justifications for rules of just conduct and distinguish between all utilitarian justifications and non-utilitarian teleological (telic) justification. Employing these distinctions on Hayek's behalf, I argue in the fourth section that he rejects *all* types of utilitarian justification and moves instead to a quite different telic justification of those norms. In the fifth section, I further describe this telic justification, especially the telos that corrected social science establishes as the rational end of social norms and their enforcement.

THE GREAT SOCIETY VERSUS THE DESIGNED SOCIETY

We need to begin by considering briefly Hayek's understanding of the liberal individualist order that has arisen in the west in the modern era and of the structure of rules that is indispensable to this social order. The liberal individualist order, which Hayek calls the "Great Society," is an immensely complex network of highly variegated interactions and relationships among individuals and the associations that individuals form in the pursuit of their diverse goals. The complexity of this network and its capacity to advance the varied ends of those who participate in it arise from the freedom that each of its members enjoys to pursue his own ends in his own chosen way – informed by his own particular understanding of his values, circumstances, and opportunities for value-enhancing voluntary interactions with other members of society. The Great Society, therefore, is founded upon respect for individual freedom – understood as ranging over both "personal" and "economic" liberties. The legal order of the Great Society is more or less limited to the articulation and enforcement of negative general rules that prohibit each agent from infringing upon the lives, personal liberties, estates, and particular contractual claims of other individuals. Indeed, for Hayek, to be free is to live under the protection of – but, also, under the constraints of – such general rules. This freedom and this correlative abstract order of rules are the two sides of the coin which is the crucial facilitating currency for the complex and rewarding concrete social and economic order that is manifest at any given time within the Great Society.

The Great Society is composed of individuals who differ from one another in their personal values, aspirations, and commitments, in their convictions, knowledge, and beliefs, in their social and economic skills and capacities, and in their particular social and economic circumstances. Yet, remarkably, they are brought together in peaceful and mutually beneficial relationships by the articulation and enforcement of rules that – whatever their specific details – preclude gains from trespass and plunder, protect individuals in their possession and chosen use of the fruits of their invested labor, forbid violation of contractual undertakings, and protect individuals in their gains from trade and contractual interactions. Anticipation of the enforcement of such general negative norms diverts individuals from strategies of plunder (or defense against anticipated plunder) and toward strategies of production and trade. Nor are the coordinating processes that take place when individuals seek to advance their diverse ends within an environment of protective norms limited to economic decisions and outcomes. That protective framework also moves individuals to use their local information about values, preferences, and available courses of action to discover and craft accommodating social relations or at least systems of peaceful coexistence. The expectation of reciprocal compliance with basic protective norms channels individuals who are not moved by shared ultimate ends into increasingly complex cooperative interactions. The information on which the emergent order depends is scattered among the participants in the Great Society; it is not and could not be possessed in synoptic form by any agent who might seek more directly to impose a comprehensive cooperative scheme upon these individuals. The overall factual order that arises from this intricate coordinating process is an unintended, non-designed, "spontaneous" order. While we can, according to Hayek, predict that some such spontaneous factual order will arise under an order of protective general norms, we cannot predict the particulars of this order. For we will not know the particular circumstances or particular perceptions of circumstances within which those many individuals will deliberate and act; and we would not know what decisions they will reach and how they will act even if we did know their particular (perceived) circumstances. For similar reasons, we cannot predict the consequences of interventions that are intended to achieve some specific concrete result within a spontaneous order.

Hayek contrasts spontaneous social order with designed social order, i.e., organization. In a fully designed social order, all the actions of the members of the order are directed toward and are to be assessed in terms of the achievement of that organization's purpose. So, each member of a fully organized firm or military force will and should perform the specific action which, in conjunction with

the specific actions performed by other members, maximally pro-
motes that firm's or army's end. The whole point of an organization
is to coordinate individuals to some common end by means of
instructions issued by the chief executive or commander to each
member about what his assigned role is. Of course, almost no actual
organization is fully organized. For it is almost always recognized
that particular members may better serve the organization's ends if
they retain some discretion to act on the basis of their own local
information and initiative. Nevertheless, the distinctive feature of
organization is that it marshals its human (and non-human) resources into a common enterprise directed as far as is thought possible by
the synoptic vision of the enterprise's leaders. A designed society
mobilizes its human (and non-human) resources toward the achievement of its (presumed) end or hierarchy of ends. The characteristic
law of an organized society will be a body of commands issued by the
sovereign authority directing each member of society to do his or her
part in the joint promotion of that society's (or sovereign's) purpose
or hierarchy of purposes. In contrast, a spontaneous social order has
no end or purpose of its own; it is a structure and a process that
facilitates the pursuit by individuals of their diverse ends and
commitments.

A great deal of Hayek's message is simply that a well-ordered
society exhibiting rational coordination among its members need
not be a designed and commanded order. Freedom and the choices
of free individuals can also be the source of rational coordination.
Indeed, a well-ordered society that is complex and pluralist *cannot* be
a designed and commanded order. Once one escapes from the grip of
the idea that coordination requires organization, one sees how much
more an environment of general protective rules expedites cooperation than does design and its associated directives. Organizations
will, however, be prominent among the associations that individuals
will form *within* the Great Society. Salient among them will be
government, which is organized (primarily at least) for the purpose
of articulating and enforcing the general protective rules that facilitate non-designed coordination. Such a government does issue directives that guide particular individuals in accordance with a deliberate
plan to sustain a regime of rules of just conduct. However, the
individuals who are subject to and guided *by those directives* are
the employees of the government, not members of the Great Society

at large. The law that governs members of society at large remains an articulation of general and fundamentally negative rules of just conduct.

Hayek, therefore, rejects the "constructivist rationalist" view that

human institutions will serve human purposes only if they have been deliberately designed for these purposes, often also that the fact that an institution exists is evidence of its having been created for a purpose, and always that we should so re-design society and its institutions that all our actions will be wholly guided by known purposes. (RO, pp. 8–9)

The most obvious form of constructivist rationalism is the belief that the concrete social and economic order of a society must be deliberately designed if it is to be rational. However, Hayek focuses on the further constructivist contention that the abstract order of rules that facilitates concrete social order must be deliberately designed if it is to be rational. Against this further contention, Hayek emphasizes the "grown" or "evolved" character of the law that makes spontaneous concrete social order possible. Law long precedes legislation. It is not the product of human will, but rather of an evolutionary process in which groups whose members tend to "follow" rules that facilitate intramural peace and cooperation are more apt to survive, expand, and be imitated than groups whose members have not stumbled onto such rules. Only gradually do individuals even perceive themselves as following rules, and only gradually are these rules articulated. Even when those rules are articulated and codified, they are perceived as discovered norms of conduct – as *laws* – the normative force of which does not derive from their being expressed or enforced by some political agency.

UTILITARIAN VERSUS NON-UTILITARIAN TELEOLOGICAL JUSTIFICATION

As Hayek portrays it, constructivist rationalism does not merely hold that only deliberately designed concrete factual orders and abstract normative orders are rational. It also demands that concrete social orders and abstract orders of norms be subjected to critical scrutiny *and* that there be a rational "demonstration" of their justification. Constructivist rationalism demands that "the traditional rules of morals and law" be subjected to critical scrutiny and that we

refuse "to recognize as binding any rules of conduct whose justification [has] not been rationally demonstrated" (RO, p. 25). According
to Hayek, this demand for demonstrative vindication, like the belief
that the deliberate use and only the deliberate use of reason can
generate a well-ordered society, embodies an overestimation of the
power of reason. In fact, Hayek appears at times to reject entirely the
enterprise of justifying fundamental social norms. For he seems to
say that it is a fundamental problem with constructivist rationalism
that it seeks to determine whether rules are "rationally justified"
(RO, p. 25).[4] Nevertheless, this cannot be Hayek's position. Although
we may be nostalgic for an era in which principles were held "as no
more than unreasoned prejudice," once "the instinctive certainty is
lost," there is no recourse except to an explicit vindicating restatement of those principles (RO, p. 60). No sensible person can reject a
call for the "rational examination of the appropriateness of existing
rules" (MSJ, p. 18). Hayek subscribes to Locke's claim in the *Essays on
the Law of Nature* that it is within the province of reason to search
for and discover the rules that constitute the law of nature.[5] We need,
then, to identify just what Hayek is rejecting when he rejects rationalist demonstration and what model of vindication for rules of just
conduct he embraces despite his rejection of demonstration.

This identification is made difficult by the dearth of precise terminology in Hayek for designating and distinguishing among alternative strategies for justifying rules of just conduct. In order to better
express Hayek's own stance and distinguish it from any stance that
is more naturally described as utilitarian, most of the remainder
of this section is devoted to terminological clarification. Let us
follow Hayek in using "utilitarianism" very broadly. Any doctrine
that bases its judgments about rightness in action on its judgments
about the relative value or ranking of alternative available concrete
social outcomes will count as utilitarian. Act versions of utilitarianism begin by projecting what alternative overall factual outcomes
will be engendered (or can be expected to be engendered) by each of
the actions under consideration and by ranking those alternative
outcomes on some scale of "utilitarian" value. Once we have that
ranking of anticipated overall factual outcomes, we can identify the
right action as the one that engenders (or can be expected to engender) the most highly ranked outcome. Rule versions of utilitarianism
begin by projecting the consequences of general compliance with

competing sets of principles. For each set of principles under consideration, we are to anticipate what overall concrete social order will ensue from general compliance with that set of rules. And we are to ascribe rightness to that set of rules general compliance with which will conduce to the best of these anticipated social outcomes. Particular actions will derive their rightness from their compliance with the set of rules to which rightness has thus been ascribed. We have here a broad characterization of utilitarianism, not only because it equally admits both act and rule forms, but also because this characterization does not at all limit what may be the scale of value for ranking alternative outcomes. In this broad sense, a utilitarian need not ascribe ultimate value only to pleasure or preference-satisfaction.

All of this is completely standard – except for the description of the alternative outcomes as overall *factual* orders or *concrete* social outcomes. The force of these Hayekian locutions is that the utilitarian ranking of competing outcomes is a ranking of arrays of particular factual states of affairs – a ranking of, for example, the array that would consist of A enjoying five units of pleasure and B enjoying seven units of accomplishment against the array that would consist of A enjoying four units of wisdom and B enjoying nine units of pleasure. (Or perhaps for each action or each set of rules under consideration what can be projected is some distribution of more-or-less probable resulting arrays of individual states of affairs. Then the ranking must be a ranking of something like the expected value of the overall outcomes of the contending actions or contending sets of rules.) Utilitarianism in the broad sense rests its judgment about the rightness of actions on a comparison of the value of alternative available concrete social worlds (or on a comparison of the expected value of alternative probability distributions of concrete social worlds).

Hayek tells us that there is a "wide sense" of the term "utilitarian" in which he, along with Aristotle, Aquinas, and Hume, counts as a utilitarian. "In this wide sense every one who does not regard all existing values as unquestionable but is prepared to ask why they should be held would be described as 'utilitarian'" (MSJ, p. 17). One might interpret Hayek here as saying that anyone who attempts *any* sort of rational vindication for rules of just conduct is a utilitarian in this wide sense. This would not quite be correct; and it would not explain Kant's absence from this list. Rather, to be a utilitarian even in this wide sense one has to seek to vindicate the rules of just conduct by identifying "the function [such rules and institutions] perform in the structure of society" (MSJ, p. 17). One needs to cite what Hayek refers to as the aim or the goal or the telos of these rules. So to be a utilitarian in this wide sense is to be an advocate of some form of teleological justification for the rules of just conduct and, thereby, for actions in accordance with those rules. Hayek's identification of the "rational examination of the appropriateness of existing rules" with inquiry into the function, aim, goal, or telos of those rules reveals his own implicit identification of all justification with teleological justification.

It should be clear that one can be a utilitarian in Hayek's wide sense without being a utilitarian in the broad sense involved in holding that the justifying aim – the telos – for the rules of just conduct or for action is the production of the best available factual social order. Since, as we shall see, Hayek rejects any vindication for actions or rules of just conduct that turns on the production of some purported best concrete social world, Hayek cannot be a utilitarian in this broad sense; he can only be a utilitarian in the wide sense that amounts to offering a justifying telos for rules of just conduct. Since, as we shall see, the justifying telos that Hayek offers for rules of just conduct is strikingly different from any justifying aim offered by utilitarianism in the broad sense just described, clarity will be served by explicitly distinguishing between utilitarianism in its broad sense and non-utilitarian teleological (or "telic") justification of rules of just conduct. Given this terminology, we can say – but still need to show – that Hayek rejects *all* utilitarian justification as being guilty of the sins of constructivist rationalism. And we can say – but still need to show – that Hayek does not reject entirely the justificatory enterprise; for he proposes a telic, but non-utilitarian, vindication of the rules of just conduct.

Although I have spoken of Hayek's appeal to the telos of rules of just conduct, Hayek himself often speaks of the rules of just conduct rather than the telos of those rules as the fundamental value that he seeks to restore. This reflects his strong interest in highlighting the importance of rules – even if they are ultimately to be vindicated by a telos that they serve. It also reflects a more strictly Kantian strand in Hayek according to which one must respect freedom and abide by rules of just conduct because to fail to do so is to treat individuals as means rather than as ends-in-themselves. "Coercion is evil precisely because it thus eliminates an individual as a thinking and valuing person and makes him a bare tool in the achievement of the ends of another" (Hayek 1960, p. 21). Still, Hayek is uncomfortable with any purely deontic doctrine; hence his pursuit of a stance that transcends standard forms of teleological vindication without abandoning the teleological intuition that rules must draw their validity from some purpose that they serve.

There is a further advantage to speaking of Hayek's project as telic but not utilitarian. For Hayek, a condition of any overall state of affairs or order being the rational end for legal rules and rule-enforcing institutions is that state of affairs or order being (at least) *ex ante* mutually advantageous. This condition is often expressed by Hayek as the condition of being rationally agreeable to all individuals. The language of telic justification more readily accommodates this mutual advantage condition than does the language of utilitarian justification. As we shall see, the abstract "order of actions" satisfies the condition of being *ex ante* mutually advantageous although no particular anticipated factual order (or distribution of possible concrete factual orders) satisfies it.

One final terminological caution is necessary. Hayek operates with only two terms to name sub-categories of teleological (in his language, "utilitarian") justification. These are "act-utilitarianism" and "rule-utilitarianism." For this reason, Hayek tends to classify whatever he rejects in the way of teleological justification as act-utilitarianism and, by paucity of sub-categories, he tends to classify whatever he accepts in the way of teleological justification as rule-utilitarianism. The result is that he often writes as though he is arguing specifically against act-utilitarianism and on behalf of rule-utilitarianism; and he is often described by commentators as an advocate of some sort of rule-utilitarianism.[6] We shall see how this description is importantly mistaken.

THE CRITIQUE OF UTILITARIAN JUSTIFICATIONS

In rejecting constructivist demonstration Hayek is most clearly and straightforwardly rejecting case-by-case determination of whether one ought to comply with a given applicable rule of conduct.

According to Hayek, such case-by-case determination, in its rationalist hubris, jettisons rather than vindicates action in accordance
with principles. This hubris is exemplified by Hans Reichenbach's
declaration that

the power of reason must be sought not in rules that reason dictates to our
imagination, but in the ability to free ourselves from any kind of rules
to which we have been conditioned through experience and traditions.
(RO, p. 23)[7]

Principles in themselves count for nothing; they are, if anything,
barriers to genuinely rational decision. Reason is directly in operation only when we determine how we should act by identifying
which available action most advances the particular ends that we
desire. Similarly, Hayek cites Keynes' account of the views that he
and youthful contemporaries embraced:

We entirely repudiated a personal liability to obey general rules. We claimed
the right to judge every individual case on its merits ... We repudiated
entirely customary morals, conventions, and traditional wisdom. We were,
that is to say, in the strict sense of term, immoralists. (RO, p. 24)[8]

As Hayek sees it, Keynes is entirely correct to say that judging every
case on its own merits leads not merely to the repudiation of general
rules but to immoralism. This is because of two converging considerations. First, the intended case-by-case assessment of available
actions turns on a ranking of the concrete factual social orders that
would respectively be engendered by those actions – the right action
being the action the results of which rank highest. Second, reason
cannot provide any such ranking of alternative factual social orders.
Thus, even if we could know what the particular results of the
various actions under consideration would be, reason could not provide an ordering of those actions. Any ranking of the available factual
orders will be an expression of non-rational will; and this non-
rational willfulness will be bequeathed to any endorsement of one
of the available actions that is based upon this willful ranking.

Not every advocate of case-by-case assessment recognizes that
this amounts to immoralism. For many such advocates have the
mistaken belief that "reason can transcend the realm of the abstract
and by itself is able to determine the desirability of particular
actions" (RO, p. 32). These advocates are under the "illusion" that

reason by itself can "tell us what we ought to do" in the sense of disclosing "common ends" that "all reasonable men ought to be able to join in the endeavor to pursue" (RO, p. 32). Indeed, the illusion is that reason discloses a formula for weighing these common ends against one another so that we can determine which array of realizations of those ends constitutes the best available factual social order. Reason is presumed to deliver a specification of one of the available factual orders as best so that "the whole of society [can be organized as] one rationally directed engine" in service of that best factual order (RO, p. 32). However, all such purported deliverances of reason are, in reality, nothing but "the decisions of particular wills" (RO, p. 32). Rationalist hubris embraces what is actually an atavistic craving for a hierarchy of common ends. Since reason cannot in fact satisfy that craving, the "over-estimation of the powers of reason leads through disillusionment to a violent reaction against the guidance of abstract reason, and to an extolling of the powers of the particular will" (RO, p. 32). "It is the over-estimation of the power of reason [to predict and know the relative value of alternative concrete social orders] that leads to the revolt against the submission to abstract rules" (RO, p. 33).

Several things should be noted here. First, although Hayek certainly thinks it is a grave error to believe that we can have knowledge or even well-justified belief about what factual order will be engendered by this or that particular action, his emphasis is not on our factual ignorance but rather on our normative ignorance. Omniscient people would be "in agreement on the relative importance of all the different ends" (MSJ, p. 8). However, as normatively ignorant beings, we lack even well-grounded beliefs about the relative importance of persons' diverse ends. To the best of my knowledge, the most extensive statement of this view appears in Hayek's very early and interesting essay, "Freedom and the Economic System":

Economic planning [for a socially best outcome] always involves the sacrifice of some ends in favour of others, a balancing of costs and results, a choice between alternative possibilities; and the decision always presupposes that all the different ends are ranged in a definite order according to their importance, an order which assigns to each objective a quantitative importance which tells us at what sacrifices of other ends it is still worth pursuing and what price would be too high ... Agreement on a particular plan requires ... for a society as a whole the same kind of complete quantitative scale of values as that which manifests itself in the decision of every individual, but on which, in an individualist society, agreement between the individuals is neither necessary nor present. (Hayek [1939] 1997, p. 201)

The ranking of alternative social outcomes

presupposes ... something which does not exist and has never existed: a complete moral code in which the relative values of all human ends, the relative importance of all the needs of different people, are assigned a definite quantitative significance. (Hayek [1939] 1997, pp. 201–2)

Constructivists say that each of these diverse ends – and not merely the various means to those ends – possess the common valuable attribute of "utility." Yet this is nothing but a futile attempt "to describe a supposedly common attribute of the different ends" that the various available means would serve and, thereby, to fulfill "the rationalist desire explicitly to derive the usefulness of means from known ultimate ends," i.e., from the utility and, hence, the value of known ultimate ends. But distinct important human ends do not have "a measurable common attribute" (MSJ, p. 18). And it is clear that Hayek means both that there is no common descriptive attribute and that there is no common sort of *value* that attaches to these different ends. The value of instantiations of one sort of ultimate human end is not commensurable with the value that attaches to instantiations of any other sort of ultimate human end. A crucial part of what is wrong with case-by-case assessment of actions is not so much its case-by-caseness, i.e., its *act*-utilitarian character, but, rather, its reliance upon rankings of alternative overall factual social orders. And a crucial part of what is wrong with reliance upon such rankings is our lack of the normative information necessary to justify such rankings.[9]

The second point to be noted is that the passages we have just surveyed reflect a central and constant polarity within Hayek's worldview between, on the one hand, reason, science, and the abstract and, on the other hand, will, ignorance, and the particular. For Hayek, scientific knowledge is fundamentally knowledge of the abstract; it is knowledge of lawful general relationships. "Evolutionary [i.e., Hayekian] rationalism ... recognizes abstractions as the indispensable means of the mind which enable it to deal with a reality it cannot fully comprehend" (RO, p. 30). The evolution of mind and rationality *is* the evolution of our propensity to act in accordance with the abstract – which includes both our propensity to recognize general lawful relationships and our propensity to abide by rules (RO, pp. 17–21, 29–31). The evolution of rationality in action as much involves an orientation toward the abstract – in the form of an evolution of our disposition to abide by general rules – as does the evolution of rationality in belief. Man is, of course, a "purpose-seeking" animal. Nevertheless, he is "as much a rule-following animal" (RO, p. 11). And his rationality as an acting being is tied to the rule-following, abstract-oriented dimension of his behavior. To be a reasonable man is to be disposed to recognize and acknowledge the directive force of the "rules which have by a process of selection been evolved in the society in which he lives" (RO, p. 11).[10] In contrast, particular states of the world are not the objects of scientific knowledge – though, of course, various individuals are acquainted with certain particular states of the world. Furthermore, particular outcomes – whether they be local factual outcomes for this or that individual or overall concrete social orders – are not the objects of rational action. In their particularity, such factual states can only be the objects of non-rational will. This polarity suggests that Hayek must hold that rational action is simply action in accordance with certain abstract rules – unless he can identify an *abstract end* that will serve as a justifying telos for those rules. As we shall see, for Hayek, the "order of actions" that is engendered by compliance with the rules of just conduct is the end that satisfies this abstractness condition.

The third point to be noted is that the basic reasons that Hayek offers against case-by-case, act-utilitarian determination of whether an individual should comply with an applicable rule applies also to rule-utilitarian proposals about the vindication of rule-abiding conduct. Both normative ignorance about our common ends and factual ignorance about what concrete social order will be engendered by our decisions and conduct cut as deeply against rule-utilitarian justifications as they cut against act-utilitarian justifications. This is especially clear if we understand rule-utilitarianism as it was explicated in the previous section, namely, as the doctrine that begins assessment of actions by ranking the concrete social outcomes of general compliance with contending sets of rules and goes on to ascribe rightness to actions that comply with the optimizing set of principles. I shall designate this as "rule-utilitarianism proper." Rule-utilitarianism proper accommodates the deontic intuition that an action can be and be known to be productive of the best available overall outcome while also being and being known to be wrong. It accommodates this intuition by insisting that such an optimizing action will be wrong if it violates a rule that is within the set of optimizing rules and will be known to be wrong if that set of rules is known to be the optimizing set. This insistence is, of course, what inspires the recurrent charge of rule worship.

Whether or not the rule-utilitarian proper has an answer to this charge, it should be clear that she presumes both the factual and the normative knowledge that Hayek denies. Just as the act-utilitarian believes he can predict what factual orders will result respectively from particular actions, the rule-utilitarian proper believes that she can predict what factual orders will result respectively from general compliance with specific sets of rules. Moreover, just as the act-utilitarian believes he can rationally rank predictable factual orders, the rule-utilitarian proper believes that she has knowledge of our common ends that enables her to rank predictable factual orders. Hayek himself provides a remarkably explicit statement of this defect within rule-utilitarianism proper:

Nor can the choice of the appropriate set of rules be guided by balancing for each of the alternative set of rules considered the particular predictable favourable effects against the particular unfavourable effects, and then selecting the set of rules for which the positive net result is greatest; for most of the effects on particular persons of adopting one set of rules rather than another are not predictable. (MSJ, p. 3)

Of course, the predictions of either sort of utilitarian may be merely probabilistic. For each action under consideration, the act-utilitarian may merely (!) attempt to ascertain the probabilities of its engendering various possible overall factual outcomes. Similarly, for each set of rules under consideration, the rule-utilitarian proper may merely (!) attempt to ascertain the probabilities that general compliance with those rules will eventuate in various possible overall factual outcomes. But these parallel attempts at probabilistic predictions will meet with parallel failure in virtue of the factual ignorance on which Hayek insists. Neither for the act-utilitarian nor for the rule-utilitarian proper does a shift to assessment based upon assignments of probabilities circumvent dependence upon information that is unavailable to the assessor. Moreover, even if the rule-utilitarian proper could justifiably assign probabilities to the relevant possible outcomes, her normative ignorance of our common ends and how they are to be weighed against one another would leave her equally unable to choose rationally between the contending sets of rules:

> Among the members of a Great Society, who mostly do not know each other, there will exist no agreement on the relative importance of their respective ends. There would exist not harmony but open conflict of interests if agreement were necessary as to which particular interests should be given preference over others. (MSJ, p. 3)

This divergence in the weighting of different interests is not subject to rational resolution – because we are ignorant of the relative value of distinct important human ends.

I have spoken of rule-utilitarianism *proper* in anticipation of discussing another doctrine that is usually taken to be a version of rule-utilitarianism, namely, "indirect utilitarianism." The crux of indirect utilitarianism is a Hayekian-sounding appreciation for the fallibility and unprofitable costs of case-by-case assessment of contending actions. Case-by-case assessment is taken to be much more fallible and costly than assessment on the basis of standing norms of commonsense morality. Of course, any act-utilitarian can recognize that these standard norms are helpful rules of thumb and that it will often be better to follow them than to enter into potentially self-deceived or self-serving case-by-case calculations. What makes one an indirect utilitarian is the conviction that case-by-case decisions are so characteristically fallible and costly that it is always – except, perhaps, for very narrowly defined circumstances – more expeditious in terms of actual or expected concrete outcomes to abide by the applicable standard norm rather than to seek to judge each case on its own apparent merits. Except perhaps under those very narrowly defined circumstances, action in conformity to the applicable commonsense norm is the best bet for realizing that "supposedly common [valuable] attribute of the different ends."[11] Within indirect utilitarianism, then, the standard utilitarian goal of engendering the best overall factual order or the best probability distribution of overall factual orders remains in place and is merely supplemented with the comforting, but highly speculative and implausible, view that action in accordance with standard norms is (almost) always our best bet for achieving this end. Indirect utilitarianism is, then, subject to the same basic criticisms that Hayek advances against act-utilitarianism. For it is committed to factual judgments about the likelihood that particular actions will yield particular concrete results and to normative judgments about the ranking of alternative distributions of possible concrete results that presume a factual and normative knowledge that Hayek denies.

In his most extended discussion of utilitarianism in *Law, Legislation, and Liberty* (MSJ, pp. 17–23), Hayek does not appreciate the large remaining gap between indirect utilitarianism and his own position. For he thinks that those who abandon the naive act-utilitarianism that justifies actions on the basis of (presumed) knowledge about what concrete results those actions will have, fully assimilate the lessons of Hayekian ignorance. He believes that these "utilitarians" thereby become intellectually "bound to assume the existence of rules not accountable for by utilitarian considerations and thus must abandon the claim that the whole system of moral rules can be derived from their known utility" (MSJ, p. 19). But, while it is true that indirect utilitarianism abandons the naive claim that the whole system of moral rules can be derived from their *known* utility, it is not true that this doctrine is bound to assume the existence of rules not accountable for by utilitarian considerations. Indeed, as I have indicated, it rests on its own highly speculative and contentious claims about the likely concrete outcomes of rule-compliant actions.

We can further see the distance between Hayek's own view and indirect utilitarianism by examining Hayek's contentions in the pivotal chapter on "Principles and Expediency" in RO. Hayek there seems to offer an indirect utilitarian case for abiding by freedom-protecting principles even when it appears that violation of those principles will procure particular benefits. The problem with deciding "each issue solely on what appear to be its individual merits" (RO, p. 57) is that the gain from the violations of a rule that is protective of freedom will almost always be more apparent and vivid than the opportunity costs of the violation. We will usually have the problem that the infringement on freedom is intended to solve directly before us (and will believe that, if we really intend to solve the problem, it will be solved), while we will hardly ever see what problem-solving activities individuals would have engaged in had their freedom not been restricted:

Since the value of freedom rests on the opportunities it provides for unforeseen and unpredictable actions, we will rarely know what we lose through a particular restriction of freedom. Any such restriction, any coercion other than the enforcement of general rules, will aim at the achievement of some foreseeable particular result, but what is prevented by it will usually not be known. (RO, pp. 56–57)

For this reason, "If the choice between freedom and coercion is thus treated as a matter of expediency, freedom is bound to be sacrificed in almost every instance" (RO, p. 57). From the point of view of expediency, one wants not to make decisions on particular issues on the basis of expediency. But it is, I believe, Hayek's view that, if expediency is the only reason one has not to decide particular issues on the grounds of expediency, one will not resist the siren call of expediency in particular cases. For, in the face of apparently great net gains through the violation of freedom-protecting norms, one will not be able to say to oneself that one ought to respect freedom *as a matter of principle*:

The preservation of a free system is so difficult precisely because it requires a constant rejection of measures which appear to be required to secure particular results, on no stronger grounds than that they conflict with a general rule, and frequently without our knowing what will be the costs of not observing the rule in the particular instance. (RO, p. 61)

Somewhat paradoxically, although expediency is a basis for wanting strict compliance with freedom-protecting principles, one will not get that compliance and that expediency if one's fundamental aim is the achievement of the expedient. This is why Hayek follows the passage just cited with the conclusion that, "A successful defence of freedom must therefore be dogmatic ... Freedom will prevail only if it is accepted as a general principle whose application to particular instances requires no justification" (RO, p. 61). Freedom and the greater advantages it brings "can be preserved only if it is treated as a supreme principle which must not be sacrificed for particular advantage" (RO, p. 57). Any appeal to expediency – including the indirect utilitarian appeal – undermines the standing of principles as principles. The recognition that expediency would be served by belief in principles as principles does not itself generate or sustain such belief.[12]

We need belief in certain "general values whose conduciveness to particular desirable results cannot be demonstrated" (RO, p. 58). Once useful "unreasoned prejudice" on behalf of such principles is lost, a vindicating restatement of those principles is needed. Such a statement must point to some overall aim to which compliance with rules of just conduct is *always* conducive. But it is not possible to show as a matter of empirical fact that compliance with a given set of norms is always conducive to any particular overall factual outcome or even to any distribution of possible overall factual outcomes. And even if this could be shown, it could not be shown that this factual outcome or anticipated distribution of possible factual outcomes is the concrete outcome or anticipated distribution of possible concrete outcomes that ought to be promoted. Hayek's commitment to the teleological character of the justification of fundamental principles requires, then, that there be *something* to which compliance with those principles is always conducive; but his insistence on our factual and normative ignorance precludes that something being any best overall factual order or any best anticipated distribution of possible overall orders. What Hayek needs, therefore, is something *between* the abstract order of norms that he seeks to vindicate and the overall factual orders or distributions of possible factual orders to which all species of utilitarian vindication appeal. He needs a telos for rules of just conduct that stands between those rules and the unpredictable and unrankable arrays of concrete outcomes that compliance with those rules might engender. This telos cannot itself be a distinct concrete factual order (or distribution of possible concrete factual orders), and it must be *non-contingently* connected with compliance with those rules so that we can know that compliance will *always* (tend to) sustain or promote that telos.

NON-UTILITARIAN TELIC JUSTIFICATION

So what is the proposed telos? As anticipated in the introductory section, it is the structure or pattern of peaceful coexistence and mutually advantageous coordination among the highly diverse members of a large-scale and pluralist society that will obtain in some concrete but largely unpredictable manifestation when there is general compliance with rules of just conduct.[13] "[T]he general rules of law that a spontaneous order rests on *aim at* an abstract order, the particular or concrete content of which is not known or foreseen by anyone" (RO, p. 50, emphasis added). Constructivist rationalism calls upon us "to reject all general values whose conduciveness to particular desirable results cannot be demonstrated" (RO, p. 58). However, this turns out to be a recipe for the rejection of all general values, i.e., all principles. Hayek's innovative proposal is not to reject demonstrable conduciveness to desirable results as the grounding of general principles but, rather, to reject conduciveness to *particular* concrete results. Independently it makes sense to turn away from particular results because the particular is not within the purview of scientific knowledge or practical rationality:

What helpful insight science can provide for the guidance of policy consists in an understanding of the general nature of the spontaneous order, and not in any knowledge of the particulars of a concrete situation, which it does not and cannot possess ... The only theory which in this field can lay claim to scientific status is the theory of the order as a whole; and such a theory (although it has, of course, to be tested on the facts) can never be achieved inductively by observation but only through constructing mental models made up of observable elements. (RO, pp. 63–64)

A social scientific understanding of spontaneous social order enables us to predict that compliance with general rules of a certain character – in particular rules that define rights of personal integrity, property, and contract[14] – will sustain and promote a pattern or structure of cooperative relationships. It is our grasp of abstractions – certain theoretical models – rather than comprehensive acquaintance with particular facts that enables us to see that

it is only by constantly holding up the guiding conception of an internally consistent model [of the overall order] which could be realized by the consistent application of the same principles, that anything like an effective framework for a functioning spontaneous order will be achieved. (RO, pp. 64–65)

Telic justification for rules of just conduct in terms of this framework for a functioning spontaneous order is available because "it is possible to distinguish between those rules and the resulting order" (RO, p. 98).

Only when it is clearly recognized that the order of actions is a factual state of affairs distinct from the rules which contribute to its formation can it be understood that such an abstract order can be the aim of rules of just conduct. (RO, pp. 113–14)

That is, it is only when Hayek recognizes this distinction that he sees a path between unreasoned affirmation of rule compliance for its own sake and rationalist demonstration with all its false assumptions about our factual and normative knowledge. Only with this recognition of a distinguishable end for which compliance with rules of just conduct is the means can he accommodate his implicit premise that all rational justification of rules or action must invoke some desirable end without stepping into the abyss of constructivism.[15]

On the account that I have advanced, Hayek proposes to provide a secure grounding for rules of just conduct – a grounding that re-enthrones them – by presenting compliance with those rules as the necessary and certain means for a newly identified fundamental value or end. Many passages in RO – especially those that describe the role of the judge within a legal order conducive to spontaneous social order – support this account. "The aim of jurisdiction [i.e., judicial decision] is the maintenance of an ongoing order of actions" (RO, p. 98). A judge operating within such an order first turns to its explicit and implicit rules:

The question for the judge here can never be whether the action [under examination] was expedient from some higher point of view, or served a particular result desired by authority, but only whether the conduct under dispute conformed to recognized rules. The only public good with which he can be concerned is the observance of those rules that individuals could reasonably count on. (RO, p. 87)

But the invocation of these rules itself serves and ultimately is governed by the guiding conception of a framework of cooperative interaction:

What must guide his decision is not any knowledge of what the whole of society requires at the particular moment, but solely what is demanded by general principles *on which the going order of society is based.* (RO, p. 87, emphasis added)

Indeed, the Hayekian judge is guided not by an attachment to those rules as such but by insight into the relationship between the body of (legally enforced) rules and the framework of spontaneous factual order served by those rules. Judges are at least to be guided by such insight when the existing explicit rules do not simply and mechanically dictate a particular decision. In such a case, the judge will not be free to pronounce as he pleases or as will advance any particular political agenda. Rather,

The rules which he pronounces will have to fill a definite gap in the body of already recognized rules in a manner that will serve to maintain and improve that order of actions which the already existing rules make possible. (RO, p. 100)

Hayek's position, therefore, constitutes an interesting stance on the question of whether judges can go beyond the existing, explicitly recognized legal norms without being willful makers of law.[16]

If the decision [facing a judge] cannot be logically deduced from recognized rules, it still must be consistent with the existing body of such rules in the sense that it serves the same order of actions as these rules ... [The judge must decide such] a case in a manner appropriate to the function which the whole system of rules serves. (RO, p. 116)[17]

This stance is available precisely because it is possible to distinguish between the norms and the order of actions that they serve.

In contrasting law that arises originally from custom and precedent with law that expresses the will of a political authority, Hayek says that the former

will consist of purpose-independent rules which govern the conduct of individuals towards each other, are intended to apply to an unknown number of further instances, and by defining a protected domain of each, enable an order of actions to form itself wherein the individuals can make feasible plans. (RO, pp. 85–86)

However, in light of the identification of the order of actions as the telos served by such rules, the Kantian characterization of these rules as purpose-independent needs to be qualified:

[I]f we include in "purpose" the aiming at conditions which will assist the formation of an abstract order, the particular contents of which are unpredictable, Kant's denial of purpose is justified only so far as the application of a rule to a particular instance is concerned, but certainly not for the system of rules as a whole. (RO, p. 113)

Further confirmation of Hayek's non-utilitarian, telic stance comes from volume 3 of *Law, Legislation, and Liberty*. In this volume,

Hayek sketches a model constitution, a crucial feature of which is that a Legislative Assembly will be charged with articulating and revising rules of just conduct that will apply to all agents within the spontaneous social order. To guide and constrain the Legislative Assembly, the constitution will contain a "basic clause" that goes beyond the requirement that the law it articulates be applicable to "an indefinite number of unknown future instances." The basic clause also will require that the law "serve the formation and pre-servation of an abstract order whose concrete contents [are] unfore-seeable" (Hayek 1979, p. 109). The constitution includes this further requirement because

government can only assist (or perhaps make possible) the formation of an abstract pattern or structure in which the several expectations of the mem-bers [of society] match each other ... It can only assure the abstract character and not the positive content of the order that will arise from the individuals' use of their knowledge for their purpose by delimiting their domains against each other by abstract and negative rules. (Hayek 1979, p. 130)

Benthamite constructivists on the one hand and Kant on the other hand were unable to conceive of an abstract order as a goal. For such an order

was too much at variance with what most people regarded as an appropriate goal of rational action. The preservation of an enduring system of abstract relationships, or the order of a cosmos with constantly changing content, did not fit into what men ordinarily understood as a purpose, goal, or end of deliberate action. (RO, p. 112)

However, the development of "social theory, particularly economics" (RO, p. 112) enables us to conceive of this abstract order as a candidate for being the appropriate goal of rational action. And, once it is avail-able, two converging lines of Hayekian argument point to the reason-ableness of its selection. The first is the rejection of any constructivist doctrine that directs us to any particular overall concrete social order (or any distribution of possible overall concrete orders) as the goal of rational action. A recognition of our factual and normative ignorance radically undermines the project of ranking such ends and identifying and securing the performance of the actions that would yield any putatively most highly ranked overall factual end. The second is the positive appreciation of our disposition to comply with rules as being a crucial strand within our evolved rationality – a rationality that has evolved so as to circumvent the problems of our factual and normative ignorance. Hayek's association of practical rationality with compliance with abstract constraining norms rather than with the pursuit of particular ends intimates a non-telic, genuinely deontic, moment within his thought. Nevertheless, his commitment to the vindication of norms having some sort of telic structure leads Hayek to search for a purpose that is predictably served by (and only by) compliance with those norms and the adoption of which is compatible with our normative ignorance. The purpose that he finds is that set of abstract relationships in and through which individuals – in particular ways that are not subject to prediction – will live peacefully and interact to mutual advantage with one another. Service to that abstract order is the rationale for compliance with rules of just conduct; and compliance necessarily serves that abstract end while violation of those rules necessarily subverts it.[18]

This abstract order is the appropriate goal of rational action for individuals who are faced with the opportunity of life within a large-scale social order inhabited by individuals who are highly diverse in their circumstances, knowledge, skills, preferences, and valued aspirations. It is the goal that is – because of its abstract character – reasonably agreeable to all individuals faced with that opportunity. "[R]ational policy" does not require "a common scale of concrete ends": rather "policy … may be directed toward the securing of an abstract overall order" (MSJ, p. 114). Given our lack of reasonable agreement upon a specific hierarchy of ends that would rank alternative particular outcomes, our factual ignorance is a blessing in disguise. For our factual ignorance prevents our rationally staking out particular and, hence, conflicting concrete social outcomes as candidates for the appropriate societal goal. Our common ignorance requires, instead, that we each give our allegiance to the abstract order of peaceful and mutually beneficial interactions that is *ex ante* advantageous to each:

There would exist not harmony but open conflict of interests if agreement were necessary as to which particular interests should be given preference over others. What makes agreement and peace in such a society possible is that the individuals are not required to agree on ends but only on means which are capable of serving a great variety of purposes and which each hopes will assist him in the pursuit of his purposes. (MSJ, p. 3)

What is crucial to the existence of the Great Society – in contrast to narrow command societies – is "the discovery of a method of collaboration which requires agreement only on means and not on ends" (MSJ, p. 3).

It should be clear that what Hayek here speaks of as agreed-upon means is what he elsewhere refers to as the ultimate ends or values – the most fundamental ends or values vis-à-vis rational policy. Speaking of the abstract rules that "serve the preservation of an equally abstract order," Hayek says that "though these rules ultimately serve particular (though mostly unknown) ends, they will do so only if they are treated not as means but as ultimate values, indeed as the only values common to all and distinct from the particular ends of individuals" (MSJ, pp. 16–17). And it is rational to treat these rules – or the abstract order they serve – as ultimate social ends or values because it is not rational to endeavor to see *through* the predictable abstract order to the particular overall factual order through which that abstract order will be manifested. Due to our ignorance, we rationally converge on the abstract order served by rules of just conduct as our common end – an end which is to be labeled "a value" because "it will be a condition which all will want to preserve" (RO, p. 104).

The "values" which the rules of just conduct serve will thus not be particulars but abstract features of an existing factual order which men will wish to enhance because they have found them to be conditions of the effective pursuit of a multiplicity of various, divergent, and unpredictable purposes. The rules aim at securing certain abstract characteristics of the overall order of our society that we would like it to possess to a higher degree. (RO, p. 105)

These abstract features alone "can constitute a true *common* interest of the members of a Great Society, who do not pursue any particular common purpose" (RO, p. 121).[19]

Hayek tells us that

It is only if we accept such a universal order as an aim, that is if we want to continue on the path which since the ancient Stoics and Christianity has been characteristic of Western civilization, that we can defend this moral system [of universal rules] as superior to others. (MSJ, p. 27)

There is no *proof* of the value of this universal order either in the sense of constructivist demonstration of its production of the best overall factual outcome or in the sense of deriving this value from some yet more fundamental (proven?) value. But that, I think, does not belie Hayek's claim that the only sensible, reasonably agreeable, end for individuals who stand as potential co-members of a Great Society is that universal order – "a timeless purpose which will continue to assist individuals in pursuit of their temporary and still unknown aims" (MSJ, p. 17).

NOTES

1. I gratefully acknowledge summer research support from the Murphy Institute of Political Economy at Tulane University. Mary Sirridge and Jerry Gaus provided helpful conversation. I have profited greatly from my involvement in colloquia sponsored by the Liberty Fund on the work of F. A. Hayek.

2. For Hayek, there is a deep connection between justice and cooperation to mutual benefit. Justice is action in accordance with norms that make cooperation possible. Part of the reason for identifying negative protective norms as the norms of *justice* is the tie between these protective norms and cooperation to mutual advantage.

3. The other candidate for culminating work is Hayek's *The Fatal Conceit* (1988). However, the extent of Hayek's authorship of this volume has been challenged. See Caldwell 2004a, pp. 316–19 and, especially, Ebenstein 2005.

4. Hayek continually conflates the claim that reason creates or designs moral norms and the claim that reason can confirm or justify those norms. Since he is so eager to deny the first, he is continually driven to deny the second as well.

5. See the passage from Locke cited in n. 25, p. 151 of RO. This passage is cited in full or in part in three essays (collected in Hayek 1967c) that anticipate the doctrine of *Law, Legislation, and Liberty*. See Hayek [1965] 1967, n. 1 on p. 84; 1967b, n. 7, p. 98; and [1963] 1967, n. 2, p. 107. A portion of this passage that does not include the claim that reason searches for and discovers the law of nature appears in Hayek 1988, p. 49.

6. See e.g. Ebenstein 2001, p. 249 and the citations in n. 27, p. 383. For Hayek's invocation of the distinction between act- and rule-utilitarianism see Hayek 1960, p. 455, n. 20, and MSJ, p. 156, n. 16.

7. The passage is from Reichenbach 1951, p. 141.

8. The passage is from a talk by Keynes entitled "My Early Beliefs." See Keynes 1949, p. 97.

9. Also see the entire section of *Law, Legislation, and Liberty* that is entitled "A Free Society Is a Pluralistic Society Without a Common Hierarchy of Particular Ends" (RO, pp. 109–11).

10. To avoid the position that a reasonable man acknowledges the directive force of *whatever* rules operate within his society, Hayek needs to emphasize that he is talking of rules that jointly facilitate an order of peaceful coexistence and mutually beneficial interaction.

11. Unlike the rule-utilitarian proper, the indirect utilitarian does not say that a given action can be known to be productive of the best overall outcome and still be known to be wrong.

12. Highly similar claims about the need for freedom or liberty to be "accepted as an overriding principle," "to be treated as the supreme principle," if the benefits of freedom are to be attained, appear in Hayek 1960. "We shall not achieve the results we want if we do not accept it [freedom] as a creed or presumption so strong that no considerations of expediency can be allowed to limit it." All these passages are on p. 68. However, nothing like the justification of freedom or freedom-protecting norms in terms of the abstract order of actions that respect for freedom facilitates appears in Hayek 1960.

13. This notion of an abstract order of actions ("a general order") first appears in Hayek's essay "The Legal and Political Philosophy of David Hume," originally published in 1963 and republished in Hayek 1967c, at p. 114. The notion is ubiquitous in Hayek's "Notes on the Evolution of Systems of Rules of Conduct" (1967a), apparently written shortly before its publication in the same collection.

14. See the characterization of rules that are conducive to the formation of concrete spontaneous social orders in RO, p. 107.

15. One is tempted to set this out in Hegelian fashion. Hayek's position is the synthesis that overcomes the conflict between the thesis of unreasoned adherence to principle and the antithesis of the need to justify principles in terms of their usefulness.

16. Chapter 5 of RO is the high point of Hayek's invocation of the abstract order of actions as the telos of judicial decision. Nevertheless Hayek slips into utilitarian-sounding pronouncements about the goal of judges being to "maximize the fulfillment of expectations as a whole" (RO, p. 103) or to achieve a "maximal coincidence of expectations" (RO, p. 106).

17. See also the striking sentences in which Hayek endorses the judicial nullification of already articulated rules that "are in conflict with the general sense of justice" (RO, p. 118).

18. There are different possible abstract orders of actions corresponding to different possible articulations of the rules of just conduct. These different abstract orders cannot be ranked against one another; but, according to Hayek, the telos for each particular set of rules of just conduct is the specific abstract order of actions that this set of rules tends to serve. No

philosophical selection of one of the abstract orders is possible or necessarily needed.

19. "A Great Society has nothing to do with, and is in fact irreconcilable with 'solidarity' in the true sense of unitedness in the pursuit of common goals" (MSJ, p. 111).

14 Hayek the cognitive scientist and philosopher of mind

F. A. Hayek's long-neglected monograph *The Sensory Order: An Inquiry into the Foundations of Theoretical Psychology* (1952b) has in recent years begun to garner some attention, most of it from economists or political scientists curious to see what bearing that work has on the foundations of Hayek's economics and social and political thought.[1] Some commentators have also noted the book's relevance to contemporary cognitive science, in particular its foreshadowing of connectionism.[2] Yet few have considered its distinctly philosophical significance – either its place in the history of twentieth-century philosophy or the light it might shed on current controversies in the philosophy of mind.[3]

This is by no means surprising, given that Hayek was not a philosopher by trade. He does not frame the issues he discusses in primarily philosophical terms, and he does not apply to those issues the methods a philosopher would. Notwithstanding his being Wittgenstein's cousin (Hayek [1977] 1992) and his friendship with Karl Popper, he appears not to have sought, nor (except from Popper) was he given, the attention of the mainstream analytic philosophical tradition that dominated the three countries – Austria, England, and the United States – in which he did the bulk of his teaching and writing.[4] Nevertheless, it is arguably as a work of philosophy that *The Sensory Order* is of the greatest interest. That it foreshadowed connectionism seems at the end of the day a point of merely historical significance; and its status as the "foundation" for Hayek's economics and politics has, I think, been exaggerated, claims for such a status typically resting on little more than the fact that the book characterizes the mind just as Hayek characterized economic and social systems, namely, as being complex, dynamic, and unpredictable in principle. (Hayek would no doubt have characterized the weather in exactly the same terms. Should we therefore regard meteorology as providing a "foundation" for his economics and politics?)[5]

The position Hayek develops in *The Sensory Order* – one anticipated in "Scientism and the Study of Society" ([1942–44] 1952) and supplemented in several other places, most importantly in the essays "Rules, Perception, and Intelligibility" ([1962] 1967) and "The Primacy of the Abstract" ([1969] 1978) – in fact constitutes an impressive philosophy of mind from which we can learn much. It is not a fully worked-out position, and it is not always presented in the jargon, or with the rigor, to which contemporary philosophers of mind have become accustomed. Still, it grapples in a highly original way with the central issues that have occupied such philosophers, incorporating (and in many cases foreshadowing) some of the most important insights of twentieth-century philosophy of mind in a synthesis whose various elements evoke the ideas of thinkers as diverse, and seemingly philosophically incompatible, as Russell and Wittgenstein, John Searle and Daniel Dennett. Indeed, a case could even be made for it as the most comprehensive and plausible attempt yet made to carry out the project of "naturalizing" the mind. If it is also in the end a failed attempt (as Hayek's friend Popper thought it was), we shall see that the failure is a uniquely instructive one.

This essay will try to substantiate these claims as follows. First, it will offer an exposition of Hayek's theory of the mind that draws out its philosophical content, lays bare its connections to some of the most important ideas put forward by philosophers both of Hayek's generation and of succeeding ones, and explores the ways in which his unusual combination of these ideas allows them, when united into a systematic whole, to withstand a number of objections that would otherwise appear insuperable when applied to them individually.[6] It will then examine what Popper took to be the fatal flaw Hayek's view shares with other naturalistic philosophies of mind, and suggest that his view nevertheless staves off the difficulties facing naturalism more effectively and heroically than these better-known philosophies do, however ultimately futile the heroism.

THE MIND–BODY PROBLEM

As a preliminary, we need to get clear on exactly what the problems are to which naturalistic philosophies of mind attempt to provide answers. Philosophers of mind typically set apart two aspects of our mental lives as being of special philosophical interest: they are, to employ the currently most widely used jargon, the phenomena of *qualia* and *intentionality*.

Qualia – the word is in the plural, the singular being "quale" – are the subjective features of conscious experience, that part of our mental lives which is directly knowable only "from the inside." If we imagine a man who has got his foot caught in a lawn mower, we might distinguish between, on the one hand, the damage to his body, the behavior he exhibits as a result of the accident (screaming, crying, flailing about), and the activity taking place in his nervous system, and on the other hand, the feeling or sensation of pain he's experiencing. The former are all objective and, in principle, publicly observable (if only via, say, X-ray or fMRI); the latter, however, is private in the sense of being directly accessible only to the man himself – and this is what philosophers would call the quale of his experience. The subjective features of the experiences of smelling a rose, tasting coffee, having an afterimage, or hearing a symphony would also be examples of qualia.

Intentionality is the directedness or "about-ness" exhibited by many mental phenomena. It parallels – and is indeed the ultimate ground of – the meaningfulness of language. The word "cat" is *about*, or *means*, something beyond itself, namely a certain kind of animal. In this it differs from, say, "gryxr," which is just a random string of letters or perhaps a meaningless sound. Even "cat" and other linguistic items, though, are in themselves just squiggles of ink on paper or noises emitted by the larynx. What meaning they have is derived ultimately from the users of language, namely us – creatures with minds, and the capacity to think about cats and the like. The thoughts we have about cats are also about, or mean, or are directed at, something beyond themselves, namely cats. And in this lies their intentionality.

Qualia are considered philosophically problematic insofar as it is difficult to see how their subjectivity can be explained in terms of the objective features of the brain and nervous system. Facts about the subjective feel of conscious experience seem clearly to be facts over and above the facts, however complex, about firing patterns of neurons in the brain, the wiring of the nervous system, or indeed physical facts of any kind; increasing knowledge of the latter would seem never to add up to knowledge of the former, to knowledge of *what it's like to experience* pain, the scent of a rose, or what have you. The mind would thus seem to be something non-physical, something existing over and above the brain; yet how could it be, given the evident dependence of mental events on brain events, and in particular the causal relations holding between the two?

Intentionality is problematic insofar as it is difficult to see how processes in the brain could have any more intrinsic meaning than squiggles of ink on paper or noises generated by the larynx. The latter have meaning only when they are taken to have meaning by thinking, language-using beings. By themselves they are meaningless. But neurons, and electrochemical signals passing between them – indeed, any material entity or process – seem as intrinsically meaningless as ink squiggles or laryngeal noises. If they have meaning, they also would have to get it from something else. But then, that something else would seemingly have to be immaterial, non-physical. Again, the mental would appear, mysteriously, to be distinct from the physical.

Explaining the relationship between qualia and intentionality, on the one hand, and the brain, body, and behavior on the other, is the heart of the traditional mind–body problem.[7] As we shall see, Hayek has something to say about intentionality, but his focus is on qualia, or "sensory qualities" as he calls them, and he characterizes the problem he aims to solve in *The Sensory Order* as that of explaining "how the physiological impulses proceeding in the different parts of the central nervous system can become in such a manner differentiated from each other in their functional significance that their effects will differ from each other in the same way in which we know the effects of the different sensory qualities to differ from each other" (1952b, p. 1). This way of framing the mind–body problem is by no means a philosophically neutral one: it incorporates a number of assumptions that are, to say the least, controversial, as does Hayek's gloss on this statement of the problem that it concerns "showing that there can exist a system of relations between . . . physiological events which is identical with the system of relations existing between the corresponding mental events" (p. 2). To explore these assumptions is to begin to see the intricate connections between Hayek's thought and the main currents of twentieth-century philosophy of mind.

PERCEPTION, INTROSPECTION, AND STRUCTURE

It is well known among Hayek scholars that his initial impetus for writing *The Sensory Order* (or at least the draft begun in the 1920s that would, thirty years later, become *The Sensory Order*) was his encounter with Ernst Mach's *The Analysis of Sensations* ([1886] 1959).[8] Mach, like Berkeley, held that it is the realm of sensory qualities or qualia alone with which we are directly acquainted in experience, and that the physical objects we ordinarily take ourselves to perceive are really nothing more than combinations of such sensory qualities. Hayek accepts the epistemological component of Mach's position – a claim that extends back, through classical empiricism, to Descartes – that acquaintance with sensory qualities forms the starting point of our knowledge of the world.

Less widely noted are the striking parallels between Hayek and several major twentieth-century philosophers concerning what he rejects in Mach's position. For instance, Hayek did not accept Mach's anti-realist metaphysical claim that sensory qualities are all that ultimately exist. There is in Hayek's view an external physical world lying beyond the veil of perceptions that constitutes the realm of sensations or sensory qualities, though we know the former only *through* the latter. But our acquaintance with the latter does not give us knowledge of the external physical world "as it is in itself" (as Kant would say), for "the progress of the physical sciences has all but eliminated these qualities from our scientific picture of the external world," leading science "to define the objects of which this world exists [*sic*] increasingly in terms of the observed relations between these objects, and ... to disregard the way in which those objects appear to us" (1952b, pp. 2–3). That is to say, the sensory qualities we encounter in perception are not truly features of external objects, but only of our experiences of those objects; what we know about the objects themselves are only their relations to each other. In taking this position, Hayek adopts a theory of knowledge that had been developed in detail by Moritz Schlick and Bertrand Russell, one that lays stress on the notion that modern science reveals to us not

the intrinsic nature of the physical world, but only its causal structure. Nor is this similarity in views accidental: Hayek was greatly
influenced by Schlick's *Allgemeine Erkenntnislehre* (translated into
English as *General Theory of Knowledge* [1918] 1985), which he had
read around the same time he read Mach, and both that work and
Russell's *Analysis of Matter* ([1927] 1954) appear in the bibliography of
The Sensory Order.[9]

Also in that bibliography is a work no less striking in its parallels
to and apparent influence on *The Sensory Order*, namely Rudolf
Carnap's *Der logische Aufbau der Welt* (1928, translated in 1967 as
The Logical Structure of the World). Carnap is generally supposed to
have been primarily concerned in this work with carrying out in
detail the project of giving a phenomenalistic reduction of physical
objects to collections of sensory qualities, *à la* Mach. As Michael
Friedman (1999) has noted, however, it is often forgotten that Carnap
was no less interested (as, it should be remembered, Mach was not) in
carrying out an analysis of sensory qualities themselves, defining
them systematically in terms of similarity relations, such that each
quality could be identified with its position in an overall structure.
This is precisely what Hayek himself advocates, holding as he did
that "the whole order of sensory qualities can be exhaustively
described in terms of (or 'consists of nothing but') all the relationships existing between them" and that "there is no problem of sensory qualities beyond the problem of how the different sensory
qualities differ from each other" (1952b, pp. 18–19).

Most instructive is the reason Hayek took this view:

[N]othing can become a problem about sensory qualities which cannot in
principle also be described in words; and such a description in words will
always have to be a description in terms of the relation of the quality in
question to other sensory qualities ... In other words, all that can be communicated are the differences between sensory qualities, and only what can
be communicated can be discussed. (1952b, p. 31)

The issue is one of cognitive intelligibility: if we couldn't describe
sensory qualities or qualia in terms of their relations, we couldn't
truly *describe* them – genuinely communicate or convey information about them – at all. If such qualities had any non-relational or
"absolute" features (p. 30), they would be strictly ineffable. This, as

Friedman emphasizes, is just the sort of concern that motivated Carnap, who took the delineation of *structure* (*Aufbau*) to be the key to the very possibility of a cognitively meaningful, and thus genuinely scientific, account of sensory qualities – indeed, to the very possibility of intersubjective communication of any sort.

The question of the grounds of the very possibility of intelligible, objective, and scientific discourse is also what motivated Schlick to focus on structure as the essence of our knowledge of the external, physical world; indeed, the link between structure and cognitive intelligibility was an important theme in the early history of the analytic movement of which Schlick was a founding father. But adherents of this structuralist conception of our knowledge of the external world, including not only Schlick but Russell and those contemporary writers influenced by him, have generally *not* adopted a structuralist analysis of sensory qualities or qualia. Instead, the view of Russellians has been that, though *perception* does not give us knowledge of the intrinsic qualities of the physical world, *introspection* of our qualia does, sensory qualities or qualia being regarded by them as intrinsic, non-relational, or absolute properties.

It is one of the most original aspects of Hayek's position that he combines the structuralism concerning the external world associated with Schlick and Russell with the structuralism concerning the internal world of sensory qualities or qualia advocated by Carnap.[10] *All* our knowledge, of both the physical and mental realms, is in Hayek's view knowledge only of structure:

[T]he order of sensory qualities no less than the order of physical events is a relational order – even though to us, whose mind is the totality of the relations constituting that order, it may not appear as such. The difference between the physical order of events and the phenomenal order in which we perceive the same events is thus not that only the former is purely relational, but that the relations existing between corresponding events and groups of events in the two orders will be different. (1952b, p. 19)

This explains why Hayek takes the mind–body problem to be formulable, and solvable, in the terms stated above: if the mind is nothing but a certain kind of structure, and that structure can be shared by something purely physical – the brain – then there is no obstacle to identifying the mind and the brain, the mental and the physical.

FUNCTIONALISM AND HIGHER-ORDER MENTAL STATES

It explains Hayek's formulation, I should say, only given one further claim of Hayek's, namely that the structure constituting the mind ought (like the structure of the external, physical world) to be regarded as a kind of *causal* structure, so that the differences between sensory qualities that define their places in the overall system of relations constituting them "can only consist of differences in the effects which they exercise in evoking other qualities, or in determining behaviour" (1952b, p. 19).[11]

This brings to mind yet another influential – perhaps the most influential – position in twentieth- (and twenty-first) century philosophy of mind, namely *functionalism*, the view that mental states are to be defined in terms of their functional roles, or the sets of causal relations they bear to each other, environmental stimuli, and bodily behavior. One of the hallmarks of functionalism is its implication that mind, given that its essence lies in the relations defining its elements rather than in the specific material character those elements happen to possess, could in principle exist in any number of substrata – not only in human beings, but in extraterrestrials, androids, even computers. That Hayek was a functionalist – a decade or more before functionalist views began to be discussed among analytic philosophers – is clear not only from his emphasis on the causal structure of the mind, but in his expression of the view that

It is at least conceivable that the particular kind of order which we call mind might be built up from any one of several kind of different elements – electrical, chemical, or what not; all that is required is that by the simple relationship of being able to evoke each other in a certain order they correspond to the structure we call mind. (1952b, p. 47)

The basic functionalist idea can be spelled out in a variety of ways. Perhaps the best-known way is to take the specific structure constituting the mind to be the sort represented by a Turing machine, an abstract specification of algorithms governing the manipulation of formal symbols, as in a computer program. But Hayek was not that kind of functionalist. His inspiration was not modern computer science but neuroscience, and like the connectionists whose work his own foreshadowed and who have challenged the symbolic processing paradigm in cognitive science, Hayek took the operations of the mind to be most aptly modeled on those of the brain, and indeed (at least in creatures with brains, like human beings as opposed to androids) to be identical to the latter.

Hayek focuses in particular on (and spends the bulk of *The Sensory Order* detailing) the way neural events may, by virtue of the causal relations holding between them, be said to *classify* events in the external environment in a manner that parallels the classification effected in perceptual experience. As the external world impinges on an organism's sensory surfaces, connections are formed between neurons and groups of neurons in such a fashion that the impulses they carry regularly occur in tandem. Different groups of impulses come to be associated with different features of the external world, as those diverse features generate and reinforce, through their effects on the senses, different sets of neural connections in the brain. It is not the intrinsic character of any individual impulse or group of impulses that gives rise to a correlation with a feature of the external world, but rather "the position of the individual impulse or group of impulses in the whole system of such connexions which gives it its distinctive quality" (1952b, p. 53). In "The Primacy of the Abstract," Hayek speaks in terms of what he calls a "superimposition" of the members of one set of neural events rather than another as being the mechanism underlying one's perceiving something as an object of a certain sort and responding to it behaviorally in the appropriate way ([1969] 1978, pp. 40–42). The fact that the superimposition is of just the sort it is – its comprising *this* bundle of impulses rather than *that* bundle (with various subsets of impulses within each bundle corre-lated with various features of the external world) – gives the percep-tual experience correlated with it (and in Hayek's view identical with it) its distinct qualitative character.

Take a simple example: your looking at an orange. What gives this experience the qualitative character it has, a character similar in some respects but not others to that of the experience of looking at an orange car, is that the orange's stimulating your sensory organs initiates some sets of neural impulses which are also initiated when you look at an orange car and others which are not, but which are also initiated when you look, say, at a billiard ball (which is similar to an orange in shape); that those impulses initiate further sets of impulses that are related to those initiated when you see other types of fruit (while failing to initiate impulses related to your seeing rocks); and that it ultimately (through such intermediate impulses) initiates some dispositions to act (realized in further neural activity) rather than others, perhaps a disposition to salivate and eat the object (which you also have when seeing a hamburger) rather than the disposition to take a drive, which you might have when seeing an orange car. In short, that it is a collection of just these particular interconnected neural impulses rather than some other ones is what makes it identical to a "roundish, orange-ish" experience rather than, say, a "reddish, square-like" experience.[12]

The possibility of combining, as Hayek does, a Schlickian–Russellian structuralism about the external world with the structuralism about the mind popularized by functionalism has, surprisingly, not been considered by many contemporary philosophers.[13] Yet such a combination seems to be supported by the very considerations that lead to structuralism about the physical world in the first place, at least in its Russellian version. Russell's insistence on that doctrine, and on the indirect realism he took to go along with it, rested on the nature of the causal chains that mediate our perceptions of the external world:

> [I]f the location of events in physical space-time is to be effected, as I maintain, by causal relations, then your percept, which comes after events in the eye and optic nerve leading into the brain, must be located in your brain ... What I maintain is that we *can* witness or observe what goes on in our heads, and that we cannot witness or observe anything else at all. (Russell [1959] 1985, p. 19)

What Russell is saying here is that in having a perceptual experience, one is directly aware only of something – an event in one's brain – that comes at the end of a long causal sequence, and thus one cannot assume that that which initiated the sequence – the external physical object one is looking at, or hearing, or whatever – itself has the qualitative features presented in the experience. We can know with confidence only that it has the structural features revealed by physical science. But surely one's awareness, in introspection, of the internal perceptual experience itself is also mediated by causal chains; certainly Russell and his followers would say so, identifying as they do mental events with brain events.[14] If so, however, then what Russell says about perception would apply also to introspection: just as the former does not reveal to us the intrinsic nature of its

objects (the denizens of the external physical world), of which we
know only their structure, so too does the latter fail to reveal to us
the intrinsic nature of *its* objects (perceptual states, and indeed other
kinds of mental state as well), leaving their structure all we know
with confidence. To use Hayek's language, if perception classifies
external events according to their relations, introspection classifies
internal (e.g. perceptual) events according to *their* relations, in an act
of higher-order classification.

This brings us to yet another anticipation in Hayek of trends in
recent philosophy of mind, namely the development of "high-order"
theories of consciousness, on which a conscious experience is analyzed as an internal state which is the object of monitoring by
another, higher-order internal state (Armstrong 1981; Rosenthal
1997). This sort of theory is a variety of functionalism in that it
takes the character of a mental state to derive from its causal relations, but its distinctive feature is its emphasis on the particular kind
of causal relation involved in a state's bringing about another state
which bears to it the same sort of relation the first state bears to an
event in the external environment.

Functionalist theories of consciousness, including higher-order
theories, are often accused of being subject to the same objections
that apply to other materialist theories. Surely, it is said, the subjective feel of your experience of seeing an orange is something over
and above, and irreducible to, any causal relations it might bear. But
the unique combination of philosophical theses comprising Hayek's
position arguably allows him considerably to undermine the force of
such objections. Standard functionalist accounts, "higher-order" or
otherwise, take for granted that physical objects – including the brain –
are more or less as we experience them in perception. It seems just
obvious, on this assumption, that an experience of an orange is
something different from a brain event and any causal relations
instantiated in it, since it clearly seems different from anything
going on in that grey, squishy lump of stuff inside your skull, no
matter how fancy is the description of those goings-on provided by
the functionalist. But Hayek, with Schlick and Russell, denies that
the greyness and squishiness are really features of the brain as it is in
itself in the first place. In imagining the brain in those terms, you're
really imagining only a *perceptual representation* of the brain –
something as different from the brain itself as is the word "brain,"

which is also but a mere (linguistic rather than perceptual) representation of the brain. Thus, noting that a perceptual experience seems different from the grey, squishy thing is of no philosophical significance. It no more shows that a perceptual experience is not a brain event than does the fact that the word "water" doesn't resemble the chemical substance H$_2$O show that water isn't H$_2$O.

Russellians conclude from this that there is after all no obstacle to identifying conscious experiences with brain events. All we really know about the brain from the point of view of physical science is its causal structure, the relations holding between the various intrinsic properties (whatever they are) that make up the brain. Why not take the qualia we encounter in introspection themselves to be those intrinsic properties, the features bearing the relations? It isn't perception that gives us knowledge of the true nature of the brain, then, but introspection. To introspect your conscious experiences just is to be directly aware of the intrinsic properties of the brain.

There is a problem with this view, though, from the point of view of defending naturalism. If the brain, conceived of as a physical object, is nothing but a certain kind of causal structure, then it isn't enough, if one wants to identify the mind and the brain, to note that qualia might be the properties that "flesh out" that causal structure. For the "identity" here still seems entirely contingent: even if qualia in fact flesh out the causal structure of the brain, it seems entirely conceivable that something else could have done so instead; and it also seems conceivable that qualia could in principle exist apart from their purported role in fleshing out this (or any) causal structure. So dualism seems to follow from the Russellian position after all. The brain and the mind really are distinct entities, even if the qualia (partially) constituting the latter contingently fill out the causal structure of the former.[15]

Hayek's brand of structuralism, extending as it does to the domain of qualia itself, is not subject to this objection. Even introspection gives us no knowledge of intrinsic properties, of the brain or of anything else; like perception, it gives us only further representations of its objects, the extra-representational nature of which we can know only in terms of their relations – as, for that matter, does any even *higher*-order, meta-introspective state. We are, in Hayek's view (as in Kant's view), never acquainted with anything but representations, whether of the external world *or the internal world*. In particular, we never encounter any intrinsic properties of the mind that could be said to be distinct from the properties of the brain.

Hayek's commitment to the epistemic priority of the internal world of the mind may also help rebut another objection to functionalist and higher-order theories, which are commonly accused of failing to do justice to the *subjectivity* of qualia, that is, their existing *for* a subject of experience and being directly accessible only to that subject from within the first-person point of view. Hayek's account clearly cannot be accused of this, holding as it does that the first-person perspective of the subject and his qualia is the starting point of all knowledge. Of course, he does hold that qualia are, for all their subjectivity, non-intrinsic properties that are analyzable in terms of their relations. But this does not entail that he is committed to "leaving out what it's like" to experience qualia, as other views which deny the intrinsicality of qualia are accused of doing (Levine 1993). For while it is easy to see what is "left out" when qualia are defined in terms of relations holding between properties of the brain – imagined as the "external," "objective," grey, squishy thing presented to us in perception, so different from what is revealed in introspection – it is much harder to see what is left out when they are defined instead in terms of relations holding between the subjective features of that introspective world itself. It is thus hard to see how there could be any aspect of qualia that Hayek's position might justly be accused of having failed to account for.

INTENTIONALITY AND THE LIMITS OF UNDERSTANDING

It has perhaps not escaped the reader's notice that our discussion of the problem of qualia has been haunted by the specter of that other problematic aspect of mind, intentionality. The idea of representation, of which so much use has been made in explicating Hayek's position, is as intentional a concept as there is. "Classification," the central notion in Hayek's analysis of perception and introspection, would also seem clearly to be an intentional process, insofar as the classifications performed are taken to have *meaning* or *significance* rather than being mere mechanical operations. And the notion of subjectivity itself seems as tied to intentionality as it does to qualia, since for qualia to exist for a subject of experience is, in the standard case, for them to have significance or meaning for that subject.

Hayek's solution to the problem of qualia would thus seem to be incomplete so long as intentionality itself remains unexplained.

Indeed, the problem of qualia seems in Hayek's theory to reduce to the problem of intentionality; or at least, his account implies that the having of qualia presupposes the having of intentionality. Acquiring a concept (a paradigmatic manifestation of intentionality) is in Hayek's view associated with, and identical to, the formation of a set of neural connections causally correlated with whatever property in the external world the concept is a concept of. What he calls the "superimposition" of various sets of neural impulses underlying a perceptual experience is just the superimposition of the various concepts associated with those sets of impulses, and determines the specific qualitative character of the experience. One set of neural impulses is associated with the concept of "orangeness," say, another with roundness, yet another with a certain texture, and so on; and when they are "superimposed" the result is the perceptual experience of an orange. Hayek concludes from this that the having of any perceptual experience (with its distinctive qualia) is possible only once one has, by virtue of the formation of the relevant neural connections, acquired concepts of the properties correlated with those connections (Hayek [1969] 1978, pp. 42–43). From this, he suggests, it follows that the having of concepts is a presupposition of experience rather than the product of abstraction from experience, as classical empiricism would have it ([1969] 1978, pp.42–43; 1952b, pp. 165–72). This is what Hayek means by "the primacy of the abstract," and it gives his position yet another affinity with Kant's. Insofar as the having of concepts is a paradigmatically intentional activity, it also makes more pressing an answer to the question of how intentionality can be explained in naturalistic terms. Does Hayek have such an answer?

Yes and no. Hayek's view was that we cannot ever fully understand the mind, in naturalistic or any other terms. But that failure of understanding follows from the very nature of mind itself, whatever its ultimate basis, natural or non-natural; it has no tendency to show that the mind is not a purely natural, physical phenomenon. We can thus have every confidence in supposing *that* intentionality, and the conscious, qualia-bearing experiences that it supports, are natural phenomena, even if we cannot fully explain *how* they can be.

The reason for the mind's inscrutability has to do with the mechanics of the classificatory process that starts with perception.

If a given perceptual experience – of an orange, say – is possible only once the relevant concepts have been acquired by virtue of the formation of neural connections corresponding to the various properties of the orange, then one's conscious, explicit knowledge of the orange presupposes in Hayek's view something implicit and unconscious, the having of the concepts themselves: "What we experience consciously as qualitative attributes of the external events is determined by relations [between concepts *qua* neural connections] of which we are not consciously aware but which are implicit in these qualitative distinctions" (Hayek 1952b, p. 167). Of course, we may go on consciously to contemplate the concepts themselves. But this just presupposes the operation of yet higher-order unconscious and implicit processes – in particular, the "superimposition" of sets of neural impulses corresponding to various aspects *of the concepts* (concepts of the concepts themselves), making possible conscious awareness of concepts in just the way that a superimposition of sets of neural impulses corresponding to the original first-order concepts makes possible conscious awareness of the orange. The same holds true of the bringing to consciousness of these *meta*-concepts, of the bringing to consciousness of meta-meta-concepts, and so on ad infinitum.

The potential for infinite regress is only half the problem, though. Perception of an external object requires, on Hayek's account, that there be a larger number of sets of neural connections corresponding to various properties of objects than there are objects themselves. For example, to perceive even a single simple object like an orange, I must possess multiple sets of neural connections, corresponding to orangeness, roundness, and the like. Something similar holds of the bringing to consciousness of concepts: there must be a larger number of neural connections corresponding to different aspects of the concepts (their inferential relations to other concepts, etc.) than there are concepts themselves. But in that case, Hayek concludes:

[A]ny apparatus of classification must possess a structure of a higher degree of complexity than is possessed by the objects which it classifies; and ... therefore, the capacity of any explaining agent must be limited to objects with a structure possessing a degree of complexity lower than its own. If this is correct, it means that no explaining agent can ever explain objects of its own kind, or of its own degree of complexity, and therefore, that the human brain can never fully explain its own operations. (1952b, p. 185)

This may have implications for Hayek's account of sensory qualities or qualia, and not just for intentionality. If the character of a sensory quality is determined by its relations to all other mental processes, as functionalists often claim and as Hayek also holds (1952b, p. 190), then the fact that we can never make conscious every tacit or unconscious mental process entails that we can never make explicit all the relations holding between any given mental process and every other one. But then we shouldn't be surprised, Hayek might argue, if even given his endorsement of the subjectivity of qualia, his insistence that they are nevertheless relational might *seem* to leave something out, and that even after we have in great detail analyzed a given sensory quality in terms of its relations, there might still seem to be some aspect of it we haven't quite captured. If there is such an aspect, it arguably just amounts to nothing more than yet further inexplicit, unconscious relations of the same sort we've already made explicit.

The implications are more stark where intentionality is concerned, however, as is perhaps most clearly conveyed in Hayek's essay "Rules, Perception, and Intelligibility," where, as the title indicates, Hayek puts things in terms of "rules" rather than concepts, neural connections, or classificatory processes. He there says that:

> It is important not to confuse the contention that any such system [as the mind] must always act on some rules which it cannot communicate with the contention that there are particular rules which no such system could ever state. All the former contention means is that there will always be some rules governing a mind which that mind in its then prevailing state cannot communicate, and that, if it ever were to acquire the capacity of communicating those rules, this would presuppose that it had acquired further higher rules which make the communication of the former possible but which themselves will still be incommunicable. ([1962] 1967, p. 62)

This is in part a gloss on the earlier point about the regress involved in making tacit processes conscious: it isn't that there is any particular process (or rule, concept, belief, or whatever) that cannot be made conscious – any given process could be conscious in principle – but rather that not all such processes could together be made explicit and conscious all at once, for any act of conscious understanding presupposes some further process or other which is left (at least at that point) unconscious and inexplicit. It is also, as the context makes clear (Hayek refers in this passage to "the problem of meaning [intelligibility, significance, understanding]"), a point about how the cognitive significance, meaning, or intentionality of conscious processes depends on their being embedded in a context that is largely unconscious and inexplicit.

John Searle (1983) has developed ideas that seem to parallel and elucidate Hayek's views. All intentional mental states, he says, have the content they do only by virtue of their place in a vast "Network" (Searle intends this as a technical term) of intentional states. The desire to run for the presidency of the United States, for example, has the intentional content it has only in the context of such other intentional states as the belief that the United States has presidential elections, the desire that people cast votes for you, and so on. But this Network of intentional states functions against a "Background" (another technical term) of capacities which are themselves non-intentional. Such capacities will for most people include, for example, the presupposition that there is an external physical world. For the average person, this presupposition isn't strictly speaking a belief or any other sort of intentional state, because it isn't consciously entertained at all; one simply behaves *as if* one had such a belief or intentional state, insofar as one acts and thinks in a way that makes sense only given the existence of an external world. Should such a presupposition become conscious and intentional, it will nevertheless operate against a Background of further capacities that remain yet unconscious and non-intentional. This is necessarily the case, in Searle's view, for if there were no Background, then in tracing the links that give any particular intentional state its content, we would be led into an infinite regress. Moreover, even if, in acting or thinking, I try consciously to follow explicitly formulated rules that would otherwise be part of the Background, these rules are capable of multiple interpretations; and the same is true of any further rules I might appeal to in order to interpret the first set. So, ultimately, I must simply *act* in accordance with some interpretation of some set of rules, without consciously or explicitly choosing to do so; otherwise I would never get started.

If the comparison with Searle is apt, then the analysis of intentionality proposed by Hayek entails that any explanation of a given intentional state or process – and by extension, of any qualia-bearing conscious experience, determined as these are by intentional states or processes – must ultimately terminate in a description of the creature having that state, process, or experience as simply acting, as a matter of brute fact, in accordance with certain rules. Adopting a distinction made famous by Gilbert Ryle (1949), Hayek concludes that all conscious, explicit, "knowing *that*" certain facts are so, including facts about the mind, necessarily rests on a tacit, inexplicit, and inarticulable "knowing *how*" to act in the world (1952b, p. 39). Since there will always be a level of mental life that cannot be made explicit, there is no way to set out a complete description of the structure of the mind, and match its elements up one-to-one with those of the structure of the brain. For that reason, even though "in some ultimate sense mental phenomena are 'nothing but' physical processes," we will never be able to reduce the mental to the physical, and "shall have permanently to be content with a practical dualism" (1952b, p. 191). But this "practical dualism" is merely epistemological, not metaphysical, "based not on any assertion of an objective difference between the two classes of events, but on the demonstrable limitations of the powers of our own mind fully to comprehend the unitary order to which they belong" (1952b, p. 191).[16] And we are at least capable of an "explanation of the principle" (p. 191) on which the mind operates – of understanding how a purely physical system like the brain could instantiate a kind of structure, the "sensory order" of the mind, which cannot be understood in all its details.[17]

EVOLUTION

The Hayek–Searle view of intentionality described in the previous section has obvious affinities with Wittgenstein's conception of "forms of life" that determine our patterns of thought and action, and this might generate a worry that often arises when such Wittgensteinian ideas are under discussion. Doesn't Hayek's position threaten to cut our intentional, mental lives off from any contact with objective reality? If we must ultimately "just act" on whatever rules happen to govern our thought and practice, aren't such rules inevitably arbitrary and unjustifiable, since any attempted justification will itself involve "just acting" on some yet higher level of rules? Are we to conclude that the rules governing our own thought and practice are determined by nothing more than the "forms of life" that have just turned out, quite contingently, to pre-dominate in our own culture? Don't relativism and skepticism loom? Not in Hayek's view. There may be no way to make explicit all the rules governing the mind, but he thinks there is a way to show that the inexplicit or tacit rules, whatever they are, do in fact put the mind into contact with objective reality: an appeal to *evolution*.

The neural connections instantiating the rules, concepts, classificatory processes, or what have you that govern our mental lives do not, after all, wire themselves up independently of the external world. They come about in part as a result of an organism's interaction with that world, and thus are bound to reflect objective features of that world. Moreover, they are also in part the product of the evolutionary history of the species to which the organism belongs (Hayek 1952b, p. 166; [1969] 1978, p. 42). The individual organism is predisposed to form neural connections corresponding to rules and concepts that have proved advantageous to the preservation of the species, and not to form those which might prove disadvantageous. These predispositions may well put constraints on what experiences are possible for an organism:

Sense experience therefore presupposes the existence of a sort of accumulated "knowledge," of an acquired order of the sensory impulses based on their past co-occurrence; and this knowledge, although based on (pre-sensory) experience [i.e. the past interactions of the organism and the species with the environment], can never be contradicted by sense experience and will determine the forms of such experiences which are possible. (1952b, p. 167)

But these constraints do not cut us off from reality, for, formed as they are by the evolutionary history of the species and the life history of the organism, they do not float free of reality. The structure of the mind can thus be presumed at least for the most part to reflect the structure of the objective world.

But what about those rules which are culturally rather than biologically determined? Surely these have no guarantee of objectivity? Hayek again demurs, on the basis of a theory of cultural evolution. Hayek's view is that those culturally based rules and practices that best enable a group of human beings to adapt to its environment will be those which tend to survive, for the groups that practice them will be the ones which proliferate and keep the practices alive; while those rules and practices which are ill suited to the preservation of a group will tend to die out, since the group that practices them either will itself shrink or die out, or will abandon those practices and adopt those of more successful groups. That certain rules and practices have survived is therefore strong evidence that they are adaptive, and reflect objective facts about the human environment. There is at least a presumption in favor of their objectivity and utility, even if we do not (and indeed, given the complexity of human affairs, often cannot) always know what that utility is. This too entails certain constraints on the mind, and in particular on the extent to which it can try consciously and radically to re-shape its basic assumptions about reality. It must forever be less *shaping* than *shaped*: "Mind is not a guide but a product of cultural evolution, and is based more on imitation than on insight or reason," Hayek argues (Hayek 1988, p. 21), and "it is less accurate to suppose that thinking man creates and controls his cultural evolution than it is to say that culture, and evolution, created his reason" (1988, p. 22).[18] But as with the constraints put in place by biological evolution, these constraints have an objective basis, and thus are bound to reflect objective reality rather than conceal it from us.

In all of this, Hayek seems very much to have anticipated the specifically evolutionary varieties of naturalism about intentionality represented by philosophers like Ruth Millikan (1984) and Daniel Dennett (1995). Their view that whatever meaning or intentional content an organism's internal states can be said to have derives ultimately from the biological function those states happen to serve, given the history of the organism and the species to which it belongs, parallels Hayek's account of rules and classificatory mechanisms which have been hardwired into us by natural selection. Dennett's advocacy of the notion of "memes" (borrowed from the sociobiologist Richard Dawkins [1989]), which are units of meaning – concepts, theories, and the like – that develop, compete, flourish, or die out via a kind of natural selection, has obvious affinities with Hayekian cultural evolution. Dennett lays particular emphasis on the idea that meaning is bound to be as indeterminate and inscrutable as any other product of evolution, given that the latter works by fits and starts, trial and error, without any preset design plan or any predetermined goal. Any given organ may well be ambiguous as to its function, given that the reasons for its preservation in an organism may have shifted through the course of the history of the species and its ancestors. The intentional processes of the mind can in his view be no less ambiguous. We are, for Dennett and Hayek alike, the products of millennia-spanning biological and cultural evolutionary processes, and cannot expect any fuller an understanding of ourselves than is warranted given the indeterminacy and complexity of the factors that went into our production. If a sense of mystery remains after even the most sophisticated and thorough naturalistic theory of the mind has done its work, this is only to be expected. It has no tendency to show that the mind is not, after all, a purely physical, natural phenomenon.

POPPER'S CRITIQUE

Or so it is claimed. It isn't clear, however, that the mysteriousness of the mind is merely an artifact of its complexity, of the ambiguity inherent in many of its representations, or of the elusiveness entailed by the potentially infinite regress of ever higher levels of meta-introspection. Complexity per se seems irrelevant: trying to fathom the complexity of the system of relationships embodied in, say, the wind and water molecules of a hurricane which give it its distinct trajectory is no mean feat either, but it just doesn't involve the *same* sort of puzzlement that the mind does. For it is the meaningfulness or intentional content of the mind that is ultimately puzzling – a feature that even the simplest of minds seems to possess, and that we are not in the least tempted to attribute to a hurricane, however complex. More to the present point, it isn't the intricacy of the neural wiring of the brain that baffles us; it's the fact that the wiring, however complex, is associated with meaning. Ambiguity is not the issue either, for to be of indeterminate meaning, a representation has to *have* some meaning in the first place, and therein lies the mystery. Something similar can be said for the regress of introspective states, or of articulations of heretofore tacit rules: introspecting and "making explicit" are themselves intentional processes, whether their regress is finite or infinite, and it is that which makes them baffling. Let a calculator be programmed to display the sequence of natural numbers out to infinity, it will not be a fraction as mysterious (if indeed it is mysterious at all) as a simpleton's ability to count no higher than five but *mean* something by it.

Both directly, in appealing to the systematic connections between neural impulses, and indirectly, in appealing to natural selection (which reduces apparent purposes in nature to complex chains of causation), Hayek sought to account for meaning in purely causal terms. This sort of approach seems inevitable if one assumes the truth of naturalism, which is why not only functionalism in general, but causal theories of representation in particular have become so prominent in recent philosophy of mind. But Popper took this to be the Achilles' heel of Hayek's theory, for as he put it in a letter to Hayek prompted by his reading of *The Sensory Order*, "I think I can show that a causal theory of the mind cannot be true ... more precisely, I think I can show the impossibility of a causal theory of the human language."[19]

Popper's reasons for this judgment are twofold (Popper [1953] 1968). The aspects of language that make it distinctively human are in his view its "descriptive" and "argumentative" functions. Human beings don't merely "signal" to one another, as bees and simple electronic devices do, but express propositions that can be either true or false. Nor do they merely attempt to get others to believe certain propositions, which might be accomplished via intimidation or propaganda, but they also, at least sometimes, appeal to objective standards of rationality. Popper argued that neither of these things can be accounted for in the causal terms typical of neuroscientific and evolutionary explanation.

Contemporary causal theories of meaning suggest that a representation encoded in the neural wiring of the brain can acquire a specific intentional content by virtue of its bearing the right causal relations to external objects and processes. Such a representation will refer to cats, for example, if it tends under certain circumstances (carefully specified so as to sidestep various counter-examples) to be caused by cats. Accordingly, our ability to grasp and express the proposition that the cat is on the mat can, on this view, be explained in terms of the having of a literal "sentence in the head" that means that the cat is on the mat. The trouble with this sort of account, in Popper's view, is that any characterization of the causal chains in question will inevitably presuppose intentionality, and thus cannot coherently be appealed to in order to explain intentionality. For example, that the causal chains associated with our use of "cat" begin with, and thus lead to a representation of, *cats* specifically – rather than the surfaces of cats, or the light reflected off cat fur, or whatever – and end specifically in our *thoughts* about cats – rather than in stimulations of the retinas and eardrums, or with a photon's reaching a point one inch away from the surface of the eyeball – is ultimately determined by our *interpreting* the chains as having those precise beginning and ending points, where interpreting is itself a manifestation of intentionality. Our characterization of such causal chains is interest-relative, not a purely objective description of features of the situation. There is nothing in the objective physical facts which makes this or that point the "beginning" or "end" of the chain, or in any other way special; there is just the continuous causal flux, out of which *we* pick certain patterns as having significance. But since "we" as thinking, interpreting beings are exactly what a causal theory is trying to explain, it follows in Popper's view that no such theory can fail to be viciously circular.

It is ironic that Hayek should have missed this objection, because in *The Sensory Order* (and earlier, and at greater length, in "Scientism and the Study of Society," [1942–44] 1952) he criticized behaviorists for failing to see that a proper characterization of the stimuli to which they would refer in explaining human behavior requires an appeal to just the sort of subjective mental phenomena they eschewed. A hammer counts as a hammer only relative to human interests, and thus cannot properly be described as a stimulus without reference to the subjective representations of observers; and the same thing is no less true in Hayek's estimation of facial expressions, scientific instruments, and other phenomena that might seem less dependent on cultural and other subjective factors (cf. Searle 1995). If Popper is right, then in presupposing that the causal chains associated with mental phenomena can coherently be described apart from human interests, Hayek's own theory is no less guilty than behaviorism is of what Hayek called "objectivism" – the tendency to ignore the irreducibly subjective element in all data pertaining to the human world.

It is also ironic that Hayek failed to foresee Popper's second criticism of causal theories of the mind. Popper held that no causal theory could account for the distinction between believing something on rational grounds and believing it as a result of such non-rational influences as intimidation, hypnosis, brain damage, drug use, and the like. This is just the sort of objection Hayek raised in

"Scientism and the Study of Society" against social theories that regard all beliefs, opinions, and theories as entirely determined by economic, historical, or other social factors.[20] Such theories are self-undermining, in Hayek's view, since if any of them were true it would show that the theorist defending it could have no reason to *believe* it to be true, given that his beliefs like all others would be determined by social forces outside his control rather than by objective standards of truth.

Popper argued that the same problem afflicts naturalistic causal theories of the mind. In order to fit mental processes into the natural order, such theories tend inevitably to characterize them in a way that makes their distinctively mental properties causally irrelevant. For example, a brain process that the theory would identify with the thought that *the cat is on the mat* will, in tandem with a brain process identical to the thought that *the cat's name is Mike*, tend to generate a brain process identifiable with the thought that *Mike is on the mat*. Yet the reason it will do so has entirely to do with its electrochemical and other neurobiological properties, and nothing to do with either the meaning of the thoughts in question or their logical connections, for only the former sorts of properties can enter into the causal generalizations formulated by physical science. But in that case, a person's having the thought that *Mike is on the mat* has nothing whatsoever to do with its logically following from the other thoughts mentioned; indeed, none of our thoughts is ever generated in a way that has anything to do with either their meanings or their logical connections to other thoughts. And if that is so, then none of our thoughts is ever really rationally justified; we think we at least sometimes believe what we do on the basis of rational considerations, but this is an illusion. But this undermines every argument anyone has ever given, including the arguments causal theorists would give in support of their theory. Accordingly, causal theories of the mind are, if Popper is right, as self-undermining as the social theories of which Hayek was so critical.[21]

CONCLUSION

Hayek began a draft of a paper entitled "Within Systems and About Systems: A Statement of Some Problems of a Theory of Communication," which, as Jack Birner has suggested, was apparently intended at least in part as a response to Popper's criticisms.²² But it was never completed, and as Birner notes, while it begins with a sketch of how his approach would account for the expressive and signaling functions of language that Popper thought could in principle be explained naturalistically, it breaks off before addressing in any detail the descriptive and argumentative functions Popper thought no causal theory could account for. So we have no clear idea how Hayek would have dealt with the one serious critique that any philosopher gave of Hayek's philosophy of mind while he was alive.

If Hayek found it difficult to account for intentionality in naturalistic terms, though, he is not alone. The idea that intentionality is *the* feature of the mind on which all naturalistic theories must inevitably founder was famously championed in modern philosophy by Franz Brentano, and goes back in one form or another to Plato and Aristotle. Contemporary philosophy has not given us much reason to doubt it – not when prominent philosophers like W. V. Quine and Paul Churchland "solve" the problem intentionality poses for naturalism by simply denying that it exists, and even purported realists about intentionality like Jerry Fodor reconcile it with naturalism by declaring that "if aboutness [i.e. intentionality] is real, it must be really something else" (Fodor 1988, p. 97). Popper himself simply concluded that some form of dualism must be true, and sought to incorporate it into his own conception of the scientific worldview (Popper and Eccles 1977).

Hayek's philosophy of mind nevertheless has value as an ambitious and systematic attempt to reduce all the diverse phenomena associated with the mind to the single category of intentionality-embodied-in-human-practice. In this too he anticipated trends in contemporary philosophy and cognitive science (Clark 1997), and (in my estimation, anyway) did so in a way that more plausibly deals with sensory qualities or qualia than any currently fashionable naturalistic approaches do. Yet his philosophy might also teach us that our reductive ambitions have an absolute limit, and that to take things down to the level of intentional human action is to reach a ground floor below which we cannot go. If a successful naturalistic theory of intentionality eluded him no less than it has eluded his successors, we cannot judge him too harshly for that. And if his failure and theirs make us warier of the scientism that has for too long dominated contemporary philosophy, we will have learned a very Hayekian lesson indeed.

NOTES

1. Of particular interest are Caldwell 2004a, Fleetwood 1995, Forsyth 1988, Gray 1998, Horwitz 2000, Kukathas 1989, and Miller 1979.

2. Smith 1997 and Weimer 1982 are two detailed treatments. The neuroscientists Edelman (1982) and Fuster (1995) also regard Hayek as having made an important contribution.

3. Some of the sources cited in the previous notes do make at least tangential reference to philosophical matters, and Smith 1994 gives a general account of the relation of some of the philosophical ideas inherent in the Austrian tradition in economics, of which Hayek was a chief representative, to the Austrian philosophical tradition. Austen Clark very briefly alludes to *The Sensory Order* in developing his own (very Hayekian) account of the nature of sensory qualities (1993, p. 117). It is also worth noting that the book was reviewed in the journals *Mind* (Hamlyn 1954) and *Philosophy* (Sprott 1954).

4. With the exception, of course, of libertarian political philosophers like Robert Nozick (1974), who are primarily interested in Hayek's economic and social thought rather than his broader philosophical views.

5. To be fair, there is, as we shall see, a sense in which Hayek's philosophy of mind has implications for social philosophy, but these implications are more evident from works other than *The Sensory Order* and are less often remarked upon than is the general – and less interesting – point that both the mind and the market are complex phenomena.

6. I do not claim that Hayek always consciously adopted these several ideas with a view to combining them in a novel fashion. In some cases the influence of other writers is direct and explicitly acknowledged, but in others it is indirect and perhaps even unrecognized, and in yet others there is no influence at all, but rather the independent development, or even anticipation, of notions more commonly associated with other theorists.

7. See Feser 2005 for a survey of these issues in greater depth.

8. See Kresge's introduction to Hayek 1994 for discussion of both the influence of Mach and the history of the development of the manuscript that became *The Sensory Order*. Hayek [1967] 1992 is also relevant.

9. For a brief and lucid exposition of the theory in question, see Maxwell 1972. As Russell's version and Maxwell's exposition of it make clear, this theory of knowledge is best thought of as a variation on the indirect realist theory of perception – "realist" because it holds that there is an objective physical world existing independently of the mind, "indirect" because it holds that our knowledge of that world is based on inference from our direct awareness of our perceptual representations of it.

Contemporary sympathizers with the view include Lockwood (1989), who emphasizes the link between structuralism and indirect realism, and Chalmers (1996) and Strawson (2003), who endorse structuralism but without committing themselves to indirect realism.

10. Carnap himself doesn't count as having combined these doctrines because he was not, as Schlick, Russell, and Hayek all were, a realist about the external world.

11. This too was a position not taken by Carnap. His structuralism about sensory qualities was not causal; he sought only to define these qualities in terms of their similarity relations to each other, and made no claim to the effect that the similarity relations could themselves be cashed out in turn as causal relations instantiated in the nervous system.

12. Hayek refers to the larger set of connections between impulses which represents one's current environment as a whole as the "model," and to the yet larger and more stable set of neural connections representing one's general picture of the world, and of which the "model" forms a subset, as the "map" (1952b, p. 112). Ultimately, it is its precise place within these larger structures as a whole – and not merely the more "local" connections just mentioned as examples – that gives any smaller-scale set of impulses (such as those correlated with seeing an orange) the distinctive qualitative character associated with it.

13. Chalmers (1996) takes note of it as a theoretical possibility, but apparently rejects it on the grounds that it seems incoherent to suppose that causal structure could be all that exists, without any intrinsic properties to flesh it out. But the view under discussion does not (or need not) in fact suppose this. It claims only that causal structure is all we *know* of, not all that *exists*. Perhaps there are, and must be, intrinsic properties of some sort fleshing out the causal structure of both mind and matter, and we just don't know what they are.

14. Chalmers, unlike Russell, Lockwood, and Strawson, is a property dualist, but he would presumably allow that both perceptual events and introspective events are identical to brain events, insisting only that some brain events have non-physical properties.

15. This seems to be part of the reason why Chalmers, though a Russellian sympathizer like Lockwood and Strawson, regards his position as a kind of dualism.

16. Here we see an anticipation of Levine's view (2001) that there is an "explanatory gap" between the mental and the physical, though not a metaphysical gap, and McGinn's view (1991) that even though there is a true theory which explains how mental phenomena can be accounted for in purely physical terms, there are inherent limitations on the powers of the mind that keep it from ever grasping that theory.

17. There is another, philosophically less interesting, sense in which Hayek thinks the mind is not fully explicable, having to do with complexity. Just as an evolutionary explanation of the origin of a particular species would not have allowed us before the fact to predict that that species would come into existence, due to the enormous number of variables involved, so too an explanation of how the mind works will, given the mind's complexity, not allow us to make any specific predictions about the course of anyone's mental life. Because this sort of point applies equally well to non-mental phenomena like the weather, it seems of little relevance to the dispute over whether qualia and intentionality can be identified with physical properties of the brain.

18. This is one reason Hayek was critical of proposals radically to alter traditional moral and economic institutions. He regarded any attempt to design a new social order from scratch as doomed to fail, given the inherent limitations on the mind's ability to understand the forces that shape such institutions. As Gray puts it, "it is Hayek's view that the impossible ambitions spawned by contemporary culture arise from a false understanding of the human mind itself" (1993, p. 33) and that "socialism and interventionism ... are but long shadows cast by a false philosophy of mind" (p. 36).

19. Karl Popper to F. A. Hayek, December 2, 1952, Hoover Institution, Hayek Archive, box 44, folder 1. Quoted with the permission of the estate of Karl Popper.

20. Hayek also criticizes historical relativism on the grounds that we could not even recognize people living in another epoch as having minds at all unless we regarded them as having epistemic standards similar to our own. Cf. Davidson 1984.

21. This is one way anyway (perhaps not the only one) of understanding the upshot of Popper's argument, which is sometimes classified as a version of the anti-materialist "argument from reason" (Hasker 1999, pp. 64–74). See Feser 2005, chs. 6 and 7, for further discussion of Popper's arguments and other objections to naturalistic theories of thought and intentionality.

22. The paper is still unpublished. The typescript is in the Hoover Institution, Hayek Archive, box 104, folder 22. Birner's thesis is cited in Caldwell 2004a, pp. 300–301.

GUIDE TO FURTHER READING

WORKS BY HAYEK

A list of all of Hayek's major works is to be found in the general list of references below. The University of Chicago Press is publishing a standard edition entitled *The Collected Works of F. A. Hayek*, now under the general editorship of Bruce Caldwell. Seven volumes have appeared so far. Hayek 1984a, an anthology of articles and book chapters by Hayek representative of various aspects of his work, is a useful one-volume reader. Many of Hayek's letters, papers, and other unpublished writings are archived at the Hoover Institution at Stanford University in California.

BIOGRAPHICAL

Ebenstein 2001 is the only full-length biography of Hayek available in English. Hayek 1994, which compiles various personal reminiscences and interviews, is the closest thing there is to an autobiography. Raybould 1998 provides an overview of Hayek's career and contains a great many otherwise hard-to-find photographs. Caldwell 2004a and Ebenstein 2003 are "intellectual biographies" recounting the development of Hayek's thought through the course of his career along with his academic life and participation in various public controversies.

SECONDARY SOURCES

There are several important scholarly works offering a critical examination of Hayek's social, political, and economic thought as a systematic whole. Caldwell 2004a is the most recent of these, and has been very well received. Other important works of this sort include Barry 1979, Fleetwood 1995, Gamble 1996, Gray 1998, Kley 1994, Kukathas 1989, and Shearmur 1996a. Butler 1983 is a semi-popular introduction.

Somewhat more narrowly focused on various specific aspects of Hayek's political philosophy are Espada 1996, Gissurarson 1987, Hoy 1984, Petsoulas 2001, Rowland 1987, and Touchie 2005. Studies focusing on Hayek's economics include McCormick 1992, O'Driscoll 1977, Steele 1993, Steele 2001, and Tomlinson 1990. Walker 1986 is an examination of Hayek's moral theory. Several works explore the relationship between Hayek's thought and that of other important thinkers. Crowley 1987 compares Hayek's views with those of Sidney and Beatrice Webb, Hoover 2003 compares Hayek with Keynes and Laski, Sciabarra 1995 compares Hayek and Marx, Smith 2005 compares Hayek and Schutz, Steele 2001 compares Hayek and Keynes, and Williams 2005 compares Hayek and Rawls.

Several volumes of essays on Hayek are available, including Birner, Garrouste, and Aimar 2001, Birner and van Zijp 1994, Bouckaert and Godart-Van Der Kroon 2000, Butler and Pirie 1987, Cunningham 1979, Frei and Nef 1994, Frowen 1997, Machlup 1976, Seldon 1961, and Streissler 1969. Boettke 2000b and Wood and Woods 1991 are multi-volume collections of previously published journal articles that are otherwise difficult to find. The journal *Critical Review* has devoted two special issues to Hayek: vol. 3, no. 2 (Spring 1989) and vol. 11, no. 1 (Winter 1997). The inaugural issue of the *NYU Journal of Law and Liberty* (vol. 1, no. 0, 2005) was devoted to the theme of "Hayek and the Law."

BIBLIOGRAPHY

Armstrong, D. M. 1981. *The Nature of Mind*. Ithaca: Cornell University Press.

Austin, John. 1954. *The Province of Jurisprudence Determined*, ed. H. L. A. Hart. London: Weidenfeld & Nicolson.

Baier, Kurt. 1995. *The Rational and the Moral Order*. Chicago: Open Court.

Baranzini, M., ed. 1982. *Advances in Economic Theory*. Oxford: Blackwell.

Barry, Norman. 1979. *Hayek's Social and Economic Philosophy*. London: Macmillan.

    1984. "Hayek on Liberty." In Z. Pelczynski and J. Gray, eds., *Conceptions of Liberty in Political Philosophy*, ch. 12. London: Athlone.

    1995. "Hayek's Theory of Social Order." *Il politico* 60: 557–81.

Bentham, Jeremy. 1907. *An Introduction to the Principles of Morals and Legislation*. Oxford: Clarendon Press.

Bianchi, Marina. 1994. "Hayek's Spontaneous Order: The 'Correct' versus the 'Corrigible' Society." In Jack Birner and Rudy van Zijp, eds., *Hayek, Co-ordination, and Evolution: His Legacy in Philosophy, Politics, Economics, and the History of Ideas*, pp. 232–51. London: Routledge.

Birner, Jack, Pierre Garrouste, and Thierry Aimar, eds. 2001. *F. A. Hayek as a Political Economist: Economic Analysis and Values*. London: Routledge.

Birner, Jack, and Rudy van Zijp, eds. 1994. *Hayek, Co-ordination, and Evolution: His Legacy in Philosophy, Politics, Economics, and the History of Ideas*. London: Routledge.

Blackmore, Susan. 1999. *The Meme Machine*. Oxford: Oxford University Press.

Boettke, Peter. 2000a. "Which Enlightenment, Whose Liberalism? F. A. Hayek's Research Programme in Classical Liberal Political Economy." In Peter Boettke, ed., *The Legacy of Friedrich von Hayek*, vol. 1, pp. xi–lv. Cheltenham: Edward Elgar.

    ed. 2000b. *The Legacy of Friedrich von Hayek*. 3 vols. Cheltenham: Edward Elgar.

    ed. 2000c. *Socialism and the Market Economy*. 9 vols. New York: Routledge.

2001. *Calculation and Coordination: Essays on Socialism and Transitional Political Economy*. New York: Routledge.

2005. "Hayek and Market Socialism: Science, Ideology and Public Policy." *Economic Affairs* 25: 54–60.

Boettke, Peter, Christopher Coyne, and Peter Leeson. 2006. "Hayek versus Neoclassicals." In Norman Barry, ed., *The Elgar Companion to Hayekian Economics*. Cheltenham: Edward Elgar.

Boettke, Peter, and Peter Leeson. 2004. "Liberalism, Socialism and Robust Political Economy." *Journal of Markets & Morality* 7: 99–112.

Böhm-Bawerk, Eugen. [1896] 1975. "Karl Marx and the Close of his System." In Paul Sweezy, ed., *Karl Marx and the Close of his System and Böhm-Bawerk's Criticism of Marx*, pp. 3–118. Clifton, NJ: Kelley.

Bouckaert, Boudewijn, and Annette Godart-Van Der Kroon, eds. 2000. *Hayek Revisited*. Aldershot: Edward Elgar.

Boulding, K. 1971. "After Samuelson Who Needs Smith?" *History of Political Economy* 3: 225–37.

Brague, Rémi. 2005. *La loi de Dieu: Histoire philosophique d'une alliance*. Paris: Gallimard.

Brittan, Samuel. 1980. "Hayek, the New Right, and the Crisis of Social Democracy." *Encounter* 54 (January): 30–46.

2005. *Against the Flow*. London: Atlantic Books.

Butler, Eamonn. 1983. *Hayek: His Contribution to the Political and Economic Thought of Our Time*. New York: Universe Books.

Butler, E., and M. Pirie, eds. 1987. *Hayek on the Fabric of Human Society*. London: Adam Smith Institute.

Caldwell, Bruce. 1988. "Hayek's 'The Trend of Economic Thinking'." *Review of Austrian Economics* 2: 175–78.

1997. "Hayek and Socialism." *Journal of Economic Literature* 35: 1856–90.

2004a. *Hayek's Challenge: An Intellectual Autobiography of F. A. Hayek*. Chicago: University of Chicago Press.

2004b. "Some Reflections on F. A. Hayek's *The Sensory Order*." *Journal of Bioeconomics* 6: 1–16.

Carabelli, A., and N. De Vecchi. 1999. " 'Where to Draw the Line?' Hayek versus Keynes, on Knowledge, Ethics, and Economics." *European Journal of the History of Economic Thought* 6: 271–96.

Caravale, G., ed. 1991. *Marx and Modern Economic Analysis*. Cheltenham: Edward Elgar.

Carnap, Rudolf. [1928] 1967. *The Logical Structure of the World*. Berkeley and Los Angeles: University of California Press.

Cassidy, John. 2000. "The Price Prophet." *New Yorker* February 7: 44–51.

Chalmers, David. 1996. *The Conscious Mind*. Oxford: Oxford University Press.

Clark, Andy. 1997. *Being There: Putting Brain, Body, and World Together Again*. Cambridge, MA: MIT Press.

Clark, Austen. 1993. *Sensory Qualities*. Oxford: Clarendon Press.

Clark, Colin. 1945. "Public Finance and Changes in the Value of Money." *Economic Journal* 55: 371–89.

Colonna, Marina. 1994. "Hayek's Trade Cycle Theory and its Contemporary Critics." In M. Colonna and H. Hagemann, eds., *Money and Business Cycles: The Economics of F. A. Hayek*, vol. 1, pp. 27–52. Cheltenham: Edward Elgar.

Colonna, Marina, and Harold Hagemann, eds. 1994. *Money and Business Cycles: The Economics of F. A. Hayek*, vol. 1. Cheltenham: Edward Elgar.

Covell, Charles. 1992. *The Defence of Natural Law*. New York: St. Martin's Press.

Crowley, Brian Lee. 1987. *The Self, the Individual, and the Community: Liberalism in the Political Thought of F. A. Hayek and Sidney and Beatrice Webb*. Oxford: Clarendon Press.

Cunningham, Robert, ed. 1979. *Liberty and the Rule of Law*. College Station: Texas A&M University Press.

Davidson, Donald. 1984. "On the Very Idea of a Conceptual Scheme." In *Inquiries into Truth and Interpretation*, pp. 183–98. Oxford: Clarendon Press.

Dawkins, Richard. 1989. *The Selfish Gene*. 2nd edition. Oxford: Oxford University Press.

Dennett, Daniel. 1995. *Darwin's Dangerous Idea*. New York: Simon and Schuster.

Desai, Meghnad. 1973. "Growth Cycles and Inflation in a Model of the Class Struggle." *Journal of Economic Theory* 6: 527–45.

   1974. *Marxian Economic Theory*. London: Gray-Mills.

   1979. *Marxian Economics*. Oxford: Blackwell.

   1982. "The Task of Monetary Theory: The Hayek–Sraffa Debate in a Modern Perspective." In M. Baranzini, ed., *Advances in Economic Theory*, pp. 149–70. Oxford: Blackwell.

   1991a. "The Transformation Problem." In G. Caravale, ed., *Marx and Modern Economic Analysis*, pp. 3–44. Cheltenham: Edward Elgar.

   1991b. "Kaldor Between Hayek and Keynes: Or Did Nicky Kill Capital Theory?" In E. Nell and W. Semmler, eds., *Nicholas Kaldor and Mainstream Economics*, pp. 53–71. London: Macmillan.

   1994. "Equilibrium, Expectations and Knowledge." In Jack Birner and Rudy van Zijp, eds., *Hayek, Co-ordination, and Evolution: His Legacy in Philosophy, Politics, Economics, and the History of Ideas*, pp. 25–50. London: Routledge.

1997. "Hayek, Marx, and Keynes." In Stephen Frowen, ed., *Hayek: Economist and Social Philosopher: A Critical Retrospect*, pp. 1–8. New York: St. Martin's Press.

2002. *Marx's Revenge: The Resurgence of Capitalism and the Death of Statist Socialism*. London: Verso.

Desai, Meghnad, and P. Redfern. 1994. "Trade Cycle as Frustrated Traverse: An Analytical Reconstruction of Hayek's Model." In Marina Colonna and Harold Hagemann, eds., *Money and Business Cycles: The Economics of F. A. Hayek*, vol. 1. Cheltenham: Edward Elgar.

De Vlieghere, Martin. 1994. "A Reappraisal of Friedrich A. Hayek's Cultural Evolutionism." *Economics and Philosophy* 10: 285–304.

Dickinson, H. D. [1933] 2000. "Price Formation in a Socialist Community." In Peter Boettke, ed., *Socialism and the Market Economy*, vol. 4. New York: Routledge.

Dostaler, G. 1994. "The Formation and Evolution of Hayek's Trade Cycle Theory." In M. Colonna and H. Hagemann, eds., *Money and Business Cycles: The Economics of F. A. Hayek*, vol. 1, pp. 147–67. Cheltenham: Edward Elgar.

Durbin, Elizabeth. 1985. *New Jerusalems: The Labour Party and the Economics of Democratic Socialism*. London: Routledge and Kegan Paul.

Dworkin, Ronald. 1978. *Taking Rights Seriously*. 2nd edition. London: Duckworth.

Eatwell, John, Murray Milgate, and Peter Newman, eds. 1987. *The New Palgrave Dictionary of Economics*. London: Macmillan.

Ebenstein, Alan. 2001. *Friedrich Hayek: A Biography*. New York: Palgrave.

2003. *Hayek's Journey: The Mind of Friedrich Hayek*. New York: Palgrave.

2005. "The Fatal Deceit." *Liberty* 19: 29–32.

Edelman, Gerald. 1982. "Through a Computer Darkly: Group Selection and Higher Brain Function." *Bulletin of the American Academy of Arts and Sciences* 36: 20–49.

Epstein, Richard A. 1998. *Principles for a Free Society: Reconciling Individual Liberty with the Common Good*. Cambridge, MA: Perseus.

Eshag, Eprime. 1963. *From Marshall to Keynes: An Essay on the Monetary Theory of the Cambridge School*. Oxford: Basil Blackwell.

Espada, Joao Carlos. 1996. *Social Citizenship Rights: A Critique of F. A. Hayek and Raymond Plant*. London: Macmillan.

Feinstein, Charles, ed. 1967. *Socialism, Capitalism and Economic Growth*. Cambridge: Cambridge University Press.

Feser, Edward. 1997. "Hayek on Social Justice: Reply to Lukes and Johnston." *Critical Review* 11: 581–606.

1998. "Hayek, Social Justice, and the Market: Reply to Johnston." *Critical Review* 12: 269–81.

2003. "Hayek on Tradition." *Journal of Libertarian Studies* 17: 1–42.

2004. *On Nozick*. Belmont, CA: Wadsworth.

2005. *Philosophy of Mind: A Short Introduction*. Oxford: Oneworld Publications.

Fisher, Irving. 1911. *The Purchasing Power of Money*. London: Yale.

Fleetwood, Steve. 1995. *Hayek's Political Economy: The Socio-economics of Order*. London: Routledge.

Fodor, Jerry A. 1988. *Psychosemantics*. Cambridge, MA: MIT Press.

Forsyth, Murray. 1988. "Hayek's Bizarre Liberalism: A Critique." *Political Studies* 36: 235–50.

Frei, Christoph, and Robert Nef, eds. 1994. *Contending with Hayek*. Bern: Peter Lang.

Friedman, Michael. 1999. *Reconsidering Logical Positivism*. Cambridge: Cambridge University Press.

Friedman, Milton, and Anna Schwartz. 1963. *A Monetary History of the United States 1867–1960*. Chicago: University of Chicago Press.

Frowen, Stephen F., ed. 1997. *Hayek: Economist and Social Philosopher: A Critical Retrospect*. New York: St. Martin's Press.

Fuster, Joachim. 1995. *Memory in the Cerebral Cortex: An Empirical Approach to Neural Networks in the Human and Nonhuman Primate*. Cambridge, MA: MIT Press.

Galston, William A. 1992. *Liberal Purposes*. Cambridge: Cambridge University Press.

Gamble, Andrew. 1996. *Hayek: The Iron Cage of Liberty*. Cambridge: Polity.

Gärdenfors, Peter. 2004. *Conceptual Spaces*. Cambridge, MA: MIT Press.

Garrison, R. W. 1994. "Hayekian Triangles and Beyond." In Jack Birner and Rudy Van Zijp, eds., *Hayek, Co-ordination, and Evolution: His Legacy in Philosophy, Politics, Economics, and the History of Ideas*, pp. 109–25. London: Routledge.

2003. "F. A. Hayek as 'Mr. Fluctooations': In Defense of Hayek's 'Technical Economics.'" *ama-gi: Journal of the Hayek Society at the London School of Economics* 5.

Gellner, Ernest. 1991. "Which Way Will the Stone Age Vote Swing?" In *Plough, Sword, and Book*, pp. 23–38. London: Paladin.

Gierke, Otto von. 1900. *Political Theories of the Middle Ages*, trans. F. W. Maitland. Cambridge: Cambridge University Press.

1934. *Natural Law and the Theory of Society 1500–1800*, trans. Sir Ernest Barker. Cambridge: Cambridge University Press.

Gissurarson, Hannes. 1987. *Hayek's Conservative Liberalism*. London: Garland.

Goodwin, Richard. 1967. "A Growth Cycle." In Charles Feinstein, ed., *Socialism, Capitalism and Economic Growth*, pp. 54–58. Cambridge: Cambridge University Press.

Grandmont, Jean Michel. 1984. *Money and Value*. New York: John Wiley.

Gray, John. 1989. *Liberalisms*. London: Routledge.

1992. *The Moral Foundations of Market Institutions*. London: Institute of Economic Affairs.

1993. *Post-liberalism: Studies in Political Thought*. London: Routledge.

1998. *Hayek on Liberty*. 3rd edition. London: Routledge.

Haberler, G. 1986. "Reflections on Hayek's Business Cycle Theory." *Cato Journal* 6: 421–35.

Hacohen, Malachi. 2000. *Karl Popper: The Formative Years, 1902–1945*. Cambridge: Cambridge University Press.

Hamlyn, D. W. 1954. Review of *The Sensory Order*. *Mind* 63: 560–62.

Hamowy, Ronald. 1978. "Law and the Liberal Society: F. A. Hayek's Constitution of Liberty." *Journal of Libertarian Studies* 2: 287–97.

Hasker, William. 1999. *The Emergent Self*. Ithaca: Cornell University Press.

Hasnas, John. 2004. "Hayek, the Common Law, and Fluid Drive." *NYU Journal of Law and Liberty* 1: 79–110.

Hayek, F. A. 1931. *Prices and Production*. London: Routledge.

1932a. "Money and Capital: A Reply to Mr. Sraffa." *Economic Journal* 42: 237–49.

1932b. "Reflections on the Pure Theory of Mr. Keynes, Part II." *Economica* 11: 398–403.

[1933] 1966. *Monetary Theory and the Trade Cycle*. New York: Kelley.

[1933] 1991. "The Trend of Economic Thinking." In *The Trend of Economic Thinking: Essays on Political Economists and Economic History*. Vol. 3 of *The Collected Works of F. A. Hayek*, ed. W. W. Bartley III and Stephen Kresge, pp. 17–34. Chicago: University of Chicago Press.

1935a. *Prices and Production*. 2nd edition. London: Routledge.

ed. 1935b. *Collectivist Economic Planning: Critical Studies on the Possibility of Socialism*. London: Routledge.

[1937] 1948. "Economics and Knowledge." In *Individualism and Economic Order*, pp. 33–56. Chicago: University of Chicago Press.

[1939] 1948. "The Economic Conditions of Interstate Federalism." In *Individualism and Economic Order*, pp. 255–72. Chicago: University of Chicago Press.

[1939] 1997. "Freedom and the Economic System." In *Socialism and War: Essays, Documents, Reviews*. Vol. 10 of *The Collected Works of F. A. Hayek*, ed. Bruce Caldwell, pp. 189–211. Chicago: University of Chicago Press.

1939a. *Monetary Nationalism and International Stability*. London: Longmans, Green, and Co.

1939b. *Profits, Interest, and Investment*. London: Routledge.

1941. *The Pure Theory of Capital*. London: Macmillan.

[1942–44] 1952. "Scientism and the Study of Society." In *The Counter-Revolution of Science: Studies on the Abuse of Reason*. Glencoe, IL: Free Press.

[1943] 1948. "The Facts of the Social Sciences." In *Individualism and Economic Order*, pp. 57–76. Chicago: University of Chicago Press.

[1944] 1962. *The Road to Serfdom*. London: Routledge.

[1944] 1991. "On Being an Economist." In *The Trend of Economic Thinking: Essays on Political Economists and Economic History*. Vol. 3 of *The Collected Works of F. A. Hayek*, ed. W. W. Bartley III and Stephen Kresge, pp. 35–48. Chicago: University of Chicago Press.

[1944] 1994. *The Road to Serfdom: Fiftieth Anniversary Edition*. Chicago: University of Chicago Press.

[1944] 2007. *The Road to Serfdom: The Definitive Edition*. Vol. 2 of *The Collected Works of F. A. Hayek*, ed. Bruce Caldwell. Chicago: University of Chicago Press.

[1945] 1948. "The Use of Knowledge in Society." In *Individualism and Economic Order*, pp. 77–91. Chicago: University of Chicago Press.

[1946] 1948. "Individualism: True and False." In *Individualism and Economic Order*, pp. 1–32. Chicago: University of Chicago Press.

1948a. *Individualism and Economic Order*. Chicago: University of Chicago Press.

1948b. "The Meaning of Competition." In *Individualism and Economic Order*, pp. 92–106. Chicago: University of Chicago Press.

1951. *John Stuart Mill and Harriet Taylor: Their Friendship and Subsequent Marriage*. Chicago: University of Chicago Press.

1952a. *The Counter-Revolution of Science: Studies on the Abuse of Reason*. Glencoe, IL: Free Press.

1952b. *The Sensory Order: An Inquiry into the Foundations of Theoretical Psychology*. Chicago: University of Chicago Press.

ed. 1954. *Capitalism and the Historians*. Chicago: University of Chicago Press.

1955. *The Political Ideal of the Rule of Law*. Cairo: National Bank of Egypt.

[1955] 1967. "Degrees of Explanation." In *Studies in Philosophy, Politics, and Economics*, pp. 3–21. Chicago: University of Chicago Press.

1960. *The Constitution of Liberty*. Chicago: University of Chicago Press.

[1962] 1967. "Rules, Perception, and Intelligibility." In *Studies in Philosophy, Politics, and Economics*, pp. 43–65. Chicago: University of Chicago Press.

[1963] 1967. "The Legal and Political Philosophy of David Hume." In *Studies in Philosophy, Politics, and Economics*, pp. 106–21. Chicago: University of Chicago Press.

[1964] 1967. "The Theory of Complex Phenomena." In *Studies in Philosophy, Politics, and Economics*, pp. 22–42. Chicago: University of Chicago Press.

[1965] 1967. "Kinds of Rationalism." In *Studies in Philosophy, Politics, and Economics*, pp. 82–95. Chicago: University of Chicago Press.

[1967] 1992. "Ernst Mach (1838–1916) and the Social Sciences in Vienna." In *The Fortunes of Liberalism*. Vol. 4 of *The Collected Works of F. A. Hayek*, ed. Peter Klein, pp. 172–75. Chicago: University of Chicago Press.

[1967] 1978. "Dr Bernard Mandeville." In *New Studies in Philosophy, Politics, Economics and the History of Ideas*, pp. 249–66. London: Routledge.

1967a. "Notes on the Evolution of Systems of Rules of Conduct." In *Studies in Philosophy, Politics, and Economics*, pp. 66–81. Chicago: University of Chicago Press.

1967b. "The Results of Human Action but Not of Human Design." In *Studies in Philosophy, Politics, and Economics*, pp. 96–105. Chicago: University of Chicago Press.

1967c. *Studies in Philosophy, Politics, and Economics*. Chicago: University of Chicago Press.

[1969] 1978. "The Primacy of the Abstract." In *New Studies in Philosophy, Politics, Economics, and the History of Ideas*, pp. 35–49. London: Routledge and Kegan Paul.

1971. *The Intellectuals and Socialism*. Menlo Park, CA: Institute for Humane Studies.

1972. *A Tiger by the Tail: The Keynesian Legacy of Inflation*. London: Institute of Economic Affairs.

1973. *Rules and Order*. Vol. 1 of *Law, Legislation, and Liberty*. Chicago: University of Chicago Press.

1975. *Full Employment at Any Price?* London: Institute of Economic Affairs.

[1975] 1978. "The Pretence of Knowledge." In *New Studies in Philosophy, Politics, Economics, and the History of Ideas*, pp. 25–34. London: Routledge.

1976a. *Choice in Currency: A Way to Stop Inflation*. London: Institute of Economic Affairs.

1976b. *The Mirage of Social Justice*. Vol. 2 of *Law, Legislation, and Liberty*. Chicago: University of Chicago Press.

[1977] 1992. "Remembering my Cousin Ludwig Wittgenstein (1889–1951)." In *The Fortunes of Liberalism*. Vol. 4 of *The Collected Works of F. A. Hayek*, ed. Peter Klein, pp. 176–81. Chicago: University of Chicago Press.

1978. *New Studies in Philosophy, Politics, Economics, and the History of Ideas*. London: Routledge and Kegan Paul.

1979. *The Political Order of a Free People.* Vol. 3 of *Law, Legislation, and Liberty.* Chicago: University of Chicago Press.

1980. *1980s Unemployment and the Unions.* London: Institute of Economic Affairs.

1981. "Foreword." In Ludwig von Mises, *Socialism: An Economic and Sociological Analysis.* Indianapolis: Liberty Classics.

1982a. *Law, Legislation, and Liberty.* 1-vol. edition. London: Routledge.

1982b. "The Sensory Order after 25 Years." In Walter Weimer and David Palermo, eds., *Cognition and the Symbolic Processes*, vol. 2, pp. 287–93. Hillsdale, NJ: Lawrence Erlbaum.

[1983] 1992. "The Rediscovery of Freedom." In *The Fortunes of Liberalism.* Vol. 4 of *The Collected Works of F. A. Hayek*, ed. Peter Klein, pp. 185–200. Chicago: University of Chicago Press.

1983a. *Knowledge, Evolution, and Society.* London: Adam Smith Institute.

1983b. "The Weasel Word 'Social'." *Salisbury Review* 2.

1984a. *The Essence of Hayek*, ed. Chiaki Nishiyama and Kurt R. Leube. Stanford: Hoover Institution.

1984b. "Introduction." In *Money, Capital, and Fluctuations: Early Essays*, ed. Roy McCloughry. Chicago: University of Chicago Press.

1984c. *Money, Capital, and Fluctuations: Early Essays*, ed. Roy McCloughry. Chicago: University of Chicago Press.

1984d. "The Origins and Effects of our Morals: A Problem for Science." In *The Essence of Hayek*, ed. Chiaki Nishiyama and Kurt R. Leube, pp. 318–30. Stanford: Hoover Institution.

1987a. "Individual and Collective Aims." In Susan Mendus and David Edwards, eds., *On Toleration*, pp. 35–47. Oxford: Clarendon Press.

1987b. "The Rules of Morality are Not the Conclusions of our Reason." In Gerard Radnitzky, ed., *Centripetal Forces in the Sciences*, vol. 1, pp. 227–35. New York: Paragon.

1988. *The Fatal Conceit: The Errors of Socialism.* Vol. 1 of *The Collected Works of F. A. Hayek*, ed. W. W. Bartley III. Chicago: University of Chicago Press.

1990. *The Denationalisation of Money.* Revised edition. London: Institute of Economic Affairs.

1991. *The Trend of Economic Thinking: Essays on Political Economists and Economic History.* Vol. 3 of *The Collected Works of F. A. Hayek*, ed. W. W. Bartley III and Stephen Kresge. Chicago: University of Chicago Press.

1992. *The Fortunes of Liberalism.* Vol. 4 of *The Collected Works of F. A. Hayek*, ed. Peter Klein. Chicago: University of Chicago Press.

1994. *Hayek on Hayek: An Autobiographical Dialogue*, ed. Stephen Kresge and Leif Wenar. Chicago: University of Chicago Press.

1995. *Contra Keynes and Cambridge: Essays, Correspondence*. Vol. 9 of *The Collected Works of F. A. Hayek*, ed. Bruce Caldwell. Chicago: University of Chicago Press.

1997. *Socialism and War: Essays, Documents, Reviews*. Vol. 10 of *The Collected Works of F. A. Hayek*, ed. Bruce Caldwell. Chicago: University of Chicago Press.

1999a. *Good Money, Part I: The New World*. Vol. 5 of *The Collected Works of F. A. Hayek*, ed. Stephen Kresge. Chicago: University of Chicago Press.

1999b. *Good Money, Part II: The Standard*. Vol. 6 of *The Collected Works of F. A. Hayek*, ed. Stephen Kresge. Chicago: University of Chicago Press.

Hayek, F. A., and Walter Weimer. 1982. "Weimer–Hayek Discussion." In Walter Weimer and David Palermo, eds., *Cognition and the Symbolic Processes*, vol. 2, pp. 321–29. Hillsdale, NJ: Lawrence Erlbaum.

Hicks, John. 1967. "The Hayek Story." In *Critical Essays in Monetary Theory*, pp. 201–15. Oxford: Oxford University Press.

1979. *Critical Essays in Monetary Theory*. Oxford: Clarendon Press.

Hilferding, Rudolf. 1975. "Böhm-Bawerk's Criticism of Marx." In Paul Sweezy, ed., *Karl Marx and the Close of his System and Böhm-Bawerk's Criticism of Marx*, pp. 121–96. Clifton, NJ: Kelley.

Hodgson, Geoffrey. 1988. *Economics and Institutions*. Cambridge: Polity.

1993. *Economics and Evolution: Bringing Life Back into Economics*. Ann Arbor: University of Michigan Press.

Hogue, Arthur. [1966] 1985. *Origins of the Common Law*. Indianapolis: Liberty Press.

Hont, Istvan, and Michael Ignatieff. 1983. "Needs and Justice in *The Wealth of Nations*." In Istvan Hont and Michael Ignatieff, eds., *Wealth and Virtue*, pp. 1–44. Cambridge: Cambridge University Press.

Hoover, Kenneth R. 2003. *Economics as Ideology: Keynes, Laski, Hayek and the Creation of Contemporary Politics*. New York: Rowman and Littlefield.

Horwitz, Steven. 2000. "From *The Sensory Order* to the Liberal Order: Hayek's Non-rationalist Liberalism." *Review of Austrian Economics* 13: 23–40.

Howard, M. C., and J. E. King. 1992. *A History of Marxian Economics*, vol. 1: *1883–1929*. London: Macmillan.

Hoy, Calvin M. 1984. *A Philosophy of Individual Freedom: The Political Thought of F. A. Hayek*. Westport, CT: Greenwood Press.

Hume, David. 1904. *Essays, Moral, Political, and Literary*. London: Oxford University Press.

1976. *Enquiries Concerning the Principles of Morals*, ed. L. A. Selby-Bigge. Oxford: Oxford University Press.

1985a. "On the Independency of Parliament." In *Essays, Moral, Political and Literary*, ed. E. Miller, pp. 42–46. Indianapolis: Liberty Press.

1985b. 'On the rise and progress of the arts and sciences.' In *Essays, Moral, Political and Literary*, ed. E. Miller, pp. 111–37. Indianapolis: Liberty Press.

1985c. "Whether the British Government Inclines More to Absolute Monarchy, or to a Republic." In *Essays, Moral, Political and Literary*, ed. E. Miller, pp. 47–53. Indianapolis: Liberty Press.

Hutchison, Terence. 1981. *The Politics and Philosophy of Economics: Marxians, Keynesians, and Austrians*. Oxford: Blackwell.

Ignatieff, Michael. 1984. *The Needs of Strangers*. London: Chatto and Windus.

Jasay, Anthony de. 1996. "Hayek: Some Missing Pieces." *Review of Austrian Economics* 9: 107–18.

Johnston, David. 1997a. "Hayek's Attack on Social Justice." *Critical Review* 11: 81–100.

1997b. "Is the Idea of Social Justice Meaningful? Rejoinder to Feser." *Critical Review* 11: 607–14.

Kaldor, Nicholas. 1937. "The Recent Controversy on the Theory of Capital." *Econometrica* 5: 201–33.

Kelsen, Hans. 1945. *General Theory of Law and State*. Cambridge, MA: Harvard University Press.

Keynes, John Maynard. [1936] 1973. *The General Theory of Employment, Interest, and Money*. Vol. 7 of *The Collected Writings of John Maynard Keynes*. London: Macmillan.

1949. *Two Memoirs*. London: Rupert Hart-Davis.

1971a. *A Tract on Monetary Reform*. Vol. 4 of *The Collected Writings of John Maynard Keynes*. London: Macmillan.

1971b. *A Treatise on Money 1: The Pure Theory of Money*. Vol. 5 of *The Collected Writings of John Maynard Keynes*. London: Macmillan.

1971c. *A Treatise on Money 2: The Applied Theory of Money*. Vol. 6 of *The Collected Writings of John Maynard Keynes*. London: Macmillan.

1972a. *Essays in Persuasion*. Vol. 9 of *The Collected Writings of John Maynard Keynes*. London: Macmillan.

1972b. *Essays in Biography*. Vol. 10 of *The Collected Writings of John Maynard Keynes*. London: Macmillan.

1973. *The General Theory and After, Part 1: Preparation*. Vol. 13 of *The Collected Writings of John Maynard Keynes*. London: Macmillan.

1978. *Activities 1939–1945: Internal War Finance*. Vol. 22 of *The Collected Writings of John Maynard Keynes*. London: Macmillan.

1980. *Activities 1940–1946: Shaping the Post-war World: Employment and Commodities*. Vol. 27 of *The Collected Writings of John Maynard Keynes*. London: Macmillan.

1981. *Activities 1929–1931: Rethinking Employment and Unemployment Policies*. Vol. 20 of *The Collected Writings of John Maynard Keynes*. London: Macmillan.

Khalil, Elias L. 1996. "Friedrich Hayek's Darwinian Theory of Evolution of Institutions: Two Problems." *Australian Economic Papers* 35 (June): 183–201.

Kirzner, Israel. 1992. *The Meaning of Market Process*. New York: Routledge.

Kley, Roland. 1994. *Hayek's Social and Political Thought*. Oxford: Clarendon Press.

Knight, Frank H. 1921. *Risk, Uncertainty, and Profit*. Boston: Houghton Mifflin.

[1936] 2000. "The Place of Marginal Economics in a Collective System." In Peter Boettke, ed., *Socialism and the Market Economy*, vol. 4. New York: Routledge.

Kristol, Irving. 1972. "When Virtue Loses All her Loveliness." In *On the Democratic Idea in America*, pp. 90–106. New York: Harper & Row.

Kukathas, Chandran. 1989. *Hayek and Modern Liberalism*. Oxford: Clarendon Press.

Laidler, D. 1994. "Hayek on Neutral Money and the Cycle." In M. Colonna and H. Hagemann, eds., *Money and Business Cycles: The Economics of F. A. Hayek*, vol. 1, pp. 3–26. Cheltenham: Edward Elgar.

1999. *Fabricating the Keynesian Revolution: Studies of the Inter-war Literature on Money, the Cycle, and Unemployment*. Cambridge: Cambridge University Press.

Lange, O. [1936–37a] 2000. "On the Economic Theory of Socialism: Part One." In Peter Boettke, ed., *Socialism and the Market Economy*, vol. 4. New York: Routledge.

[1936–37b] 2000. "On the Economic Theory of Socialism: Part Two." In Peter Boettke, ed., *Socialism and the Market Economy*, vol. 4. New York: Routledge.

Larmore, Charles. 1987. *Patterns of Moral Complexity*. Cambridge: Cambridge University Press.

Laski, H. J. 1934. *The State in Theory and Practice*. London: Allen and Unwin.

Lavoie, D. 1985a. *National Economic Planning: What is Left?* Washington, DC: CATO Institute.

1985b. *Rivalry and Central Planning*. New York: Cambridge University Press.

Layard, Richard. 2005. *Happiness: Lessons from a New Science*. London: Allen Lane.

Lerner, A. [1934–35] 2000. "Economic Theory and the Problems of a Socialist Economy." In Peter Boettke, ed., *Socialism and the Market Economy*, vol. 4. New York: Routledge.

[1936–37] 2000. "A Note on Socialist Economics." In Peter Boettke, ed., *Socialism and the Market Economy*, vol. 4. New York: Routledge.

[1937] 2000. "Statics and Dynamics in Socialist Economics." In Peter Boettke, ed., *Socialism and the Market Economy*, vol. 4. New York: Routledge.

Levine, Joseph. 1993. "On Leaving Out What It's Like." In Martin Davies and Glyn W. Humphries, eds., *Consciousness*, pp. 121–36. Oxford: Blackwell.

2001. *Purple Haze: The Puzzle of Consciousness*. Oxford: Oxford University Press.

Lockwood, Michael. 1989. *Mind, Brain, and the Quantum*. Oxford: Basil Blackwell.

Lomasky, Loren. 1987. *Rights, Persons and the Moral Community*. Oxford: Oxford University Press.

Löwe, A. 1997. "How is Business Cycle Theory Possible at All?" *Structural Change and Economic Dynamics* 8: 245–70.

Lukes, Steven. 1997. "Social Justice: The Hayekian Challenge." *Critical Review* 11: 65–80.

Luxemburg, Rosa. [1913] 1951. *The Accumulation of Capital*, trans. Agnes Schwarzchild. London: Routledge and Kegan Paul.

Macedo, Stephen. 1990. *Liberal Virtues: Citizenship, Virtue, and Community in Liberal Constitutionalism*. Oxford: Oxford University Press.

Mach, Ernst. [1886] 1959. *The Analysis of Sensations*. New York: Dover.

Machlup, Fritz, ed. 1976. *Essays on Hayek*. Hillsdale, MI: Hillsdale College Press.

Maitland, F. W. 1911. *Collected Papers*, vol. 3, ed. H. A. L. Fisher. Cambridge: Cambridge University Press.

Marx, Karl. [1859] 1904. *A Contribution to the Critique of Political Economy*, trans. N. Stone. Chicago: Charles Kerr.

[1867] 1887. *Capital*, vol. 1, trans. from the 3rd German edition by Samuel Moore and Edward Aveling. London: Swan Sonnenschein, Lowry, and Co.

[1885] 1919. *Capital*, vol. 2, trans. N. Stone. Chicago: Charles Kerr.

[1894] 1909. *Capital*, vol. 3, trans. N. Stone. Chicago: Charles Kerr.

1967. *Capital*, vol. 1. New York: International Publishers.

1975. *Early Writings*. Harmondsworth: Penguin.

Maxwell, Grover. 1972. "Russell on Perception: A Study in Philosophical Method." In D. F. Pears, ed., *Bertrand Russell: A Collection of Critical Essays*, pp. 110–46. New York: Anchor Books.

McCormick, Brian. 1992. *Hayek and the Keynesian Avalanche*. New York: St. Martin's Press.

McGinn, Colin. 1991. *The Problem of Consciousness*. Oxford: Blackwell.

Menger, Carl. [1950] 1976. *Principles of Economics*. Translated by James Dingwall and Bert Hoselitz. New York: New York University Press.

Mill, John Stuart. [1844] 1874. *Essays on Some Unsettled Questions of Political Economy*. 2nd edition. London: Longmans, Green, Reader, and Dyer.

Miller, David. 1989a. "The Fatalistic Conceit." *Critical Review* 3: 310–23.

1989b. *Market, State, and Community*. Oxford: Oxford University Press.

Miller, Eugene F. 1979. "The Cognitive Basis of Hayek's Political Thought." In Robert Cunningham, ed., *Liberty and the Rule of Law*, pp. 242–67. College Station: Texas A&M University Press.

Millikan, Ruth. 1984. *Language, Thought, and Other Biological Categories*. Cambridge, MA: MIT Press.

Mises, Ludwig von. [1912] 1934. *The Theory of Money and Credit*. London: Jonathan Cape.

[1920] 1935. "Economic Calculation in the Socialist Commonwealth." In F. A. Hayek, ed., *Collectivist Economic Planning: Critical Studies on the Possibility of Socialism*, pp. 87–130. London: Routledge.

[1922] 1951. *Socialism: An Economic and Sociological Analysis*. 2nd edition. New Haven: Yale University Press.

1966. *Human Action: A Treatise on Economics*. 3rd revised edition. Chicago: Henry Regnery.

Mueller, Dennis C. 2003. *Public Choice III*. Cambridge: Cambridge University Press.

Mulhall, Stephen, and Adam Swift. 1992. *Liberals and Communitarians*. Oxford: Blackwell.

Nell, Edward J., and Willi Semmler, eds. 1991. *Nicholas Kaldor and Mainstream Economics*. London: Macmillan.

Neumann, J. von, and O. Morgenstern. 1944. *The Theory of Games and Economic Behavior*. Princeton: Princeton University Press.

Nietzsche, Friedrich. 1994. *On the Genealogy of Morality*, ed. Keith Ansell-Pearson. Cambridge: Cambridge University Press.

Nozick, Robert. 1974. *Anarchy, State, and Utopia*. New York: Basic Books.

1986. "Robert Nozick." In *The Harvard Guide to Influential Books: 113 Distinguished Harvard Professors Discuss the Books that have Helped to Shape their Thinking*. New York: Harper and Row.

Nurkse, Ragnar. 1934. "The Schematic Representation of the Structure of Production." *Review of Economic Studies* 2: 232–44.

Oakeshott, Michael. 1962. *Rationalism in Politics*. London: Methuen.

1975. *On Human Conduct*. Oxford: Clarendon Press.

1991. "The Political Economy of Freedom." In *Rationalism in Politics and Other Essays*, pp. 384–406. Indianapolis: Liberty Press.

O'Driscoll, Gerald P. 1977. *Economics as a Coordination Problem: The Contributions of Friedrich A. Hayek*. Kansas City: Sheed, Andrews, and McMeel.

O'Hear, Anthony. 1997. *Beyond Evolution: Human Nature and the Limits of Evolutionary Explanation*. Oxford: Oxford University Press.

   2004. "The Open Society Revisited." In Philip Catton and Graham Macdonald, eds., *Karl Popper: Critical Appraisals*, pp. 189–202. London: Routledge.

O'Malley, Joseph. 1970. "Introduction." In Karl Marx, *A Contribution to the Critique of Hegel's Philosophy of Right*. Cambridge: Cambridge University Press.

O'Neill, John. 1998. *The Market: Ethics, Knowledge, and Politics*. London: Routledge.

Orosel, G. 1987. "Period of Production." In John Eatwell, Murray Milgate, and Peter Newman, eds., *The New Palgrave Dictionary of Economics*, vol. 3, pp. 843–46. London: Macmillan.

Panico, Carlo. 1987. "Interest and Profits." In John Eatwell, Murray Milgate, and Peter Newman, eds., *The New Palgrave Dictionary of Economics*, vol. 2, pp. 877–79. London: Macmillan.

Patinkin, D., and G. Clark Leith. 1977. *Keynes, Cambridge, and the General Theory*. London: Macmillan.

Paul, Ellen Frankel. 1988. "Liberalism, Unintended Orders, and Evolutionism." *Political Studies* 36: 251–72.

Peacock, Alan, and Hans Willgerodt, eds. 1989. *German Neo-Liberals and the Social Market Economy*. New York: St. Martin's Press.

Petsoulas, Christina. 2001. *Hayek's Liberalism and its Origins: His Idea of Spontaneous Order and the Scottish Enlightenment*. London: Routledge.

Pettit, Philip. 1997. *Republicanism: A Theory of Freedom and Government*. Oxford: Clarendon Press.

Pinker, Steven. 1999. *How the Mind Works*. New York: W. W. Norton.

Pinker, Steven. 2002. *The Blank Slate: The Modern Denial of Human Nature*. New York: Penguin.

Plant, Raymond. 1994. "Hayek on Social Justice: A Critique." In Jack Birner and Rudy van Zijp, eds., *Hayek, Co-ordination, and Evolution: His Legacy in Philosophy, Politics, Economics, and the History of Ideas*, pp. 164–77. London: Routledge.

Plumptre, A. F. W. 1947. "Keynes in Cambridge." *Canadian Journal of Economics* 13.

Popper, Karl R. [1945] 1966. *The Open Society and Its Enemies*. 5th edition. 2 vols. London: Routledge and Kegan Paul.

   [1949] 1968. "Towards a Rational Theory of Tradition." In *Conjectures and Refutations: The Growth of Scientific Knowledge*, pp. 120–35. New York: Harper and Row.

[1953] 1968. "Language and the Body–Mind Problem." In *Conjectures and Refutations: The Growth of Scientific Knowledge*, pp. 293–98. New York: Harper and Row.

1957. *The Poverty of Historicism*. London: Routledge and Kegan Paul.

[1959] 1968. *The Logic of Scientific Discovery*. New York: Harper Torchbooks.

Popper, Karl R. and John Eccles. 1977. *The Self and its Brain*. London: Routledge and Kegan Paul.

Rawls, John. 1971. *A Theory of Justice*. Cambridge, MA: Harvard Belknap Press.

1993. *Political Liberalism*. New York: Columbia University Press.

2001. *Justice as Fairness: A Restatement*. Cambridge, MA: Harvard Belknap Press.

Raybould, John. 1998. *Hayek: A Commemorative Album*. London: Adam Smith Institute.

Raz, Joseph. 1979. "The Rule of Law and its Virtue." In Robert L. Cunningham, ed., *Liberty and the Rule of Law*, pp. 3–21. College Station: Texas A&M University Press.

Reichenbach, Hans. 1951. *The Rise of Scientific Philosophy*. Berkeley and Los Angeles: University of California Press.

Reinach, Adolf. [1913] 1983. The A Priori Foundations of the Civil Law. Translated by J.F. Crosby. *Aletheia: An International Journal of Philosophy* 3: 1–142.

Reisch, George. 2005. *How the Cold War Transformed Philosophy of Science: To the Icy Slopes of Logic*. Cambridge: Cambridge University Press.

Ricardo, David. [1817] 1821. *On the Principles of Political Economy and Taxation*. 3rd edition. London: John Murray.

Richardson, Ray. 1997. "Hayek on Trade Unions: Social Philosopher or Propagandist?" In Stephen F. Frowen, ed., *Hayek: Economist and Social Philosopher: A Critical Retrospect*, pp. 259–74. New York: St. Martin's Press.

Robbins, Lionel. 1971. *Autobiography of an Economist*. London: Macmillan.

Röpke, Wilhelm. 1960. *A Humane Economy*, trans. Elizabeth Henderson. Chicago: Henry Regnery.

Rosenthal, David. 1997. "A Theory of Consciousness." In Ned Block, Owen Flanagan, and Guven Guzeldere, eds., *The Nature of Consciousness*, pp. 729–54. Cambridge, MA: MIT Press.

Rosser, J. Barkley, Jr. 1999. "On the Complexities of Complex Economics Dynamics." *Journal of Economic Perspectives* 13: 169–92.

Rowland, Barbara M. 1987. *Ordered Liberty and the Constitutional Framework: The Political Thought of F.A. Hayek*. Westport, CT: Greenwood Press.

Russell, Bertrand. [1927] 1954. *The Analysis of Matter*. New York: Dover.

[1959] 1985. *My Philosophical Development*. London: Routledge.

Ryle, Gilbert. 1949. *The Concept of Mind*. New York: Barnes and Noble.

Scheler, Max. 1998. *Ressentiment*, trans. L. B. Coser and W. W. Holdheim. Milwaukee: Marquette University Press.

Schlick, Moritz. [1918] 1985. *General Theory of Knowledge*. La Salle, IL.: Open Court.

Schmitt, Carl. [1922] 1985. *Political Theology: Four Chapters on the Concept of Sovereignty*, trans. and intr. George Schwab. Cambridge, MA: MIT Press.

Schumpeter, Joseph. 1908. *Das Wesen und der Hauptinhalt der theoretischen Nationalökonomie*. Leipzig: Duncker & Humblot.

1942. *Capitalism, Socialism, and Democracy*. New York: Harper and Row.

Sciabarra, Chris Matthew. 1995. *Marx, Hayek, and Utopia*. Albany, NY: SUNY Press.

Scitovsky, Tibor. 1976. *The Joyless Economy*. Oxford: Oxford University Press.

Scruton, Roger. [1990] 1998. "Gierke and the Corporate Person." In *Philosopher on Dover Beach: Essays*, pp. 56–73. South Bend, IN: St. Augustine's Press.

2000. *England: An Elegy*. London: Chatto and Windus.

2002. *The West and the Rest*. London: Continuum.

Searle, John R. 1983. *Intentionality*. Cambridge: Cambridge University Press.

1995. *The Construction of Social Reality*. New York: The Free Press.

Seldon, Arthur, ed. 1961. *Agenda for a Free Society: Essays on Hayek's* The Constitution of Liberty. London: Institute of Economic Affairs.

Shearmur, Jeremy. 1986. "The Austrian Connection." In Barry Smith and Wolfgang Grassl, eds., *Austrian Economics: Historical and Philosophical Background*, pp. 210–24. London: Croom Helm.

1996a. *Hayek and After: Hayekian Liberalism as a Research Programme*. London: Routledge.

1996b. *The Political Thought of Karl Popper*. London: Routledge.

1997. "Hayek, Keynes and the State." *History of Economics Review* 26: 68–82.

Forthcoming. "Hayek, *The Road to Serfdom* and the British Conservatives." *Journal of the History of Economic Thought*.

Skidelsky, Robert. 1983. *John Maynard Keynes: Hopes Betrayed 1883–1920*. London: Macmillan.

1992. *John Maynard Keynes: The Economist as Saviour 1920–1937*. London: Macmillan.

2000. *John Maynard Keynes: Fighting for Britain 1937–1946*. London: Macmillan.

Skinner, Quentin. 1998. *Liberty Before Liberalism*. Cambridge: Cambridge University Press.

Skyrms, Brian. 1996. *Evolution of the Social Contract*. Cambridge: Cambridge University Press.

2004. *The Stag Hunt and the Evolution of Social Structure*. Cambridge: Cambridge University Press.

Smith, Adam. [1776] 1976. *An Inquiry into the Nature and Causes of the Wealth of Nations*. Chicago: University of Chicago Press.

Smith, Barry. 1994. *Austrian Philosophy: The Legacy of Franz Brentano*. La Salle, IL: Open Court.

1997. "The Connectionist Mind: A Study of Hayekian Psychology." In Stephen Frowen, ed., *Hayek: Economist and Social Philosopher: A Critical Retrospect*, pp. 9–29. New York: St. Martin's Press.

Smith, Mark J. 2005. *Situating Hayek: Phenomenology and the Neo-Liberal Project*. London: Routledge.

Smith, Peter. 1998. *Explaining Chaos*. Cambridge: Cambridge University Press.

Sprott, W. J. H. 1954. Review of *The Sensory Order*. *Philosophy* 109: 183–85.

Sraffa, Piero. 1932a. "Dr. Hayek on Money and Capital." *Economic Journal* 42: 42–53.

1932b. "A Rejoinder." *Economic Journal* 42: 249–51.

Steele, G. R. 1993. *The Economics of Friedrich Hayek*. London: Macmillan.

2001. *Keynes and Hayek: The Money Economy*. London: Routledge.

Stockman, David. 1986. *The Triumph of Politics: Why the Reagan Revolution Failed*. New York: Harper and Row.

Strawson, Galen. 2003. "Real Materialism." In Louise M. Antony and Norbert Hornstein, eds., *Chomsky and his Critics*, pp. 49–88. Oxford: Blackwell.

Streissler, Erich, ed. 1969. *Roads to Freedom: Essays in Honour of Friedrich A. von Hayek*. New York: Kelley.

Streit, Manfred E. 1997. "Constitutional Ignorance, Spontaneous Order, and Rule-Orientation: Hayekian Paradigms from a Policy Perspective." In Stephen F. Frowen, ed., *Hayek: Economist and Social Philosopher: A Critical Retrospect*, pp. 37–58. New York: St. Martin's Press.

Sweezy, Paul, ed. 1949. *Karl Marx and the Close of his System*. New York: Augustus Kelley.

Taylor, F. [1929] 2000. "The Guidance of Production in a Socialist State." In Peter Boettke, ed. *Socialism and the Market Economy*, vol. 4. New York: Routledge.

Tomlinson, Jim. 1990. *Hayek and the Market*. London: Pluto Press.

Touchie, John C. W. 2005. *Hayek and Human Rights: Foundations for a Minimalist Approach to Law*. Cheltenham: Edward Elgar.

Trautwein, Hans-M. 1994. "Hayek's Double Failure in Business Cycle Theory: A Note." In M. Colonna and H. Hagemann, eds., *Money and*

Business Cycles: The Economics of F. A. Hayek, vol. 1, pp. 74–81. Cheltenham: Edward Elgar.

Vanberg, Viktor 1994. *Rules and Choice in Economics*. London: Routledge.

Vaughn, Karen. 1999. "Hayek's Theory of the Market Order as an Instance of the Theory of Complex, Adaptive Systems." *Journal des économistes et des études humaines* 9: 241–56.

Waldrop, Mitchell. 1992. *Complexity: The Emerging Science at the Edge of Order and Chaos*. New York: Simon and Shuster.

Walker, Graham. 1986. *The Ethics of F. A. Hayek*. Lanham, MD: University Press of America.

Watkins, John. 1997. "Parsons on Two Theses of Hayek." In Stephen F. Frowen, ed., *Hayek: Economist and Social Philosopher: A Critical Retrospect*, pp. 87–94. New York: St. Martin's Press.

Weimer, Walter B. 1982. "Hayek's Approach to the Problems of Complex Phenomena: An Introduction to the Theoretical Psychology of *The Sensory Order*." In Walter Weimer and David Palermo, eds., *Cognition and the Symbolic Processes*, vol. 2, pp. 241–85. Hillsdale, NJ: Lawrence Erlbaum.

Whitman, Douglas Glen. 1988. "Hayek contra Pangloss on Evolutionary Systems." *Constitutional Political Economy* 9: 450–66.

Wicksell, Knut. [1901] 1934. *Lectures on Political Economy*, vol. 1, trans. E. Classen. London: Routledge and Kegan Paul.

[1906] 1978. *Lectures on Political Economy*, vol. 2, trans. E. Classen. New York: Augustus M. Kelley.

[1936] 1965. *Interest and Prices: A Study of the Causes Regulating the Value of Money*. London: Macmillan.

Williams, Juliet. 2005. *Liberalism and the Limits of Power*. New York: Palgrave Macmillan.

Witt, Ulrich. 1994. "The Theory of Societal Evolution: Hayek's Unfinished Legacy." In Jack Birner and Rudy van Zijp, eds., *Hayek, Co-ordination and Evolution: His Legacy in Philosophy, Politics, Economics, and the History of Ideas*, pp. 178–89. London: Routledge.

Wood, J. C., and R. N. Woods, eds. 1991. *Friedrich A. Hayek: Critical Assessments*. 4 vols. London: Routledge.

Zweig, Stefan. 1943. *The World of Yesterday: An Autobiography*. New York: Viking.

INDEX